Fine WoodWorking *on* Bending Wood

35 articles selected by the editors of *Fine Woodworking* magazine

The Taunton Press

Cover photo by Seth Stem

20 19 18 17 16 15

ISBN-13: 978-0-918804-29-7
International Standard Book Number-10: 0-918804-29-9
Library of Congress Catalog Card Number: 84-052100
Printed in the United States of America

A Fine Woodworking Book

Fine Woodworking® is a trademark of The Taunton Press, Inc., registered in the U.S. Patent and Trademark Office.

The Taunton Press, Inc.
63 South Main Street
PO Box 5506
Newtown, CT 06470
e-mail: tp@taunton.com

Contents

Introduction

Wood is stiff, unyielding stuff. Yet over the centuries, woodworkers have devised three different ways of bending it into smooth and permanent curves.

When wood is freshly cut from the living tree, it's limber with sap and easy to coax into curved shapes. If you clamp it curvy while it dries, it will stay curvy. This is the oldest, least precise, but easiest, way to bend wood.

When one must start with lumber that's already dry, all is not lost. Cooked awhile in hot, wet steam, it regains some of the plasticity it had when alive. The dance of the steam-bender must be practiced and quick: this is the most challenging way to bend wood.

When the woodworker wants a curve that's really strong and precise, the best strategy may be to slice the boards into thin, supple strips. Thin laminates may easily be bent and glued around a form. This is the most controlled way of bending wood.

This book reveals the trade secrets and expert shop tips behind all three of these wood-bending strategies. In 35 articles reprinted from the first nine years of *Fine Woodworking* magazine, authors who are also craftsmen tell exactly how they've applied each of these methods to wood-bending problems in their own workshops. They also explain how you can make the tools and acquire the skills you'll need for successful wood-bending in your shop projects.

John Kelsey, editor

Making a Basket from a Tree

Splints from black ash, in the Shaker tradition

by Martha Wetherbee

The completed basket is 12 in. by 9½ in. by 5 in., excluding the handle.

In my shop at Shaker Village in Canterbury, N.H., I make wooden baskets the way they were made 100 years ago. I make cheese baskets, egg baskets and laundry baskets. I reproduce Shaker kitten heads, cat heads, hexagons and chip baskets, also measures of all sizes from ¼ pint to ½ bushel. Openwork baskets with pegged wooden swivel handles swing from the ceiling on Shaker pegs. Most are filled with onions, garlic and shallots drying. I make other types, including the old-style basket that I stamp in color with potato prints. All are constructed without nails, staples, tacks or glue. The three surviving Shaker sisters at the Canterbury community (in their 80s in 1980) remember very little about the basketmaking industry that died during their childhood. I have been reassembling the facts about the old crafts so that my baskets will continue in the Shaker tradition as simple, functional products of the highest possible quality.

Choosing a tree — Baskets made in New England are usually made from black ash, also known as brown ash. This tree is particularly suitable for basketmaking; its yearly growth rings can be loosened by pounding them with a sledge. Strips of separated ring can be pulled from the log and woven into baskets, chair backs or seats because they bend easily without splintering or cracking. When finished smoothly they can be used to panel frames in cabinet doors or room dividers.

Black ash is an unattractive tree that seldom grows straight. Its butt is short with branches beginning eight or ten feet up. The branches are scrawny and crooked, and the top of the tree bends downward as though it were dying. Few live longer than 80 years, and few are cut commercially. Years ago black ash was known as the basket tree.

Healthy black ash trees grow beside good-sized free-flowing streams. Once I cut a tree by a stream that had at one time flowed briskly, but five years before had been dammed and rerouted by beavers. As the flow of water declined, so did the health of the black ash. Its annual rings were extremely difficult to separate when pounded.

The ideal basket log is a 10-ft. knot-free black ash butt about 12 in. in diameter. For the beginner a 6-ft. length, 6 in. to 8 in. in diameter will do. I don't recommend using a tree less than 5 in. in diameter. When I began making baskets I used whatever logs I could find—some of them crooked and knotty. The rings separated quite well, but many of the splints had to be rejected because they tore around a knot or were too curved. A few knots the size of a penny can be worked around.

When you find your tree, contact the landowner and tell him he has a basket tree growing in his wetland; a basket for the tree is usually an agreeable trade. When I select a tree for my next-year's baskets I feel that I am giving it a second chance in life—the opportunity to be converted into 50 baskets that will be cared for, admired and used for many more years than the tree would live.

Pounding apart the rings — Cut an ash in spring, the Indians say; there is a good deal of water in the tree and the sap has loosened the bark. Irwin, a full-blooded Penobscot Indian living in Indian Town, Maine, told me that years ago his father would start out early in the morning to search for a black ash. He would cut it and pound the splints from the entire log in that day. In the evening he would return with great bundles of splints on his shoulders. For me it takes 10 days of rigorous pounding, eight hours each day, to pound apart one log.

Although the Indians traditionally cut black ash in the springtime, I have had success all year round. A tree cut in any season should separate easily if pounded within a week of being felled. A log that cannot be pounded immediately or one that still has lots of good splint on it should be submerged in water to keep it from drying out, though soaking for more than a year may rot the inside.

I recommend using the back of an ax for pounding. Grind the edges of the end round to avoid sharp corners that might perforate the splints. The back end of a splitting maul, a hatchet or a sledge hammer might also be used.

Set the log on the ground or in *V*-grooves cut in the ends of two stout stumps. Shave off the bark with a drawknife. Pound a section 2 in. or 3 in. wide along the log from one end to the other. Strike with the same force you would use to split cordwood. Allow each impact to overlap the one before it.

The first few layers below the bark, which include the cambium and some of the youngest sapwood, will need a good deal more strenuous beating than deeper layers. Don't become discouraged if the growth rings don't cooperate. The farther you get inside the log, the easier they will separate. These first layers are too brittle for splints and tear easily. Sometimes it is easier to shave these layers off with a drawknife. It may take as long as two hours for one person to get the outer portion off the log. You will know when you have arrived at good splint wood by the strength and flexibility of the material. Now the careful work begins.

Give the end of the log some extra tapping to begin separating the splint. You will be able to lift the outer ring with your fingers and pull off a strip that is 2 in. or 3 in. wide, though wider strips are possible if enough of the log has been pounded. Continue pounding and stripping the entire circumference of the log before starting the next layer. Sometimes more than one growth ring can be lifted at a time, de-

Photos: Richard Starr; Illustrations: Christopher Clapp

pending on the wood and the force of the blow. I have taken as many as six layers of splint up at one time. If you have difficulty getting layers to separate just keep pounding, being sure not to miss a spot. You can't skip around; there are no shortcuts to making good splint.

The thickness of the annual rings will vary according to favorable or difficult growing conditions during the year they were formed. I have found no differences in working qualities between heartwood and sapwood, though heartwood splints, which come from deeper in the tree, are darker in color.

Occasionally annual rings won't separate from one another. Such layers may look pithier than the others on the end grain of the log. Remove these rings with a drawknife and resume pounding on good layers. I once acquired a log discarded by another basketmaker who'd encountered sticky layers halfway through.I took it home and submerged it in a pond, weighing it down with logs. A month later I cleared the sticky section by shaving and pounding for an hour. The splints below this section pounded with ease. There were 40 good years left in the log, which made 25 baskets.

Preparing the splints — Sort splints according to their thickness. I once wove a large laundry basket using thin splints, and a heavy load of laundry permanently ballooned out the sides. Make the basket from heavy splints if you expect it to carry heavy loads.

Cut the splints with heavy scissors to proper width and length for the style of basket you choose to make. The Indians built their own stripping tools by embedding a clock spring with sharpened edges in a block of wood. A leatherworker's tool for cutting strapping works; it costs about $8 (1980).

All wood grows in annual rings, and each ring has two layers: earlywood, which grows rapidly in the spring, and latewood, which is formed more slowly in the summer. Black ash is a ring-porous hardwood, which means that the earlywood layers contain many large, sap-conducting tubes called vessels. There are fewer vessels in the latewood and they are much smaller. Because of this structure, earlywood is more coarse and less dense than latewood. When ash is pounded, the earlywood collapses and comes apart.

Black ash basket splints, as they come off the log, are composed of smooth, strong latewood with a stringy coating of earlywood on their outer surfaces. Growth rings can be used as basket splints in their natural state, but you can split thick layers into thinner pieces. When you do this, you get two splints, each with a smooth surface of latewood on one side. Very thick splints can be split into thirds or quarters, yielding interior splints that are satiny on both sides. The advantage of

Black ash (Fraxinus nigra), *also known as brown ash, splits easily, and therefore is a perfect basket tree. It is found in Northern wet areas and is 40 ft. to 80 ft. tall. Its pinnate, elliptic leaves number seven to eleven, its bark is shaggy and its buds are dark brown. At upper right, Wetherbee pounds a black ash log that has been soaking for a year, which is why it appears so dark. Note the overlapping impact marks. Right, she peels off an outer-ring strip.*

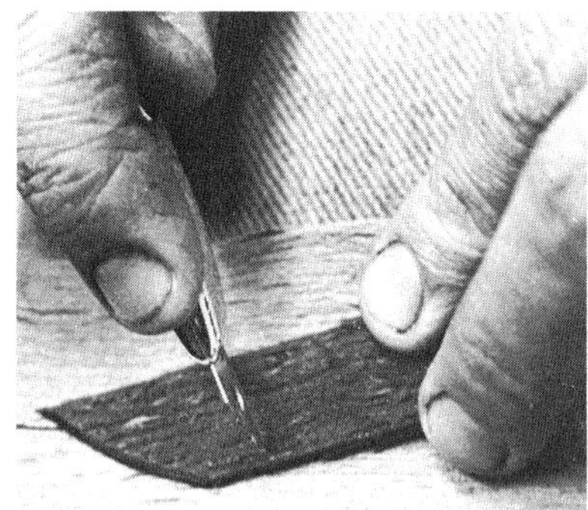

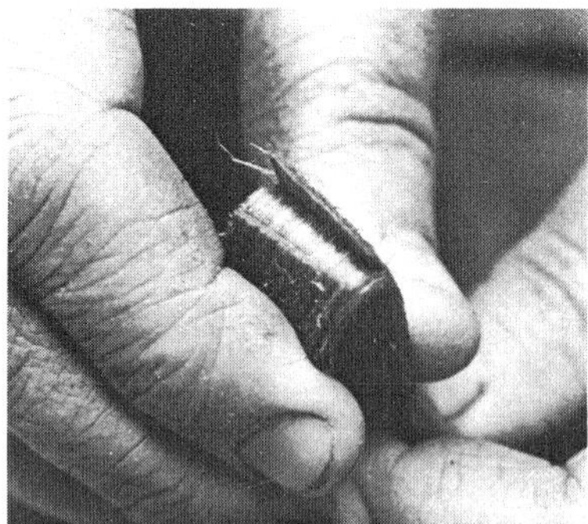

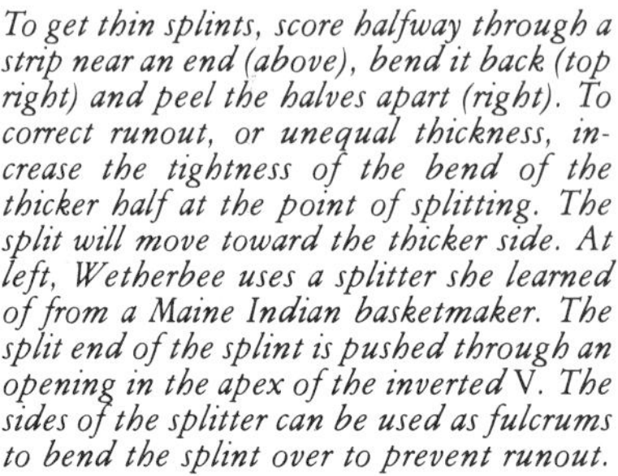

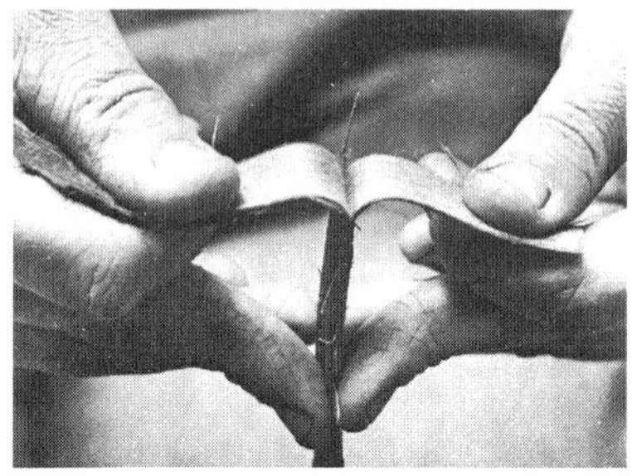

To get thin splints, score halfway through a strip near an end (above), bend it back (top right) and peel the halves apart (right). To correct runout, or unequal thickness, increase the tightness of the bend of the thicker half at the point of splitting. The split will move toward the thicker side. At left, Wetherbee uses a splitter she learned of from a Maine Indian basketmaker. The split end of the splint is pushed through an opening in the apex of the inverted V. The sides of the splitter can be used as fulcrums to bend the splint over to prevent runout.

splitting is twofold: You get smooth surfaces and, if you care to conserve material, several splints from one. Mixing satiny splints with the coarse, as the Shakers did, can create textures extraordinarily pleasing to the eye and to the touch. Rough splint surfaces may be scraped smooth. I use a paint scraper or a drawknife to remove the fuzzy outer layer.

Weaving the body of the basket — Weaving the basket is not difficult or time-consuming. In fact, most of the time in basketmaking is spent selecting the ash, pounding it and carving handles and rims. Some baskets have round bottoms, others are square or rectangular. I will describe how to weave a basic, rectangular market basket about 12 in. long, 9½ in. wide and 5 in. deep. The only tools you will need are a work table, scissors and a bucket of water.

The vertical members of the basket are thick splints called uprights. This basket will need 7 splints that are 25 in. long, ½ in. wide by $\frac{1}{16}$ in. thick and 11 splints the same width and thickness but 22 in. long. (Baskets with handles must have an odd number of uprights so the handle sits centered on an upright.) The horizontal members of the basket are called weavers. You'll need 32 weavers about 41 in. long and about ¼ in. wide by $\frac{1}{32}$ in. thick.

Soak the uprights until they are pliable—up to 30 minutes. Weave them into a tight mat about 9½ in. by 6½ in., with the long splints running in one direction and the short in the other. The tightness of the mat is limited by the thickness of the splint; little square openings will remain between the strips. Soak the weavers until they are workable. The first weaver helps to hold the bottom mat of the basket together. Weave it around the mat, over and under. The ends of the weaver will overlap, and this overlap should cross two consecutive uprights.

When wet, the sides of a basket can be bent to whatever shape you desire. Making sure the uprights are pliable, bend all the uprights upward and then inward toward the center of the basket. As you add courses of weavers you must continue to persuade the side splints to take the shape of the basket. As the rows accumulate, the uprights begin to stay in position without help.

Each weaver should begin and end under a different pair of uprights from its neighbors so that the overlaps are staggered around the basket. With all the weavers in place, the wet basket should be about 6½ in. high. Set the basket in a sunny window to dry for at least two weeks. You will find that the basket has become loose because the splints have shrunk in width as they lost moisture. Tighten the basket by pushing the weavers toward the bottom, one row at a time. With scissors, cut the uprights that end inside the top weaver flush with the top of the basket. Trim the outside uprights to form points a couple of inches above the edge of the basket. Invert the basket and immerse the projecting uprights in a shallow sinkful of water for a few minutes to soften them. Tuck them down into the weavers on the inside of the basket. The body of the basket is now finished and ready to be rimmed.

Making rims and handles — For me the most exciting part of making a basket is carving and shaping wood for rims and handles. I use white ash or hickory, trees fairly easy to find in New Hampshire, for the inner rim and handle. White oak, red oak or brown ash could also be used. For the outer rim, because it has little structural value, I use a heavy piece of ash splint rather than split and shave wood.

Choosing a good tree is important. If you select the right one, your handles will bend with ease; if not, they are likely to break. The perfect tree for handles is healthy, knot-free and 3 in. to 8 in. in diameter at chest height. The bark of a healthy tree looks young, tight and vibrant. It is best to use the wood as soon as it is cut, though a log will remain fresh for up to a month if kept whole. Once split up, the wood becomes too dry to use for basket parts in less than a week. I go into the woods in the morning to select a tree and usually have made four or five handles and rims before the afternoon has passed.

The length of the log you'll need is determined by the size of the basket to be rimmed. For our basket the rim is 40 in.

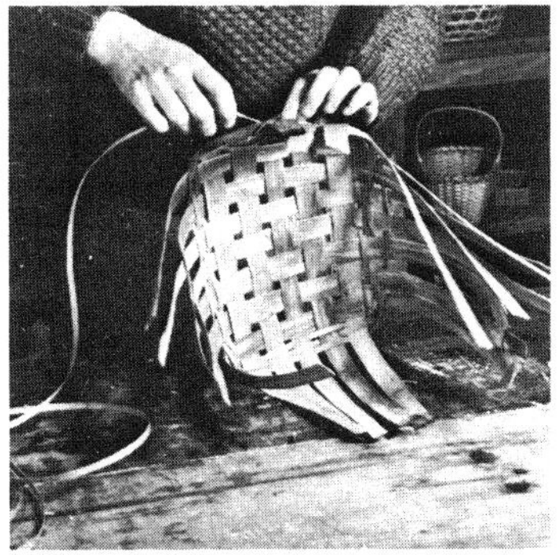

After the uprights have been woven into a mat, left, weave a weaver around it, right, and bend the uprights up and in. Successive courses of weavers begin to hold the uprights in shape to form the sides of the basket. The handle (figure 1) is shaped on a shaving horse with a drawknife, notched and attached to the basket (figure 2).

1. Basket handle before bending

Not to scale

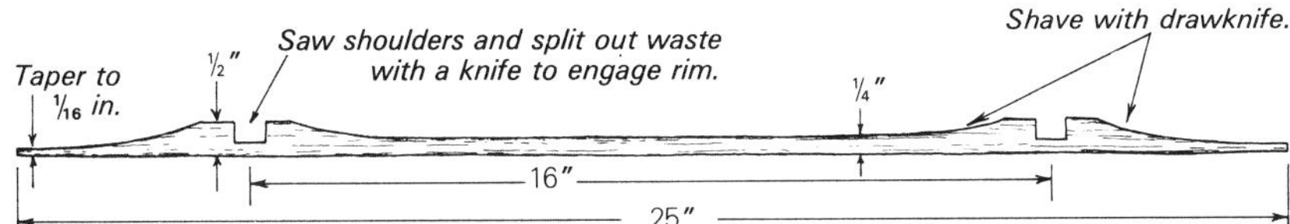

2. Basket construction

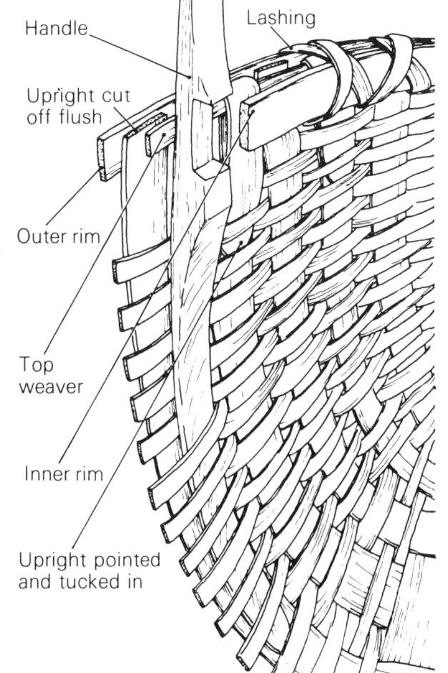

and the handle needs 25 in., so cut a section about 40 in. long from the butt of the tree. Split the log into quarters with a sledge and a wedge until you can split the pieces further with a froe and a wooden maul. The closer the piece is to the size of the handle and rim, the less time you will spend shaving it out with the drawknife. The best part of the wood for bending is the sapwood closest to the bark. Try to split out a section that is 1 in. to 1½ in. square or pie-shaped, but a 2-in. piece will do if splitting gets difficult.

To make the inner rim, clamp the stick in the shaving horse (an example can be found on page 8) with the bark side down. Holding the drawknife bevel side down, shave wood off the heartwood side of the stick, a single growth ring at a time. The drawknife can shave away lots of wood quickly, so be cautious. Your aim is to obtain a stick ½ in. wide and ⅛ in. thick. Follow the growth rings as closely as possible to maintain continuous grain. Working just inside the bark is easiest because the bark side of the stick is true to the grain. Hold the stick at arm's length and sight along its edge. The piece must be uniformly thick to make a smooth and even bend. When the stick is almost down to size, turn it over and shave off the bark and cambium layers, trimming the stick to its final thickness. When the piece is perfect, chamfer the edges with the drawknife, then use a hand knife to round the edges of the rim.

Green wood cannot be bent abruptly; it must be coaxed to take a new shape. With the sapwood side of the stick on the outside of the curve, begin at the center of the stick and work outward, bending the stick at 2-in. intervals. I use the end of the shaving horse as a fulcrum when I begin to bend and later hold the wood in my thumb and forefingers. With repeated coaxing, being more forceful each time, the stick will loosen up. When the shape is nearly round, form it into a complete circle and hold the overlapping ends together with two spring clamps. Now you can form the rim into an oval, matching it to the shape and size of the inside top of the basket.

If at any stage of the bending you discover sections of the rim that need to be shaved thinner to bend properly, don't be afraid to unbend the rim and put it back on the shaving horse; green wood will return to its bent shape easily. When you are satisifed with the shape of your rim, return it to the shaving horse and taper the ends in thickness so that no lump forms where they overlap.

Carving the handle is similar to shaping the rim. Start with a piece about 25 in. long and shave it into a ½-in.-square section. The arch of the handle is 16 in. long, with 4½-in. ends that project into the basket. Center the 16-in. measurement on the heartwood side of the stick. Shave away this section until its thickness is a uniform ¼ in. Chamfer the edges of this underside surface with the drawknife and round the chamfers. Leave the top surface of the handle flat. Taper the ends of the handle to about 1/16-in. thickness, as shown in figure 1.

Coax the handle to its bent shape as you did the rim. When you are satisfied with the curve, tie the ends of the handle together with wire or string and let it dry overnight. After drying, the once supple wood retains its form and no longer feels workable. To cut the notches to fit the rim, clamp the handle in the shaving bench. Use a fine-tooth saw to cut two slots to accommodate the width and thickness of the rim. Split out the waste with a knife.

The basket is finished by attaching the rims and handle to the body with spring clamps. Prepare the lashing from thin splint cut to 3/16-in. widths. Slide one end of the lashing splint down along an upright, fold it up and tuck it under a couple of weavers. Then bring the lashing up over the rim and down between two uprights. Wind the entire basket in one direction and tuck the end of the lashing into the body of the basket. This basket has a second lashing wound the other way around the rim, over the first lashing, creating a crisscross pattern and adding strength. The rim and handle form a rigid framework. The woven body flexes to resist shock. In combination, they make a durable and attractive vessel. □

Martha Wetherbee, of Sanbornton, N.H., is a former elementary-school teacher who turned to basketmaking several years ago.

Splitting Out a Firewood Tote

This project gets you started with green wood

by Wayne Ladd

The first time I met Vermont chairmaker Dave Sawyer, he was sitting on a shaving horse making a pitchfork. The only sounds were the creaking of the horse and the hiss of his drawknife. Having played at woodworking myself, I looked around the shop for the familiar router, bench saw and jointer, but saw only bits, braces, hand planes and, against one wall, a fine bench. Sawyer asked if I knew of any ash trees for sale. As it turned out, a huge, straight ash had blown over on my land. The following week, wedges in hand, Sawyer came over to split the trunk. We carried the splits to my car, then to his shop. The next day, I was amazed to find that he had a pitchfork made from my tree.

I was so impressed with Sawyer's skill and practiced eye for simple, sturdy woodworking that I spent the following year as his part-time apprentice. One of the first projects I learned was the log carrier shown here. Though the graceful bow gives the tote a fragile look, I've discovered that it can carry more wood than I care to heft at one time. And you can wrap twine around the foot rails and hang it from a rafter to make a wonderfully sturdy indoor child's swing.

Green-wood tote holds all the wood you want to carry.

Splitting green wood—Making the log carrier from riven green wood affords some important advantages over sawn, kiln-dried wood. First, you can go straight to your woodlot, fell a tree, and then split, shave and assemble it into a finished product, all in a matter of hours. Split along the grain instead of being sawn across it, riven wood is stronger than sawn wood, and satisfyingly easy to cut, bend and shape while green. You don't have to glue your projects together, either. Whittled tenons, dried over the woodstove, slip into mortises bored in wet wood, where they swell and lock the joint. For working green wood, you'll need two steel wedges, a mallet and a froe for splitting. A drawknife, spokeshave, brace and bit, and shaving horse complete the toolkit. For a shaving horse design, see the box on page 8.

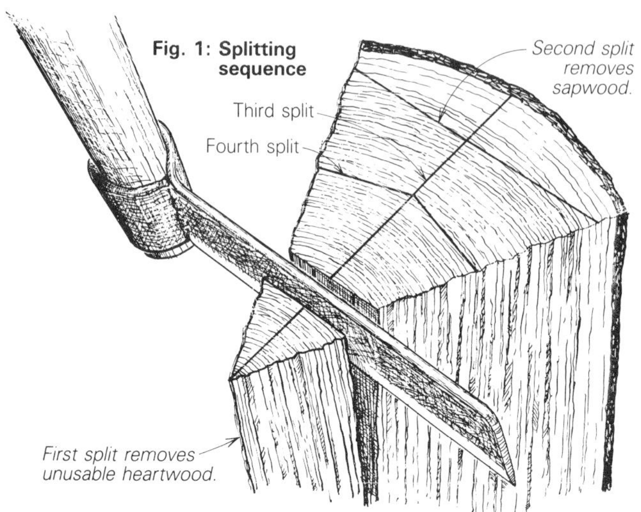

I use white ash for my carriers because it's the best bending wood that grows on my land. Hickory and oak also bend well. Whatever wood you choose, it should be straight-grained. Read the bark. If it's free of swirls and scars, chances are the wood will be the same. A 5-ft. log, 6 in. in diameter, will provide enough wood for a dozen carriers.

Quarter your log by first driving a wedge into one end and then leapfrogging the wedges up the side. If you've got a big log, split it into eighths. I use wedges only to get the log into manageable splits or bolts, which I then carry to the shop, where I split the parts closer to the final size with a froe. You'll need a brake—a mechanism that props the bolts at about 35° from the vertical for froeing. The crotch of a fallen tree or two heavy logs adjacent to each other make a suitable brake. Work with the bolt angled toward you.

Learning to froe is easy if you remember that this tool doesn't cut the wood, but rives or splits it along the material's natural fibers. Start the froe with a wack or two from the mallet. Then set the mallet aside, and continue the split by alternately levering the fibers apart and advancing the tool into the split. Split the unusable heartwood off the point of the quarter first. Then follow the sequence shown in figure 1, splitting in halves so that an equal amount of wood on each side of the froe will keep the cleave going straight down the length of the bolt instead of running off and exiting where you don't want it to. If the split does run out, put the heavy side down, and with the heel of your hand, put weight on this side of the split only. This will make the heavier half "give up" its grain. You can tell by the sound whether you

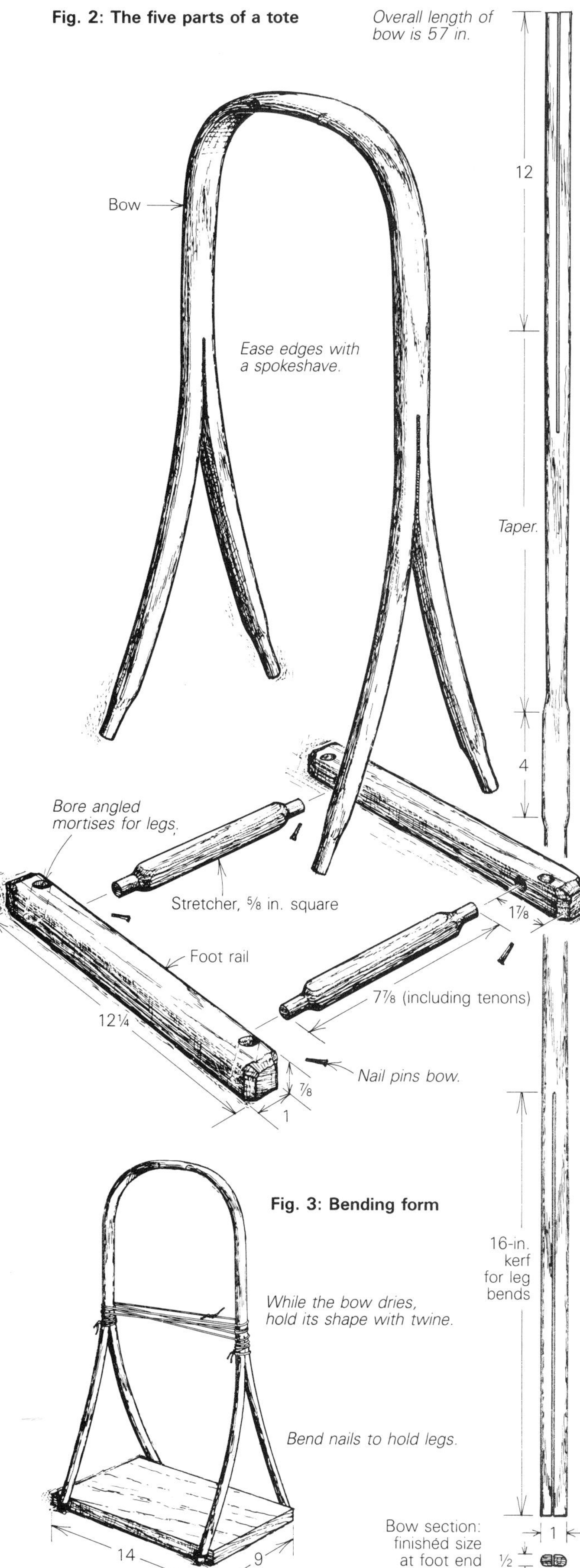

Fig. 2: The five parts of a tote

Fig. 3: Bending form

are following the grain. If it goes *tic, tic* and gives a little at a time, you're on. When it sounds like a branch breaking, it's jumping the grain and you need to straighten it out.

Make your rough splits ¼ in. oversize in section; you'll be shaving them down to finished dimensions with the drawknife. The bow will be steam-bent later, so keep grain direction in mind. Whether the growth rings are radial or tangential to the bend is up to you. I prefer a tangential split—it looks nicer and it makes it easier to follow the grain.

Drawknifing to size—Now the pleasant work can begin. Clamp the bow in your horse and shave one face smooth with the drawknife. Shave with the grain as much as you can and watch for tearing. You may not be able to read the grain, but your drawknife will. Downhill, the cut will be deliciously smooth; uphill, the knife will dig in. Pull in long, even strokes, sliding the drawknife sideways as you go. If you're doing it right, the slicing motion will peel off long shavings of even thickness. On each piece, smooth one face first, then square up an adjacent edge and shave the opposite face and edge to yield the finished dimensions. It's the same order of cuts you'd follow using a jointer, tablesaw and thickness planer. Keep the rails in a cool, damp spot so that they'll retain enough moisture to swell the tenons later. Dry the stretchers and the bow over a woodstove.

Define the handle's shape with graceful, ⅛-in. radius scallops on each side. By using the drawknife with the bevel down, you can control the depth and the shape of the scallop. Otherwise, the knife will want to dig in. Starting about 12 in. from each end of the bow, drawknife a taper toward the handle, as shown in figure 2. Also, hollow the inside (compression side) of the bow a little, maybe $\frac{1}{16}$ in. at the handle tapering to zero about 19 in. from each end.

Shape the handle to your liking, then ease the edges of the bow, rails and stretchers with your spokeshave. Finally, with a handsaw or bandsaw, rip 16-in. long kerfs at each end of the bow so that it can be wishboned into the rails after steaming.

My steamer is a stainless steel tube capped at one end, half filled with water and placed in the firebox of my woodstove. Any steel pipe or even an old steel drum will work. While the bow steams, make up the simple bending form shown in figure 3. It should be constructed to overbend the leg splits a little so that they'll have to be sprung back in to fit into the rails. This tension will stop the legs from splitting further.

With gloved hands, remove the bow from the steamer and limber up the bends by forming them over your knee. First put bends on each side of the handle about 4 in. from the center. This creates a bow with two "shoulders" rather than one that's a perfect half-circle. After you've defined the shoulders, bend the bow like Superman would bend a bar of steel. Make adjustments where needed—the handle has to look right, and you can't change the bend when it's in the form.

To keep the wood from splitting as you limber the leg bends, clamp the top of the kerf in your shaving horse and flex the legs into a graceful sweep from a point 1½ in. below the end of the kerf. Watch for kinks. A couple of turns of twine at the end of the kerf will keep the split from advancing when you release it from the shaving horse. Put the bow in the form and pull its sides in with a twine wrap.

Assembling the carrier—I assemble the stretchers to the rails after first whittling ⅝-in. long by $\frac{7}{16}$-in. diameter tenons at the ends of the stretchers. Trim the tenons for a squeaky-tight fit in a test mortise bored into scrap. To avoid splitting out the mortises, flatten the top and bottom of the tenon with your knife, bore the mortises in the rails and then tap the pieces together. The dry tenons swell, so I don't use glue, but if you feel that this is tempting fate, use some.

The legs fit into angled mortises bored through the rails. I eyeball the angle by clamping the base assembly in my vise, boring 7⁄16-in. mortises from the top inside corner of each rail with a brace and bit. The mortises should be located about 7⁄8 in. in from the end of each rail. I angle the brace so that the edge of the mortise will exit about 3⁄16 in. from the outside bottom edge of each rail. Just as the point of the bit breaks through, I withdraw it and complete boring from the bottom up. This eliminates splintering.

Before you whittle the tenons on the bow, it needs to be cleaned up with a scraper. Any splinters or hairline cracks in the bends will show up when you put a finish on, so examine the bow closely. To trim it, I stand it on the bench between two sticks clamped 8¼ in. apart. Nails driven into the sticks stay the bow while I stand back and take a look. If the bow appears crooked, I raise one leg or the other until it looks good. Then, using a compass to scribe them, I trim the ends of the long legs at an angle that will sit them flat on the bench.

The leg tenons should be 1 in. long. I shape the leg to taper right into the tenon. Shoved home at assembly, the joint fits tightly without fussing. Since these joints carry most of the stress, I glue them and drive a cut-nail pin from the inside of the foot perpendicular to the bow. Before pinning the joints, though, turn the carrier upside down and sight the legs. Align them by pushing one or the other beyond its mortise.

The final step is to trim the projecting leg tenons flush and to flatten the bottom, which always twists a little from the tension of the bow. I shave the feet with my drawknife, testing for flatness on the benchtop. When the carrier sits right, I sand out any dirty marks and put an oil finish on it. I mix a little stain in the oil to bring out the grain of the ash. □

Wayne Ladd turns trees into totes, treen and chairs at his home in East Calais, Vt.

Plans for a Swiss shaving horse

by Drew Langsner

These plans are adapted from the shaving horse used every day for the past 60 years by Swiss cooper Ruedi Kohler (see pages 9 to 14). This has several advantages over other shaving horses. The position of the pivoting arm provides great leverage. The treadle extends forward for a comfortable reach, the bridge extends a generous 4 in. past where the head contacts it, and the angle of the head provides direct downward pressure, important because drawknifing tends to pull the stock forward. With the pivot holes at the front of the arm, the head swings open automatically when you release the treadle, so that it's easy to reposition stock. The central arm with the head open on both sides is a pleasure when turning long stock end-for-end.

Keep in mind that the shaving horse is a folk tool, and lots of variations are possible. Bridge height, for instance, can range from 7 in. to 11 in., depending on your own height (I'm 5 ft. 8 in., and the height as drawn is good for me). The head and treadle are held by tusk tenons, which I find easy to construct, but I've bolted and face-glued heads to arms. All versions work well. One advantage of tusk-tenoning the parts is that it makes the arm easy to detach for transportation. □

Drew Langsner operates Country Workshops in Marshall, N.C.

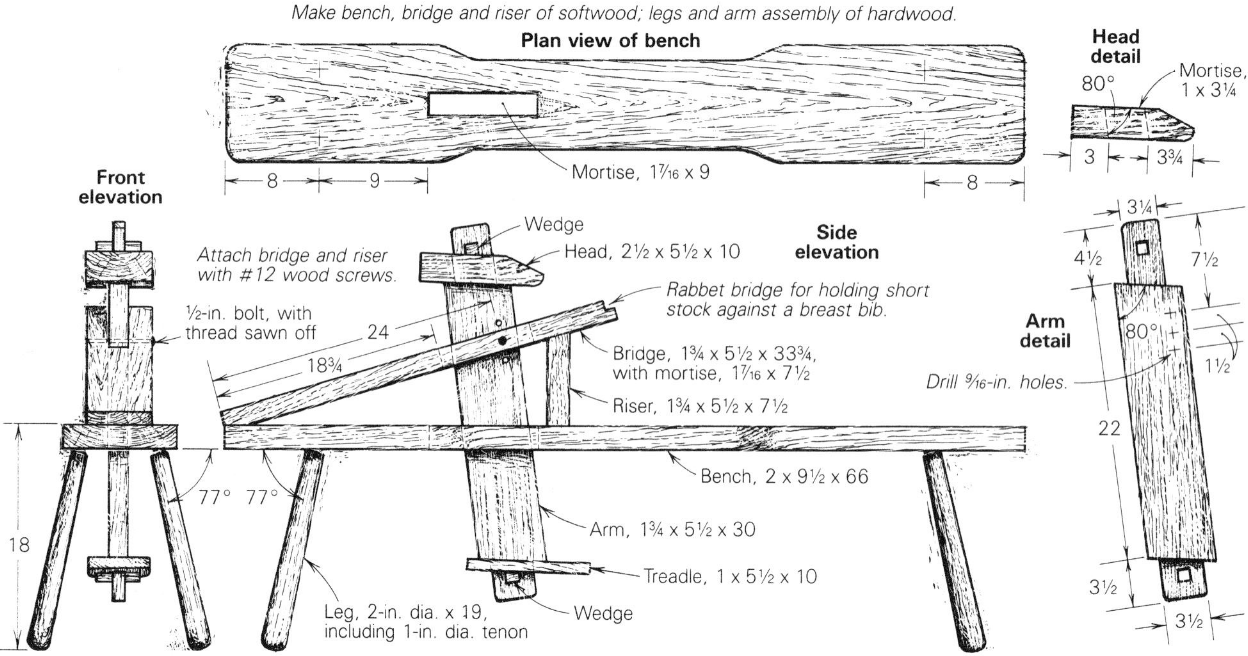

Making Wooden Buckets

White cooperage, the Swiss way

by Drew Langsner

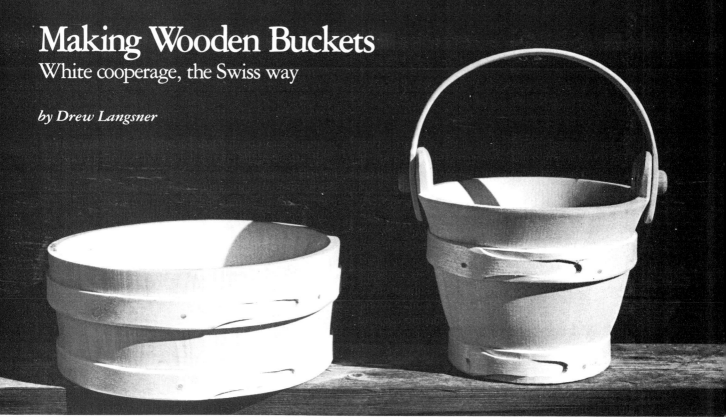

Swiss-style buckets of close-grained pine, with maple hoops. Traditionally used in small dairies, these liquid-tight containers are known as 'white' cooperage. The sculpted bucket, right, is carved from extra-thick staves after the staves have been glued together.

Coopered containers range in volume from huge wine vats to pint-size beer steins. Whatever their size, they are all basically tapered cylinders made of vertically arranged wooden staves with mitered edges. The staves are held tight by two or more hoops made from wood or metal. Bottoms consist of one or more boards which fit into a groove cut into the staves. Because of their cylindrical shape and the compression/tension relationship among staves, bottom and hooping, coopered containers are remarkably strong and durable.

As a trade and technique, cooperage may be divided into four overlapping areas: Wet cooperage is for holding liquids. Dry (or "slack") cooperage is for such less demanding needs as transporting or storing grains, fruits or nails. Of greater importance to woodworkers is the distinction between single-bottom and double-bottom cooperage. Double-bottom containers have bowed staves whose mitered edges are curved. Whiskey barrels are typical. In single-bottom cooperage—called "white cooperage" because the buckets are traditionally used to hold milk in small dairies—the staves are straight, as are the mitered edges.

The methods for single-bottom cooperage described in this article were taught to me by Rudolf Kohler, an 83-year-old cooper who lives and works in the Swiss Alps. I met Kohler in 1972, while I was searching for a traditional Swiss milking bucket to purchase as a souvenir. I'd not done much woodworking, but I became so fascinated with his work (and his beautiful shop) that I asked if it would be possible to study with him. He agreed and we managed well, even though I speak little German and Kohler knows no English; we put a great deal of positive energy into the relationship. Ten weeks later I wasn't a cooper, but I had become a woodworm. In 1980 I returned to Switzerland and worked with Ruedi Kohler again, this time for three fast-moving, hard-learning weeks.

Cooperage in the Swiss Alps was traditionally a winter trade practiced by farmers who were occupied with outdoor work from spring to fall. When Kohler was 22, having practiced alpine farming and cheesemaking with his father, he paid an old cooper fifty Swiss francs for four months of winter training. At the time (1923) the wage for a day's work was three francs. The next winter Kohler returned for another session. This time his usefulness earned back the fifty francs, and he was presented with a set of coopers' tools, which he still uses. Kohler says that when he got into cooperage the craft was in its decline. New factory-made metal containers were cheaper than coopers' woodenware, and modern health regulations gradually prohibited using old dairy vessels except high in the Alps. World War II was a good time for coopers, because metal was scarce. But after the war cheap plastics were introduced, and cooperage almost died out. During the last 15 years, interest in traditional crafts has renewed the demand for woodenware. In 1967 Kohler retired from farm-

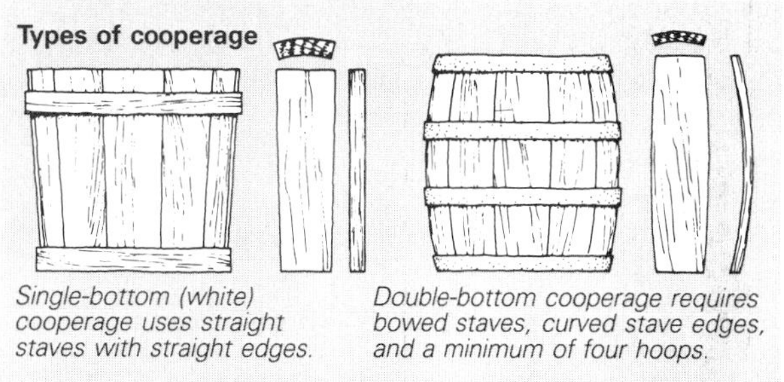

Single-bottom (white) cooperage uses straight staves with straight edges.

Double-bottom cooperage requires bowed staves, curved stave edges, and a minimum of four hoops.

ing and cheesemaking to become a full-time cooper. He still makes a few coopered vessels for farm use, but the greater part of his output goes to the tourist trade: milk buckets, bowls and butter churns that will never be put to work.

Cooperage techniques are closely related to those of many other traditional woodcrafts. Most of the work is done at a shaving horse, although a workbench with a vise and bench dogs is also useful. Many cooperage tools are shared by other crafts—hewing hatchets, froes, carving knives, drawknives, spokeshaves, planes, saws, drills, etc. Coopers also use several specialized tools—curved (hollowing) drawknives, convex-soled planes, and a device called a *croze,* which cuts a groove for the bottom board inside the assembled staves. I'll discuss each as it comes to hand when making a typical, single-bottom, staved container, 220mm (8⅝ in.) in diameter and 120mm (4¾ in.) high.

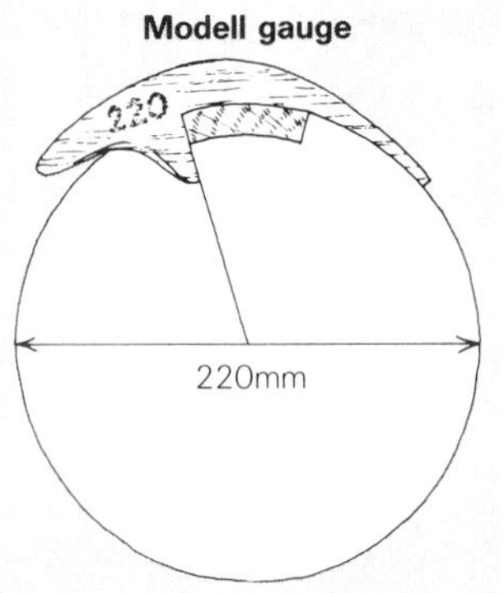

Wood selection—Many woods can be used for cooperage, but there are definite qualities that all coopers look for. The wood must be straight-grained and must work easily with hand tools. Cooperage requires well-seasoned wood, because shrinking staves leak and loosen the hoops. Double-bottom cooperage requires wood that bends easily; the best is white oak. For single-bottom cooperage, the favored wood in Switzerland is arve (*Pinus cembra*), known in English as Swiss stone pine. It is a slow-growing conifer found at altitudes generally above 3,300 ft. Arve growth rings average about 1mm (1/25 in.) per year. The fibers are extremely small, and the wood works easily, even across end grain and through knots. Arve does grow in the United States (it's planted as an ornamental), but any straight-grained softwood will do: pine, cedar, redwood, Douglas fir. Linden (basswood) can also be used. One of the appeals of cooperage is that the wood is readily available, and you need only a few board feet to make a bucket.

Traditionally, coopers buy wood as bucked logs, either round or split. A neighbor tells Kohler about some pine firewood of extra-fine quality, or a local sawmill puts aside an arve log. Kohler used to begin with a crosscut saw, but today he bucks out sections with a chainsaw, working around major knots, sawing suitable stave lengths. Staves for our 120mm high bowl are initially cut 150mm (6 in.) long. These rounds are then radially split into pie-shaped billets, which are air-seasoned in a drafty hayloft for at least a year.

Kohler sometimes buys wood that has been plain-sawn into thick, unedged planks. Sawmill edging often wastes much wood. The advantage of lumber is that it is easy to handle. The disadvantage is that some staves will not be quarter-grained, which is never the case with split-out stock. After air-seasoning, the wood is roughed into stave blanks—split along a radial plane using a small froe and a maul. Stave width varies. For our small container, widths can range from 35mm (1⅜ in.) to 80mm (3 in.). Kohler uses a broad hatchet for trimming and roughly tapering the sides, perhaps 3mm to 6mm (3/16 in.) wider at the top than at the bottom. This produces a taper in the finished bucket such that the diameter of the bottom is about 10% less than that of the top.

Kohler next stacks the blanks against a south-facing outdoor wall for further air-drying. Then a few days before he needs them, he takes the staves indoors for a final drying on a rack above the stove. He often groups stave blanks in bunches according to length, for single projects. At this stage the aggregate width of the staves should be about four times the bowl's diameter—in this case about 880mm (35 in.).

Shaping the staves—Swiss coopers find the correct edge angle of a stave with a simple gauge called a *modell.* The modell is a thin crescent-shaped piece of wood whose inner contour matches the exterior curve of the container. The perpendicular edge guide at one end of the modell represents the radius line of the curve.

Staves are shaped at a shaving horse, using a flat drawknife, a hollowing drawknife, a long jointer plane and an appropriate modell. Shaping begins with drawknife work on the exterior face. Hold the modell across the top end of the blank to gauge the curvature, then with the blank in the shaving horse, shave the top third of the stave to fit the modell. You could pencil in the shape on the end grain, but Kohler just judges by eye. The first cuts should be light, to verify grain direction and irregularities. Block out the curve from the sides toward the center, keeping the stave as thick as possible. Turn the blank end for end and drawknife the rest of the outside face. The curve for the bottom end is gauged by eye to match that of the top end. The modell is not used at the bottom end because stave taper results in a tighter curve there. Fair the whole outside face. If necessary, use the drawknife in reverse, as a push tool, to handle grain that runs into the wood. Or reposition the stave in the shaving horse, to get the most from your pull stroke. Then turn the stave over.

Rough out the inside face with a hollowing drawknife. This is a deeply curved coopers' drawknife with an exterior bevel. Shave from both ends, to approximately 18mm (11/16-in.) thickness. Do not attempt to cut thinner walls at this stage. If you don't have a hollowing drawknife, you can use either a scorp or a narrow inshave ground with an outside bevel. Or you can reshape (and retemper) a flat drawknife to an appropriate curvature, about 35mm (1⅜-in.) depth across a circular arc that spans about 120mm (4¾ in.). Another method (which Kohler uses for the inside of his oval milking buckets) is to dog individual staves to the workbench and hollow them with a convex-soled plane.

Edge angles are roughed out with a flat drawknife and the modell, which is always gauged at the upper rim. To hold the stave and have tool access along the full length of the edge, Kohler sets one end against a rabbet cut across the near end of the work ledge on his shaving horse. He holds the other end tight against a breast bib, a small flat board that hangs by a string around his neck. Stave edges must be flat, not twisted or curved. Any container has to be tapered so that the hoops can be driven tight, but more than an 8mm (5/16-in.) taper for a 150mm (6-in.) long stave results in a container with too much taper, which won't hold its hoops.

Stave edges are finished with a jointer plane set upside down on the edge of the shaving horse, or secured in a vise. Run the stave over the plane, checking the angle between passes. For safety, grip the staves well above the plane sole, and spit on your fingertips to increase your hold. Besides the

Drawings: Christopher Clapp

correct angle, check for flatness. Hold pairs of staves side by side and look for uniform contact. Try wiggling them back and forth, making sure they don't wobble or roll.

Once the staves are jointed, lay them out side by side in a flat shallow arc to check for correct circumference (3.14 times intended diameter). The proper length, measured with a tape or a folding rule, which can follow the arc, should be the circumference you are aiming for, plus or minus 2%. If the series is too long, drawknife and plane one or more staves down to size. If too short, substitute a slightly larger stave.

Test assembly—Two wooden hoops will hold the completed container together. To position the staves for setting the hoops, Kohler drills mating holes and inserts small hardwood pegs into the sides of each stave. The pegged staves won't shift while the hoops are hammered tight.

Two temporary metal hoops are used in an initial test assembly, and to hold the staves in place for further shaping before the wooden hoops are fitted. Kohler makes his own metal hoops (see drawing, below right), and keeps a large collection of them in various diameters. To test-assemble, peg the staves together and place the cylinder on a workbench, bottom rim facing up. Fit the larger metal hoop onto the assembled staves first, and drive it tightly in place with a square-headed hammer or a coopers' hoop driver. A hoop driver looks like a blacksmiths' hammer with a notch ground along the peening edge. I made one by taking a small rock-climbing hammer and filing a groove into the face of its pick end. Set the groove over the hoop edge and hit the head of the driver with a second hammer. Work round and round until the hoop stops moving downward. The correct test-fit should be about one-fourth from the top rim of the container. When the first hoop is in position, fit the second, smaller hoop.

Although the staves are pegged, they can pivot in and out on those pegs. If a stave protrudes, hammer it in—but place a second hammer inside to dampen the blows, and vice versa—until you have averaged out the differences.

Check the container for roundness by measuring across the upper rim from two perpendicular locations. You can live with a discrepancy up to 5mm (3/16 in.). Look for openings between staves. If you find any, knock off the temporary hoop and check all edge angles against the modell. Reassemble. If there are still spaces on the inside, disassemble and plane one stave narrower. If gaps show on the outside, remove a stave (save it for your next container) and substitute a new one that's wider. This is your last chance to be sure that the staves fit together perfectly.

Dressing the assembled staves—Once you have the stave edges flush, you can dress the rims and the interior surface. Slightly moisten the end grain of the upper rim with a wet sponge, to soften the wood. Then plane the rim flat. A block plane works nicely. Check by eye or by placing the container upside down on a flat surface.

The lower rim of the assembled staves generally requires sawing before planing. Pencil a series of marks measuring from the (now flat) upper rim, in this case at 120mm (4¾ in.). Set the container on its side and begin a shallow sawcut aimed from one pencil mark to the next. Kohler uses a small backsaw. Make a series of shallow passes around the container. For a flat cut, hold the saw parallel to the plane of the rim, not perpendicular to the side of the staves. With the

The outside curve and edge bevel of a bucket stave are checked with a gauge called a modell, *drawn on facing page.*

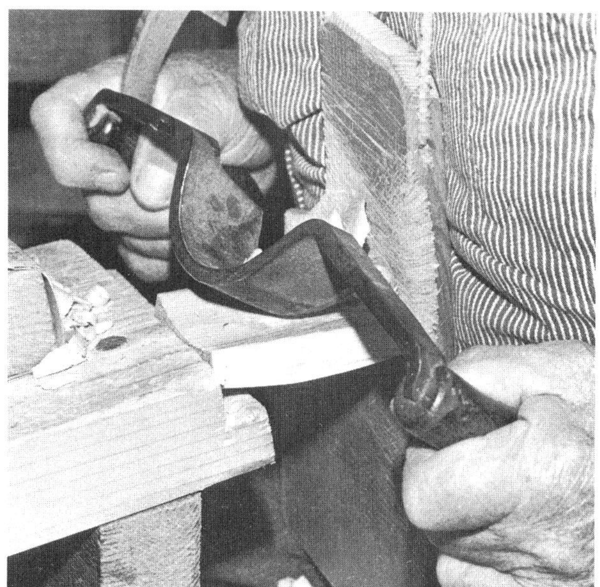

To shave short staves, cooper Ruedi Kohler supports one end of the blank in a rabbet on the front of his shaving-horse ledge, the other against a wooden bib.

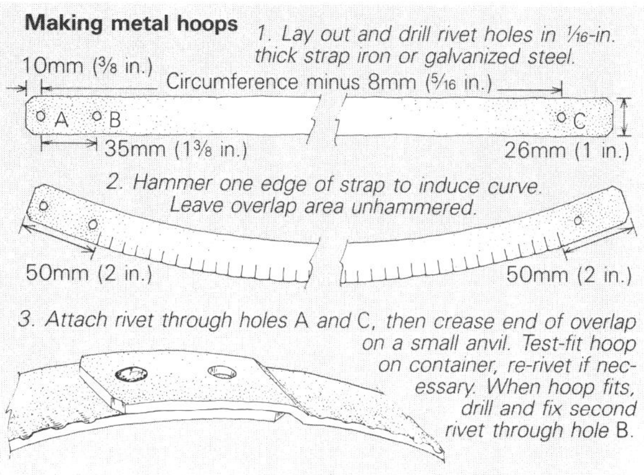

Making metal hoops
1. Lay out and drill rivet holes in 1/16-in. thick strap iron or galvanized steel.
10mm (3/8 in.)
Circumference minus 8mm (5/16 in.)
A
B
C
35mm (1 3/8 in.)
26mm (1 in.)
2. Hammer one edge of strap to induce curve. Leave overlap area unhammered.
50mm (2 in.)
50mm (2 in.)
3. Attach rivet through holes A and C, then crease end of overlap on a small anvil. Test-fit hoop on container, re-rivet if necessary. When hoop fits, drill and fix second rivet through hole B.

The staves are test-assembled and temporarily held in place with two metal hoops, so that the inside of the cylinder can be smoothed either with a Surform, as shown in the photo above, or with a convex-soled plane.

This croze *is like a marking gauge with teeth. Instead of merely scribing the groove for the bottom, it cuts it directly into the assembled staves.*

Shaping bottom board

1. Use a marking gauge to scribe the edge of the bottom board, and drawknife to this shape.

4.5mm (3/16 in.)
5.5mm (1/4 in.)
8mm (5/16 in.)

2. Use a slotted hardwood stick (called a fümel) to compress the edge to 4.5mm.

4.5mm
Fümel

waste sawn away, plane the lower rim smooth.

At this point the staves are still of various thicknesses. To indicate their dressed thickness, bevel the rims inside and out, leaving the upper rim 15mm (5/8 in.) thick and the lower rim 17mm (11/16 in.) thick, to accommodate the groove for the bottom of the container. For the outside bevel, use a spokeshave held about 30° from the staves and produce a rim line as close to a circle as possible. Gauge the proper thickness and bevel the inside, using a sharp carving knife, held point down in your fist like a dagger.

Some white coopers dress the inside with a scorp, but Kohler uses small wooden planes with convex soles and irons. He planes along the length of the staves, first from the upper rim, then from the lower, until the inside surface is worked down to the rim guidelines. Difficult grain can be shaped with a convex Surform. Sand the inside with 80-grit, then 120-grit paper, working across the grain. The outside of the container will be dressed later.

The bottom—Kohler's croze, the tool that cuts the bottom groove in the assembled staves, resembles an enlarged marking gauge with a row of coarse teeth in place of the scriber (photo, below left). This cutter is held by a setscrew or a wedge in the sliding arm. The cutter's teeth are filed much like coarse crosscut-saw teeth, having 5 points to the inch. Kohler made his from an old plane iron. The groove can be cut in a number of other ways, including scribing the edges with a marking gauge and excavating it with a chisel.

On our container, the groove is 13mm (1/2 in.) above the lower rim, 5mm (3/16 in.) wide and 5mm deep. Set the assembled staves bottom up on the shaving-horse bench, secure between your thighs and against a block between the container and the upright supporting the shaving-horse work ledge. Be sure to hold the croze flat against the bottom rim. Press down hard to avoid chatter (and scratching the dressed staves) and take a series of shallow passes around the rim. The 5mm width of the groove requires resetting the distance between cutter and fence for a second round of passes.

Bottoms can be split from a wide straight-grained billet, taken from a clear sawn board, or glued up from narrower stock. The bottom wood is planed smooth on one side, scribed with a marking gauge to 18mm (11/16 in.) thick and planed to thickness.

You can find the radius for the bottom with straight-leg dividers. Open them to the approximate radius, judged by eye. Place one leg in the bottom of the groove and walk the dividers around the groove. By trial and error, readjust the dividers until you can walk off six equal divisions. The dividers are now set for the exact radius of the bottom.

Scribe the circumference on one face of the bottom and saw it out just outside the scribed line. Put the bottom in a vise, and spokeshave the rim to just inside the scribed line, rotating the wood in order to spokeshave with the grain. The bottom should be 0.5mm (0.02 in.) undersize.

With your marking gauge, scribe two lines 5.5mm (1/4 in.) apart on the edge of the bottom board, and then drawknife the board to the shape shown in the drawing at left. With the board still in the vise, use a hardwood stick with a 4.5mm (3/16-in.) slot and compress the rim to 4.5mm thickness. Then sand the bottom board across the grain.

With the bottom shaped, you are ready to glue up. Knock off the metal hoops and disassemble the staves, laying them on the workbench in order. Spread a thin coat of white glue on both edges of each stave. Glue is used so that the exterior can be dressed with the hoops removed. Do not use yellow glue. It sets too fast and complicates knocking the staves apart again if you run into trouble fitting the bottom. Reassemble the staves with glue and pegs, and lower the bottom board (chamfered edge down) into the container from the top. Spread the lower rim until the bottom board snaps into its groove. Hold the staves in place with a loose-fitting, temporary upper hoop. Tap the staves around the bottom, replace the lower metal hoop, and tighten it with hammer and hoop driver. Hammer the staves in or out as necessary. Then tighten the upper hoop. Allow the glue to set at least one hour before you remove the metal hooping, so you can spokeshave the exterior of the staves to the beveled upper and lower edges. Sand the outside of the container.

Wooden hoops—The most distinctive feature of Swiss milk buckets is their beautiful wooden hoops. The design is a refined variation of the so-called arrow-lock pattern. Hoops can be made from maple, walnut, oak, even pine limbs. Traditionally, hooping stock comes from the trunk of a choice young maple, 120mm (4¾ in.) to 200mm (8 in.) in diameter at the butt. A tree that is growing in an open area is preferred because its limbs grow outward, perpendicular to the stem, yielding minimal grain deformity around knots. In thick woods, tree limbs reach up to the light, causing irregular stem grain.

Buck the bole to a length at least 200mm longer than the circumference you will need. The bottom hoop will fit flush with the container's bottom, and the top hoop will be about a hoop's width below the rim. Hoop length includes an overlap of some 160mm (6⅜ in.), plus about 50mm (2 in.) for waste and end-cuts. Each bole length will yield 20 to 40 hoop blanks, and it may be possible to take two clear lengths from a single tree. Seal the end grain, and split the bole in half and then into eighths as wood is needed. Green wood is easiest to work and to bend, but air-dried wood can be used. Maple splits easily, but its grain is rarely straight, so bandsaw two radial strips 8mm to 10mm (about ⅜ in.) thick, and 30mm to 35mm (about 1⅜ in.) wide; the growth rings will cross the thickness of the strips. Blanks from ring-porous hardwoods can be split to size. Drawknife the bark side to a smooth and straight, or slightly bowed, edge. You will have to support the hoop wood on an extension stick sandwiched between shaving-horse ledge and jaw.

Next, decide which will be the outside face of the hoop. This can be either side of the blank, but the wood often takes a natural bow. Drawknife the outside face smooth, then scribe a line 26mm (1 in.) from the dressed edge and drawknife the blank to width.

To fit the tapering shape of the container, the hoop in section must be thicker at the bottom than at the top. Mark and then drawknife the hoop 7mm (¼ in.) thick at its top edge, 9mm (⅜ in.) thick at its bottom edge.

The next step is to measure the exact length of the hoop. Wrap a piece of stout string around the container where the center of the hoop will lie. Add 8mm (5⁄16 in.). Transfer this length to the hoop blank, leaving room for the 80mm (3-in.) overlap at each end. The drawings at right detail the steps for first shaping the same side profile at each end of the hoop, and then shaping the female and male pattern in plan view.

Assemble and fit the longer upper hoop first. Ladle boiling

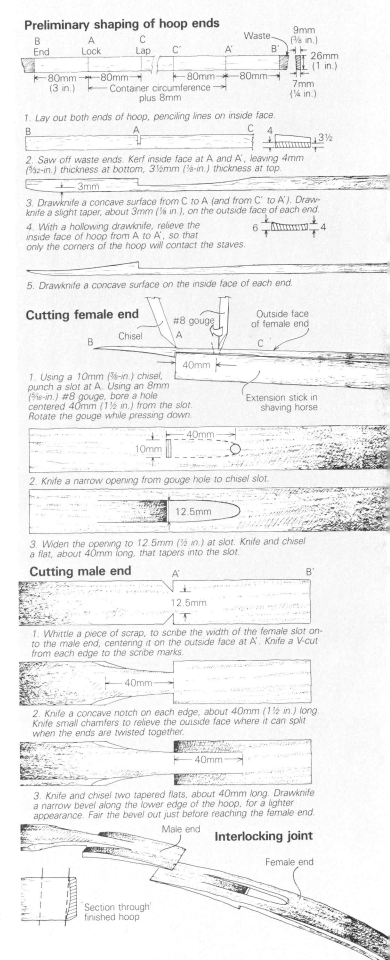

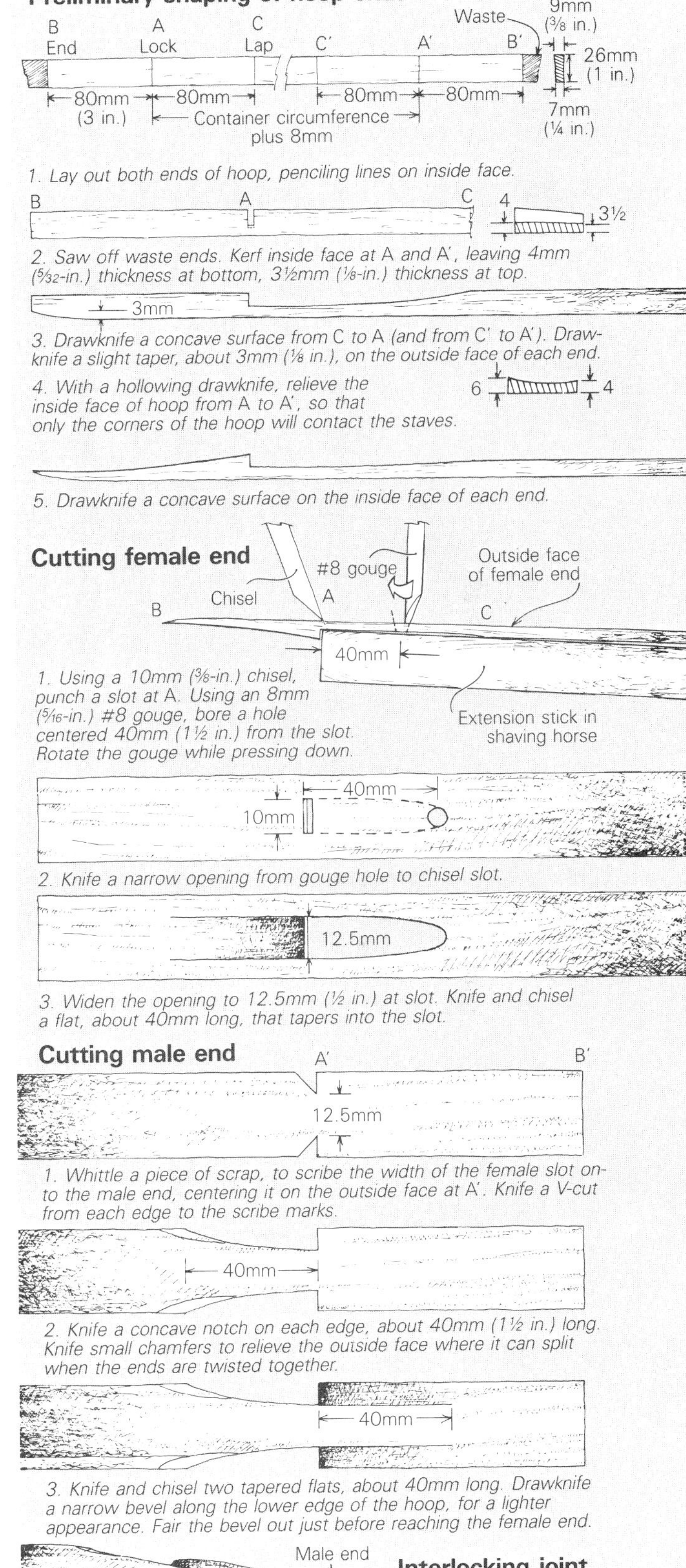

Preliminary shaping of hoop ends
B
End
A
Lock
C
Lap
C'
A'
B'
Waste
9mm
(⅜ in.)
26mm
(1 in.)
7mm
(¼ in.)
80mm
(3 in.)
80mm
80mm
80mm
Container circumference
plus 8mm
1. Lay out both ends of hoop, penciling lines on inside face.
B
A
C
4
3½
2. Saw off waste ends. Kerf inside face at A and A', leaving 4mm (5⁄32-in.) thickness at bottom, 3½mm (⅛-in.) thickness at top.
3mm
3. Drawknife a concave surface from C to A (and from C' to A'). Drawknife a slight taper, about 3mm (⅛ in.), on the outside face of each end.
4. With a hollowing drawknife, relieve the inside face of hoop from A to A', so that only the corners of the hoop will contact the staves.
6
4
5. Drawknife a concave surface on the inside face of each end.
Cutting female end
Chisel
#8 gouge
Outside face of female end
B
A
C
40mm
1. Using a 10mm (⅜-in.) chisel, punch a slot at A. Using an 8mm (5⁄16-in.) #8 gouge, bore a hole centered 40mm (1½ in.) from the slot. Rotate the gouge while pressing down.
Extension stick in shaving horse
40mm
10mm
2. Knife a narrow opening from gouge hole to chisel slot.
12.5mm
3. Widen the opening to 12.5mm (½ in.) at slot. Knife and chisel a flat, about 40mm long, that tapers into the slot.
Cutting male end
A'
B'
12.5mm
1. Whittle a piece of scrap, to scribe the width of the female slot onto the male end, centering it on the outside face at A'. Knife a V-cut from each edge to the scribe marks.
40mm
2. Knife a concave notch on each edge, about 40mm (1½ in.) long. Knife small chamfers to relieve the outside face where it can split when the ends are twisted together.
40mm
3. Knife and chisel two tapered flats, about 40mm long. Drawknife a narrow bevel along the lower edge of the hoop, for a lighter appearance. Fair the bevel out just before reaching the female end.
Male end
Interlocking joint
Female end
Section through finished hoop

Ladling hot water over the hoop blank, above, limbers it for bending. The blank must be twisted, below, in order to fit one end through the other.

A knife sizes the rim line by beveling the waste away. Both the inside and the outside of the container will be thinned to meet these top and bottom rim lines.

water over the hoop for about one minute. Limber the hoop by flexing it. Limber the joint ends by inserting them in a vise opened about 10mm (3/8 in.); bend toward the interior face. Reheat the hoop by ladling more boiling water. Bend the hoop into a circle and twist the ends to insert the tab through the outside face of the slot. Any small splits should be immediately pared off with a knife so they don't run into the hoop.

With your container upside down on the bench, fit the hoop. Drive it into place by hammering on a small hardwood block. The hoop should become tight 25mm to 30mm (about an inch) from the upper rim. If the hoop is too tight (short), remove it from the container, and with the joint still assembled, saw 2mm to 3mm (up to 1/8 in.) from one of the locking edges of the tab. An alternative is to thin the overlapping section by paring the inside faces with a knife. If the hoop is loose (too long), add a thin spacer between the male and female locking edges.

Now heat, limber and lock the lower hoop. Fit it so that the bottom of the hoop is flush with the bottom of the container. With a knife, trim the edges of the overlapping ends. Nail or peg both hoops in place. For pegs, drill 3mm (1/8-in.) diameter holes through the hoops and into, but not through, the staves. Locate one peg on each side of the lock joint, plus two evenly spaced pegs on the opposite side of the hoop. Nails are generally brass with round heads.

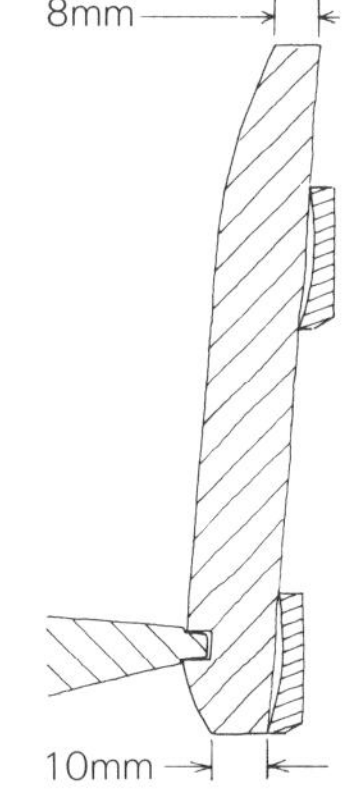

After the wooden hoops have been fitted, the inside face of the rims can be dressed with a knife for a lighter, more finished look. Take long, smooth slices, beveling them about 65mm (2½ in.) from the top rim. The final thickness at the rim should be 8mm (5/16 in.). Make a similar bevel around the interior of the bottom rim.

A handle is optional. If you want one, make it from maple and secure it with wooden pegs. Note Kohler's clever arrangement in the photo on page 9: the two extra-long staves are relieved, so the handle moves freely and doesn't bind against the rim. This photo also shows how the sides of a bucket are sometimes sculpted. While the effect is decorative, the purpose is really practical—it allows the bucket to be made more tapered, while still using a basically circular hoop of minimum inside taper. Kohler begins such a bucket with thicker, more tapered staves, gluing up the bucket as usual. Where the top of each of the two wooden hoops will be, he makes a sawcut about 3mm (1/8 in.) deep. With a skew chisel, he carves flat the area where each hoop will land. Above the area for the top hoop, he drawknifes the outside of the bucket concave. Above the area for the bottom hoop, he drawknifes the bucket convex. He then fits the wooden hoops as usual.

For farm use, staved containers are not given any surface treatment. The hoops of bowls and buckets sold as gifts or prizes are often chip-carved, and the whole is given a coat of quick-dry semigloss lacquer. Lacquered ware is easy to keep clean, but it is decorative, never used on the farm. Under continuous wetting and drying, it would soon deteriorate. □

Drew Langsner operates Country Workshops in Marshall, N.C. For details on course offerings, write Country Workshops, Rt. 3, Box 262, Marshall, N.C. 28753. Photos by the author.

Bending with Ammonia

by Bill Keenan

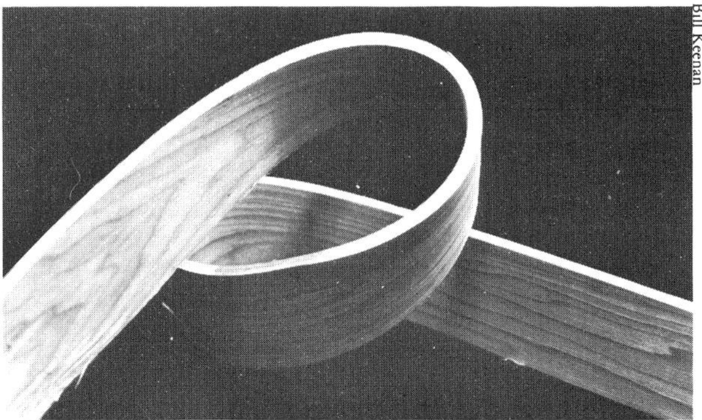

After plasticizing in anhydrous ammonia, the ¼-in. stock above was easily bent into a pretzel shape.

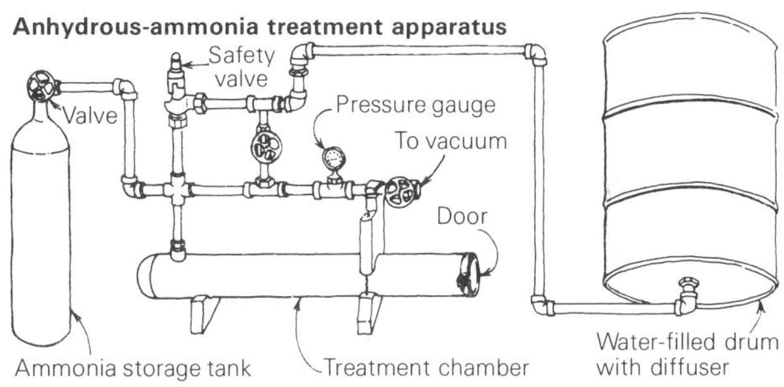

Consider the possibilities if wood were as pliable as leather. Form could be added to the beauty of wood without having to use subtractive methods of shaping. With this in mind, Huff Wesler, at the University of Wisconsin's Art Department, has experimented with wood that is plasticized by immersion in gaseous anhydrous ammonia. After exposure to the ammonia, wood can readily be coaxed into fantastic forms.

The underlying principle of this process is not hard to understand. A solvent applied to the wood diffuses into the cell-wall structure. The bonds that clamp the wood's microscopic components together are disassembled. The wood becomes flexible, and when bending force is applied the components are physically displaced. As the solvent diffuses out of the wood, these microscopic cell components bond together in their new positions. The piece regains its rigidity in the new shape, like hair after a permanent-wave treatment.

Steam has traditionally been used to soften wood, but ammonia plasticizes the fibers more quickly and more completely; yet ammonia is not so strong that it will dissolve cell tissue as might a stronger solvent. Only the cell components are separated, allowing movement with minimal bending stresses.

The process Wesler uses derives from research conducted over the past 15 years at Syracuse University, and commercial applications of it are covered by a number of U.S. patents. It's important to note that anhydrous ammonia (anhydrous means without water) is chemically pure NH_3, whereas household ammonia is a dilute solution of ammonia gas in water. Experiments with household ammonia will not bend wood.

Ammonia vapors are extremely dangerous to the eyes and lungs, and this process releases quantities of these noxious fumes. A fume hood and goggles are essential parts of the apparatus. The original Syracuse experiments were conducted atop a tall building, where strong winds carried the fumes away. Despite the awful vapors, Wesler believes the process holds real potential for the craftsman and sculptor.

He built a treatment chamber (see drawing at right) for introducing ammonia into wood; using parts acquired from ordinary plumbing suppliers and stainless-steel fittings from dairy suppliers, he spent under $1,000. The unit was welded together to withstand a pressure of 800 PSI as a safety measure. Pure, anhydrous ammonia at room temperature and at approximately 130 PSI pressure is used in the chamber.

The first step in treatment is selecting the right piece of wood. In general, woods good for steambending are also good for ammonia bending. Certain species work better than others; oak works well whereas maple does not. Bending stock should be straight-grained and flatsawn. Surface irregularities and such defects as knots should be avoided, because they tend to concentrate stress. Moisture content of the wood is also important. Wesler prepares his bending stock in a plastic enclosure into which moist heat is fed, like a steam room. The stock stays there for about a month, until its moisture content is raised to an optimal 20%.

To demonstrate, Wesler places a ¼-in. thick hickory board in the chamber, exposing it to the gaseous ammonia for about 45 minutes. (Time varies according to thickness and species of wood; generally, an hour per ¼-in. thickness is adequate.) When he removes the piece, it's soft and ready to be shaped.

The bending rate can mean the difference between success and failure. If the piece crumples or kinks along its concave face, bending should be halted for about 30 seconds to allow the wood to flow. But there is also a time constraint, as the wood will begin to stiffen in about 15 minutes.

Ammonia-treated wood requires significantly less force to bend than steam-treated wood. Pieces ¼ in. thick can be bent by hand and then restrained by taping or clamping. There are other methods of bending, such as form bending, for which a mold is required. A pipe makes an excellent form for a helix or circle. Thicker pieces require a bending strap.

Once the bending is completed, the piece is dried until it reaches equilibrium with surrounding humidity conditions. A temperature and humidity-controlled drying room is best, but air-drying works well too. Warping and distortion can be controlled by leaving restraints on the piece until it is dry. This may take from hours to weeks, depending on the size and type of wood, and on the drying conditions.

Following exposure to ammonia, wood is changed in several ways. It is often denser and harder than before, a condition you can augment by compressing the wood while it is still soft. The color of the wood usually darkens slightly, but this can be an asset, as some plain woods come to life. Color change can be prevented with a sulfur-dioxide pretreatment.

There are a lot of variables involved in plasticizing wood, but the results are worth the trouble. The ease with which ammonia-treated wood can be bent, molded, embossed, densified or any combination of these processes offers a new horizon for the wood craftsman. □

Bill Keenan is a woodworker and forester in Milwaukee, Wisc.

EDITOR'S NOTE: Commercial applications of the ammonia bending process are covered by patent. For more information, contact the Director, Invention Administration Program, Research Corp., 6840 East Broadway Blvd., Tucson, Ariz. 85710.

Steambending

Heat and moisture plasticize wood

by William A. Keyser, Jr.

Ever wonder how old bentwood furniture parts were made or how ribs for boats are formed? Probably by steam bending. This process uses steam or boiling water to plasticize the wood so that it can be bent, usually over a form or mold. Upon cooling and drying, the bent piece retains its shape. The distinct advantage of steaming is that the grain of the wood follows the curve, thus eliminating the short-grain problems associated with bandsawn curves.

Of course a lamination, i.e., several thin pieces glued together in the curved position, will also do the job. But there is something nice about one integral piece of wood making the bend, with the grain following the curve. The time required to resaw and surface all the laminations is saved, no wood is lost to saw kerfs and ugly glue lines don't surface if the bent piece is subsequently carved or shaped. Also, a lot fewer clamps are required.

Steam bending has shortcomings. The most troublesome is accurately predicting springback. A laminated member will conform very closely to a mold; the greater the number of laminations, the less it will spring back. In steam bending the results depend upon the grain structure of each piece of wood. Local eccentricities—knots, checks and cross grain—will affect the final curve much more than in lamination, where the process itself tends to homogenize the structure of the member. This disadvantage becomes critical when exact duplicates must be made. Also, some breakage or rejects can be expected in steam bending. If ten pieces are required, bend twelve or thirteen.

When deciding whether to steam-bend or laminate, reason it out this way: If the member must start precisely at some point *A*, negotiate a specific curve and end up exactly at point *B*, and do so repeatedly, the odds are better if you laminate. If the relative positions of *A* and *B* are not critical, or if their relationship is maintained by the rest of the structure and if there is some tolerance in the path taken from *A* to *B*, then the integrity of a single piece would justify steam bending. Where either process is appropriate, the material and time saved in steam bending by not resawing settle the question.

The piece of wood to be bent is placed in a closed container or steam box and bathed in steam generated by boiling water. The steam gradually softens the structure of the wood and makes it flexible. The wood is then forced around a mold and clamped in position. The outside circumference of the wood must usually be reinforced with a metal strap. The shape of the mold is determined by the curve desired, with due allowance for springback. The bent piece is either left clamped on this mold to cool and dry, or it is immediately placed on a separate jig to hold it in position during drying.

When the piece has cured and is removed from the mold or drying jig, it usually springs back slightly. With luck, it now

Bill Keyser is professor of woodworking and furniture design at Rochester Institute of Technology. He's currently writing a woodworking textbook.

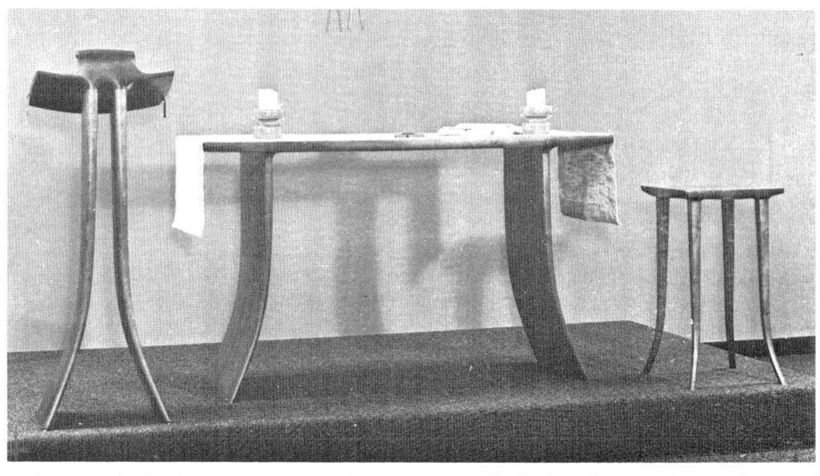

Ark at Interfaith Chapel, University of Rochester, is 8 ft. high and made of steam-bent teak angled and then joined edge-to-edge to create the shell's compound curve. Pieces bent off-the-corner become legs of small table in chapel at Geneseo, N. Y.; plain bends joined edge-to-edge support altar and lectern.

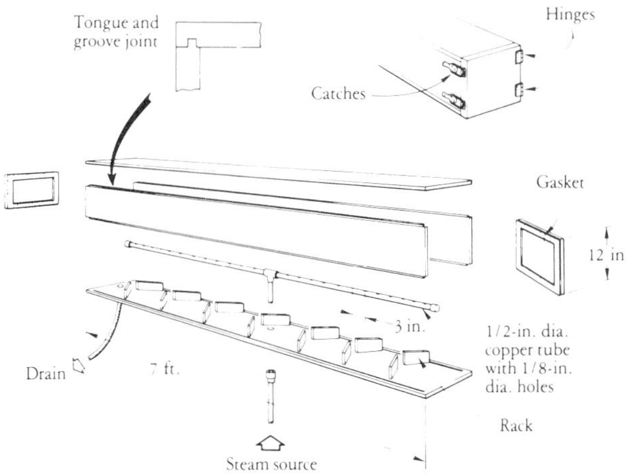

Keyser's steam box is made from one sheet of ordinary 3/4-in. plywood and is supported on sawhorses.

Wet steam for bending can be generated in a variety of ways. Keyser uses a kerosene-fired wallpaper steamer.

coincides with the desired curve. Machining, cutting of joints and shaping can then be done on the bent piece of wood.

When wood is steamed, the heat and moisture soften its fibers and allow them to distort with respect to one another, thus permitting the piece to bend. Steam at 212° F warms the wood and whatever moisture is already in the fibers; the moisture in the steam supplements the initial moisture content of the wood, especially in those fibers near the surface. Apparently, pressurized steam doesn't help much; in fact, there is some evidence that it makes the wood brittle and is detrimental to successful bending.

It's important to make sure the steam is saturated with moisture. Bubbling the steam through a trough of water or leaving some free water lying in the bottom of the steam box will ensure this. Generally, the wood should remain in the steam for about one hour per inch of thickness. Steaming for longer periods of time doesn't increase the bendability much.

Generating steam

Steam can be generated in a variety of ways; I use a kerosene-fired wallpaper steamer. Electrically heated versions are available from Warner Manufacturing Co., 13435 Industrial Park Blvd., Minneapolis, Minn. 55541. Local paint and wallpaper stores often rent them. The steam-generating units from home sauna baths can also be used. One unit, the Hot Shot model MB4L, is available from Automatic Steam Products Corp., 43-22 34th St., Long Island City, N.Y. 11101. A lidded 5-gal. can with a filling cap and a hose fitting brazed or soldered into the lid also works well. It can be heated on a large camp stove, plumber's furnace or open fire.

The steam box can be made from one sheet of 3/4-in. exterior fir plywood, either C-C, B-C or A-C grade, depending on how much you want to spend, with the best face toward the inside of the box. You could use marine exterior grade, but it's not necessary. Tongue and groove the corners, or butt and screw them. A manifold can be made from 1/2-in. dia. copper tubing drilled with 1/8-in. dia. holes every 3 in. Introduce the steam through a hose adapter and tee midway along the length of the manifold, to equalize distribution. A drain hole for the condensation should be provided at one end, with a hose adapter to carry the water to a floor drain or outside the shop. A rack or some other method of supporting the wood above the manifold should be provided so the wood doesn't lie in the condensate. I use blocks of wood screwed to the bottom and angled toward the drain end of the box. A coat or two of porch and deck enamel or marine paint, inside and out, will preserve the steam box for years. Assemble the bottom and two sides, install the manifold, drain and rack, and paint the interior surfaces before putting on the top. Use a good waterproof glue and brass screws at the corners. Both ends should have hinges, gaskets and catches. Thus, the box can be loaded from either end if short pieces are being steamed, or very long pieces can be run right through the open-ended box and the gaps stuffed with burlap or rags to contain the steam. When the box is supported on sawhorses or on a permanent stand, slant it slightly so the condensate runs toward the drain.

Selecting wood

Some species of wood steam-bend better than others. I've found that white and red oak, walnut, ash, hickory, pecan and beech bend well. Cherry is not quite as good, and it's just barely possible to bend teak and mahogany. Softwoods do not bend well. The tables below show the relative bendability of various species, expressed as a percentage of unbroken pieces, and the limiting radii of supported and unsupported bends in 1-in. stock. Such tables have been compiled to guide industrial users and are only approximations—the craftsman's best guide is experience.

Bendability of Domestic Hardwoods

	% Unbroken Pieces
Ash	67
Beech	75
Birch	72
Elm, soft	74
Hackberry	94
Hickory	76
Magnolia	85
Maple, hard	57
Oak, red	86
Oak, white	91
Pecan	78
Sweetgum	67
Sycamore	29
Tupelo	42
Walnut, black	78

U.S. Forest Products Laboratory, *Wood Handbook: Wood as an Engineering Material*, 1974.

Limiting Radii of Curvature (in inches for 1-in. stock)

	Supported By Strap	Unsupported
Afrormosia	14.0	29.0
Alder	14.0	18.0
Ash	4.5	13.0
Beech	1.5	13.0
Birch, yellow	3.0	17.0
Douglas fir	18.0	33.0
Ebony	10.0	15.0
Elm, white	1.7	13.5
Hemlock	19.0	36.0
Hickory	1.8	15.0
Mahogany	36.0	32.0
Oak, white	0.5	13.0
Oak, red	1.0	11.5
Spruce, Sitka	36.0	32.0
Teak	18.0	35.0

W.C. Stevens and N. Turner, *Wood Bending Handbook* (Princes Risborough, England: Forest Products Research Laboratory, 1970).

Industrial research has also found that air-dried wood at a moisture content of 15% to 20% is best for steaming. But I have bent some species of kiln-dried wood at 8% to 12% MC with good success. If difficulties arise and the wood seems too dry, try soaking it in water for a day before steaming. The added moisture is absorbed mainly by the fibers near the surface and will evaporate quickly when the heated wood cools.

Stock for bending should be selected for straight grain and must be free of cross grain, knots, checks and other defects. I have found that flatsawn stock bends better than quartersawn; that is, the annual rings of the board should run parallel to the mold, as closely as possible.

Preparing the stock

It is best to place the heartwood side of the board on the inside of the bend. The board should be jointed and thicknessed, but usually not to finished dimension, particularly if the stock is thick. With cross sections 1-1/2 in. x 4 in. and larger, it is best to leave a little extra stock so the final profile can be sawn or otherwise worked to final form after bending. But having the stock smooth on four sides before bending prevents cracks and splits from propagating from a surface irregularity such as sawmill or circular-saw marks. A small chamfer, perhaps 1/16 in., on all four edges of the stock also helps prevent splits from starting at points where the grain might be slightly crossed. On thin stock or where curvature is not great, I sometimes presand the parts before bending. Although steam raises and sometimes discolors the grain, at least the mill marks are gone and all that is required after bending is light scraping and final sanding.

The piece of wood to be bent should always be several inches longer than the desired finished length. During bending the ends frequently are distorted and these defects can be cut off later. An end coating (such as that used around kilns, or ordinary oil-base paint or roofing cement) spread on the end grain before presoaking or steam bending prevents excessive absorption of moisture and subsequent end-checking during drying.

It is usually better to cut joints after the piece is bent; however, I have cut mortises and tenons before bending where they occurred on the straight portion of a member.

In any bend, the distance *L* around the outer convex side of a curve is longer than the distance *l* around the inner concave side. Ordinarily, when stock of length *l* is bent around a curve the outer fibers stretch (or go into tension) to attain the addidional required length (*L-l*). Wood plasticized by steam will stretch only very slightly before fracturing (failing in tension), but it can be compressed to a much greater degree. The fibers in compression slip, compress, bend and distort without failing. Therefore, the objective is to begin with the plasticized stock at length *L*, prevent the outer convex fibers from stretching (going into tension), and force the inner concave fibers to compress (and therefore shorten to length *l*). This is done by fitting the outer surface of the stock with a heavy steel strap securely welded or bolted to steel end blocks. Assuming the strap does not stretch as the wood is bent, the end blocks push against the inner fibers, compressing them to length *l*.

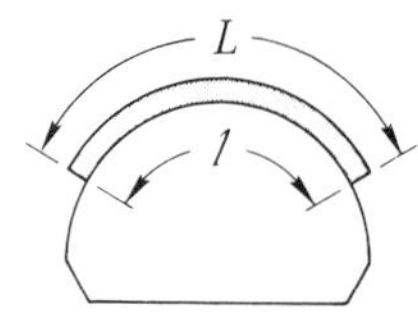

Wood fits tightly against strap between solid steel end blocks, which extend outward from small clamps to provide leverage. Then assembly is clamped to center of mold to prevent initial buckling and quickly pulled around. After setting for 15 minutes, wood is clamped overnight to drying jig, left.

Straps and molds

I use 16-gauge cold rolled steel for straps on stock up to 1/2 in. thick, 1/16-in. hot rolled steel for stock 1/2 in. to 1 in. thick and 1/8-in. hot rolled steel for stock 1 in. to 2 in. thick. I make end blocks from angle iron or channel iron at least 1/4 in. thick, or solid steel bar stock when available. Don't underestimate the amount of force the end blocks must withstand when bending heavy stock. Frequently the force is great enough to bend the angle iron. Welding corner blocks behind the angle iron helps prevent this.

The strap must be wide enough to cover the full width of the stock being bent, and end blocks must be large enough to cover the entire end of the piece. When bending stock thicker than 1 in., I fasten each end block to the bending strap with at least three 1/2-in. dia. bolts. When I buy the strap material, I get it long enough to accommodate quite long stock. Then I can redrill the holes and rebolt the end blocks to reuse the strap for other bends. Chemical reaction with the steel strap will discolor the surface of most woods. Discoloration is usually removed in subsequent shaping and finishing, but if it is objectionable, use stainless steel straps or cover them with polyethylene sheeting.

The plasticized wood member must be bent around a mold. This mold must be very strong, must support the full width of the bent piece and must accommodate some clamping arrangement for drawing the wood around the curve. A male mold is always used, so that it will support the inner fibers of the bent wood. I make many of my molds from discarded telephone-pole crossarms (about 4 in. x 5 in.) glued into a blank and bandsawn to shape. Stacked 3/4-in. thick fir plywood or laminated 2-in. construction lumber also works well. Regardless of construction method, strength is the key word, because incredible forces can be generated in bending a piece of wood around the mold.

It is important to allow for springback when shaping the mold, so that after the bent part is released it assumes the intended shape. Only experience will teach how much to overbend in compensation for springback. Among the variables are the nature of the curve, thickness of the wood and species. Usually the more gentle the curve, the more one must compensate. It seems that the more the fibers on the concave side of the member are displaced, the less they spring back.

Keyser puts the hot wood into the strap, which has been warming atop the steam box. A clamp at each end secures it to the heavy channel-iron reverse levers, tight against the end blocks. Speed is essential; do a dry run to make sure mold, clamps, tools are handy.

When making molds, I work from the full-size drawing of the piece and guess at the amount of springback. I cut the mold, bend a trial piece and then revise the mold if necessary.

If only one piece is to be bent, the strap and wood can be left clamped to the mold for a day until the piece cools and dries thoroughly. If several pieces must be bent, it saves time to construct a drying jig. This allows you to bend, remove the clamp and strap after about 15 minutes, and clamp the wood onto the drying jig. This frees the bending strap and mold for the next piece to be bent.

I usually allow one day per inch of thickness (or fraction thereof) for the bent piece to cool, dry and set before removing it from the mold or drying jig.

Bending in one plane

The simplest bend is a single curve in one plane. In bending a 1-1/2-in. x 5-in. x 56-in. piece of walnut around a 10-in. radius mold, I've used a giant cross-bow arrangement. Be careful with this method; don't take a chance on lightweight equipment failing and recoiling. I use two 1-ton heavy-duty chain hoists for the job. The wood is removed from the steamer and placed between the end blocks of the bending strap, which has been warming on top of the steam box. The strap is secured to the wood by a clamp at each end, then the strap and wood piece are aligned and clamped to the center of the mold. This is important because as bending progresses, the wood will try to pull away from the mold at the tangent point and will immediately crack if not clamped tightly there. Continue to wind the chain hoists and pull the piece around the mold as quickly and smoothly as possible, until the bend is complete. You have only a few minutes to work, for the longer the bending operation takes, the more the piece cools and dries, and the greater the risk of failure.

When the curve is this severe, the compressive forces against the end blocks become great enough to overturn the

Cross-bow mold is made from telephone-pole crossarms and fitted with one-ton chain hoists. Center clamp at base of mold and two more clamps hold wood firmly in place as hoists pull it around.

Bend is complete. Enormous compressive forces are apparent in slight curve away from mold's ends, despite heavy reverse levers.

After two days on mold, wood still springs back, left. Bar clamps, right, shackle bent pieces to minimize further springback.

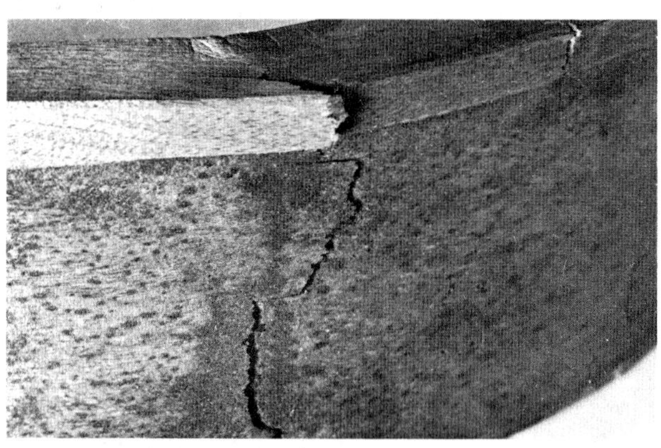

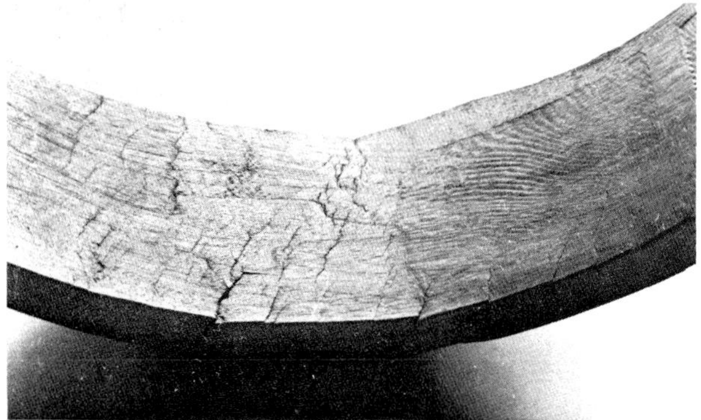

Catastrophes: Tension failure, top, indicates loose or overturned end blocks and too-narrow strap (discoloration); compression failure, bottom, occurs when bend is too tight or wood is too plastic.

steel blocks and allow the strap and wood to recurve away from the mold. To counteract this tendency, a reverse lever made from heavy channel iron is bolted through the strap to the end block. This lever, pushing against the back of the strap, prevents the end block from overturning.

In good weather and when a helper is available, the mold may be staked to the ground and a car or truck used to pull the bent piece around the mold. The steamed piece with the strap in place is clamped to the mold on one end of the curve, and the other end of the strap is fastened to a tow chain. The advantage is that the piece can be pulled around very quickly; the danger is that lightweight chains can snap and recoil.

A few cautions are in order; live steam is dangerous stuff. The steam box and steam generator should not seal tightly, to avoid building up pressure inside. You must be sure the generator doesn't run dry and burn up. Wear heavy gloves when handling the steamed wood, and when opening the box, beware of scalding your face in the blast of steam. If you wear glasses, the steam will fog them.

Failures

Much can be learned from pieces which have failed during bending. In tension failure, the fibers on the outside surface of the bend simply pull apart. It is the result of reduced end pressure caused by the end blocks not fitting tightly against the ends of the wood or distorting during bending. The outer fibers go into tension instead of the inner fibers being compressed. If the bending strap is not wide enough to cover the entire piece of wood, a crack is liable to start at the unsupported edge. Wrinkling, or compression failure, occurs on the inner surface because of over-plasticization, too tight a bend or a bad choice of species for the particular bend.

Bends without a strap

Bending without a strap and end blocks is possible only when the curve is slight or the stock is very thin. I have found that the difference between the lengths of the outer and inner faces of the bent piece should be less than 3%, although this varies from species to species. For 1-in. stock, the minimum radius I would bend without straps and end blocks is about 33 in. Bends made without straps are less stable and more springback can be expected. The bends are not as predictable for duplication because complete distortion of the fibers has not taken place and the "memory" of the wood cells will straighten it out. I seldom bend without a strap.

For shallow bends, or when stock is very thin, bending can be done without a strap. The steamed wood is clamped directly to a combination mold and drying jig such as the one shown above.

Complex curves

Bending a single piece of wood in a reverse, or S, curve or bending in two planes requires only a more complicated mold and strap. The principles remain the same: the strap must follow the convex side, or outside, of each portion of the curve, and end blocks must force the wood fibers on the inside of the curve to compress. Extensions of the end blocks, welded or bolted to the strap, provide handles to help in pulling the wood around the mold. Then it is clamped in place and left to set.

Bending off the corner

Table or stool legs can be bent off the corner by using a 1/2-in. x 1/2-in. x 1/8-in. angle iron as the bending strap. It fits over the outside corner of the steamed piece. Near the ends, the strap is fortified by welding on short lengths of a larger-size angle iron, to which is welded the solid steel end blocks. The small angle iron is flexible enough to bend around a gentle curve. The bending mold is made of two pieces of solid wood bandsawn to the desired curve, with the bandsaw table tilted 45°. The steamed stock is placed in the bending strap, the strap and stock are inserted under a shackle at the end of the bending mold and then the piece is simply forced around the mold and clamped. □

For a reverse curve in one plane, strap iron is fastened to each portion of mold where curve changes direction. Steamed wood is clamped at end blocks, then to mold, and quickly pulled around. End blocks are angle iron, backed up with hardwood fastened by bolts.

For a bend in two planes, ends of two pieces of strap iron are overlapped at right angles and welded edge-to-edge—in effect, forming a few inches of angle iron at point where curve changes direction. Three clamps hold overlapping iron and hot wood to mold; end blocks and handles are lengths of tee iron welded to straps.

Further Reading

Forest Products Laboratory, *Wood Handbook: Wood as an Engineering Material.* Agricultural Handbook No. 72, Washington, D.C.: U.S. Government Printing Office, 1974.

Forest Products Laboratory, *Wood Handbook. Basic Information on Wood as a Material of Construction with Data for Its Use in Design and Specification.* Agriculture Handbook No. 72, Washington, D.C.: U.S. Government Printing Office, 1955.

Peck, Edward C., *Bending Solid Wood to Form.* Agriculture Handbook No. 125, Washington, D.C.: U.S. Government Printing Office, 1968.

Stevens, W.C. and Turner, N., *Wood Bending Handbook.* London: Her Majesty's Stationery Office, 1970.

Wangaard, Frederick J., *The Steam-Bending of Beech.* Beech Utilization Series No. 3, Northeastern Forest Experiment Sta., 1952.

Off-the-corner strap, left, is welded from two sizes of angle iron. Steamed wood fits tightly between end blocks, is tucked under shackle on mold, and forced into place, above. After 15 minutes it is removed, placed in drying jig, and clamped with the aid of blocks notched at 45°.

Fixtures for Steambending

Adjustable end-stop and versatile table control breakage, springback

by Michael C. Fortune

Steambending allows me to work with simply curved pieces of wood that I can shape and blend together. Most of the curves I bend happen in one plane and are not exercises in pushing the limits of the process; most of my jobs are multiples, like sets of dining chairs. The trouble with steambending is the inconsistent and unpredictable results—breakage during the bending and springback afterward.

Since I cannot afford to cut extra blanks in anticipation of rejects, I've had to devise techniques that will ensure uniform results. I also required a high degree of design flexibility, a reasonable rate of productivity, quick set-up time and easy operation by one person, and low capital investment. The system I'll describe is based upon an adjustable end-stop that's attached to the usual steel back-up strap, and a special clamping table to which I can bolt a variety of bending forms.

When I've worked out a design, an integral part of my sequence for building the object is making a complete technical drawing. For steambending, this provides the length of the blanks to be bent, their cross-sectional dimensions so that I am sure of having enough material to shape and carve around joints, the joinery details and index points for the machine jigs I use, and the size and shape of the bending form itself. The way I work, it is not practical to guess about springback, nor to accommodate each part individually, nor to discard parts that do not match. In some cases, the grain in a bending blank is part of a visual composition and could not be substituted without sacrificing other components as well.

Immersing a straight piece of wood in hot steam plasticizes its fibers. When the steamed wood is bent, the fibers on the inside of the curve are compressed while those on the outside must stretch. Since the wood is much stronger in compression than in tension, a steel back-up strap with fixed end-stops is commonly used to restrain the length of the blank, thus shifting most of the stress into compression. If the strap is too loose, tension failure is the likely result—the wood fibers on the convex side of the bend stretch until they break. If the strap is too tight, the fibers on the inside of the curve may wrinkle and buckle, called compression failure.

In my early experiments, using fixed end-stops on the back-up strap, I got a few pieces of furniture and a large pile of rejected parts. Although I had machined all the blanks to the same length, some of the rejects failed in compression, while others failed in tension. I attributed these inconsistent results to the strap's having stretched during repeated use, and to my having used kiln-dried wood, which could have had such baked-in defects as casehardening or surface checking. The steaming time was also marginally inconsistent, since I put several pieces into the steam box at once, then used them one at a time. Eccentricities that grow into most pieces of wood also contributed to these inconsistent results.

To control these variables, I discarded the fixed end-stops for an adjustable end-fixture that could respond to each blank as the bend progressed. Also, I now use only air-dried wood, which in Ontario ranges in moisture content from 12% to 20% out-of-doors. Since severe bends may require more moisture, say 25% M.C., I may pre-steam the blank for an hour and let it sit in the steam box for a day before bending. I've successfully bent white oak, black walnut, cherry, ash and red oak, but the bending stock must be high quality, straight and free of defects.

Adjustable end-stop—The end-stops on the steel strap are subjected to considerable force as they compress the wood fibers around the bend. The end-stop must accommodate this force. The ones I am now using are shown in figure 1, on the next page, and an earlier version of the adjustable end-stop is shown in the photo. The principal material in both is ¼-in. and ⅜-in. by 2-in. bars of hot-rolled mild steel. My current version is welded from three thicknesses of bar. The adjustable end-stop fixture is not welded to the strap, but is detachable, so it can be mounted on straps that range from 1 in. to 6 in. wide according to the stock to be bent. The bottom of the fixture includes a 45° step that interlocks with a 45° step on the bending strap. A machine screw holds the fixture in place but does not receive any lateral force; if it did, it would quickly shear off. The adjusting thread is ⅝-11 N.C. running through a coupling nut about 2 in. long. The end-stop itself is made of ¼-in. or ⅜-in. angle iron with a short length of black iron pipe welded onto it. The pipe both locates the stop on the threaded rod and reinforces the angle iron. I generally make the stop 2 in. wide, but I add a steel reinforcing plate to the working face of the angle to make it larger than the end of the stock I am bending.

The strap is 1⁄16-in. steel, wide or wider than the stock, and able to take a bend without kinking. Holes are drilled ⅜ in. or ½ in. in diameter on 4-in. centers down the length of the strap, so its overall length can be grossly adjusted by the location of the fixed, hardwood end-stop, which is bolted on. Two holes are drilled through the end-stop for this purpose, with about 1½ in. overhanging on the end that faces the stock and 3 in. on the other end.

Bending table—I used to bend steamed wood around a form clamped to my workbench. To gain mechanical advantage, I attached levers to the end-stop and back-up strap assembly. My body weight was the main force, plus anyone willing to hang on for 15 minutes until the bent part could be removed and clamped to a drying jig. I needed a better way.

The versatile cast-iron table with square holes that welders use seemed appropriate. With this in mind, I fabricated a plywood table 4 ft. by 5 ft. by 3 in. thick to which I could

---

Michael Fortune designs and makes furniture in Toronto, Ont. He has also taught at Sheridan College.

Fig. 1: Steambending fixture

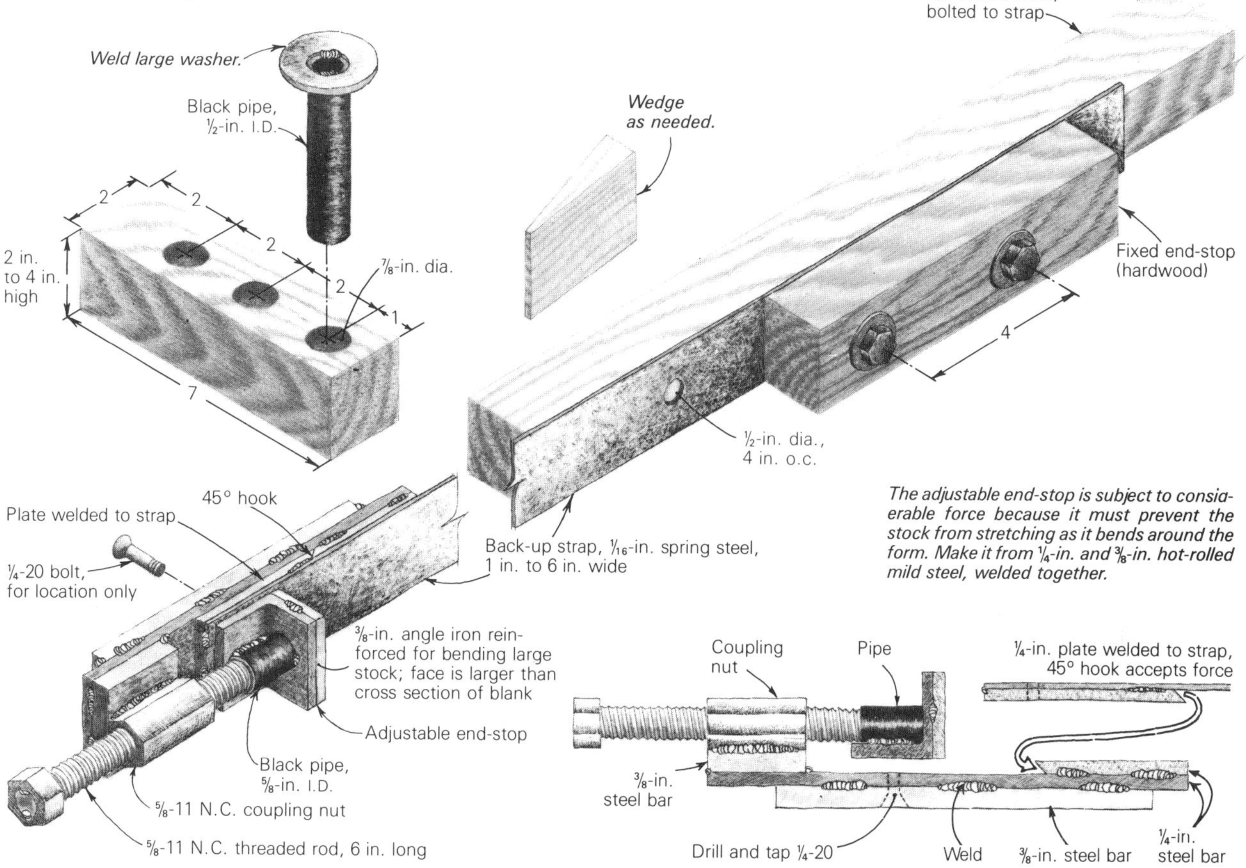

The adjustable end-stop is subject to considerable force because it must prevent the stock from stretching as it bends around the form. Make it from ¼-in. and ⅜-in. hot-rolled mild steel, welded together.

Fig. 2: Drilling jig

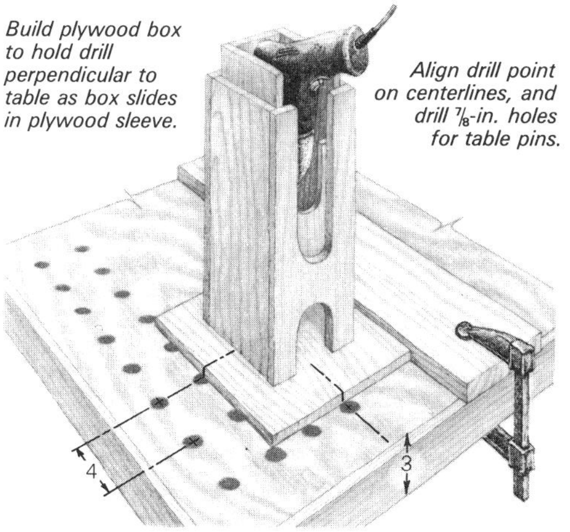

Build plywood box to hold drill perpendicular to table as box slides in plywood sleeve.

Align drill point on centerlines, and drill ⅞-in. holes for table pins.

Bend has been levered from fixed-stop end, left, by block and tackle (not visible); adjustable end-stop is clamped to block at right, which is attached to the table by one pin. Strap and stops pivot away from the form for easy insertion and removal of stock.

fasten bending forms. My table was laminated from four sheets of ¾-in. plywood, hardwood ply for the faces and floor sheathing for the core. Not having a veneer press, I laminated the sheets one at a time, using wood screws to provide clamping pressure. I removed the screws before adding the next layer, so I could drill holes anywhere in the table without hitting embedded hardware. For design flexibility, I drilled a regular pattern of ⅞-in. holes through the table, and holes in my bending forms and adjustable end-stop fixture. These accommodate short lengths of iron pipe, ½-in. I.D., which act as locating pins. They can handle the substantial shear forces of the bending process and have a large washer welded to the top for easy insertion and removal. Half-inch bolts pass through the table pins to secure the bending forms and adjustable end-stop fixture to the table.

To drill perfectly perpendicular ⅞-in. holes through the large table, I constructed a tight-fitting box around a ½-in. hand drill. It slips into a sleeve mounted on a square of plywood, as shown in figure 2.

The pattern of holes eliminates the need for large, reinforced bending forms, because most forms can be bolted to the table at several points. I prefer plywood forms, as the less dense core of particleboard will crush after repeated use. I cut the inside shape of the form parallel to its face so that clamps can be applied wherever they might be required.

The photo, above, shows how I mount the assembly. Note

Photos, except where noted: Michael C. Fortune

Above, Fortune begins to pull in the block and tackle for the first bend of a chair seat. The stock is first steamed in the plywood box in the background; steam is generated by a salvaged boiler containing a 4.5-kilowatt immersion heater. Below, with the first corner turned, Fortune slackens off the adjustable end-stop before levering the wood around the second bend.

Walnut dining chair, one of a set of eight with dining table, has steambent arms and rear legs, laminated back slats.

David Allen

that the adjustable end-stop is at the starting point of the bend, and the fixed stop is at the free end of the blank. The adjustable end-stop is clamped to a wooden block, which in turn is located on the table by a table pin and a bolt. This arrangement allows the strap with both end-stops to pivot away from the form for quick installation of the heated blank, and easy removal of the bent piece. Index marks can be made on the form and transferred to the bent piece for later reference when machining joints. A dozen wooden clamping blocks, drilled with ⅞-in. holes, will come in handy, as they can be bolted down anywhere and wedged against the bent blank.

The final piece of the assembly is a lever bolted to the back of the bending strap at the wooden fixed-stop end. It provides mechanical advantage and supports the blank, which otherwise might compress locally or overturn off the strap. The lever reaches several inches beyond the stop toward the blank (see figure 1). It can be clamped to the blank here if trouble starts to develop, then the clamp removed when the blank is bent close to the form. A block and tackle can be attached to the lever at its far end, for additional leverage. This can be tied off in mid-bend, freeing the operator to adjust the end-fixture or to place clamps. A marine hardware spring-loaded cinch would be useful here too.

The bending process—Before bending, make sure that all forms, fixtures and clamps are in place. Set the steamed blank (steam an hour for every 1 in. of thickness) in the strap, making sure it's in line with the strap and with both end-stops. Tighten the threaded rod on the adjustable end-fixture. I use a ratchet, tightening until it's secure, then giving it another half-turn. This should flatten any kinks out of the strap.

The photos at left show a U-shaped bend around a chair-seat form. The first curve and first corner can be bent without backing off the adjustable fixture. However, upon approaching the second corner, the straight portion of the blank will start to arch away from the strap or to deform in an S-shape. I loosen the fixture just enough to relieve the excessive compression forces that have built up. The second bend can then be made.

I've found that springback can be minimized by leaving the bent part to cool on the form for 15 minutes, bathed in a slow stream of compressed air. Then it's quickly transferred to a setting jig of the same shape as the form before it has time to spring back. It is clamped there, and left for a week or preferably two weeks. The setting jig should be wide enough to accommodate all the parts being bent; clamps spanning the bend will maintain the distance between the ends of the blanks but do not help to maintain the shape. I accommodate the setting time by proceeding with other parts of the job according to my drawings.

It's important to allow the bent fibers to relax, and the wood to reach moisture equilibrium with the atmosphere. Since pieces may come out of the strap at 20% moisture content or higher (for severe bends), they must dry slowly, else they'll check. This problem is acute when bending red and white oak. I cover the setting jig with a blanket to restrict air flow for a few days, and this seems to control the problem. □

Further Reading

Wood Bending Handbook, W.C. Stevens and N. Turner. Woodcraft Supply, 313 Montvale Ave., Woburn, Mass. 01888, 110 pp.

A Time and Motion Study

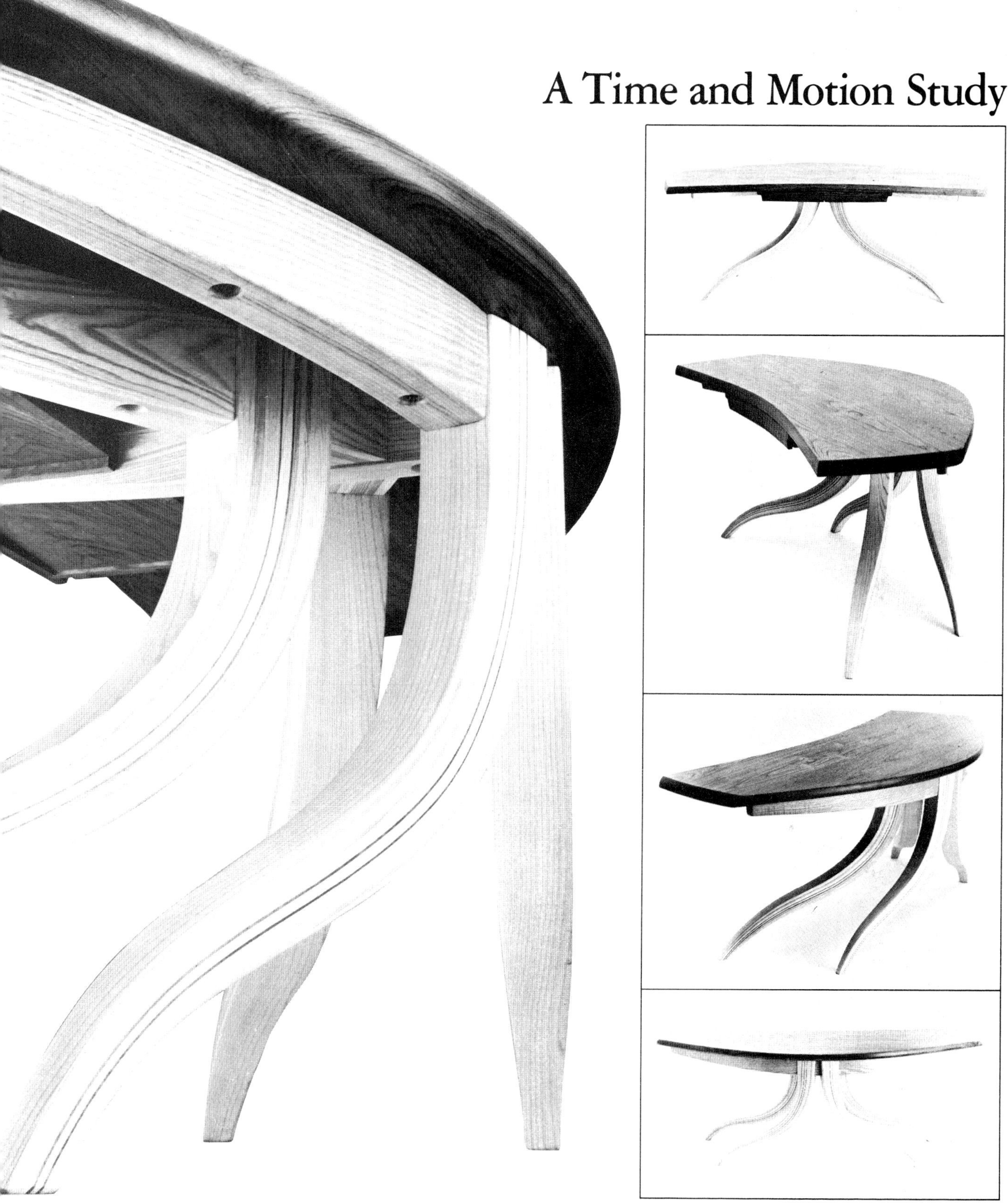

Photos: Michael Germer

The show's catalog calls Jere Osgood's new desk "light and graceful, with an anthropomorphic spring that defies weight." Osgood himself calls it a pedestal table with the pedestal shoved off to one side. Kept away from his bench for 18 months by his job as acting director of Boston University's Program in Artisanry, Osgood practically leapt into his shop when he returned to full-time teaching. Out popped this desk. Osgood says the design is a step in a definite direction, one of a series built with the bent tapered lamination techniques he explains on pages 62 through 73. To support the solid teak top, he bent and glued thin, tapered layers of ash and walnut around particleboard forms, using as many as 40 clamps on each leg. To determine the commercial feasibility of the design and the techniques, Osgood made its production a time and motion study—a desk like this, built in limited runs by a small shop, could retail for about $5000. □

Oval Boxes

How to make steambent containers

by Tom McFadden

I designed my oval boxes and carriers after studying Shaker examples. Typically, the sides of Shaker boxes were made of maple and splayed into three or more tapered fingers in the area of the scarf joint, where the two ends overlap. In my boxes the sides are of cherry, maple, madrone, mahogany, oak, ash or walnut, and I leave the outside overlapping end square, instead of cutting fingers on it. All these woods steambend easily in a thickness of 1/8 in. Before bending, the inside end involved in the scarf joint is tapered to produce a smooth surface when assembled. I fasten the joint with copper tacks and yellow glue, and attach the handles on carriers using the same. (The tacks are available from Fasco Fastener Co., 2023 Clement Ave., Alameda, Calif. 94501.) The pine tops and bottoms fit into the bent sides of the box and rim, and I secure them with round-head brass brads. The completed pieces are finished with two coats of polyurethane followed by an application of paste wax. I make the boxes in seven sizes and the carriers in five sizes.

When selecting stock for bentwood boxes, you should use only straight, even-grained wood for the side pieces. Imperfections such as curl, knots (sound or otherwise) or slanting grain may cause the pieces to break or to bend unevenly. You can use kiln-dried stock, but lumber that has been air-dried to 10% or 12% moisture content will respond to the steam more readily and produce more consistent results. Resawn, a good 4/4 board will yield three side pieces.

Before resawing, crosscut each board to within 3 in. or 4 in. of its finished length; then joint one face and edge, and plane the unjointed face. Now rip the boards to width, then resaw and plane them to produce blanks 1/8 in. thick. Take ten of the 1/8-in. blanks, align and stack them one atop another and tape them together with masking tape. Mark out the narrow part of the outside end of the scarf joint and the location of the tacks by laying a pattern on top of the bundle. The ends of the pieces can now be stack-sawn to shape and the 1/16-in. dia. pilot holes drilled for the copper tacks. Smooth the end-grain edges with a stationary belt or disc sander.

Next separate the pieces and with a hand plane taper the inside end of each overlap down to 1/64 in. over the last 6 in. After tapering, sand each side piece inside and out with a 100-grit belt in a belt sander, and round the edges by hand slightly with 120-grit paper. Mark the inside of each piece with a pencil so you'll know which way to bend it after it comes out of the steam box. The completed side pieces are again taped into bundles to await steaming.

I made the bending forms for the boxes and their tops from stacked 3/4-in. hardwood plywood, sanded and varnished to facilitate removing the completed side pieces. I use hardwood plywood for the forms because of its stability in the

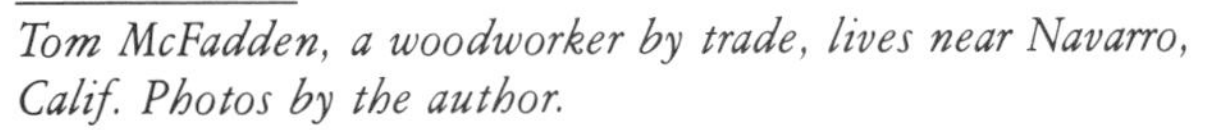

Tom McFadden, a woodworker by trade, lives near Navarro, Calif. Photos by the author.

Author's Shaker-style oval boxes and carriers are steambent from various hardwoods, glued and nailed at the splice. Boxes nest one inside another. Below, rack of dowels inside steambox holds the stock, sawn and planed to about 1/8 in. thickness, on edge for a 15-minute soak in unpressurized steam.

For seven sizes of box, McFadden has made seven sizes of mold, plus seven more slightly larger molds for their lids. The molds are hardwood plywood, sanded smooth and varnished. Stainless-steel plate let into each mold is an anvil against which first row of tacks may be clinched.

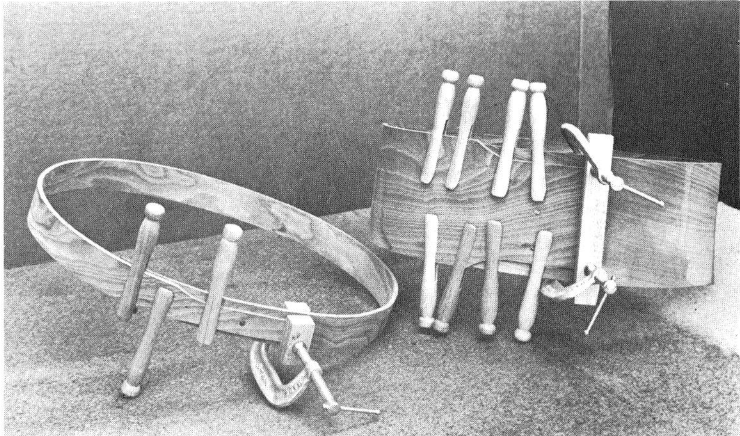

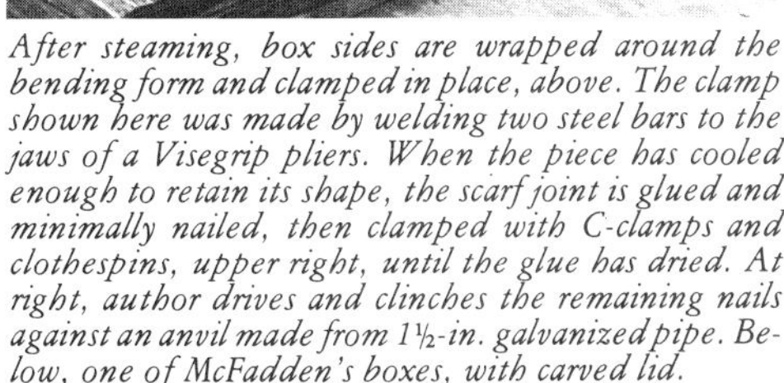

After steaming, box sides are wrapped around the bending form and clamped in place, above. The clamp shown here was made by welding two steel bars to the jaws of a Visegrip pliers. When the piece has cooled enough to retain its shape, the scarf joint is glued and minimally nailed, then clamped with C-clamps and clothespins, upper right, until the glue has dried. At right, author drives and clinches the remaining nails against an anvil made from 1½-in. galvanized pipe. Below, one of McFadden's boxes, with carved lid.

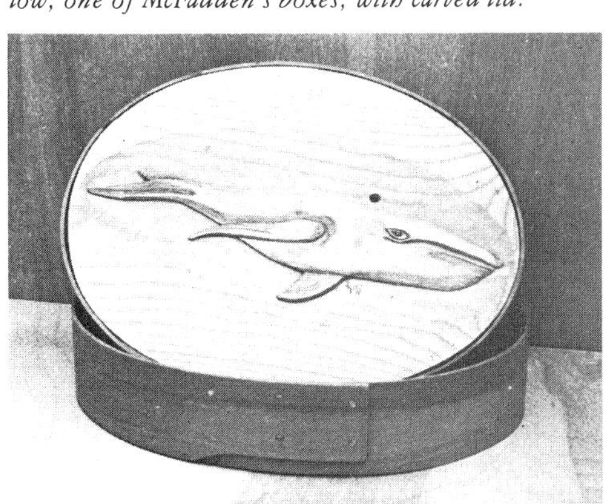

face of temperature and humidity changes. Each form is fitted with a stainless-steel plate in the area of the scarf joint that lets me drive tacks through the wood without damaging the form. Stainless steel is used to ensure against staining the steamed wood. The plate is let flush into the surface of the form and attached with stainless-steel screws. At one end of the plate the form is notched to accept an adapted Visegrip which clamps the steamed sides in place while they cool and are glued and riveted with the tacks. Further, each form is mounted on a plywood base plate which fits interchangeably into a frame screwed onto a table. Two cleats hold the form ½ in. above the base plates so that the completed sides can be easily gripped from below and slid upward off the form.

The side pieces are placed in the steam box and subjected to unpressurized steam for 15 minutes. After steaming, quickly remove each piece from the box, wrap it tightly around the form and clamp it with the adapted Visegrip. After the piece has cooled enough for its shape to set, remove it from the form. Apply glue to the scarf joint and then reclamp it on the form for tacking. Only the center vertical row of tacks is driven at this time; these will fix the size of the oval and will hold the overlap in place while the side is removed from the form and the overlap is clamped with C-clamps and clothespins. Drive the remaining two rows of tacks after the glue has dried. The points of the first row of tacks are turned over and mushroomed against the stainless plate in the bending form; the remaining tacks are hammered in against an anvil made from 1½-in. galvanized pipe. The finished side pieces are hand-sanded with 120-grit paper to remove the raised grain caused by the steaming.

Handles for the carriers are resawn and shaped in the same manner as the side pieces. They are steamed and bent around

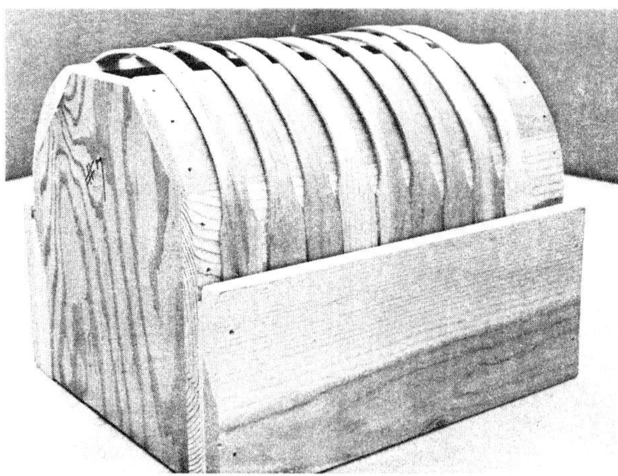

Rack keeps carrier handles bent while they cool and dry.

a form, then placed in a drying rack until they are attached to the sides with glue and copper tacks.

Cut the tops and bottoms from pine (quartersawn is best) with a moisture content of 6% to 7%. It is essential that this material be very dry or it will shrink away from the side pieces and leave ugly gaps. Place the side piece for the box on the pine bottom, trace the inside shape and bandsaw along the line. Make final adjustments in the fit with a disc sander. Round the edges of the pieces slightly, and sand them. Use dividers to mark the location of the brass brads that will hold the top and the bottom in place. Then drill the pilot holes through the side pieces, and drive the brads. □

Shaker Carrier

Dovetail box, steambend handle

by John Kassay

This not-so-difficult-looking project offers two challenges—the hand-cut, through-dovetail corners and the sculptured, steam-bent bail (handle). Carrier is the Shaker name for a box fitted with a bail. Those carriers that exhibit pleasing form, fine construction, and quality craftsmanship were made for the Shakers' own use, whereas carriers made for sale in Shaker stores, though well crafted, look mass produced. With the exception of the manner in which the bail is fastened, this carrier is a fine example of one made for communal use.

To make the carrier, thickness-plane enough pine (wood species is optional) to make the sides (A), ends (B) and bottom (C). All surfaces should be hand-scraped and sanded. Those surfaces that will be on the inside of the carrier should be finished surfaces and so marked. Now lay out the sides and ends and add $\frac{1}{32}$ in. to their widths and lengths, and cut accordingly. The extra length allows the ends of the dovetails to project minutely beyond the outside surfaces. After the sides and ends are assembled, these projections are planed or sanded off, resulting in a better appearing dovetail joint. The extra width is used for truing up the edges at the top and bottom of the carrier, again after assembly.

Mark out and cut the bottom ¼ in. longer and wider than the overall length and width of the carrier sides and ends. Sand the inside surface and shape the upper edges as shown in the drawing. Nail the bottom in place—a nice touch here would be to use ⅞-in. fine-cut headless brads (available from Tremont Nail Corp., PO Box 111, Wareham, Mass. 02571.

Nailing the bottom onto the carrier sides may seem to contradict all we have been taught about wood movement, but it is the way the Shakers did it—and they had central heating too. It has been suggested that the bottom ought to be let into a groove in the sides, like a frame-and-panel. However, I have rarely seen good results from altering a Shaker design. In this particular case, inletting the bottom would eliminate a characteristic Shaker form, the molding created by the protruding bottom, and it would greatly complicate the carrier's joinery. I think that when the bottom worked loose, the Shakers would just nail it on again.

The bail is made of ash; red or white oak or hickory could be used instead. Mill straight-grained stock to overall thickness, width and length (detail 2), then steam it and bend it around a mold before tapering it to shape. Although it's difficult to shape the bail after bending, it's more frustrating to lose a pre-shaped bail during the bending process.

The photo on the facing page shows my bending jig, with a back-strap made of four strips of 24-gauge galvanized sheet steel, spot-welded together at the center. (For more on backstraps, see pages 16 through 24.) This apparatus will bend

John Kassay is the author of The Book of Shaker Furniture, *available from University of Massachusetts Press, Box 429, Amherst, Mass. 01004.*

kiln-dried white oak that's been steamed for about two hours under low pressure (5 PSI to 10 PSI). If you use split-out green wood, the chance of a successful bend is greatly increased; you can probably substitute an ordinary band clamp for the steel back-up strap and end blocks. I leave the bent stock on the jig to set for a couple of days. When removed, it springs back just the right amount to fit the carrier.

Now make a full-size pattern of half the length of the bail, trace it onto the bent wood and cut out the shape. With a block plane and a scraper blade, taper the bail in thickness from the center to the ends, as shown in the edge view, then spokeshave it to the cross-sections shown. Note that the undersurface is rounded, while the outer surface is left flat. Both ends of the bail are flat where they attach to the carrier ends, and chamfered on their outer corners. Fine-sand all the surfaces and ease any sharp corners, except those where the bail meets the carrier. Fasten the bail with four brass rivets and washers, two at each end; you could substitute countersunk flat-head woodscrews.

The inside surface of the original carrier was protected with a wash coat of yellow milk-paint, while the outside was left natural. The bail was varnished. □

John Kassay

Wedges hold bent stock against bending form while it cools and sets. Steel back-up strap with end blocks helps make the bend, but once bent, the strap can be tipped away from the stock, as shown.

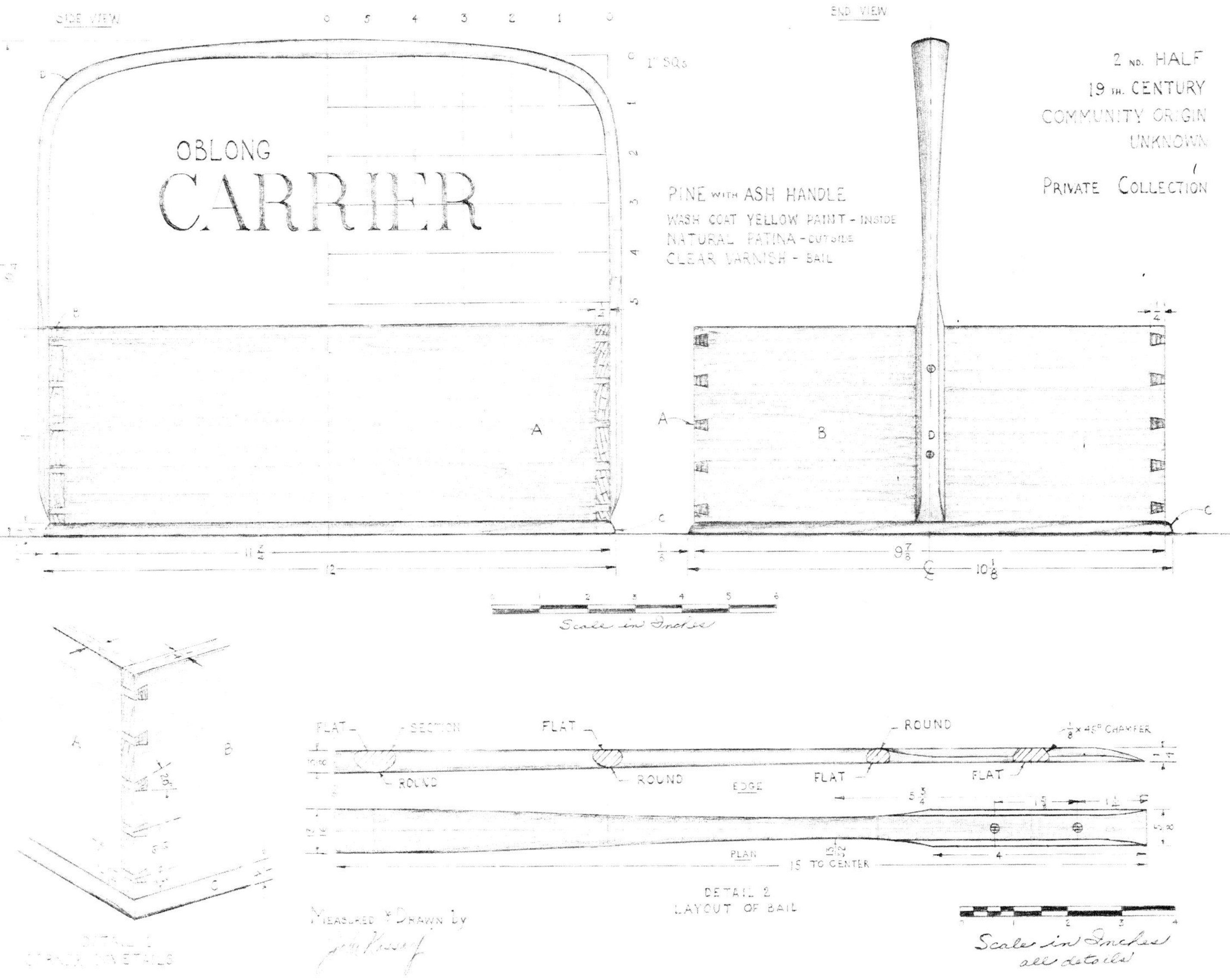

OBLONG CARRIER

2 ND. HALF 19 TH. CENTURY
COMMUNITY ORIGIN UNKNOWN
PRIVATE COLLECTION

PINE WITH ASH HANDLE
WASH COAT YELLOW PAINT - INSIDE
NATURAL PATINA - OUTSIDE
CLEAR VARNISH - BAIL

Scale in Inches

DETAIL 2
LAYOUT OF BAIL

Measured & Drawn by John Kassay

Scale in Inches all details

From *Indian Artists at Work*, 1978, courtesy Douglas & McIntyre, Vancouver.

Kwakiutl storage chest kerf-bent in red cedar by Larry Rosso of Vancouver.

Kerf-Bent Boxes

Woodworking techniques and carving tools of the Northwest Coast

by Susan J. Davidson—Photographs by Ulli Steltzer

Although the art of the Pacific Northwest Coast Indians has long been recognized, little attention has been given to how they actually made things. Most people will think of their massive totem poles, dugout canoes and sculptural masks, but the kerf-bent wooden box is the more ingenious example of a woodworking technology developed through eons of practice. It consists of just two planks of cedar. One is the flat bottom, rabbeted all around to receive the sides. The other is a single plank that has been deeply kerfed in three places, plasticized by controlled steam and bent at right angles to form four sides. The last corner is sewn or pegged together. The result will hold water.

These richly decorated boxes range in size from a few inches to several feet. Some have flat sides, some bulge outward. Some have lids, some have sweeping curves cut into their top edges. They stored the food and possessions of everyday life as well as the ceremonial regalia of the winter dances, they were cooking pots and serving dishes, and finally they were coffins. But they were not merely containers as we think of containers, for their intricate motifs also represented the personal crests of the owner. These crests were displayed proudly, for they served to verify rank as well as spiritual power.

The Indian population probably never exceeded 100,000 on the whole coast of Alaska, British Columbia and Washington. They lived scattered in hundreds of villages separated by at least six different languages and dozens of dialects. (Major tribal groups and villages are shown on the map, facing page.) That this sparse population had the time to make great quantities of boxes testifies to the material richness of their seacoast and rain-forest habitat. As Haida carver Bill Reid, who spent two years carving a 57-foot totem pole, has written, "Even today, only a stupid man could starve on this coast, and today is not as it was." They could support a whole class of artisan specialists who, freed from the urgency of subsistence work, transformed the gifts of the forest into concrete expressions of their cultural values. The elite, in turn, would hoard the treasures they had commissioned and convert this wealth into status at the potlatch, by giving it all away, in the expectation of receiving even more in return.

Although it used to be thought that the woodworking arts were quite unsophisticated until the introduction of iron tools by European explorers after 1770, recent archaeology shows otherwise. This culture and its art has been on a high level for several thousand years. Iron tools had been known on the coast for about two hundred years before direct European contact. When Europeans traded metal tools in quantity for furs and artifacts, the Indian culture reached a lavish sophistication previously not feasible. Yet this coast was still the remotest corner of the world, and remained essentially intact for almost another century. About 1850, gold was discovered inland. White settlers came to stay. There followed a century of terrible repression, while the Canadian authorities tried to "civilize" the heathens by outlawing their language, customs and ceremonies. Finally, as scholars began to recognize the value of what was being crushed, the political changes of our own era also stirred the Indian people.

The last 30 years have seen a genuine cultural renaissance. The elders have brought out their hidden wealth and memories, and young men and women have been struggling to reclaim their heritage. Historical techniques are being supplemented by modern methods. While power tools such as the router and band saw are used by native carvers for rough work, they prefer the old forms of hand tools, updated with metal blades, for finishing and detail cuts. For this article I have drawn heavily on ethnographic reports (see *further reading,* page 36), but my best resource has been this new generation of craftsmen, and it is their work I wish to document.

In the old culture, a deep respect for the spirits of all living beings pervaded daily life and work. The spirit world was close at hand, especially in the grey winter. Before taking a salmon from the ocean, or bark from a tree, a person would ask permission from its spirit. Even today, after the Haida artist Robert Davidson had carved a 40-ft. Bear Mother totem pole for the village of Masset, the first part of the erection ceremony was for him to dance around the pole with all his tools tied to a rope draped over his shoulder. He chanted a raven's cry, which he later said was his victory song at having conquered the pole by completing it.

Cedar was, and remains, the material of choice—western red cedar and yellow cedar, known in the timber trade as Alaskan cedar. Some craftsmen today buy milled boards from the lumberyard, culling the piles for tight, clear, straight grain. Others use chain-saw mills to quartersaw planks from logs that wash up on the beach. Some still split out boards with wedges and mauls. The old way was to burrow two deep holes into the living trunk, one near the ground and the other as high up as the boards would be long. Planks could then be split off using a graduated set of seven yew-wood wedges and a stone maul, and the tree would live on. The trees were much bigger then, 10 ft. and more in diameter.

Aside from living memory and contemporary experience, information about the old ways of woodworking comes mainly from Franz Boas, the German-born anthropologist who studied the Northwest Coast tribes between 1885 and 1930. There is also a film (made by the University of California at Berkeley anthropology department) about steam-bending a wooden box, featuring the late Kwakiutl (pronounced *kwa-gyulh*) chief Mungo Martin, one of the last carvers to have had direct continuity with the traditional technology. By the time of Boas' observations, metal tools were readily available and the trees were usually felled. They were made to lie with their smooth, weather side upward. The seven graduated wedges were driven in along a line four finger-widths above the center of the log. When the tree began to open, a round crab-apple or yew-wood stick about 6 in. thick was inserted across the horizontal crack, and two men pounded on blunt wedges that were hollowed to fit around the "spreading stick." Planks were always split from the branch end down, to prevent the plane of fissure from

Haida chest, kerf-bent with bear design, 36 in. by 19 in. by 23 in., collected in 1870. Courtesy Museum of Anthropology, Univ. of British Columbia, accession no. A-7103.

turning outward, and to avoid producing a plank that was short and thin at one end.

The first plank removed was three finger-widths thick, because it never ran quite parallel to the splitting plane. Subsequent planks ran more nearly parallel and could be as thin as one finger-width—if the cedar was good. If the plane of separation dipped downward, the upper surface of the log was loaded with logs and stones. If it turned upward, the tree was turned over so the weight of the wood could change the inner stresses, dipping the plane downward again. Planks of 20 ft. and longer were split this way. Most boards were split tangentially, that is, the growth rings intersected the face of the board at a small angle. But the boards destined to become bent boxes were split radially, through the center of the tree, crossing the growth rings at right angles.

Twisted boards were piled in a level spot and weighted with heavy stones. A second method of straightening was to drive two pairs of stakes into the ground, a pair at each end of the plank, slanting away from each other. The plank was forced between the stakes and twisted to counteract the warp. After some time in traction, it usually would remain flat.

Boas, unfortunately, was not woodworker enough to note the moisture content of timber, although it is not likely that any amount of air-drying would bring it below about 15% in this damp climate. Green stock is easy to bend into a gentle curve, but green wood is liable to shatter when forced into tight bends like these, as a result of hydraulic pressure within the cells. Doug Cranmer of Alert Bay has made boxes of maple, yew, alder, yellow cedar and pine. He believes any seasoned wood can be bent if it is steamed long enough. But whatever wood is used, Cranmer says, "It must die first, dry right out and relax before it can be bent."

To smooth and thickness the board, a chisel with a bone or stone blade was used to shave off long splints. The final planing was done with a hand adze, working with the grain. The finished board might be only half a finger thick. Using an ingenious geometry dependent on cedar-bark strings and charcoal markings, the craftsman made a rectangular template from a large flat board. This pattern was traced onto the newly prepared board and the shape reproduced by adzing down the edges.

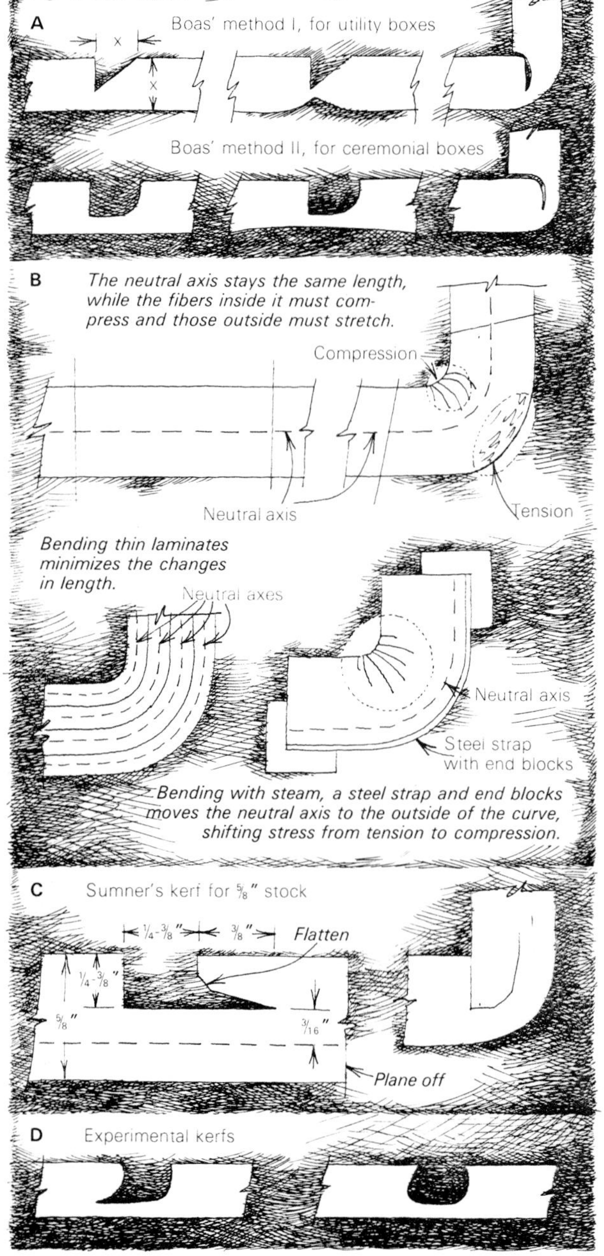

The next step was most critical, that of cutting the kerfs where the future corners would be. Boas describes two styles of kerfing (figure 1A). The simplest is a *V*-cut with one vertical side, about halfway through the board, as wide as the board is thick. The outside of the board would be shaved back on both sides of the *V*-cut. Museum specimens show that this method was reserved for utility boxes for gathering, storing and cooking food. The wood at the corners is quite thin and would have bent easily with a minimum of steaming, but the result is fragile—many surviving examples are cracked or broken. In the second method Boas recorded, the kerf looks like a dado with one rounded corner. It was made by incising a narrow vertical kerf, then working it wider with the knife along a curve reaching down to the original cut. The board was also thinned opposite the kerf. This method was reserved for decorated chests and serving dishes. It required more skill to make, but produced a more durable and aesthetically pleasing wrapped corner.

Kerf-bending can be explained by contemporary technology. As shown in figure 1B, when a piece of wood assumes a curve, the fibers on the inside of the curve must become shorter, and those on the outside must stretch. Only the fibers in the middle of the stock, along its so-called neutral axis, stay the same length. Laminating many thin layers minimizes the distance between the neutral axis and the surfaces in compression and tension, and therefore results in less stress. (For a more extensive discussion on bending laminates, see the article on pages 62 to 65.) Wood, however, is considerably easier to compress without failure than it is to stretch. Thus another way to bend is to plasticize the fibers with steam and confine the length of the stock by means of end-blocks fastened to a steel strap (see pages 16 to 24). This effectively shifts the neutral axis to the outer surface of the bend, putting most of the fibers into compression rather than tension. Kerf-bending marries both approaches.

A study of 99 boxes at the National Museum of Man in Ot-

Fig. 1: Kerf styles

tawa isolated 11 different kerfing styles. The deeply undercut kerf as used by Roy Hanuse shown below, right, and in the photos on pages 38 and 39 is the most common today; the version used by Richard Sumner of Alert Bay is shown in figure 1C. Sumner's dimensions apply to a plank 23¼ in. long by 3⅝ in. wide and ⅝ in. thick, the size he recommends to anyone experimenting with the technique. Like Hanuse, Sumner roughs out the kerf with a router, then finishes it with straight and curved knives. He also sands out the undercut. Instead of shaving a relief opposite the kerf, however, he runs the flat side through a planer to leave about 3⁄16 in. of wood. Sumner and Cranmer agree that the key to perfect boxes is a uniform kerf, and Cranmer is experimenting with router bits to design one that will do the whole job, including undercut. Box-makers at the reconstructed village of 'Ksan (near Hazelton, B.C.) use other varieties of kerf (figure 1D).

Larry Rosso of Vancouver has made many boxes, including large chests (see photo, page 30), using the undercut kerf, but he makes the wood even thinner toward the back side—no more than ⅛ in. Rosso recommends that the undercut start two-thirds of the way down the kerf and extend as far as possible into the wood. Rosso has bent alder, red cedar, yellow cedar, pine, spruce and fir. He finds that the softer woods, like cedar, spruce and pine, are easier to bend accurately, and that tight-grained woods are superior.

In old boxes, as today, the fitting at the fourth corner is a rabbet joint, the rabbet being as wide as the kerfed board is thick, and half as deep. The other end was and is left blunt to butt up against this tongue. Hanuse bends so that the undercut kerfs point away from the rabbet, whereas Rosso always sets up so that he is bending into the kerf, on grounds that this makes it easier to end up with a truly square box.

According to Boas, when the board was prepared—and this included as much shaping as possible in advance of bending—it was sandwiched between two level planks weighted with stones and left to soak overnight in hot water or steam. When all was ready, a big store of medium-sized stones was gathered from the beach and a large driftwood fire built to heat them. Seaweed and eelgrass were also collected. Three ditches four fingers wide, a short span deep and as long as the width of the board were excavated in the earth. Hot stones were transferred into each hole until it was nearly full. Seaweed was used to fill up the holes, and eelgrass was heaped on top. Then the board was laid on with a kerf directly over each miniature steam pit. Eeelgrass was piled thickly on top of the board, along the kerfs. The board was lifted up at one end, water poured into the three holes and the board lowered onto the steam. Red-hot stones were placed on top of the eelgrass last piled on and then more grass. More water was poured along the kerfs, and a final layer of eelgrass was used to cover the steaming plank.

These days, a hot plate or a camp stove is generally used to boil water in a tank, and the live steam is fed to the wood via a rubber hose. Some use a plywood box for steaming, while others, like Hanuse, simply put the wood inside a tent made from a plastic bag, the hose tied tightly at one end.

Contemporary craftsmen bend the steamed wood with the aid of asbestos gloves, belt clamps and strips of inner tube. The old way relied on two wooden implements and a length of cedar-bark rope. The two tools were what Boas called "a board protector" and "the implement for bending corners;"

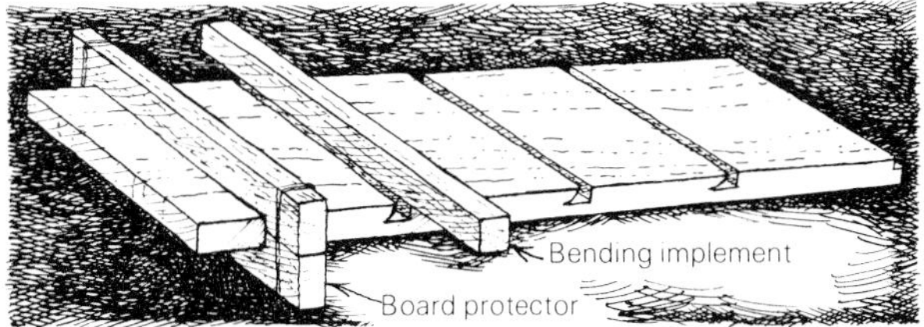

they are shown in the drawing above. The first was a piece of red pine the size of a 2x4 and several feet long, split in half and hollowed out to receive the steaming plank, then lashed together. The second was simply a square length of red pine, about a foot longer than the width of the steaming plank.

While the board steamed, the boxmaker split out many thin, tapered cedar pegs, each about four fingers long. These would be used later to peg the last corner together. When the board had steamed long enough, the eelgrass and hot stones were removed, the board protector slipped over one end of the plank, and the bending implement laid behind the vertical edge of the kerf. The craftsman stood astride the plank, one foot on each end of the bending implement, grasped the board protector in both hands, and pulled it up until the corner was bent slightly more than the required 90°. He repeated the procedure with the corner at the other end of the plank, and lastly with the middle corner. The rope was quickly wrapped around the bent form, the last corner fitted together, and the rope tightened up and wound several more times around so the box would not twist. To keep it square, four cedar sticks of equal length were wedged diagonally inside—two across the top and two across the bottom.

While the box was cooling, the open corner was pegged

Cedar box was made by Roy Hanuse of River's Inlet, B.C. How he steamed and bent it is shown in the photos on pages 38 and 39. The box is cubical, 12½ in. on a side. The carved design represents a person—the head, chest and hands on the left, the pelvis, legs and feet on the right. The same designs are repeated on the other two sides. This style of carving traditionally fills all the available space, by splitting and spreading out the elements of the figure depicted. The designs are usually bilaterally symmetrical and show anatomical details as if the artist had X-ray vision. Strong, thick 'formlines' define the patterns; variations of the ovoid and U-shape are also characteristic. A little creature, dubbed Mighty Mouse by one anthropologist, appears in the chest area on the left, his 'ears' suggesting lungs.

Tackle box by Doug Cranmer was bent as shown in sketch below.

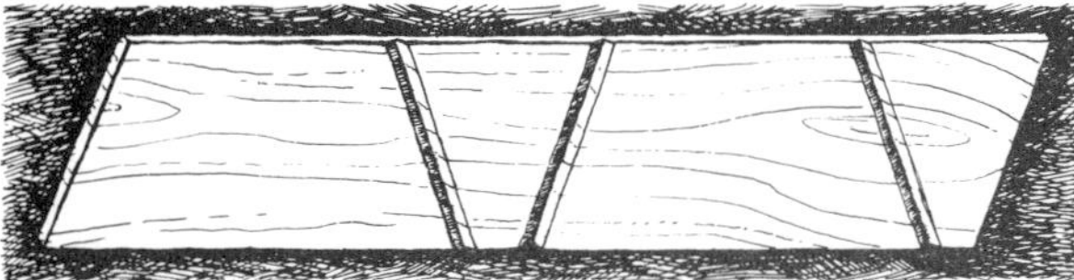

Twelve-sided box by Larry Rosso, kerf-bent from one long board.

A medium-sized canoe, hollowed out but not yet filled with boiling water for spreading to final shape. Photo was taken in 1902 by C.F. Newcombe, courtesy British Columbia Provincial Museum, Victoria.

closed. Holes were drilled at angles alternately one above and one below the horizontal plane, three fingers apart, through the rabbet into end grain. The pegs were covered in saliva before they were hammered in. An alternate way of closing this corner was to "sew" it by lacing cedar withes through drilled holes. Shallow grooves were made to recess the lacing, protecting it from abrasion.

The bottom was shaped from a block of wood rabbeted down half a finger-width around the edge. It was made to fit up tightly into the box and then pegged securely to the sides. The lid was sculpted to fit tightly over the top.

The corner joint, lid and bottom had to be fitted with precision if the box were to be water tight. This was accomplished by "spotting." Charcoal mixed with oil was rubbed along one of the adjoining edges. The two edges were pressed together. Black spots on the clean edge revealed the uneven places, which were then shaved off. Before the final fitting, the joints were rubbed with tallow and rotten pitch wood.

Although the board protector and bending implement were meant to create enough counterpressure to prevent the outer fibers from breaking, there was often some raggedness, or "sprizzling," along the bends. This was cleaned off as the last step in preparing a box to receive its decoration. The skin from dogfish, a member of the shark family, was used to sand wood to a smooth finish.

All the contemporary boxmakers emphasize that if a corner does not bend into place within a minute of coming out of the steam, the risk of fracture is very high. The wood should be re-steamed to avoid disaster. Sumner has isolated four common pitfalls. Cutting the undercut too far down, which leaves the wood too weak, and not using enough steam, are the main reasons a corner will crack. Inaccurate measurements and uneven undercutting cause the box to be off-square. Rosso evaluates a box by how evenly the corners are wrapped and how well the kerfs close. If there is a lid, it should fit in equally well in any direction.

Box-making was a highly evolved art, especially among the Kwakiutl, Tsimshian, Haida and Tlingit people. Unusual designs were developed for specific purposes—by varying the positions of the kerfs, for example, it was possible to make a box that would fit up into the bow of a canoe, for hooks, knives and other gear (photo and drawing, top left). Some unknown Haida artist once made a twelve-sided box, perhaps for a shaman, which Rosso has duplicated (photo, middle left).

Although the use of hot rocks for generating steam has largely disappeared, solar experimenters are rediscovering the heat-storage potential of a mass of rock. The Indians cooked in kerf-bent boxes by filling the box with water and food, and bringing to a boil by tossing in hot rocks. Great canoes up to 80 ft. long were made using the same techniques (photo, bottom left). A cedar log of appropriate size was felled, making sure it landed on its belly, the side with fewest branches. The outside was adzed to form and the inside was roughed out, sometimes using controlled fire for the preliminary hollowing. Holes of specified depths were drilled into the hull from the outside and plugged with twigs that had been charred at the tips. As the craftsman adzed out the interior he encountered charcoal smudges, indicating he had gone far enough. The sides were as thin as the breadth of one forefinger, while the bow, bottom and stern were two fingers thick. The cavity was filled with a mixture of one-third human urine and two-thirds water, and hot rocks were added

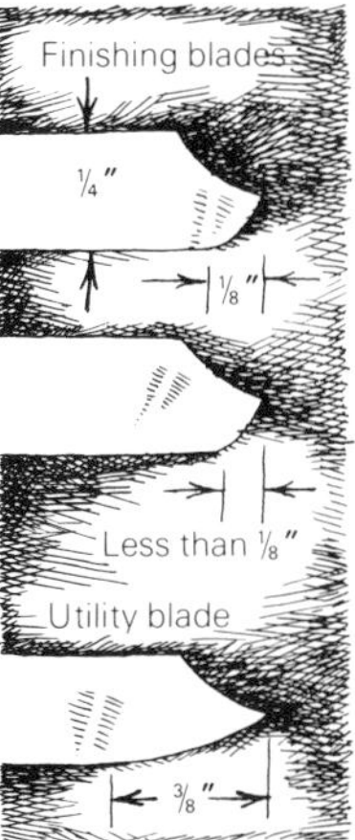

Traditional D-*adze, left, and adze with carving-gouge blade. Drawing, right, shows typical blade profiles.*

until the liquid boiled. A careful fire built under the canoe kept it boiling until the wood became pliable. When the sides could be spread the thwarts were pressed into place, the canoe allowed to cool, and the liquid poured out. The thwarts were then sewn into place by lacing spruce withes through predrilled holes. Extra pieces to extend the height of the prow and stern were pegged and sewn onto the main hull.

A carver's tools were so important to him that he often made them into beautiful works of art themselves. The handles became animal forms or were engraved with personal crest designs. The prehistoric materials for tools were animal bones, horns and teeth, shell, stone and wood. When European trade goods arrived, the superiority of iron blades was readily acknowledged but the traditional tool forms did not change.

The three distinctive tools still used by Indian carvers are the *D*-adze, the elbow adze and the curved knife. Traditional wedges, chisels, drills and mauls have largely been replaced by their modern counterparts, and power tools have found ready acceptance, in particular the electric router and the gasoline chain saw.

The *D*-adze, shown above, is named for the shape of its handle. It fits comfortably into a loosely closed hand, with the thumb extended over a knob on the front. The tool balances on the outer surface of the palm behind the little finger. The knob, which often becomes an animal's head, absorbs some of the impact from each chopping stroke and helps direct the next. *D*-adzes can be made for utility work—removing big chunks of wood at each stroke—or for finishing. A finishing adze is used in a very precise way to create a regular, dimpled surface as the final texture on large areas such as structural timbers, totem poles and canoes. Sevveral variables can be adjusted, according to the tool's purpose.

The method of fastening the blade to the handle determines how the adze responds to impact. A utility adze should be rigid, and the blade is commonly bolted on. For a finishing adze, it helps to use a more flexible lashing. The rebound from each stroke helps establish the steady rhythm that will produce a uniform pattern. Old tools sometimes have quills or cedar wedges bound into the lashing, to increase elasticity.

When making a blade, consider four variables: its width, the curvature of the sharpened edge, the bevel on the bottom side, and the weight. An average *D*-adze blade is 1½ in. wide, 6 in. long and ¼ in. thick. A narrower blade will cut deeper. Blade metal often comes from car leaf springs, old files, or ³⁄₁₆-in. mild tool steel. The business end is splayed by grinding away width on either side, and by rounding the tip. A flat curve is better for utility work, biting deeply and creating a chip that must be broken off. A rounder curve allows shallow scooping, freeing a shaving with each stroke.

The top side of the blade (toward the handle) is beveled to the middle of the metal's thickness, which mostly helps to thin out the blade. The working edge is then created by grinding a second bevel on the bottom side. For a finishing adze, this bevel starts about ⅛ in. back and is rounded in cross section, as shown in the drawing above. If the bevel is made shorter, the tool bites deeper. The bevel for utility blades is long and flat, starting about ⅜ in. back from the edge.

Ultimately, experience and personal preference determine how a tool should be made. Carver Roy Hanuse uses a German #5 gouge lashed to a *D*-adze handle and weighted with an extra piece of steel. He made it for finishing, to create a deeper, more shadowed texture. This it does but it's also an excellent utility adze for roughing out concave forms, especially across the grain.

Mastering the adze requires endurance and patient practice. Utility work is less painstaking than finishing, but both depend on coordination and concentration. For finishing, the shoulder, elbow and wrist joints are locked. A controlled swing from the elbow and shoulder allows the tool to strike the surface repeatedly from a height of about three inches. The finishing texture is created by moving down the surface with the grain, in parallel rows that slightly overlap. Control is easier if the blade is angled 10° or 20° to the grain direction. To keep each cut uniform, the same section of the blade must make contact each time. Cross-grain texturing is done only on sculptured pieces.

The elbow adze is named for the shape of its haft. The branch of a tree becomes the handle, and a piece of the main stem becomes a platform for the blade (photo, next page). If a branch of the proper angle is not available, the haft can be steamed, bent and lashed in place, or a wedge can be placed on top of the blade. Traditionally the blade was lashed on with sinew, but bolts are more common now. Crab apple, willow, alder and cedar are all used for handles.

Elbow adzes are also used for both utility and finishing work. The angle between blade and haft is partly personal preference and partly functional: utility adzes around 30°; finishing adzes, 25°. A short grip is effective for utility work,

Isabel Adams Rorick, of Masset, makes the haft for an elbow adze.

while a longer grip puts more bounce in each stroke. Some utility adzes are large enough for a two-hand grip. The angle at which the blade contacts the wood determines the bite of each stroke. For utility work, 35° to 40° is about right. For shallow texturing, 15° is more like it.

When Hanuse showed us how to adze out hollows for the sides of a box (page 38), he unclamped the board and allowed it to respond to the blows. If we perceive that tools are simply specialized extensions of the hand, and the *D*-adze more so than most tools, we can understand his statement, "You can go on adzing for hours if you work at the same beat as your heart. Until you get something going for you, you're just hacking all over the place."

Different tribes preferred different tools. The northern groups used the elbow adze exclusively, while the southern peoples used both styles. According to the late Haida carver and boatbuilder, Robert Davidson, Sr., 25 or 30 different adzes were used for making canoes. When traveling, the carvers left their adze handles behind and made new ones as needed. To lash on a blade, the sinew or string was tied to a fixed object and the adze rotated into the string while the toolmaker kept it taut.

There are many varieties of curved knife (photos, next page), but the basic blade is about ½ in. wide and up to 3 in. long, sharpened on both edges and curving up toward the tip. It can be pulled or pushed and is extremely versatile, doing most of the work ordinarily given to spokeshaves, planes and carving gouges. Although its origins are uncertain, this style of knife definitely postdates European contact. It may derive from the farrier's knife used to trim horses' hooves, or from the canoe knife (crooked knife) used in the fur trade.

These knives are not available commercially, so carvers have become adept at making their own. The metal from a circular-saw blade makes a good knife, as does Keewatin mild tool steel in ⅛-in. bars. First a strip of metal the desired width is ground to make point and tang, then the bevel is shaped on both edges by grinding the top surface only. The metal is heated to the purple color just before cherry red, and the desired curve imparted by gently pressing on a piece of wood. Quenching the blade in oil and then water completes the tempering—a delicate business easily ruined, especially when using recycled steel. The edge is made keen with emery cloth and stropped on leather with Chromeglantz, an abrasive paste normally used for polishing pots. Cutting a clean, crisp outline in woods as soft as cedar requires a very sharp blade.

Knife handles can be straight, for two-handed use, or contoured, for one hand. The shape is carved in dry alder, then split in half. A niche is hollowed out to receive the tang, both sides of the handle and the tang are covered with epoxy, and the knife is clamped together to set.

A curved knife is usually gripped underhand, the thumb braced against the end of the handle opposite the blade for leverage and guidance. Power is gathered by the whole forearm and directed by the wrist. When pulling the knife toward the body, the wrist is firmly locked but carries through the stroke by twisting inward until the shaving falls free. When pushing, the wrist again follows through by swinging away from the body. The tip of the knife is vulnerable. If you drag it through the wood instead of forcing the edge to cut, the tip gets caught and can snap off.

To bring this article full circle, I wish to note the Indians' use of stale human urine in bending wood and preventing checking, which seems to be on the same track as current scientific research on bending wood with anhydrous ammonia. Wood that is immersed in liquid ammonia (NH_3) or in gaseous ammonia under pressure of 150 PSI becomes as

Further reading

Boas, Franz. *Ethnology of the Kwakiutl.* Bureau of American Ethnology, 35th Annual Report parts 1 and 2, Washington, D.C., 1921; and *The Kwakiutl of Vancouver Island,* 1909, reprinted by AMS Press, New York, 1975. These sources are difficult to locate. The AMS reprint, though expensive, is full of nuggets about the woodworking and other technologies of the Northwest Coast.

Codere, Helen. *Kwakiutl Ethnography.* University of Chicago Press, 1966. In this summary of the writings of Franz Boas, Kwakiutl woodworking traditions are described in the chapter "Technology and Economic Organization."

De Menil, Adelaide, and Reid, Bill. *Out of the Silence.* Amon Carter Museum of Western Art, Fort Worth, Tex., 1971. A photo-poem describing the totems that remain in their original locations.

Drucker, Philip. *Cultures of the North Pacific Coast.* Chandler & Sharp, Novato, Calif., 1965. An introduction to the ethnography of the Pacific Northwest Coast. Also by Drucker is *The Northern and Central Nootkan Tribes,* Smithsonian Institution Bureau of American Ethnology, bulletin 144, 1951.

Holm, Bill. *Northwest Coast Indian Art: An Analysis of Form.* University of Washington Press, Seattle, 1965. A clear introduction to the symbols and art styles.

Sturtevant, William C., comp. *Boxes and Bowls: Decorated Containers by Nineteenth-Century Haida, Tlingit, Bella Bella and Tsimshian Indian Artists.* Smithsonian Institution Press, Washington, D.C., 1974. A catalog published for the exhibition of the same title at the Renwick Gallery. Good introductory essays.

From left: double-curved knife, hooked blade, and slightly curved knife. Right, double-curved knife smooths an eye socket.

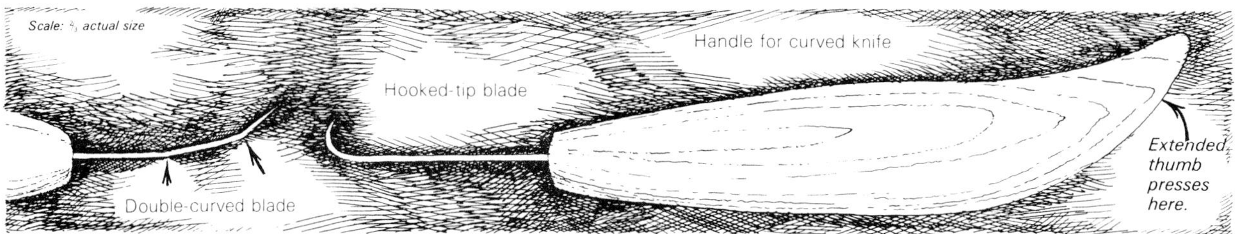

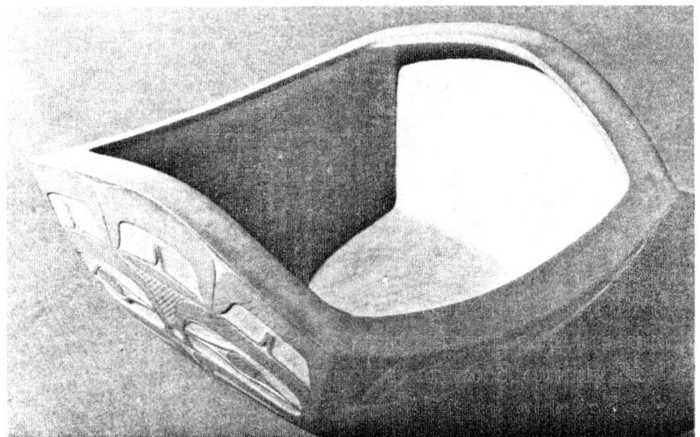

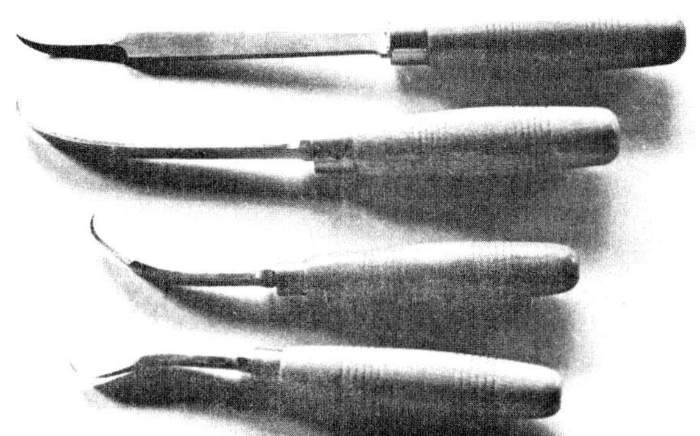

Eagle feast dish carved (not bent) by Haida artist Robert Davidson. The dish required four special knives (photo right, top to bottom): a straight knife with sharply hooked tip for carving out the bottom inside corners, a long-curved 'floor knife' for flattening the bottom, a delicate double-curve for shaping the interior of the sides, and a reverse-bent for undercutting the lip around the top.

pliable as spaghetti. This is not the same as household ammonia, a solution of ammonia in water, and the procedure is both difficult and dangerous.

Ethnographic accounts refer to the use of a stale urine mixture in spreading canoes as well as in steaming boxes, and Boas reports that canoes were less disposed to checking if steamed this way. The active component of stale urine is urea (NH_2-CO-NH_2), chemically similar to ammonia (NH_3). Both are powerful denaturing agents, although ammonia desorbs rapidly, leaving no active residue in the wood, while urea is a liquid at room temperature and likely to remain in the wood. This gives credence to Boas' report, as the urea residue could trap water in the cells and prevent the wood from drying out completely.

Cellulose fibers have a helical form, held relatively stable by cross-bonding among hydrogen atoms. The hydrogen in ammonia interferes with the hydrogen bonds in the cellulose, allowing its micromolecules to flow past one another. However, scientific attempts to increase the plasticity of wood by impregnation with a saturated solution of urea, then heating in an oven to 100°C, have not been successful.

All this has led researcher Robin Wright of the University of Washington in Seattle to make experimentally some 400 kerf-bent boxes by soaking the wood overnight in a 1:10 solution of industrial ammonia in water. She concluded that this preparation made the fibers more pliable, although it did not eliminate sprizzling along the corners. Robert Free of the Burke Museum in Seattle has continued this project, with the aim of making small boxes for sale rather than of settling the question. He soaks the wood in ammonia solution for up to two weeks. □

Susan Davidson, of Vancouver, is an anthropological researcher and freelance writer whose principal interest is Indian art of the Pacific Northwest. Ulli Steltzer's books are Indian Artists at Work *(Douglas & McIntyre, Vancouver) and* Coast of Many Faces *(Douglas & McIntyre/University of Washington Press, Seattle).*

Kerfing and Bending a Box

Roy Hanuse, a Kwakiutl, is a carver who has only recently taken up box-making. He is also a carpenter and no foe of power tools, but he always returns to his traditional tools for the finishing touches.

(A) Hanuse begins by laying out the kerfs and side profiles along one edge of his stock, a select piece of clear, tight-grained yellow cedar. The box is to have bulging sides, hollowed on the inside, and the shaping is done before bending. First, though, he routs the rabbet for the fourth corner (7/16 in. deep by 7/8 in. wide). He turns the plank outside up and (using a 1/2-in. straight-flute bit) routs channels 7/8 in. deep above the center marks for each corner. These channels limit the undulations of the sides, bandsawn next. He shapes the curves with his elbow adze **(B)**, and cleans up the valleys with a curved knife. Now Hanuse turns the board inside up and roughs out the bending kerfs **(C)**, first with the 1/2-in. straight bit to a depth of 7/16 in., then with a modified dovetail bit **(D)**. The undercuts point toward the blunt end of the plank. He cleans up the kerf with a jackknife, and extends the undercut with a curved knife **(E)**.

Hanuse returns to the outside of the box and uses a *D*-adze to enlarge and shape the valley above each kerf **(F)**. Thinning the wood here is what allows it to bend. With elbow adze, curved knives and gouges, he finishes shaping the outside, then turns the plank again to rout and adze most of the waste from the inside.

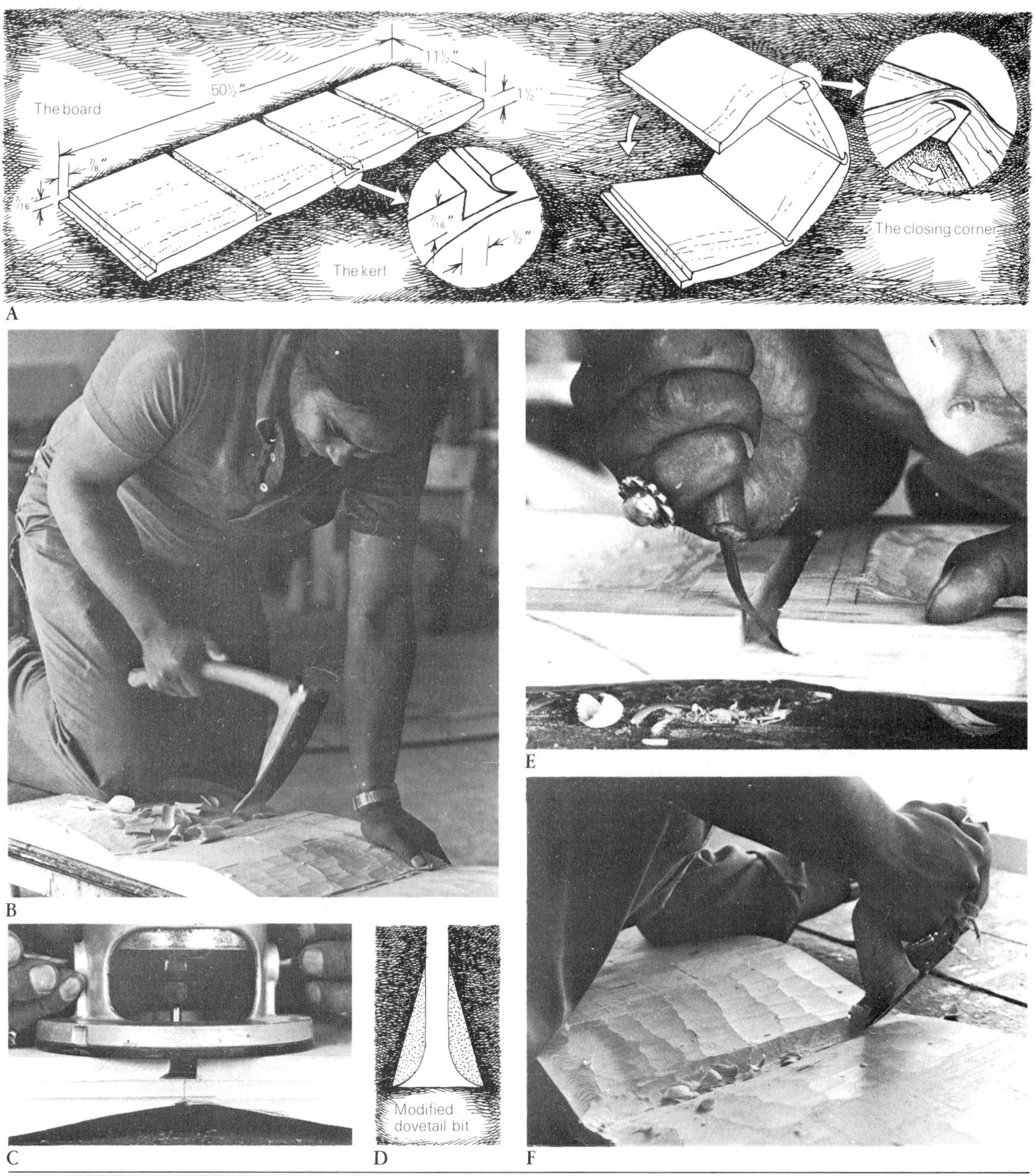

A
B
E
C
D
F

Hanuse's steam source is an old spray tank heated on a gas burner. A rubber hose delivers steam to a heavy plastic bag, in which the stock rests on nails hammered into a plank. He adjusts the bag to the job by wrapping the excess plastic around another plank.

Hanuse warms the stock in hot running water, pours a kettle of boiling water over the kerfs, then pops it into the steam (G). He keeps the tank three-fourths full of water, and occasionally flexes the joints through the bag to judge how it's going. It steams about an hour. Quickly out of the bag and bent (H), one corner at a time. Two belt clamps cinch the form; pipe clamps on the diagonal brace the open corner (I).

When the wood cools, Hanuse trims the open corner to a precise fit. Then he clamps up again, adding a pressure block to push the fourth corner tight for pegging. He's whittled about 15 conical pegs, from $\frac{5}{16}$-in. square sticks of kiln-dried yellow cedar. Using a $\frac{3}{16}$-in. bit, Hanuse drills five holes into the corner from the blunt side, at various angles, and ten angled holes in through the rabbet. He paints the mating surface and the peg holes with white Bondfast glue (polyvinyl acetate), hammers in the pegs (J), and shaves them flush.

The box dries for several days, the steamed wood shrinking around the pegs. Then the pegged corner is recessed with curved knives to match the other three. Hanuse then cleans up the exterior contours, trims broken fibers at the corners, sands the outside to 80 grit, and pares off a thin shaving all around to make a clean surface for carving. Finally, he completes hollowing and thinning the inside (K) and attaches the rabbeted bottom board with angled pegs and glue. □

G

H

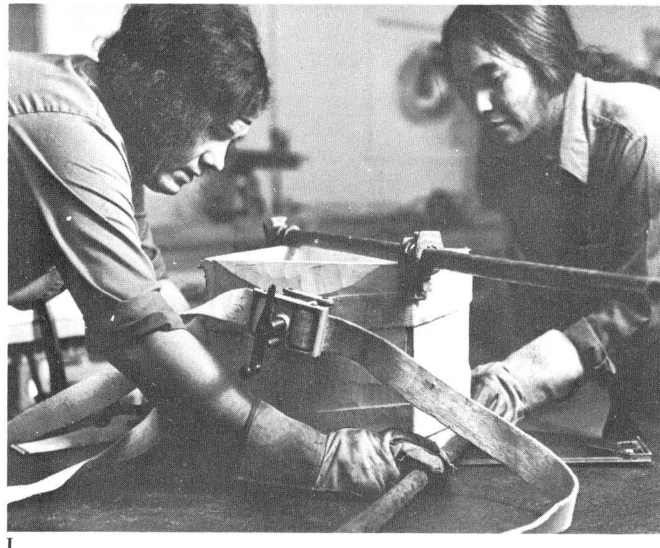

I

J

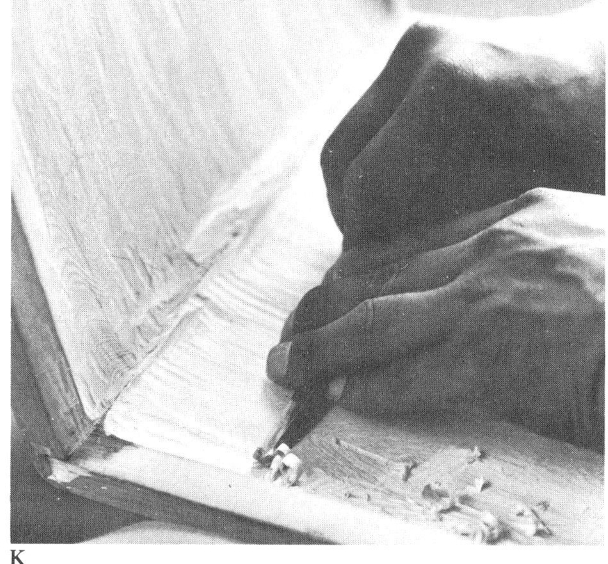

K

Hot-Pipe Bending

Coordination, concentration and practice ensure success

by William R. Cumpiano

Bending guitar sides on a hot pipe is the most dramatic and challenging of all instrument-making techniques. All your senses come into play in the "dance" in front of the bending iron. You feel the intense heat radiating onto your face and chest. You can smell the sweet aroma of hot wood and the quite different odor of a singed surface. You hear the creaking sound of straining wood fibers, and the change in sound that tells you the wood is about to break. In hot-pipe bending, one hand moves a thin, wet piece of wood over a hot pipe in short hops, while the other hand pushes down on the heated wood to bend it. The operation is tricky and requires coordination, concentration and practice. There is nothing quite as heart-stopping as watching a select Brazilian rosewood guitar side turn in an instant into expensive scrap—accompanied, of course, by its unbent matching side.

Not surprisingly, many professional hand-builders resort to various molds and hydraulic/electric devices to circumvent hand-bending. But such devices limit their production to one or two body shapes. Those who have mastered the technique of hand-bending can custom-bend to the purchaser's specifications. One might also bend sides for boxes and trays, or to create sculpture.

The first step is to make a template of the curve to be bent. Stiff paper is fine for making other templates or for keeping a record of different body shapes, but for bending, something more durable and stiffer is needed. Tempered Masonite ⅛ in. thick is adequate; it does not get wrinkled and soggy when wet. The ideal material, albeit expensive, is 1⁄16-in. aluminum sheet. Score the outline from the paper original onto the aluminum. After cutting as close to the line as possible with a tinner's snips, mill-file to the scored line.

Study the template. Your success at capturing the outline in the bent wood depends on your familiarity with its shape. The two types of curves found most commonly are "fair" curves (sections of a circle) and accented curves. An accented curve is one that seems to have the force of a point straining to push it outwards. A fair curve has no accent. Mentally subdividing the template into straight-line segments, fair curves and accented curves will help you during bending.

Even with ideal facilities and the best guidance, your efforts will come to naught with poorly selected side blanks. Textbook-perfect side blank material is flawlessly quartersawn wood of perfectly even and homogenous consistency. Such material is indeed difficult to break accidentally. On the finished instrument it is superior for its stability and its ease of repair. But perfect side blanks are rare and one must often compromise. My criteria vary with the species. Maple can be used even if not well quartersawn, providing it is soaked a short time, because it is extremely tough and flexible in thin sheets. However, curly maple must be flawlessly surfaced, lest a small chip or dig allow a crack to start. Mahogany is the most forgiving of all: I select primarily for appearance and homogeneity. However, failure can occur along sap lines and pieces containing them must be avoided.

Because rosewood is often brittle, vitreous and non-uniform, it must be selected with the most care of all. What may appear to be fine, even material may actually hide long, fine cracks that render it useless. Gently flex and probe the entire

William Cumpiano, a professional luthier and teacher in North Adams, Mass., is coauthor of Guitarmaking: Tradition and Technology *(Van Nostrand Reinhold).*

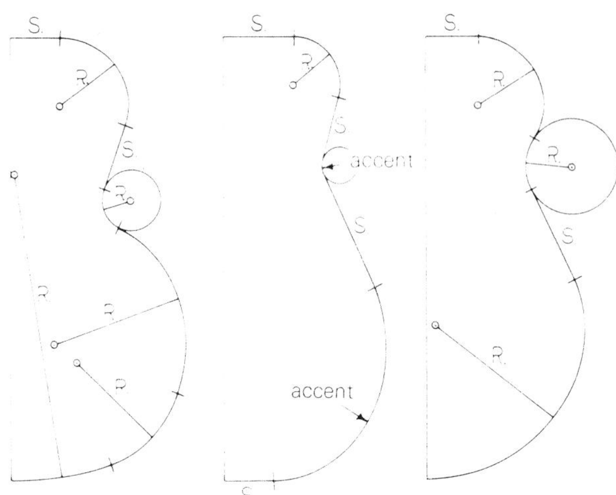

Typical guitar profiles include straight-line segments (S), *fair curves, or sections of a circle* (R *indicates a radius to an imaginary center), and accented curves.*

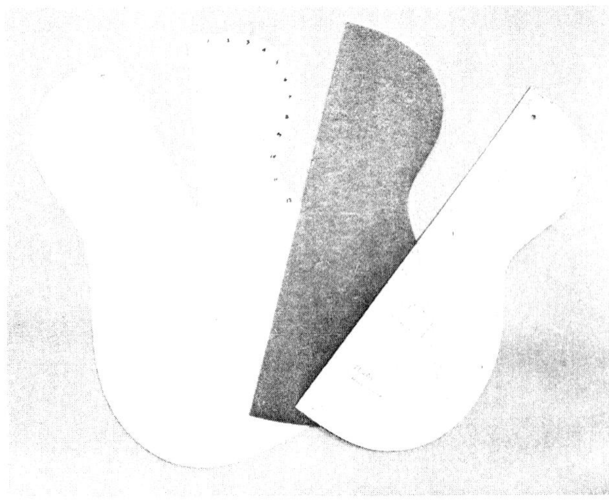

Templates may be made of (left to right) paper, cardboard, Masonite or aluminum. Beginners should start with gentle, large-radius bends, as in classical or 'dreadnaught' guitars.

Bending Irons

The simplest bending iron is made from a 2½-in.-diameter by 6-in. long pipe nipple, available in plumbing supply shops. Thread one end of the nipple into a flange. Screw the flange onto a sturdy board on which is mounted a ceramic bulb socket holding a heating coil. Bulb-socket heating coils can be obtained from an electric supply house; they may be difficult to find because they are the heating elements on infrared lamp fixtures and old-fashioned electric space heaters, which may be illegal in your state. A cylindrical coil is better than a cone-shaped one.

The round bending iron shown here is a beginner's apparatus. It is cheap, adequate and easy to throw together, but unsatisfactory in the long run, since the coils burn out frequently. A round bending iron offers only a line-contact source of heat. The pipe cannot bend a curve with a radius tighter than 1¼ in. Also, you must manually shut the iron on and off to maintain the correct temperature, a very troublesome and clumsy hindrance.

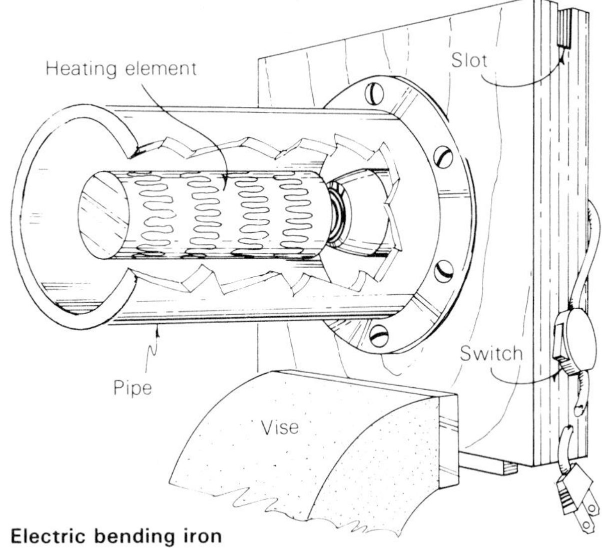

Electric bending iron

If you have started bending with a round pipe, you may be able to become proficient, in time. However, bending is easier if you replace the pipe nipple with an oval, or even better, egg-shaped bending iron. Start with an 8-in. length of thick-walled, large-diameter (about 6 in.) pipe. It can be made egg-shaped in a large vise, beaten to shape with a sledge, or taken to a scrapyard and pressed by having the wrecker's magnet dropped on it from the height of a few inches. You can improve heat transfer by filing the contact surface flat. Iron pipe is fine, but I've also used copper and aluminum. With a hacksaw, cut tabs that can be bent back and drilled for mounting. Asbestos "washers" at the tabs will prolong the life of the unit.

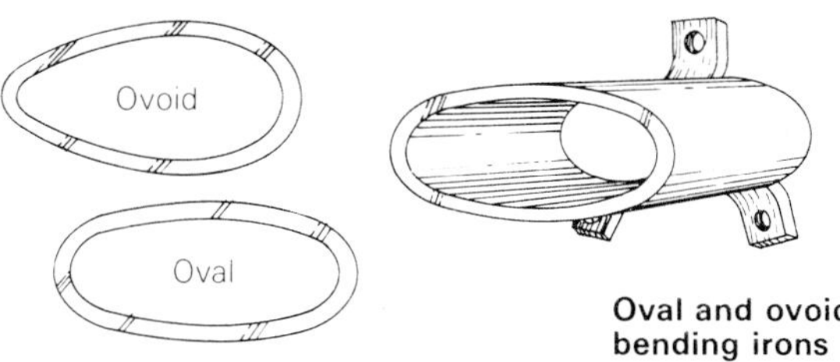

Oval and ovoid bending irons

As with the round pipe, an electric heating coil may be used. The entire scheme can be greatly improved by hooking up a thermostatic device. I have seen various successful arrangements using lighting rheostats, electric-iron rheostats, and electric frying-pan controls. However, a heating coil may require as much as 1000 watts and whatever rheostat you use must operate within this capacity. You can purchase one of several electric bending irons, thermostatically controlled, that work very well but are frightfully expensive.

Bottled gas can be a heat source for the pipe. Build a small carriage behind the bending-iron platform to support the gas torch bottle valve upwards, with its nozzle inserted into a large opening in the platform. The nozzle controls heat effectively. Partially closing the oval opening at the end of the iron with a bent rectangular baffle of thin metal sheet will conserve heat that would otherwise be lost, protect your skin (which is usually directly in front of the opening) and reduce your gas bill. I use an ordinary propane torch. A refill costs less than $3 (1978) and lasts me about a month.

When installing a new torch, remember never to tighten the valve with force. One or two firm tightenings will ruin the valve seats and cause the torch to operate erratically. It will flare dramatically and unexpectedly, creep open or closed while in use, and make it impossible to maintain low settings.

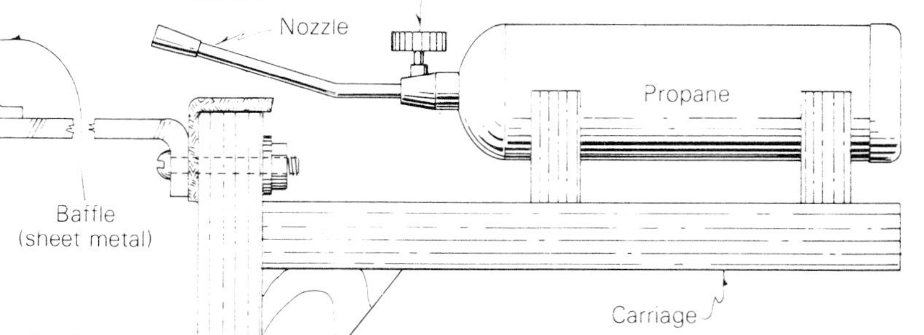

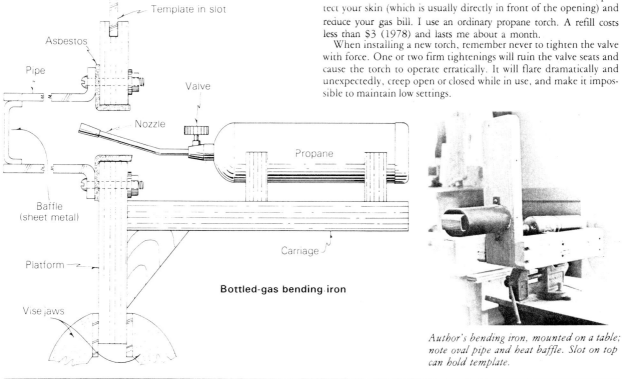

Bottled-gas bending iron

Author's bending iron, mounted on a table; note oval pipe and heat baffle. Slot on top can hold template.

surface. A small end check may cause the whole blank to split dramatically in twain when flexed during bending. Beware of uniformly textured rosewood that has a single, very black line running down its length. This is an interface between two varying densities, a line of stress that may split the blank. Start with material as straight and uniform as possible. If well-quartered yet dramatically grained material is used, its pattern should likewise be even and uniform. Do not use edge grain that wiggles and runs off quickly. Edge grain that runs off gently over a reasonable length of stock is acceptable.

The thin wood (1/16 in. to 1/8 in.) used in instrument making must be stored with fastidious care. Plates must be separated with dry spacers of uniform thickness placed accurately and neatly. The first slat in the pile must be similarly spaced from the supporting shelf, as must the last from the heavy weight above the entire pile. Rosewood and ebony blanks must have both ends parafinned or painted. Improperly stored material, however select and expensive, is liable to check or warp and will have to be discarded.

Various guitarmaking texts suggest that side blanks must first be treated vigorously and harshly to persuade them to bend, for example, by immersing them in boiling water for an hour, or soaking rosewood blanks in hot solvents and soapy water for days. I have observed that a great many problems in hand-bending in fact stem from overwetting and boiling thin slats. For example, maple falls apart under tension as the too-soft material simply separates away from itself under even the mildest pressure. Mahogany that has undergone too much soaking loses its "memory" and must be rebent time and again. Thin, waterlogged maple and mahogany will ripple across the grain after drying. Leaching out the resins by boiling leaves the wood lifeless and crack-prone.

Immersion time varies directly with blank thickness. Blanks of average thickness (.095 in. to .080 in.) need only be immersed in tepid water for a short time: rosewood for 30 to 40 minutes, mahogany for 15 to 20 minutes and maple for as little as 1 to 10 minutes. Side blanks thinner than .080 in. should be used on only the smallest guitars, although modern lute ribs may be as thin as .060 in. Marquetry strips should be immersed in very hot water for 60 to 90 seconds. No prebending is necessary for properly stored strips if the template curves are moderate; strips can be eased into place on the guitar immediately after wetting during the binding process. An ordinary 36-in. sheet metal window-box planter makes an excellent soaking trough.

You must remove all encumbrances and place the bending iron conveniently. You will be bending, taking the piece off the pipe at intervals and comparing it to your template. The template must be firmly secured; a slot in the platform that holds it snugly at eye level will minimize your movements. Another way is to clamp the template to an adjacent tabletop. Having it flat will help discourage the common tendency to bend a skew, or twist, into the blank. Keep handy a small dish with water and a sponge for wetting the wood, to minimize scorching.

Several reference marks in yellow crayon on your blanks will help ensure the proper bookmatch on right and left sides. I find the bookmatch, put the sides together and joint only the common edges, leaving the opposite edges rough or even wany. This helps prevent the mistake of accidentally bending two right or two left sides. The straight, true edge will be glued to the guitartop; the rough edge will be hand-planed and sanded to the proper arch just before the instrument's back is assembled. Allow no less than 1/4-in. extra width.

I also find it helpful to mark the finished length on the blanks (allowing not less than a 1-in. overhang at each end) and to mark "outside" and "inside" on both pieces. If you choose to bend the waist first, a clear mark on the blank at the apex will keep you from running out of material while bending the upper and lower bouts. This point can be calculated by measuring with a string from the template centerline to the waist apex. Another way is to mark off 1-in. increments on the template perimeter with a compass and transfer the waist measurement directly to the side blank with a ruler.

While the iron is heating, take stock of yourself and your task. Choose a time when you will be at your most alert. Take your phone off the hook and lock your shop door.

If you have planned correctly your pipe heat should be just right by the time the blanks are sufficiently wet. If you are a slow bender remove both sides from the trough. As you get faster, you will find yourself leaving the second side in the water while you bend the first.

Pipe heat is critical. The pipe should be the hottest that will not burn the wood on immediate contact. Remember that you will be constantly moving a wet piece of wood over the pipe. If it burns in spite of this, your pipe is too hot. A good test for correct heat is to sprinkle a few drops of water on the pipe. If they sit calmly or boil on the surface, the pipe is too cold. If the drops hop about, sizzling loudly, it is hot enough. If they instantly pop or vaporize, the pipe is too hot.

Even at the right temperature, the pipe may burn the wood if you pause for more than several seconds while bending a tight curve, since the side sometimes must be stopped and wrapped tightly around the pipe. Here additional moisture and short lifting and pressing movements are called for. Some singeing is inevitable, and lightly singed wood can be scraped away later. A tight bend demands some experience, so a beginner should choose a template with only gentle, large-radius bends (such as classical or "dreadnaught" shapes).

The two common procedures are bending from one end to the other and bending the waist first, followed by the upper and lower bouts. The first is considered to be the more difficult, but both will give excellent results when mastered.

If you are right-handed, feed the blank horizontally over the pipe with your right hand in a rapid succession of short up-and-down movements, which will advance the side in short hopping increments. A tight curve will require a slower feed, with faster hopping movements. A broad, gentle curve will require a faster feed, with slower, longer hops. You should rarely, if ever, stop the blank on the pipe. This will cause a kink or lump in the curve. An educated right hand advances the blank at an even, machine-like pace.

Your left hand determines the amount of pressure to apply, and thus the tightness of the resulting curve, by the angle at which the hot blank leaves the pipe surface as it is advanced by the right hand. Apply pressure square to the pipe, and keep the blank square to the pipe. The tendency is to angle the blank as it advances, and to tip the blank surface toward you as you grasp and press it. This results in a complex, changing twist in the finished piece, which in turn results in an instrument with one shape when viewed from the front and a different shape when viewed from the back.

The most valuable "feel" that you should be anticipating is the feedback given you by the change in springiness of the material as heat is applied. As you advance the blank over the top surface of the oval pipe, the rate of feed must be matched to the rate at which the wood absorbs enough heat to become plastic, or "relax." You should attempt to feel this change in stiffness, for it is at this point where the best bending occurs. If you are not sensitive to this change you may be applying pressure ineffectively—at best, the blank will simply not take the bend; at worst, the blank may crack.

If you have mentally subdivided the template into simplified steps, deciding when and where to apply pressure is likewise simplified. At the end of each step, or even more frequently, you should compare the piece with the template. But unless you maintain tension as you take the blank to the template, the piece will not hold the desired shape. Hesitate momentarily and allow the piece to cool slightly under tension. This pause is critical: The wood is "curing" at this time and the fibers are returning to a rigid state in the new shape. If you relax tension here, the piece will return to a random shape, and there will be no bending progress.

Take advantage of this curing interval by flexing the piece to match the template segment, then holding it still for a few moments against the template. The piece will retain the correct shape with little springback. Springback can be remedied at this point (after letting go of the piece) by gently and rhythmically flexing the piece while it is still warm until it springs back to the desired shape.

Bending mistakes can be corrected by reverse bending, but if you unbend too frequently and guess poorly at the place to rectify your error, the piece will take on a tortured, lumpy shape that is impossible ever to correct.

Acceptable deviation from the template should not exceed the ability of the material to flex after bending. Your criteria should be the wood's ability to be coaxed to the template line with only the gentlest pressure. Some builders feel that all the parts of an instrument should be under moderate tension during and after assembly, the justification being that the stress adds energy to the acoustic vibrations rippling through the guitar. Others feel exactly the opposite. This is a moot point, because there is no practical way of testing these contradictory assumptions. I choose to approximate the template to the best of my ability and reduce the variation to a minimum for other reasons: ease of assembly and the resulting improvement in the final appearance of the instrument.

Occasionally cracks and surface tearing of fibers at tight bends can occur. Some can be repaired. Cracks that appear as straight lines along straight-grained material can be closed by gentle clamping with glue and reinforcement from the back with a strip of tightly woven fabric saturated in white glue and pressed behind the glued crack. If jagged cracks occur in flatsawn materials, discard the piece. Moderate tearing of the surface fibers on tight bends can be repaired by working glue into the fracture and pressing the fibers down with a clamp and a gently curved caul.

Wet material locked into a mold over extended periods may mildew. I let the pieces air-dry for several hours and then tape them tightly to each other until assembly. Springback can be corrected by touching up dry on a moderately heated iron just before assembly. □

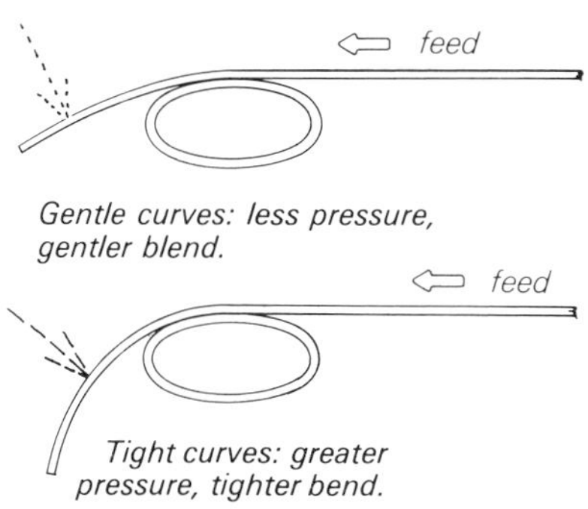

feed
Gentle curves: less pressure, gentler blend.
feed
Tight curves: greater pressure, tighter bend.

Amount of pressure and rate of feed determine tightness or curve. Fast feed with slow, long hops makes broad, gentle curve.

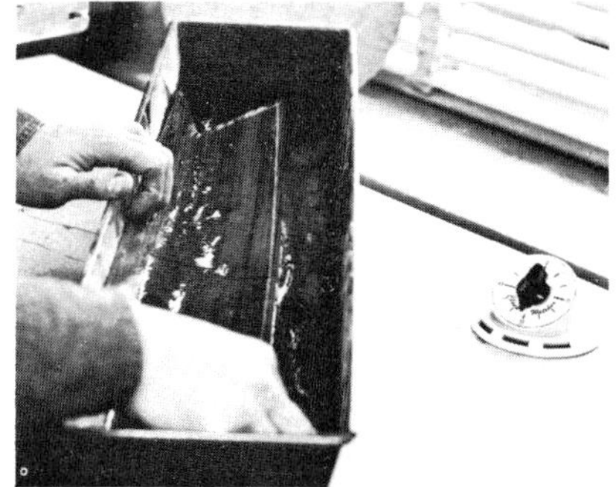

Side blanks are immersed in water in window-box planter; kitchen timer keeps track of minutes, prevents overwetting.

Right hand feeds evenly while the left fans rapidly (note blur) to advance the blank in small hops across the pipe.

Waist-first bending: Mark at center of blank, where waist will be, ensures sufficient length for upper and lower bouts.

Neck-to-tail bending: Major curve section of upper bout is held in tension momentarily to permit wood to 'cure' in new shape.

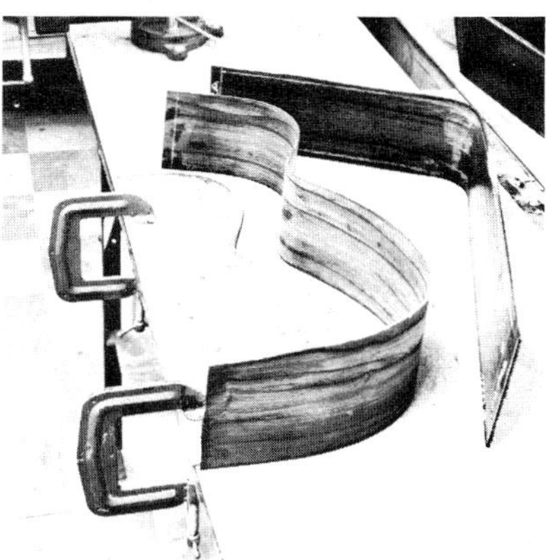

Finished side is checked against template. Some deviation is acceptable; reverse bending, in moderation, can correct mistakes.

An Adaptable Instrument Form

Bob Mattingly's straightforward route to a musical box

by Jim Cummins

I'd had in mind building a vielle, a sort of modern medieval fiddle, ever since I traced and sketched one about six years ago, but the project kept stalling. I'd done enough repair work to know that the intimidating complexity of most musical instruments is an illusion—that instrument building is basically simple, depending more on common sense and sharp tools than on magic and secrets. I already knew something about the separate procedures involved—bending the sides, thicknessing the back and top, what woods instrument makers use. What I lacked was a straightforward way to fit all the procedures together.

Then, at the 1982 annual Guild of American Luthiers Convention, which was held in Colorado that year, I met Bob Mattingly, a guitar maker from Long Beach, Calif., who has developed a course aimed at non-woodworkers who want to make guitars. His best trick is two clever forms built up from layers of plywood and/or particleboard. When the stack is bandsawn, it yields both a bending form for the instrument's sides and an assembly form—an outside mold the exact size and shape of the instrument—that will hold the pieces of the project for clamping. The bending form comes out of the center waste from the assembly form, so both are economical and quick to make. They allow for shortcuts, ingenuity, and whatever tools or clamps you may have around your shop, even rubber bands. The principle can be applied to making any hollow shape with top, bottom and curved sides: ukuleles, dulcimers, guitars of all styles and sizes—any curved box (such as the one on page 47), whether or not it's intended to make music. The whole process seemed so accessible that I dug out my old drawings and cleared my workbench. With help from my wife, Karen, I got the fiddle ready for pegs and strings over a three-day weekend.

Figure 1 shows how simple the basic construction is. The instrument has a flat top and back, bent sides reinforced by strips called linings, and blocks inside the body at the neck and tail for strength. Guitars and other modern instruments have a series of internal cross-braces to stiffen the back and the top. The vielle, with its relatively heavy, ⅛-in. thick pieces, needs none.

Template—Whatever your project, draw or trace its outline, and make an exact template of half its top—mine was of plexiglass. If the box is not symmetrical, make a full template. Determine the depth of the finished box, and pile up enough plywood or particleboard to match, with the pieces at least 1 in. larger all around than the body of the instrument. The middle sheet in the stack should be thick and sturdy, and about 3 in. larger. This sheet will act as

Fig. 1: Parts of a vielle

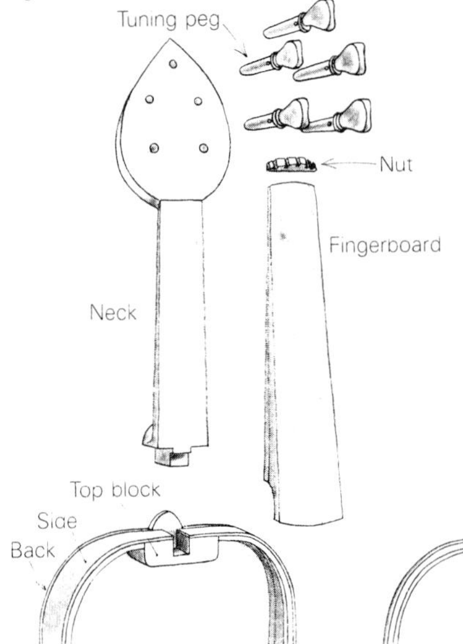

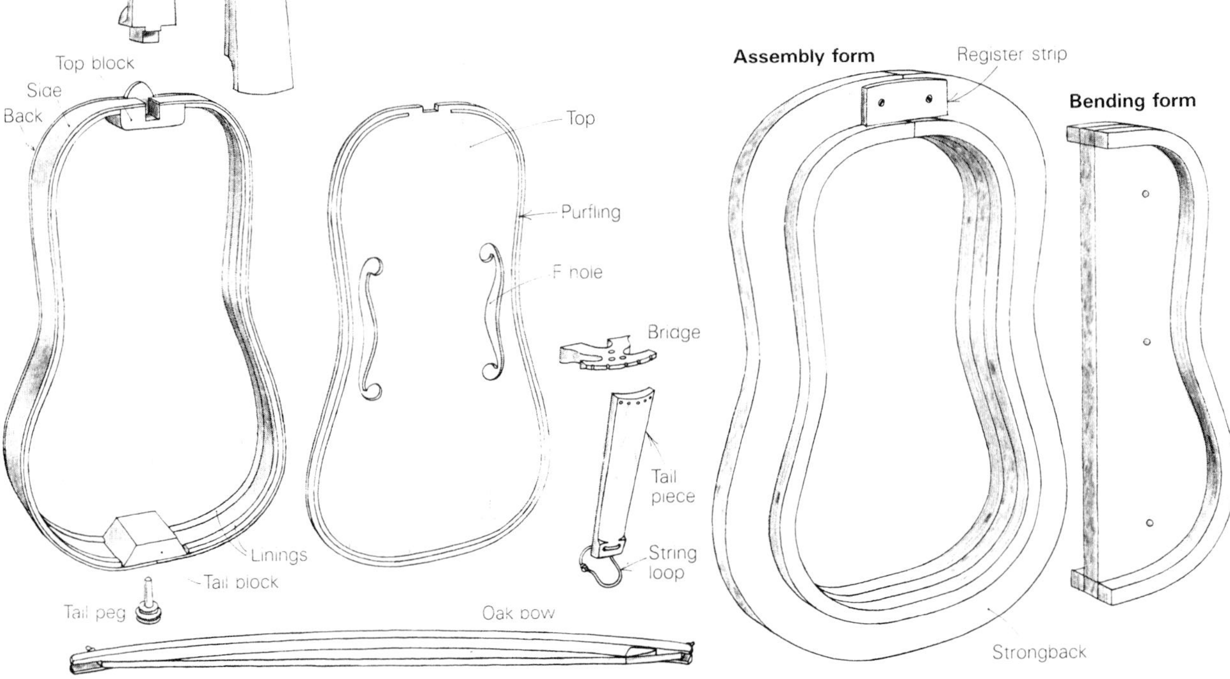

a strongback, an oversize, wider lamination that will make the thin walls more rigid. I used particleboard for the strongback, but something as large as a guitar needs ¾-in. plywood instead. The stack should be at least the height of the deepest part of the instrument; later the box's walls can be trimmed down to exactly the right height or even tapered. Figure 2 shows the steps that get you both forms from the stack.

Register strip—As seen in steps 4 and 5, a register strip placed over the entrance kerf solidifies the assembly form and compensates for the sawkerf, keeping the form the exact size of the template. The shape of a vielle is a straightforward curve that can be made with one continuous bandsaw cut. For more difficult shapes, including those with right-angle corners or other tight spots that require you to back up the blade and reapproach from another direction, you can design various inserts, held in place by additional register strips, that will restore the assembly form to one piece, as shown in figure 3. Thus you can adapt the form to other methods of attaching the neck, as well as to cutaway guitar styles.

Sanding—The assembly form is so accurate that it exactly reproduces any error. Take care to sand the bandsaw marks away without distorting the shape or flaring the walls. If you want the instrument to be tapered in depth (many guitars are deeper at the tail than at the neck), be sure to taper the bottom side of the assembly form rather than the top, otherwise the neck's top surface won't lie in the right plane. Mattingly's students make an extra-long sanding block to help them keep the mold's top and bottom surfaces flat and even. Shellac and wax the form so it will resist glue.

Using the forms—I'll move quickly through the following steps to show how the forms are used. Rather than trying to give a crash course in luthiery, I have put a list of references on page 47. The basics of instrument making are simple enough to cover here, although the fine points can be argued forever.

Bending wood—You have to prebend the instrument's sides and the linings in order to be sure of a tight glue joint when you clamp them in the assembly form. I made a steamer from a

Fig. 2: Making the forms

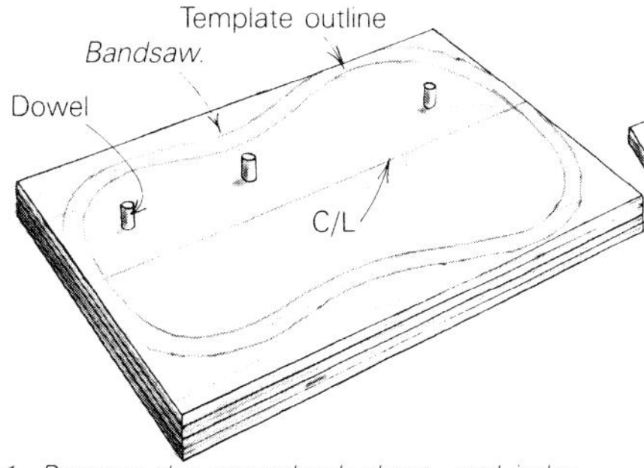

Template outline
Bandsaw
Dowel
C/L
Bandsaw
Strongback

1. Remove the strongback sheet, and index the stack with dowels. Trace the template on the stack, then trace a contour ½ in. larger than the template. Bandsaw the outside line.

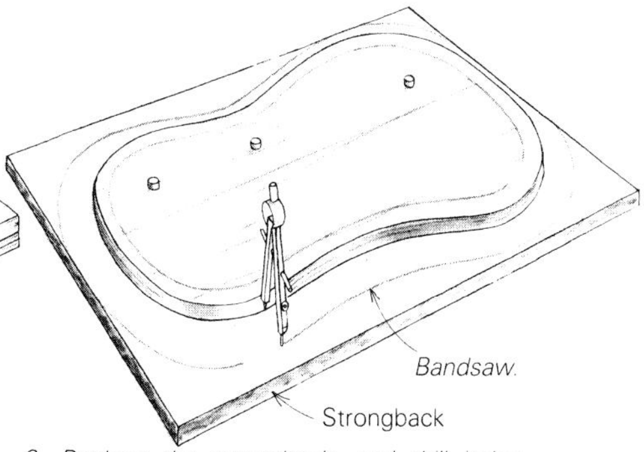

2. Replace the strongback, and drill index holes, using the previous holes as pilots. Draw the outline of the strongback, about 1½ in. wider than the previous cut. Bandsaw.

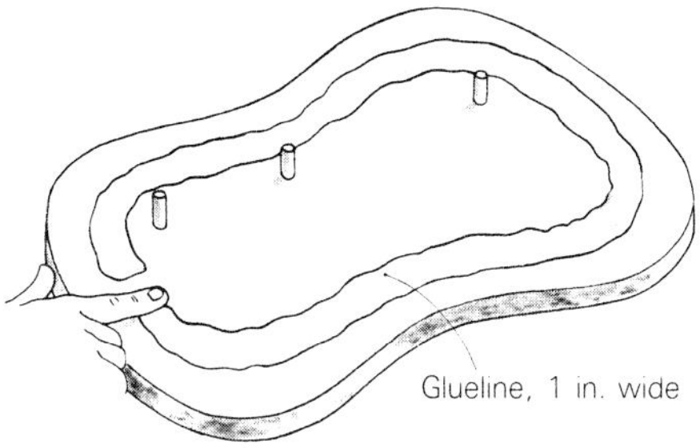

Glueline, 1 in. wide
Register strip

3. Use the dowels to glue the layers to the strongback one at a time. Spread a 1-in. wide band of glue around the edge of each layer. Clamp up.

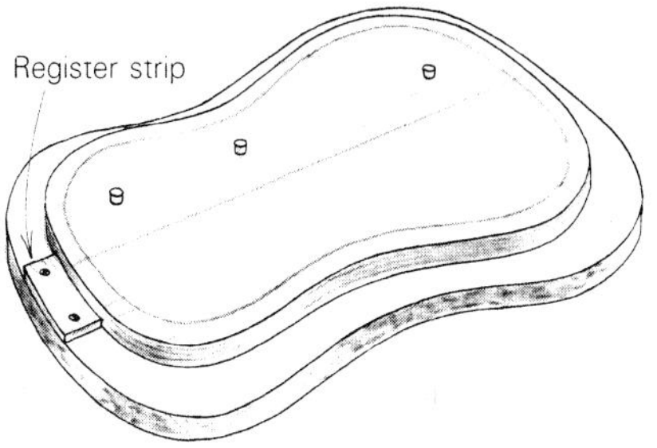

4. Screw a register strip across the top of the strongback, then remove it. Later on the strip will hold the mold at its original dimensions and strengthen it.

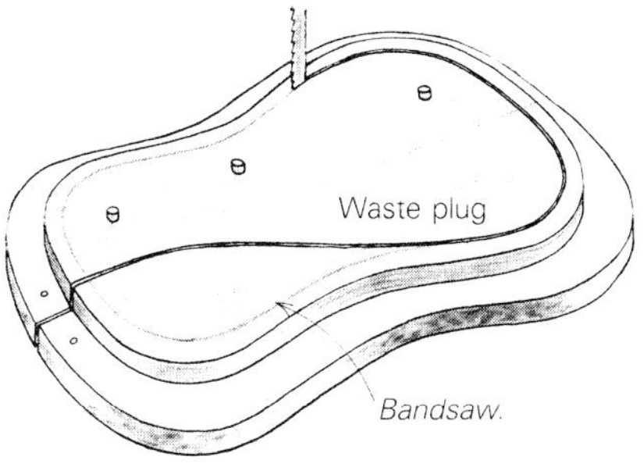

Waste plug
Bandsaw

5. Beginning the cut at the top, bandsaw around the template outline.

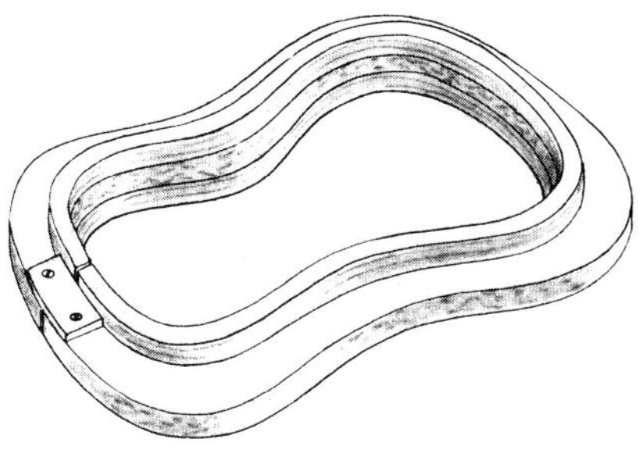

6. Reattach the register strip. This completes the assembly form.

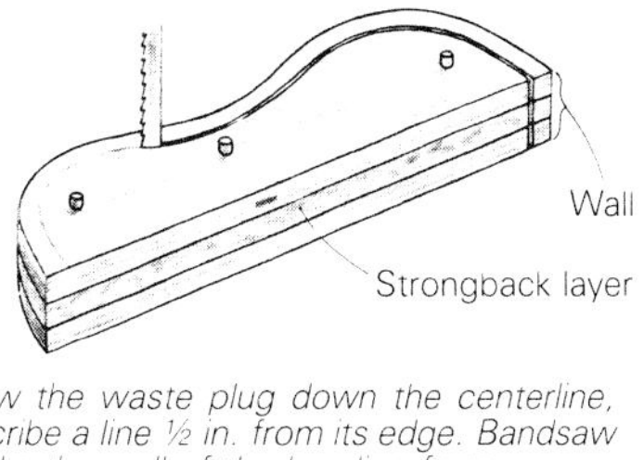

Wall
Strongback layer
Bending form
Glue strongback

7. Saw the waste plug down the centerline, and scribe a line ½ in. from its edge. Bandsaw to make the wall of the bending form.

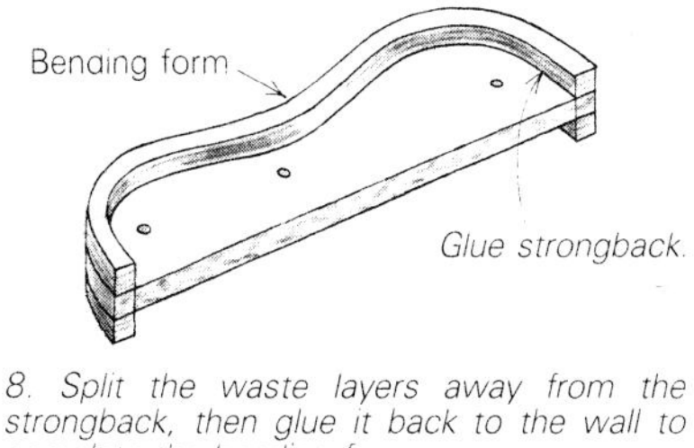

8. Split the waste layers away from the strongback, then glue it back to the wall to complete the bending form.

Fig. 3: Variations **A** *shows the Spanish method of attaching neck to body, with a removable, neck-size section in the mold.* **B** *shows a cutaway guitar.*

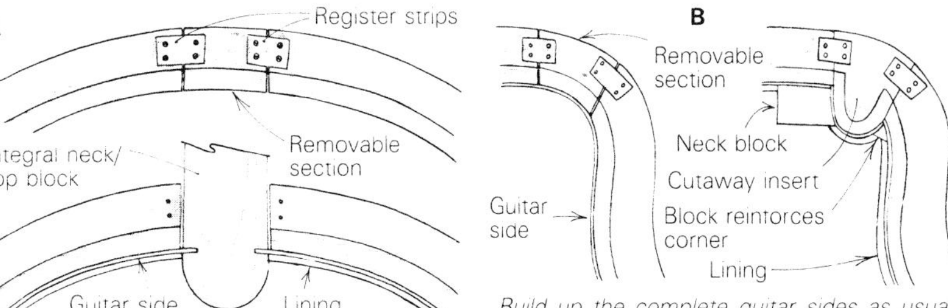

After the linings have been glued to the bent sides, remove the section and install the neck.

Build up the complete guitar sides as usual. Then remove the section where the cutaway will fit, miter the sides, install the cutaway insert and complete the shape.

hot pot and a rolled-up-cardboard tube (photo, below), and steamed a single $1\frac{1}{2}$-in. strip of dogwood (it was handy, though maple would have done fine) to make the linings. They will eventually be glued around the inside of the sides, as shown at right, to provide more gluing surface for attaching the top and bottom. Don't slice and taper the linings before you bend them, or they'll twist. In the bending-form photo below, the wood is being heated with an industrial hot-air gun to set the bend. After the bend had set, I bandsawed the piece into four narrow strips (about $\frac{1}{4}$ in. wide), and then tapered them so they would blend smoothly into the instrument's sides.

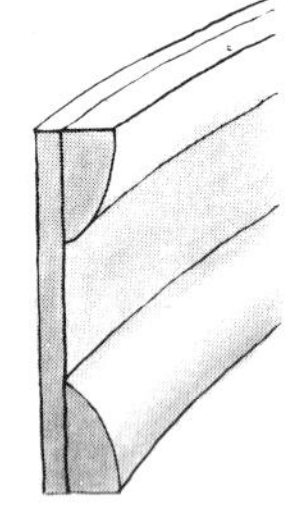

Mattingly bends guitar sides on the bending form, too, using a natural-gas flame to steam up the damp wood as he clamps along. But a vielle's sides are thicker than a guitar's. It turned out that my clamps were not strong enough to hold the sides on the form. So I prebent mine around a bending iron I rigged up—the hot-air gun held in my vise, shown in the photo, below left.

Clamping the sides in the mold—The sides are butt-joined and glued at the bottom of the instrument, but at the top, at this stage, they just float free. Figure 1 shows the maple tail block, which strengthens the joint and will later be drilled to hold the peg to which the tail piece is tied. The linings butt against it, and I clamped and glued them one at a time to the sides as shown below. The tail block could be smaller in an instrument with less string tension, or it could be replaced by another lamination if you were building a box. In fact, for a box, you could dispense with linings entirely by double-laminating the sides, perhaps with one lamination narrower than the other to form a rabbet for the box's top.

After the glue had dried, I removed the sides from the assembly form to check that I hadn't glued them in, and I found that there was little springback.

Fitting the neck, top and back—I shaped the maple neck with bandsaw, jointer and belt sander, then cut its tenon on the tablesaw. Next I made a top block with a matching mortise and glued it in place in the assembly form. The tenon is stepped down so the top

An improvised bending setup: An industrial hot-air gun can plasticize the wood as it is levered around the vise's tommy bar. The steamer in the background is a cardboard tube in an electric hot pot.

The bending form: Linings are first steamed, then clamped and heated with a hot-air gun or a gas flame to set the bends. Guitar sides can be bent the same way.

The assembly form: Pre-bent sides and linings are laminated with spring clamps, while the handscrew secures the tail block. The top block will be glued in last.

can overlap it, but I left a little of the tenon showing as a clue to anybody who might ever try to remove the neck. I made the back from bookmatched maple and the top from bookmatched spruce. I know people who've made instrument tops by quartersawing red cedar construction lumber, but it makes a quieter instrument.

The next step was to plane the linings, sides and blocks to make a good glue joint with the top and back. Most of the truing-up can be done with the sides in the assembly form, which provides stability and reference points.

I clamped the neck to the top block with the instrument outside the mold, as shown below. While the glue dried, I cut the F holes in the top with a knife. Since spruce grain is alternately hard and soft, which makes for a jumpy cut, I made a light cut around the outline, and gradually deepened the cut by making wider and wider Vs until it went through. I'm tempted to try some filigree the same way.

I clamped the back and top to the instrument using rubber bands for tension around the sides and Jorgensen handscrews over the blocks.

Odds and ends—Figure 1 shows the other parts needed to complete the vielle. The relationships between the tail piece, bridge, fingerboard and nut are interdependent, and determine how easily the instrument will play. The player must be able to bow each string separately and to fret the strings on the fingerboard easily. I made my vielle wider than the one I'd traced because I thought it looked better, but this meant that I had to change the height of the strings at the bridge. The dimensions and curves of the parts I'd traced six years before no longer worked. It was late Monday before I finally got most of the pieces roughed out.

I spent the next Saturday chiseling out a groove for the dogwood and poplar purfling, which I first laminated on the bending form. Then I experimented with a series of maple bridges until the arc and the height worked out right. Eventually, I raised the fingerboard by putting a full-length wedge between it and the neck. I bought viol strings from an early-music store, and a neighboring luthier turned me a nicer set of tuning pegs than I could have managed. Then I varnished the vielle.

While the varnish was drying, I made a crude bow from some synthetic horsehair I'd stashed away. I rosined the bow, touched it expectantly to the strings, and was rewarded with an intermittent squeaking wail that sounded like a dried-out bearing sounding its death rattle. I didn't find out until weeks later that the sound was all my fault and not the instrument's. In the hands of a string player, it sounded fine. Making the box was the easy part. Now I have to learn how to play it. □

Jim Cummins usually makes and plays flutes. He is on the editorial staff at FWW.

The neck can be clamped to the top block outside the assembly form. For an alternative neck joint, see figure 3.

The finished vielle next to another shape that can be made by adapting Mattingly's assembly form, a little dogwood-and-ash box.

Further reading

De Paule, Andy. *Country Instruments: Makin' Your Own.* Van Nostrand Reinhold, 1976.

Ford, Charles. *Making Musical Instruments: Strings and Keyboard.* Pantheon, 1979.

Data sheets from the Guild of American Luthiers, 822 South Park Ave., Tacoma, Wash. 98408.

The Shape of a Violin

It is, and it isn't, as simple as it looks

by Harry S. Wake

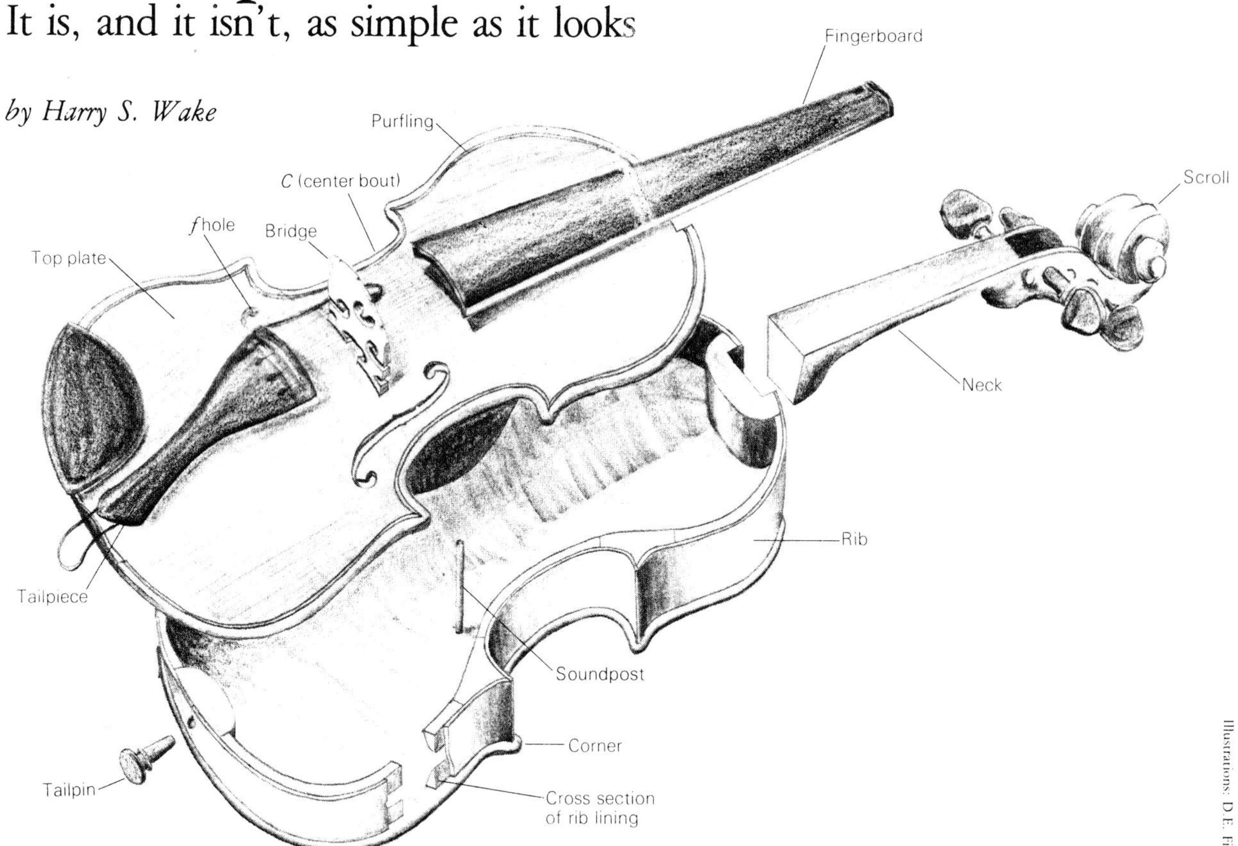

There has always been an aura of mystique and romance about the violin, and it is surprising how relatively simple its construction is. On the other hand, it is not quite as simple as some are apt to believe—for example, the top and back plates are not given their delicate contours by moisture, heat and pressure; they must be carved with chisels and gouges and measured to micrometer thicknesses. This is the question: "How is the shape of a violin arrived at?"

The violin as we know it was established in the 1600s and except for a couple of minor changes conducive to improved playing technique has remained unchanged for over 300 years. The conventional materials used for the body of the instrument are quartersawn maple for the back, neck, head (or scroll) and ribs or sides, and quartersawn straight-grain spruce for the top or table. The fittings—pegs, tailpiece and fingerboard—are usually made of ebony, although other hardwoods are sometimes used. The bridge is always made of maple or sycamore.

The back and top plates are usually made of two pieces of wood joined on the centerline. Quartersawn maple with nice grain markings joined in this manner creates a beautiful effect. Sometimes a piece of maple can be found that is wide enough to make a back without a centerline joint, but these pieces are much prized and quite expensive.

All wood for violin-making must be air-seasoned and at least 10 to 15 years old. European suppliers have been cutting and seasoning wood for violin-making for a couple of centuries or more, and most of the wood used today originates there. It appears, however, that their supplies are running low: German suppliers are now buying Oregon maple and British Columbia spruce and sending it to Europe for processing, then returning it to us for violin-making.

The maple and spruce logs are cut to suitable lengths and split into wedges. These wedges are split again and put together in pairs to make one violin top or back. They are then trimmed—sufficient material is sliced off the top face of the maple lengthwise of the grain to make the violin ribs, which eventually finish to a width of about 1½ in. and a rough thickness of 3/32 in. or less. This width allows enough material for trimming after the ribs are bent and formed on the mold. The finished depth of the violin ribs will be 1¼ in. all around; some makers modify this a little by reducing the depth slightly at the upper end.

The two halves of the top and back are trimmed and joined on the centerline. One half of the wedge is placed in a vise with the thicker edge uppermost and quickly brushed with a plentiful coat of glue. Traditionally, hide or animal glue was

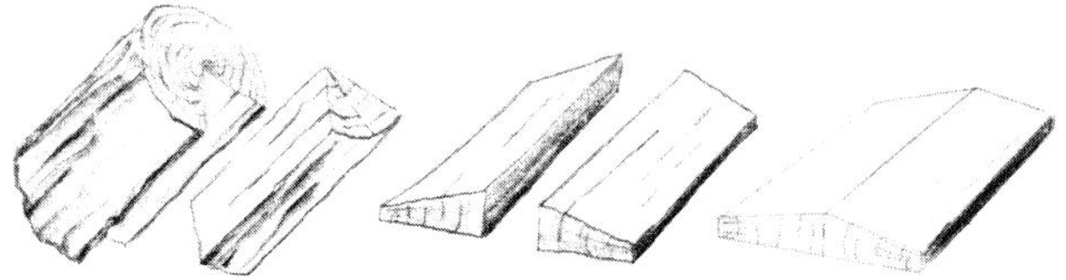

For violin top or back, split wedge from a log, then split wedge into two. Trim, place thick edges together, join on centerline.

Photos: Gene Fran

Front, back and scroll of violin No. 62, made by Wake.

Tony Doubek

Wake playing cello he made in 1976.

used in violin-making. Today, plastic resin glue can be used for the centerline joint, and for a few other places. The top plate must be glued to the ribs with hide glue, however, because someday the top will be taken off for repairs. I object to the use of common white household glue anywhere on a violin, because most parts of a violin are under constant tension, and white glue will not hold. I've seen too many violins with their necks pulled out of their mortises. The glued halves are rubbed together and left to set overnight. This is better than using clamps, unless you devise a special frame. Top and back pairs are now joined, but before going further with these we will go to the mold on which the ribs will be built. These ribs will be used as a template to develop the outline of the top and back plates.

Of all the different variations of the basic violin outline that have been developed, those of the Italian makers Amati, Stradivari and Guarneri are probably used most. After the violin-maker has decided on a model, he prepares a pattern for the mold. Allowing for the thickness of the ribs and for overlap of the edge of the plate, a half-pattern is made from thin-sheet aluminum or plastic. This is actually a pattern for the inside of a violin. The half outline is transferred to the mold wood, then flipped over and the other half drawn. This ensures that both sides from the centerline of the violin will be the same, in opposite.

The mold is a sandwich of two pieces of plywood, measuring about 9 in. by 15 in. Use pieces that are each ⅝ in. thick, or one of ½ in. and one of ¾ in. The mold must be a sandwich because it will be separated later on, as the violin is being assembled. Many different types of mold are used, but all act as a foundation on which the violin is built.

The two pieces of plywood are held together with four bolts. In addition, the top piece has three tapped holes on its centerline for push-out bolts that will help separate the two plates. The half-pattern is used to draw the outline on the mold, which is then carefully sawn and finished true and square to the line.

Some means must be provided for attaching the bent rib pieces to each other at the corners and at the top and bottom of the instrument. With the two plates of the mold firmly bolted together, holes are drilled to accommodate clamps, and cutouts are made at top and bottom and at each corner, as in the drawing. Squared blocks of willow or spruce are then attached to the mold in place of the cutouts, with the wood grain running vertical to the face of the mold. In the end, these blocks will become part of the violin and remain inside it. Therefore they are attached with only a small touch of glue, and they are fastened only to the lower section of the mold. The blocks must be finished flush to the top and bottom of the mold. Now the half-pattern is used to transfer the outline to the top face of the blocks, so they can be trimmed to the drawn outline.

Bolt two pieces of plywood together for the mold. The three holes down the centerline are through only the top half of the mold and will help separate it later on. The other holes accommodate clamps.

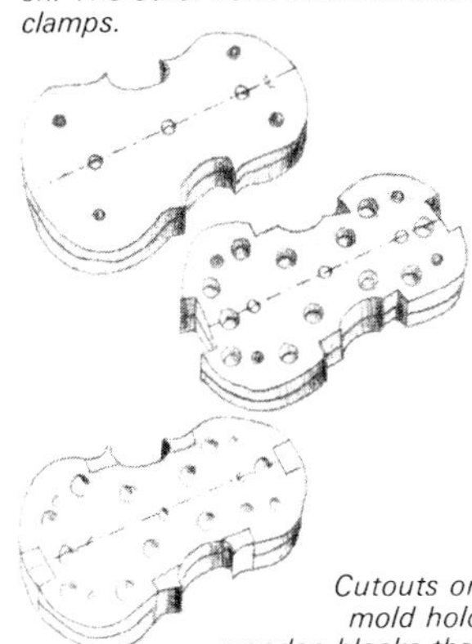
Cutouts on mold hold wooden blocks that separate from mold to become inside gluing surfaces of violin.

Gene Truax

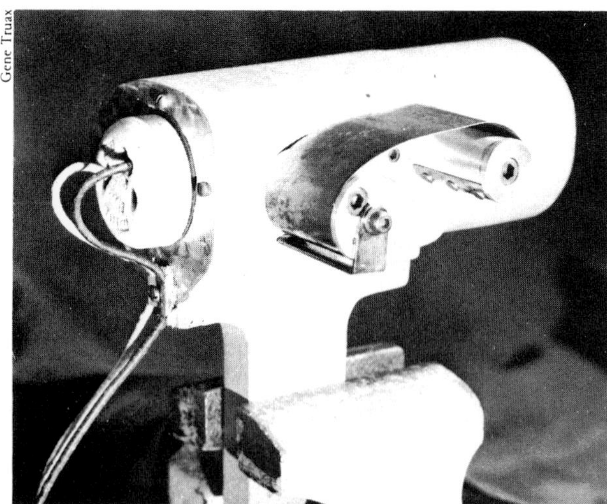

Electrically heated, adjustable bending iron, designed by Wake, can bend C's for any size violin.

The next operation is bending the ribs, the stock for which, it will be recalled, was cut from the wedge-shaped maple bottom plate. Six pieces are cut to lengths sufficient for upper and lower right and left sections and the two *C's* (center bouts). They will be sanded down to a final finish of 0.040 in., or about 1 mm. These pieces are soaked in water for about a half hour and formed by wiping them over a hot iron or pipe section; each maker develops his own methods, and it becomes quite simple with practice. I have designed and patented an adjustable, electrically heated bending iron that makes it possible to bend *C's* for any size violin or viola.

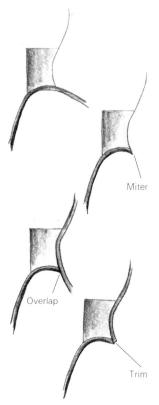

The ends of the bent C-pieces are mitered to accommodate overlapping of the upper and lower sections.

The mold is prepared by applying a coat of soap or silicone grease adjacent to the blocks, to prevent any excess glue from sticking where it is not wanted. The *C's* are glued in place first, clamped securely and left to set. The ends of the *C's* are trimmed to a miter at the corners to accommodate the overlap of the upper and lower sections of the ribs, and those sections are next glued in place only at the corners of the *C's*. The left and right upper sections of the ribs are trimmed at the ends, brought snugly around the mold and glued to the upper block. The ends don't have to come close together because a mortise will later be cut here for the neck.

Gluing the lower rib sections to the bottom block is a little different, because a perfect butt joint must be achieved right on the centerline. Bring one of the ribs down tightly around the mold and clamp it at the bottom. Make a mark right on the centerline and trim off the end of the rib square and true. This end will not be glued down yet, but the other lower rib will be brought down and around and the end of it placed underneath the one that has been cut. Use a sharp knife to score a line on the rib underneath, using the upper rib as a guide. The second rib is then cut off at the scored line, and both can be glued in place.

The corners are trimmed off square and at a true right angle to the face of the mold. The completed rib assembly is then put aside, and work resumed on the top and back.

The bottom of the top and back plate assemblies is now cleaned up to a flat and level surface. The mold assembly top face is laid face down on the flat face of the top wood, centerline to centerline, and secured with a clamp at each end. The mold face should make close contact all around on the face of the wood. The overhanging edge of the finished violin top should be just about 3/32 in.; if a small washer with this wall thickness is placed against the rib and a pencil point placed in the hole, the pencil point can "ride" the washer completely around the ribs to mark the top outline on the face of the wood. The back plate is laid out the same way and an extension is left at the top center that will be finished later as the base of the neck.

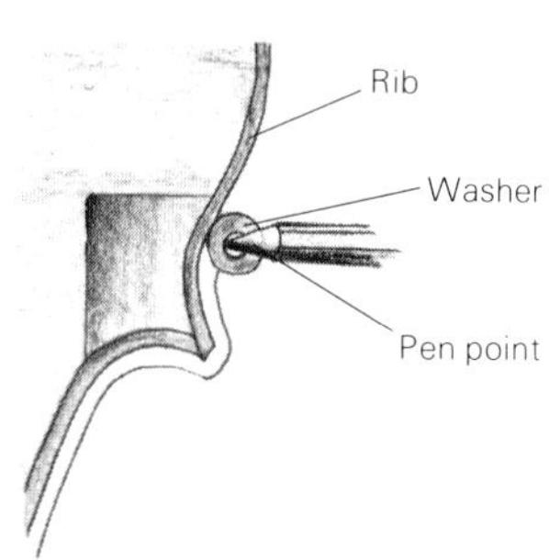

With the point of a pen, ride a washer around the ribs to mark the outline of the top of the violin on the face of the wood.

The plates are bandsawn, but not too close to the line at this stage, taking care not to cut off the extension at the top of the back. The outside surfaces of both plates are next brought to final dimensions and contours and the edges finished to the line with gouges, finger planes, scrapers and sanding. The arching and thickness patterns are different for top and bottom plates, and an experienced maker doesn't use guides or patterns for the outside contours. Some makers, however, use transverse and longitudinal arching guides. The average height of the plates from the bottom face to the highest point of the arching is about 5/8 in. After the outside arching and contours are finished, the undersides of the plates are scooped out with the use of the same gouges, finger planes, etc., and carefully calibrated—the top plate to a thickness of less than 3 mm. The exact thickness depends on the density of the wood being used: It should weigh about 68 grams, and by working with the weight, a plate that is denser will finish thinner than one of a less dense wood. The thickness of the back plate will be different, because the central area is usually left fairly thick, about 4 mm to 5 mm, and the plate gradually thins towards the outer edge to 3 mm or less. It will weigh about 110 grams.

During this stage, the violin-maker suspends the top plate by forefinger and thumb and taps it lightly in the central area, listening for the "tap tone." This is an important procedure, and as the work is brought to final thickness he will continue to monitor it in an effort to bring it within desired frequency. When the plate is finished, he will note the tap tone frequency for future reference. The back plate should have a finished frequency just about a half tone higher than the top. If the top tap tone, for example, was *F*, then the back would be *F* sharp. If the top was *E*, the back would be *F*.

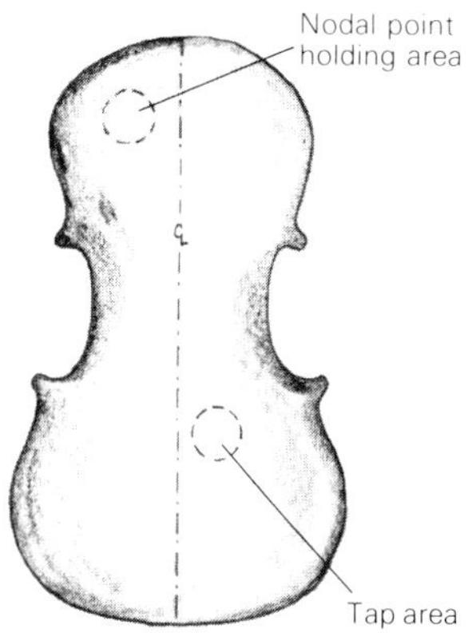

Through the research of scientists and violin-makers in recent years, new electronic methods have gained wide use in frequency testing and matching top and back plates of violins. The sensitive ear is no longer essential, although it still helps a great deal.

With the top and back plates having clean, scratchless surface finishes both inside and out, the next step is inserting the three-layer purfling trim into a shallow groove cut just inside the edge. The purfling material can be purchased either in wood or fiber. It has a white piece sandwiched between two black pieces, and is supplied in strips about 1/16 in. wide and deep, by about 3 ft. long. Although it is brittle and more difficult to work, I prefer wood purfling.

Different methods are used to cut the purfling groove: Some makers draw a two-bladed cutter around the edge, then use a narrow chisel to remove the wood, forming a channel just a little less deep than the material to be inserted. Others, like myself, devise machine methods for cutting the groove.

It is difficult to fit the purfling into a tight groove that is swollen with glue, so the groove should be wide enough so that the purfling will drop in easily. In fitting wood purfling, the corners are critical and can make or mar a piece of work. All pieces are bent over a hot iron, but cannot be presoaked in water because the layers will separate. Considerable care must be taken while bending.

The pieces should first be fitted into the grooves dry and neatly mitered at the corners. When all the pieces fit, glue them in, pressing them down with a smooth round object like a wooden tool handle, and wipe away the glue with a damp cloth. The plates are then put aside for the glue to set. Cleanup is next, then the edges all around are neatly rounded off. The back plate is now finished. The top plate has yet to have the *f*'s or sound holes cut and the bassbar fitted.

The *f*'s will be centered at a point 7⅝ in. down from the top edge; the *V*-nicks on the inside edge of the *f*'s are the index points. A template for a single *f* is positioned with the index nick of the *f* on the crossline marked lightly across the top. The *f* is traced through the template. Then the template is flipped over and the opposite *f* traced. Cutting the *f*'s requires care for a neat job with a sharp clean outline, but with a little practice and a sharp blade it becomes routine.

The bassbar is a longitudinal support that is fitted and glued to the underside of the top at a slight angle to the centerline, almost in line with the *G*, or lowest string. Along with the soundpost, it supports the top against the pressure of the strings on the bridge. Some makers put counter-tension into a bassbar by leaving a slight gap under each end before gluing the bar down.

The tap tone or frequency of the finished plate will probably be lost when the *f*'s are cut. However, by careful trimming of the bassbar and constant checking of the tap tone, the clear ring of the original frequency can be restored.

Harry Sebastian Wake is author of The Technique of Violin Making *and several other books on violin construction, plans and repair, which may be ordered from him at 4171 Stettler Way, San Diego, Calif. 92122.*

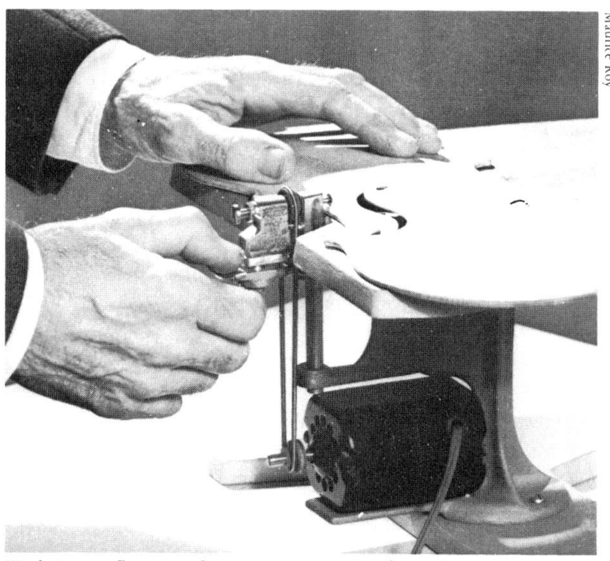

Wake's purfling machine cuts a narrow channel around edge of violin plate.

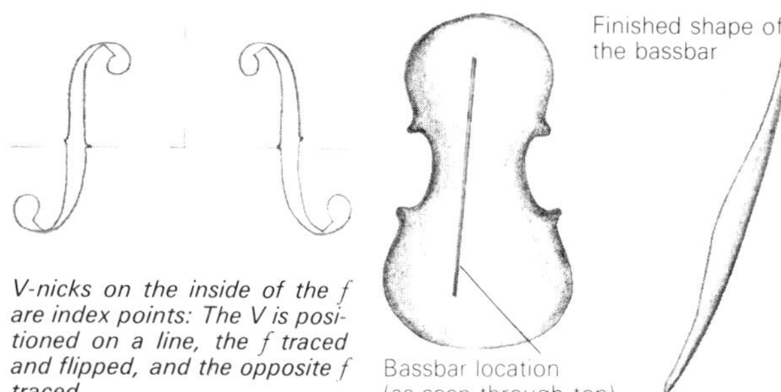

V-nicks on the inside of the f are index points: The V is positioned on a line, the f traced and flipped, and the opposite f traced.

While the sides are still secured on the mold, the finished top plate is placed in position and secured with a clamp at each end. A small hole is drilled at the bottom and top just to one side of the centerline, through the top and into the blocks on the mold about ¼ in. deep. Round toothpicks are thinned slightly and pushed into the holes, then cut off, leaving a short end projecting. The same procedure is performed on the violin back—these small dowels position the top and back plates when the assembly is glued together.

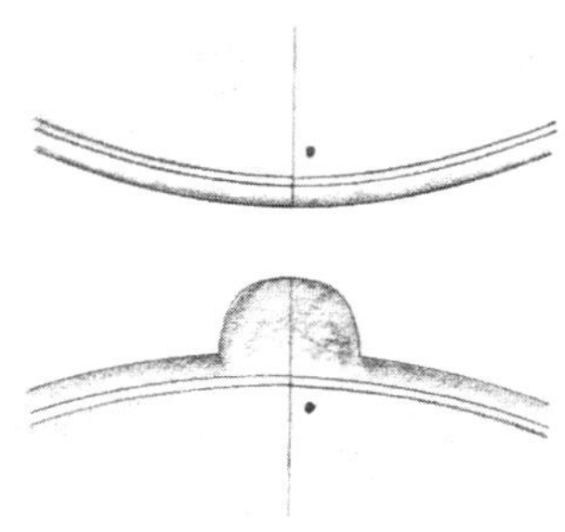

Bottom and top, back and front holes hold tiny positioning dowels.

Remember that there are three tapped holes on the centerline, through the mold's top plate only; inserting machine screws and tightening them down after the four bolts that hold the two sections together are removed, pushes the upper plate of the mold out of the rib frame. The lower section of the mold remains attached to the ribs at the blocks.

The now exposed upper edges of the ribs offer too little surface area for gluing, so lining strips are prepared and glued inside the edges. There are six pieces: two for the upper sections, two for the *C*'s and two for the lower sections. These are preferably willow, in strips about 3/32 in. thick by 5/16 in.

wide, bent with heat to conform to the curvature of the inside of the ribs. They are glued in place using spring clothespins for clamps and left to set. The top edge is cleaned off flat and true to leave a good gluing surface, and the linings are tapered down to a thin edge on the inside.

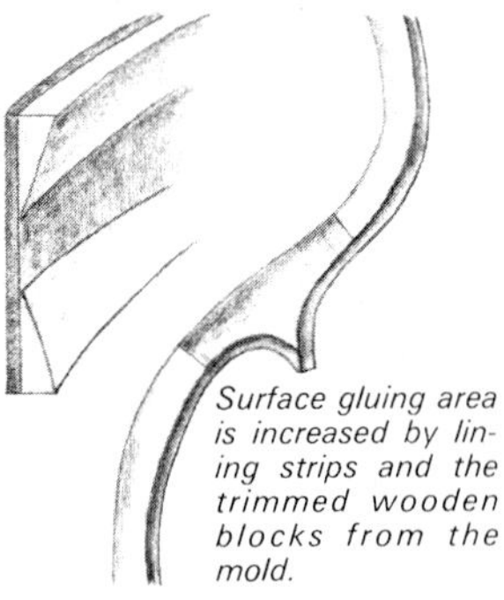
Surface gluing area is increased by lining strips and the trimmed wooden blocks from the mold.

With a thin knife blade the blocks are carefully separated from the mold, and the lower section of the mold is removed from the rib frame. Six more linings are fitted to the lower edge, the blocks trimmed to the inside contours and the rib frame cleaned up for assembly with the top and back plates.

The back plate is glued onto the rib frame first, using bobbin-type clamps all around and C-clamps at the end blocks. Bobbin or spool clamps are easy to make. They consist of two freely moving spools mounted on a threaded bolt together with leather washers and an easy-running wing nut. About fifty of these clamps are required to go around the corpus when gluing the top or bottom plate to the ribs. The clamps are usually set close together with light pressure. A violin-maker can make his own spool clamps from 1-in. diameter dowel rod and ¼ in. by 4 in. stove bolts. The stove bolts have squared shoulders underneath the oval-type head and prevent the lower spool from turning when the clamp is tightened.

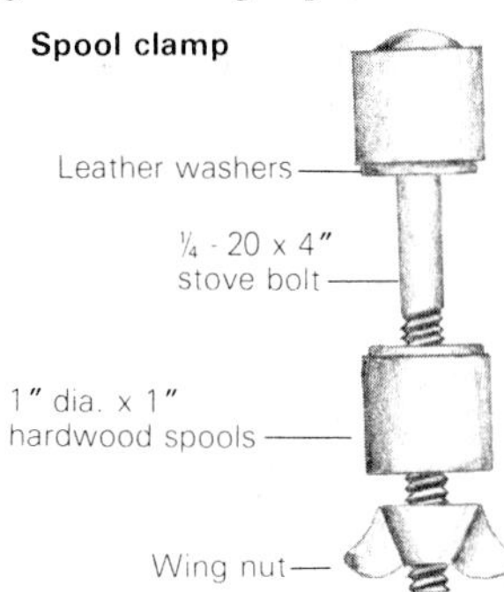

The toothpick dowels now are useful in positioning the plate for gluing. Before the top plate is attached, glue a label showing the maker's name and the date to the inside of the back where it will be visible through the *f* hole on the bassbar side. Gluing the top on completes the assembly.

For the neck and head or scroll, a block of quartersawn maple, 2½ in. by 2½ in. by about 10 in., is trued up and all layout lines are drawn directly on the material. A band saw is used to remove most of the excess wood and the profiles of the scroll are traced on opposite faces of the block. Pilot holes for the peg holes are drilled through while the block is still square. Dimensional tolerances are carefully observed and the heel of the neck fitted into a mortise cut into the top center of the violin body.

All fittings, such as pegs for tuning, bridge, fingerboard and tailpiece, can be purchased ready-made for fitting to the instrument, but some makers prefer to cut these parts themselves. The violin can be completed and set up for testing in the unvarnished condition. Then it will be stripped down and the maker will use either his own formula or a commercial varnish to finish his masterpiece. Many commercial brands are available from violin-making materials suppliers, but I make and formulate my own. It's no secret, but the basic ingredient might be a little difficult to come by—I was given a supply a few years ago. I crush fused fossil amber to a fine powder, dissolve it in turpentine and blend it with linseed oil with or without heat, depending on the color desired. □

Plywood

Kerf-bend fair curves

by Karl Seemuller

Plywood is a much overlooked and often abused material for building furniture, largely because of the horrible production furniture pumped into the market by shortsighted designers. But plywood has a lot to offer and is relatively easy to work with. The key to using it successfully lies in understanding its strengths and weaknesses, and in designing work specifically for the material. It does not help to think of plywood as a substitute for solid wood or as its poor cousin. Such an approach can result only in a finished piece that is a substitute for the real thing. If you are going to use plywood make the full commitment and design for it.

Why bother to use plywood when you have the technical skill to use solid woods? Cost is a major consideration. The cost in time and material of a plywood piece is a fraction of that of a solid wood piece. I am speaking in terms of a small shop that produces furniture many people can afford. If you design one-of-a-kind pieces for yourself or for museums, plywood is probably not the material for you.

Plywood offers quite a few advantages to the designer. It is available with just about any veneer. It comes in nice flat finished sheets ready to be cut into components. It is designed to resist seasonal changes in dimension. And plywood joinery tends to be very simple, though exacting. The cost is about the same per square foot as the board foot cost for solid wood in the rough. But solid wood needs to be rough dressed, edged, glued up, surfaced and sanded to bring it to an equivalent stage.

On the other hand, the very flatness of plywood dictates planes or simple curves. Solid wood offers much more versatility. Adding solid wood edgings to plywood softens some of its harsh quality. Solid wood also provides better colors and grain variation in the finish. The finish surface of plywood is veneer only about 1/32 inch thick, so there is not enough depth for the colors to develop fully. And the wetting or steaming process tends to bleed or leach colors out of finished veneer. However, a careful selection of veneered plywood can often bypass this problem.

Hardwood plywood is available with either a veneer core or a lumber core. In the veneer core, the core has a plywood construction. In lumber core, the core is solid wood, usually mahogany, poplar or basswood. The staves are glued side by side, and covered on both sides by layers of crossbanding and a face veneer. Veneer core is suitable for most applications; it is stable, uniform, and cheaper than lumber core. Lumber

Karl Seemuller has taught at Philadelphia College of Art. When he isn't busy using plywood he works with sculptural form in solid woods.

core is used where additional strength is required. There is also hardwood plywood with a core of particle board, with all of the latter's advantages and disadvantages.

Several machines are used for working plywood. In addition to a table saw, either a shaper or a router is necessary. Carbide blades and bits are a must as the glue in plywood quickly dulls steel. Either a set of tongue-and-groove shaper cutters or a slotting bit for the router is helpful. If you do more than an occasional piece, a shaper and a good set of tongue-and-groove cutters are indispensable. An invaluable asset of these cutters is that they joint the edge of the plywood at the same time that the tongue is cut, thereby ensuring a perfect fit.

It is in the realm of joinery that plywood is most abused. You can cut and join plywood in almost any way you desire and it will go together. Unfortunately, this is precisely what many people do. The result is a product that deteriorates quickly. In solid wood, no one considers cutting dovetails out of short grain, but plywood is often equally misused.

A major problem is how to cover the ugly raw edges that pop up everywhere. The most common solution is simply to glue a strip of veneer over it. Ouch! You are just asking for trouble. We are working with wood, not plastic laminate. One basic design consideration is to avoid any sharp veneered edges or corners. The veneer must be protected from sharp blows or knocks that could easily chip or crack it. Veneer is not fragile, but it does need some help if it is going to give proper service. This problem is solved by using a piece of solid wood edging. It can simply be glued in place, but it is better to attach it with a sturdy joint. I prefer the simple tongue and groove.

This creates another problem. We now have an obvious strip applied to the edge. I take the easy way out. I cannot hide the edging, so I make it an important part of the design. Now, the fact that it is hiding the core and protecting the veneer becomes secondary to its visual importance.

The next problem is joining the plywood at the corners. While the standard solutions are variations of a mitered corner, either spline or locked (never plain), a better solution is to use solid wood in the corners, joined to the plywood with tongue and groove joints, and left square or rounded off. Or you can use a spline miter and inset a small square "wear" strip along the outer edge to give the protection needed. Interior partitions of plywood are best joined by a tongue and groove, so that inevitable variations in the thickness of the plywood don't affect the fit.

Precise joinery is crucial to successful plywood construction. An error might result in cutting through the thin veneer. If you should cut through, do not get into a sweat figuring how to fix it; you cannot. Avoid the error. Work carefully and precisely so there is no need to fudge the joints. Proper use of the router and shaper will prevent these errors. Always keep the important surface of the work against the shaper table or router base to ensure a uniform dimension from the veneer to the tongue. Always use hold-downs on the shaper to keep the work in firm contact with the table. When cutting solid wood edging, keep it slightly fuller than the plywood. In this way you can sand the solid wood to meet the veneer rather than the reverse. When using a one-shouldered tongue and groove in a partition, sand the member before cutting the tongue. This will prevent a sloppy fit later.

Plywood can easily be bent into simple curves. If the curve is shallow it can be made by laminating several 1/4 or 1/8-in. pieces together over a form. As you might expect the springback will be quite large, but the resulting piece will be very strong and stable.

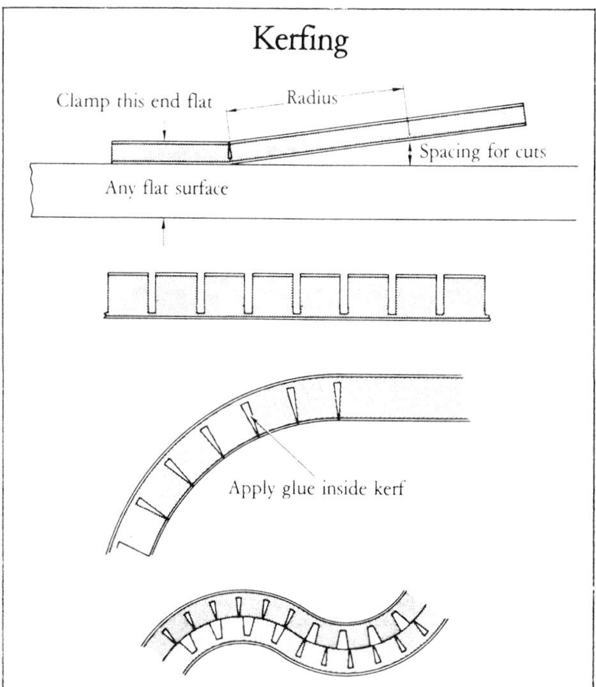

Tongue-and-groove joints can be made with a carbide-tipped slotting cutter in a router, left. At right, shaper cutters shown in the tongue-cutting configuration. Groove cutter is not shown.

Another method is to run a series of kerf cuts in the plywood. In this way a 3/4-in. piece of plywood can be made into a curve with less than a 5-in. radius. For this operation I prefer a lumber core. Use a carbide blade, preferably one with a thin kerf—the thinner the better. The procedure is simple and economical. Large jigs or forms are often unnecessary. The kerf cuts must be spaced properly so that once the curve is made, the cuts all close up tight, restoring strength to the plywood.

If the inner surface is important visually, two thin kerfed pieces can be used instead of a single thick one. This is particularly helpful with an "S" curve. For example, instead of a single 3/4-in. kerfed piece, use two 1/2-in. or 3/8-in. pieces. Kerf them in the same manner as before, and bend them into shape with the kerfs facing each other. The result is a very strong form, finished both inside and out.

Plywood is limited and cannot offer the same potential as solid wood. But remember, it is not a substitute but a distinct material. Design for it specifically and you will have come more than half the way to a successful piece. □

Michael Thonet

One hundred and fifty years of bentwood furniture

by John Dunnigan

The Vienna Chair, made of only six parts, is the result of the experiments of Michael Thonet, the Viennese cabinetmaker who in 1856 perfected a process by which solid rods of wood could be steam-bent into complex curves. By this process, the rear legs and backrest of a chair could be made out of one long piece of wood, eliminating much of the joinery chairs previously required and avoiding the short-grain problems of carved joints.

Called Armchair #9 when first produced in 1870, the Vienna Chair was successful from the start. The architect Le Corbusier selected it for use in several of his buildings, including his pavilion "L'Esprit Nouveau" at the 1925 Paris Exposition—more than 55 years after it was designed. Long before the tenets of Modernism were accepted, in Michael Thonet's furniture form and function were one. Twentieth-century designers such as Breuer, Aalto and Eames, as well as many contemporary designer-craftsmen, have been inspired by Thonet's bentwood techniques and timeless designs. But perhaps his most profound effect, fully realized with the introduction of tubular steel, plastics and other modern materials ideally suited for curvilinear design, is in his success at mass-producing furniture.

The Vienna Chair, designed more than 10 years before the invention of the bicycle, popular ever since.

Michael Thonet (pronounced like *sonnet* and with a silent *h*) was born the son of a tanner in Boppard-am-Rhein, Germany, in 1796. He was apprenticed to a cabinetmaker, and by age 23 opened his own shop. By 1830 he was building furniture in the Biedermeier style, a provincial version of the Paris *meubles de luxe.* Like Empire in France, Regency in England and Federal in America, Biedermeier was high fashion for the first half of the 19th century.

Before long Thonet had established a reputation for technically skillful, innovative executions of traditional work. His earliest known bent work is in applied decorative elements on otherwise typical Biedermeier pieces. An engraving in the Technisches Museum in Vienna, on the facing page, shows a set of his furniture made between 1830 and 1840; the applique on the sofa and bed is probably typical of the kind of work Thonet produced a decade earlier as well.

With the exception of the front and back seat rails and the back support, his chairs of this period are made entirely of laminated strips of veneer. The lamination was done by loosely tying a stack of veneer strips, each measuring about ¹⁄₁₆ in. by 1 in. by 84 in., into a bundle and soaking it in a bath of hot glue. The glue, made from animal hide and bone, differed little from today's product. Once the bundle of veneer was completely saturated, it was removed from the bath and, before the glue started to set, pressed into a heated mold of the desired shape. After it was satisfactorily fastened to the form, the whole was left to cool and harden in place. After a couple of hours, Thonet had a curved piece of wood that was cheaper to make, lighter and more durable than anything he could have carved out of solid wood. In addition, the inner laminations could be cut from less expensive wood than the outside surfaces.

His Boppard chairs, made in the 1830s, reflect this technique. The rear and front legs, the side stretchers and most of the seat rail are one continuous lamination; the loops at the feet and slits in the stretchers compliment the construction. These chairs were a unique approach to a traditional design which, although full of new curves and innovative in profile, still looked somewhat stiff. Their curved sides are in single planes and are connected by flat horizontals at the seat and back—Thonet had not yet figured out how to make the compound bends for which he would later become famous.

He continued to experiment with new methods of bending, while taking out patents to protect his new laminating process (1840-41). Securing these patents in England, France and Belgium was expensive, requiring financial backing. Thonet invested everything he owned in developing his furniture and in marketing it around Europe.

In 1841 at a fair in Koblenz where he was exhibiting, Thonet made a favorable impression on Prince Metternich,

John Dunnigan makes furniture in Saunderstown, R.I.

Photos, except where noted: Thonet Industries

MÖBEL
IN DEN JAHREN 1836–1840 VON MICHAEL THONET IN BOPPARD ANGEFERTIGT.
TAFEL I

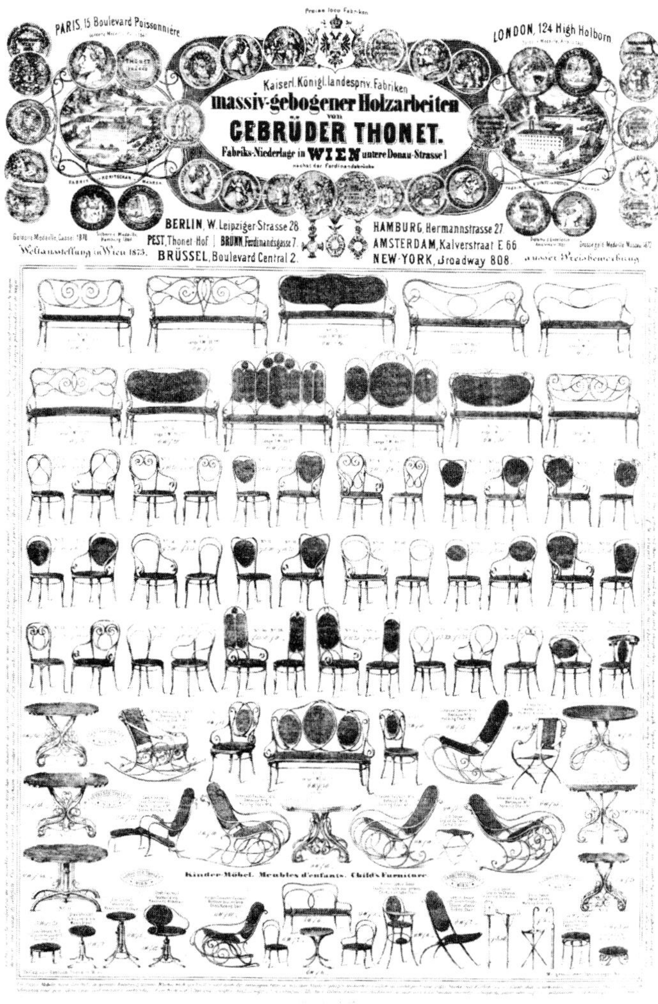

Set of furniture (center left) from the 1830s includes the Boppard chairs and represents Thonet's early work in the Biedermeier style, but with innovative bentwood construction and appliqué. Hot hide glue was used to bend the laminates that make up the chairs; bundles of veneer were soaked in a glue bath, then removed and pressed into a heated mold. This technique makes possible construction such as in the detail at left. Top left, a cradle made in the 1850s and a folding chair from the 1860s. A Thonet catalog cover from the 1870s, above, reflects the fashionable styles of the day.

chancellor to the Austro-Hungarian Empire. It was Austrian policy to seek out inventors and assist them in pursuing their ideas in the interest of the Empire; Metternich invited Thonet first to his castle in Johannesburg to learn more about his work, then to Vienna. In the spring of 1841, Thonet left the business with his wife and eldest son and traveled to Austria to secure a patent for production. The Prince recommended him to the court, Thonet writes his wife, "with such spirit about our things that he really let no one add a word; he rocked back and forth on the chair; he took the little bent rod he'd gotten from me in Johannesburg and described its strength as combined with remarkable thinness. He explained the construction as if he had worked with us himself, especially in explaining the merits of the [wheel] rims."

The Austrian court granted the patent Thonet requested a few months later; it gave him the right "to bend the most brittle kinds of wood in a chemical-mechanical way into desired forms and curves." However, for all his good fortune in Austria, Thonet had problems with his backers in Boppard who, having begun to worry about the apparent lack of success of the patents in England, France and Belgium, precipitated Thonet's bankruptcy. By the fall of 1842, Thonet moved his family to Vienna. After working a year for the established cabinetmaker Franz List, Thonet met Carl Leistler, a prominent parquet manufacturer. When Leistler saw Thonet's execution of a difficult, circular-patterned parquet floor, he engaged both Michael and his son Franz to work in their own section of his factory. The men worked together until 1846 on the renovation of the Palais Liechtenstein under the direction of the English architect P. H. Desvignes, and Thonet laminated parquets, furniture and moldings.

Over the years Thonet tried several techniques in an attempt to perfect his laminating process. Not satisfied with the one-plane bends of the earlier Boppard chairs, he tried resawing an already laminated curve perpendicular to the glue lines and regluing it on a second curved plane. This process was slow and impractical; the reapplication of hot glue weakened the first set of glue joints, and there was also the problem of trying to bend all the hard glue in the first lamination. The resulting pieces were too costly to be marketed widely.

As a next experiment, Thonet cut thin rods of square cross section and tied them into a bundle. Sixteen rods ¼ in. by ¼ in. made a 1 in. by 1 in. part. The bundle was cooked in a hot glue bath and bent to a mold, as in the first process. Although these strips bent easily, it was difficult to achieve a uniform glue line, so this approach was also impractical.

Thonet kept returning to his original method using a single stack of flat laminates and eventually found that simply by twisting it he could obtain the compound curves he wanted. Rectilinear surfaces, when twisted, lie in different planes and thus a wood-strip laminate can be bent easily in more than one direction, depending on the amount of twist. It was the logical next step, but it took 20 years to figure out.

Thonet applied this new technique while working with the architect Desvignes on the Palais Liechtenstein. He designed three chairs, apparently the first of their kind, each composed of six bundles of laminates. The first bundle goes up one rear leg, forms part of the back, and continues down the other leg; another bundle forms the seat frame and part of the back; the legs and seat rails are made from a series of laminates going up one leg, across to support a section of the seat, and down the other leg. Each leg is thus made up of two bundles glued in turn to one another with triangular inserts in the corners. Entirely laminated, these chairs seem to be without mechanical joints or fasteners.

The Liechtenstein chairs reflect various furniture styles from about 1650 on. Their lines build upon the Louis XIV and Queen Anne styles of the late 17th and early 18th centuries and were influenced by the Rococo as well—in fact they were made to be used in a Rococo Revival setting in the palace. The Classical Revival was also a major ingredient—archeological discoveries after 1750 brought ancient Egyptian, Greek and Roman furniture to the eyes of a fashion-conscious public. The Greek *klismos* chair particularly attracted the attention of furniture makers, whose attempts to copy its graceful leg curves proved problematic: Shaping from solid wood necessitated choosing grain configurations with too much discrimination for large-scale production; techniques like bending and laminating were solutions. Products of early industrial technology as much as of an older desire to imitate the art of the past, Thonet's Liechtenstein chairs constitute a crucial bridge between 18th and 20th-century furniture.

After the work on the palace was completed in 1846, Thonet continued to make unusual parquets and experimental bentwood furniture at Leistler's in Vienna. In 1849, when Leistler refused his offer of partnership, Thonet, then 53 years old, formed his own company. In a house in Vienna he and his sons set to work mass-producing bentwood furniture. At first he had to rely on the financial assistance of his friend Desvignes, with whose support he developed another new chair in 1850. This one, for the Palais Schwarzenburg, had lathe-turned front legs doweled into the seat frame; the rear legs and backrest were laminated as in the Liechtenstein chairs. Certain changes in the process, however, make these chairs an important step toward solid bentwood furniture. Instead of a dozen or so thin layers of veneer cooked in glue, the backs use only four thicknesses of ⁵⁄₁₆-in. mahogany; the seat rings have five layers. Thonet cooked the laminates in boiling water, bent them on the forms and dried them for a few days, then glued them together; this required fewer laminates, which saved time, and the glue was under much less stress. This is the first chair Thonet constructed using the boiling-water technique, and it eventually appears as chair #1 in the Gebruder Thonet catalog (page 55).

In 1850 the family turned its attention to preparing for the great world exposition to be held the following year at the Crystal Palace in London. Thonet exhibited several pieces of furniture there, including a set of rosewood chairs and a settee with caned seats and backs in the Liechtenstein style. He sent pieces in mahogany and palisander as well, and tables with inlays of brass and tortoise shell. Thonet came away with a bronze medal (the highest awarded to an industrial product) and many important marketing contacts.

About this time Thonet received his first major public commission from the famous Cafe Daum in Vienna. From this point on, the bentwood chair would be known by many as the Cafe Chair (shown at bottom left on the facing page). The back is made of four layers of twisted mahogany laminates, while the front legs appear to be bent from solid stock with turned capitals, which act as shoulders for the tenon of the leg into the seat. The seat frames are made of five layers of mahogany, as they were in the Schwarzenburg chairs. Because of its lightness, durability and accommodating design, the bentwood chair was perfectly suited for public places. According to Hermann Heller, Thonet's biographer, Thonet shortly thereafter did a similar set of 400 chairs for a hotel in Budapest.

In 1853, Thonet founded Gebruder Thonet, registering the company in the names of his five sons. They were the proprietors, but Thonet still held directorship. Business was good enough to employ nine cabinetmakers, one lathe-turner, eight veneer-cutters, two gluers, eight sanders, two stainers, ten finishers and two assemblers. They rented a large building and, before the year was out, had installed a 4-HP steam power plant to run the machines.

It was in this shop over the next three years that Thonet, then almost 60, began to realize his lifelong goal of mass-producing solid bentwood chairs. He had been experimenting all along with solid-wood bending and had earlier tried with little success to bend slats for chair parts by cooking them in hot glue. It worked with the veneer but not with thicker stock. Having perfected the laminating process in the 1840s, Thonet continued to use thicker and fewer laminations in each successive design and with every passing year. In the mid-1850s he made a chair for the Palais Schwarzenburg which had a solid bentwood back made of one continuous rod that was full thickness in the rear legs but tapered to a thin strip at the top of the back where the bend was most critical. After it was bent, two additional thin strips were laminated to this top section to regain the desired thickness. The seat frame was made up of only three layers, which probably were also boiled, bent and dried before being glued.

The success of these products—not only Thonet's chairs but all kinds of furniture—was remarkable. The impetus gained from the Crystal Palace exhibition propelled the company into a worldwide market, and this, perhaps more than any other factor, conditioned the final form of the solid bentwood chair. Thonet had successfully shipped laminated chairs to several countries, but when he sent his first shipments to North and South America, he found that the glue wouldn't stand up to prolonged heat and excessive moisture. Although Thonet had been working diligently to solve such problems

Collection of the Royal Prince of Liechtenstein

The Liechtenstein chairs, above and right, 1843-1846, are each made of six bundles of laminates and without mechanical fasteners. They are probably the first of their kind, combining graceful compound curves and simple construction. The engraving at bottom right shows furniture Thonet exhibited at the Crystal Palace Exhibition in 1851. The Cafe Daum chair, lower left (also from the early 1850s) was Thonet's first major public commission. The back and seat rim were made of only a few laminates; the front legs were turned and bent from solid stock. Bracing between seat bottom and legs was an improvement in all later models.

TAFEL II.
MÖBEL
AUSGESTELLT AUF DER WELTAUSSTELLUNG LONDON 1851.

Gebrüder Thonet

for most of his life, it is no small coincidence that the fate of the solid, steam-bent chair was resolved at the moment when the vast American market was to be gained or lost.

The problem with bending solid wood of substantial thickness was that it always broke first on the convex surface, regardless of how much boiling water or steam it was subjected to. The fibers stretched and tore apart on this outside face, while their compression on the inside or concave surface usually caused no damage. The very center of the piece probably remained constant in length and therefore neutral. To solve the problem, Thonet needed a way to keep the convex side of the bend from stretching, to make it act more like the neutral layer, and to transform the force of the bend entirely into compression. He fastened a strip of sheet iron to a still-straight piece of wood on what would be the convex surface and squeezed it at the ends with screw clamps. When the piece was bent, the convex side of the curve could not stretch, and the whole piece was under uniform compression—as though the neutral layer of fibers had been moved to the outer edge of the wood. Bending in more than one direction simply required additional straps.

To apply this technique to his furniture, Thonet first had to find a suitable wood. Mahogany, rosewood and palisander, which laminated well, did not bend in solid rods as easily as ash or beech. The long, straight grain of beech, coupled with its low cost, made it the logical choice. The process followed these lines: A straight-grained, branchless beech butt was crosscut to the desired length in the forest to avoid hauling

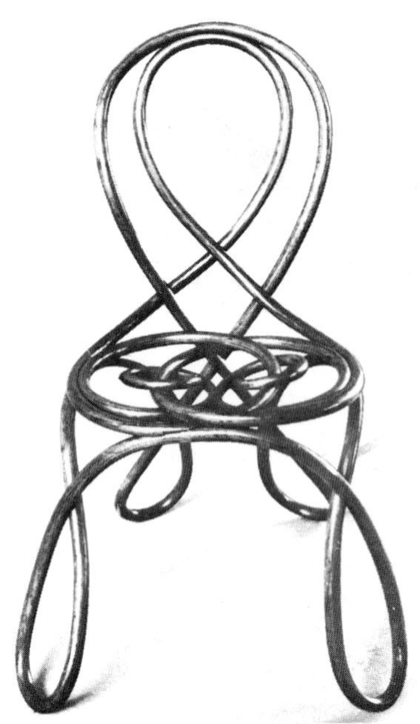

A demonstration chair made in 1870 out of two pieces of steam-bent solid beech, by Michael's son August, responsible for many of the company's later designs.

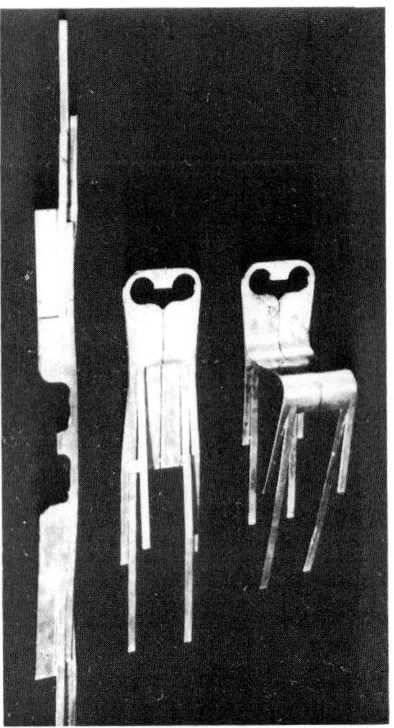

Thonet made this experimental chair from only two pieces of ash—it is shown here at four stages of construction. Designed in the 1870s, this piece turned out to be impractical for mass production because of the large, clear-grain pieces of wood necessary. *For a successful one-piece chair, see page 98.*

unnecessary wood back to the shop. The log was ripsawn into rods of square section (approximately 2x2) and then turned to the desired shape on a lathe. Next, a rod was selected, probably before drying, and steamed for one to two hours, depending on its thickness. When the rod was pliable enough, it was quickly placed in the iron strap (or straps) and bent by hand on a cast-iron form to the desired shape. This could take only a couple of minutes. After the wood and strap were clamped to the form, the whole thing was placed in a heated room for a few days to dry. By this method Thonet could make the rear legs and back of a chair out of one long piece of solid wood. The front legs and seat rims went through an identical process on their way from log to chair. The legs were turned and tapered before they were bent, but the seats were bent, glued and screwed with a scarf joint and then finally the edges were rounded.

Thonet built his first factory at Koritshan in Moravia (now Czechoslovakia) in 1856; he designed not only the factory but much of its machinery (multi-bladed saws to mill the stock and a mechanical spoke-shaver to round and taper the rods) as well. The factory was situated at the edge of a beech forest, and it was powered completely by water and steam. Some craftsmen were still needed, of course, but most of the work could now be done by cheaper, unskilled labor from the village of Koritshan. Before long, the factory employed virtually all the village men, women and children who went to work in the forests, the factory, and even in their homes.

Thonet's factory made the transition from the artisan's small workshop to mass production, and by 1859 the technique of bending solid wood into almost any shape had been perfected. In that year Thonet designed his most popular chair, the #14 side chair, (at right on facing page). The refinement of his earlier chairs, #14 retains the fluid lines of the Liechtenstein chairs while reinterpreting them as mass-produced items. As in the #9 armchair, Thonet reduced the chair to a minimum of six parts, easily produced, shipped and assembled, since the members were bolted or screwed together. The front legs no longer had capitals at the joints, and they were screwed into the seat with threaded mortise and tenons. The chair cost less than the average worker earned in a week, and it became the company's best seller—fifty million sold in the first fifty years. Here was a chair elegant enough for the finest salons and inexpensive enough for the masses.

Thonet designed his first bentwood rocker in 1860, at which point rockers were still a novelty in Europe although they had been popular for more than a century in America. In rocker #1 the parts were bent of solid beech and then laminated to one another. Most of the joints were also laminated (only a few screws appearing in this piece), although in later models all parts were fastened by screws. The Gebruder Thonet catalog of 1873 features more than 30 different models of bentwood rockers, testifying to their growing popularity. Unlike most rocking chairs, which are just chairs with two curved pieces stuck on the bottoms of the feet, Thonet's rocker expresses in detail and overall image that its very essence is to rock; it looks always in motion.

At his death in 1871, Thonet had achieved his goal—to perfect the process for making furniture from bent wood. He

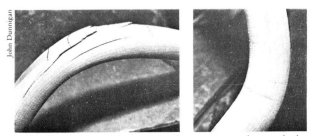

John Dunnigan

In bending, tearing on the convex surface occurs more frequently than collapse on the concave surface.

had developed a product that was affordable, functional and beautiful. He left behind him a furniture empire consisting of four large factories, as well as showrooms in many major cities of the world. Although he was not the only one in the 19th century to use lamination and steam to bend wood, he was certainly the most successful. The simplicity, efficiency and grace of Thonet's work, techniques and designs have helped pave the way both for modern methods of large-scale production and for the design styles of the 20th century.

Thonet's legacy — Gebruder Thonet continued in the vanguard of design, with an impact on the Vienna Secession, Art Nouveau and Art Deco movements as well as on the Bauhaus. Many leading designers and architects collaborated with Gebruder Thonet, among them Otto Wagner, Josef Hoffman, Marcel Breuer, Ludwig Mies van der Rohe, Pierre Jeanneret, Charlotte Perriand, Mart Stam, Anton Lorenz and Walter Gropius. In the 1920s the Thonet Company pioneered tubular-steel furniture and merged with Kohn-Mundus to form a conglomerate of 21 factories throughout Europe.

In 1938, with the world on the brink of war, the company decided to move to the United States. After the war a large nationalized bentwood furniture industry grew up in Poland, Czechoslovakia and Romania and still operates in many of the old factories. The original Thonet family continues to operate two of its factories in West Germany and Austria and maintains headquarters in Frankenburg, West Germany.

In the United States the third of the separate companies is Thonet Industries (pronounced *Thonay*). With plants in Sheboygan, Wis., Statesville, N.C., and York, Pa., Thonet Industries makes furniture in wood, metal and plastic, and still produces the old bentwood classics.

Today the steam-bending of furniture is done very much the same way it was a century ago. However, the same quantity and quality of beech is not available in the U.S. as it was in Europe, and consequently one of the biggest problems in producing bentwood furniture in America is in obtaining the raw materials. For thirty years Thonet Industries used northern rock elm. Lately because of supply difficulties they've begun using southern elm and ash. How the people at Thonet Industries in Statesville, N.C., produce a bentwood chair is shown in the photo-essay on the following pages.

Here are some of Thonet's most popular designs, along with the first tubular-steel chairs they inspired. The 1926 Mies van der Rohe chair (top right) and 1928 Breuer chair (bottom left) show their indebtedness, especially to Rocker #1, 1860, (top left). Thonet's #14 sidechair, 1859, (right) became the first widely accepted, mass-produced chair; by 1900 forty million had been sold. A recently revived version of the #18 sidechair (center), called the Export Chair when designed in 1876 for long-distance shipping, is probably the best known in the U.S.

Thonet's chair in production

1. The wood is air-dried to 20% (moisture content) before milling to size and shape. Only straight-grained, clear stock can be used, so there is a good deal of waste. Leg-back units for a Cafe Chair are crosscut to 90 in. and then run through a variable cam-rod machine that turns out round pieces tapering from 1¼ in. in diameter at the ends and in the center to 1½ in. diameter at the two points between which they will join the seat. They are heaviest where the joints will be. The rods are soaked in water overnight to raise the moisture content of the outer shell to 30% to 40% while keeping the center of the rod at about 20%. Softening the shell allows shorter steaming time.

2. The rods are put into the steamboxes and subjected to wet steam pressurized at 5 PSI, kept at 200°F. The steaming time for different chair parts might be anywhere from 10 minutes to an hour, depending on the extent of the bend and the size of the stock; the leg-back rods usually stay in for about 30 minutes. The rods must be flexible but not soft. Too little cooking leaves the wood brittle and, when it is bent, the fibers will snap on the outside; too much cooking destroys the bond between the fibers and compression cracks and crumpling on the concave surface result. There are many steam retorts throughout the Statesville, N.C., plant, so there is always a piece ready for bending.

Photos: John Dunnigan

3. When pliable, the wood is removed from the steam and bent, one piece at a time. The benders work in teams of two in the department where they make the leg-back unit. The 90-in. tapered rod is taken out of the retort, quickly placed in an aluminum strap, and both are clamped in the center to the stationary form. A centerline marked on the form, strap and rod facilitates this part of the operation, and the benders know from experience how best to orient the grain of the wood to the bend. Next the bending clamps are attached to the ends, pulling the strap tightly against the rods and applying pressure to the ends of the rod to prevent the fibers from stretching. The strap acts as the convex surface of the wood and consequently keeps the whole piece in compression during the bend.

Thonet's techniques are basically the same today as they were in the 19th century, when these three benders wrestled with a chair part.

4. The rod is bent in and up; then it is twisted slightly and pulled back down in order to make it fit the complex curve of the form. The benders work one side at a time, with a steady, smooth motion; experience tells them instantly if a breakage occurs. If it is only a minor split, they will attempt to repair it, but many pieces do not survive the bend and there is a high failure rate in the move from rough stock to finished product. The return curve shown here is the most critical part of the bend.

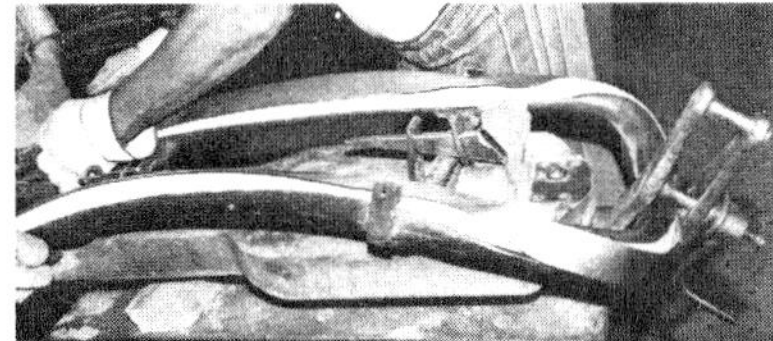

5. When the operation is completed, wedges are driven between a block on the end of the strap and a bracket on the form that holds the wood in place; then the bending clamps are removed for re-use. The bending process, from steamer to clamp removal, takes less than two minutes.

6. The bent wood, still on the form, is stacked on a cart, which, when full, will be wheeled into the kiln for overnight drying. About 120 of these leg-back members are bent each day. Generally the moisture content of the wood is reduced to 8% after about 16 hours in the kiln.

7. The seat rims are soaked and steamed a little longer than the legs because they are much thicker. Seat rims can be successfully bent only by machines that wind the wood around a circular form.

8. The smaller parts, like the hairpin back inserts shown above, are bent eleven at a time in a simple machine press. To adapt steam bending techniques for smaller runs, see pages 16 to 21 and 22 to 24.

EDITOR'S NOTE: *The 150th anniversary of furniture by Thonet was celebrated in 1980. In observance of this milestone, Dover Publications reprinted the original 1904 Thonet catalog, and Barron's published* Thonet: A History of the Firm, *by Christopher Wilk.*

Before Thonet, and afterward

In Boston Samuel Gragg (1772-1855) patented his "elastic chair," right, in 1808—the first piece of American furniture to feature a bentwood, cantilever back. It is modeled after the ancient Greek *klismos* chair, a design for which appeared in Thomas Hope's *Household Furniture and Interior Decoration* (London, 1807). Hope's design used a continuous laminate curving from the top back rail to the front seat rail. Gragg carried the bentwood concept further by bringing the back member down past the front rail to become the front leg. The chair is steam-bent hickory, assembled with mortise and tenon, dovetails and screws. Gragg was a Windsor chairmaker who was probably trained as a wheelwright in New Hampshire before moving to Boston around 1800. In a recent piece Seth Stem, of Marblehead, Mass., made the continuous leg and back members of his asymmetric chair, shown from the front and side, by free-bending black cherry laminates, clamping with stretched inner tube wrapped around them in a candy-cane arrangement that permits adjustment under pressure. The front foot of a leg laminate is clamped to a 2x4 fixed to a particle-board base. Then the laminate is bent over, twisted (on the left) and brought down to be clamped to another 2x4 fixed where he wants the back leg. The seat rim is joined to the two leg arches by face-glued gussets, which are subsequently doweled and shaped. Stem simultaneously free-bent the three laminates that form the back, sitting in the chair with a glue-covered *T*-shirt to adjust their position to comfort. The chair is 39 in. by 32 in. by 21 in.

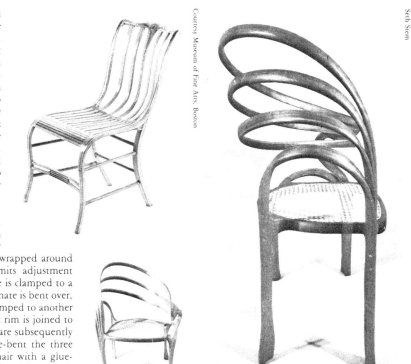

Courtesy Museum of Fine Arts, Boston

Seth Stem

Bent Laminations

Slice and glue the wood to make it curve

by Jere Osgood

Samples of laminated wood have been found dating from the 15th century B.C. Lamination means a layering process. All the layers are aligned with the grain going in the same direction, and are held fast by a glue. Thin slices of wood can be laminated flat or to a curved form.

It is important to distinguish lamination from veneering. The grain of the laminate layers is always oriented in the same direction. In contrast, in veneering or plywood the grain directions alternate and an odd number of layers must be used. In lamination the layers, when glued together, will act like solid wood, expanding and contracting across the long grain. In veneering, grain alteration stabilizes the unit and there is no movement across or with the grain. (Stacking, also a form of lamination, is a separate subject. Stacking is usually carved rather than bent to achieve a curve.)

Furniture-related examples of lamination are flat or curved cabinet panels, tabletops, and curved leg blanks. The simplest lamination is the use of a fine figured wood as an outer layer on a tabletop or cabinet panel.

In many cases I find laminations more acceptable than solid construction. For example, one plank of an unusual figured wood could be resawn into many layers. These could perhaps cover all the sides of a cabinet, if backed up by layers of wood of lesser quality or rarity. If used at full thickness, many planks of this unusual wood would be needed to achieve the same effect.

Jere Osgood teaches woodworking at Boston University. He lives in New Milford, Conn.

Lamination is an economical way of obtaining curved forms. Members can be thinner when laminated as opposed to sawn because of the inherent strength of parallel grain direction. Steam bending is of course an alternative for curves and is an important process. However, lamination offers the advantage in many cases of more accurate reproduction of the desired curve. Modern glues have eliminated the bugaboo of delamination—the glue lines are as strong as the wood itself. An excellent use of laminated wood is in chair or table legs where short-grain weakness might inhibit design. It is important in some cases to make the layer stock thick enough so that any shaping or taper can be done in the outer two layers because going through the glue lines might be unsightly. In addition to counteracting short-grain weakness, laminating a curved leg also saves scarce wood, because a laminated leg can be cut from a much narrower plank than would be required for sawing the curved shape out of solid stock.

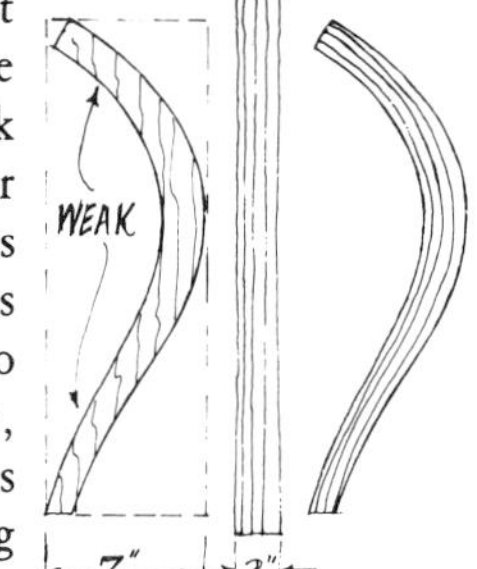

For flat panels such as a tabletop or a cabinet panel, a core of some stable wood (poplar or mahogany) is used. A face wood, which can be veneer or resawn stock, is glued on both sides with the grain directions the same. It is important to cover both sides to forestall warp and to use the same species

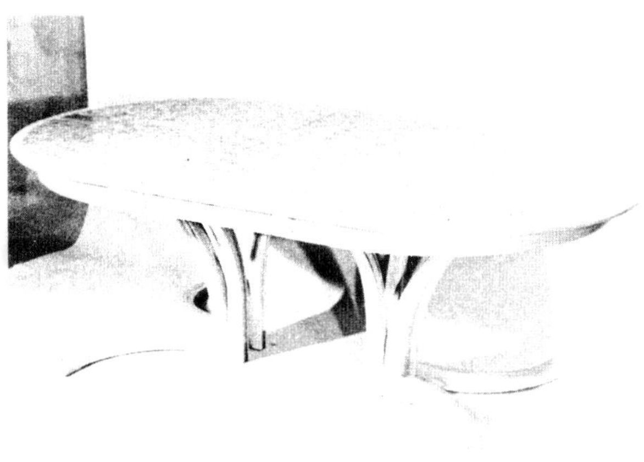

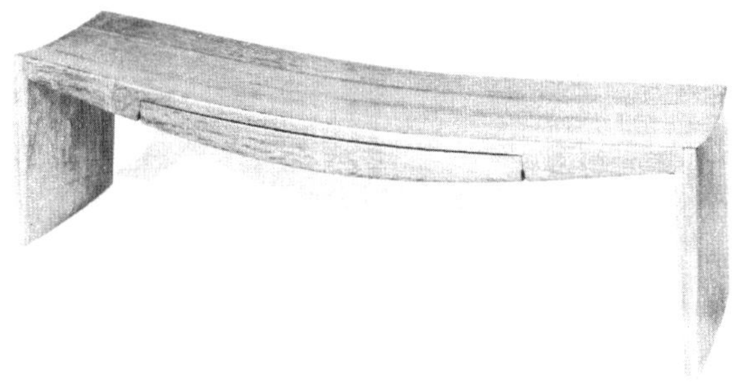

Dining table by James Schriber: Top is simple laminate faced with tamo veneer; apron and legs are laminated ash. Bench by Osgood: Curved ends, top and front are all bent laminates.

Chest of chair, laminated curly maple, by Jere Osgood.

on both sides. However, if the densities are kept the same, substitutions can be made. Typical veneer thicknesses are 1/30 in., 1/28 in., 1/16 in. and 1/8 in. Resawn stock is thicker—perhaps 1/8 in., 3/16 in., 1/4 in. or 3/8 in. The core thickness in a cabinet panel might be 1/2 in. and in a tabletop, 13/16 in. The core requirements disappear when laminating something like a drawer front, which might typically be two layers of 3/8-in. material or three layers of 1/4-in. stock.

When panels are curved the thickness of the layers is important. A thick core might not be possible. Whatever size layers are used, they must each be able to take the desired curve. For example, 1/16-in. layers might be needed to bend a 3-in. radius, but for a lesser bend of, say 1-in. deflection over a 36-in. drawer front, 1/4 in. or 3/8 in. might be thin enough. The appearance of the visible edge of something like a drawer front is also a design factor to consider.

A general rule is to keep layers of the maximum thickness that will take the desired bend. This not only saves time and money (each time a lamination is cut, a slice the thickness of the saw blade turns into dust) but also aids in gluing evenly. A multitude of thin layers of, say, 1/28-in. veneers risks a surface unevenness from disparate clamp pressure marks resulting from a poorly bandsawn form or from unevenly spread glue. But you don't have any choice if you have 2000 square feet of very thin veneer that will fulfill the stock requirement for a specific piece of furniture.

First, determine the thickness needed by testing the bend with a sample. Narrow or simple cuts, say for chair legs, are usually possible with a single pass on a table saw, the limitation being the diameter of the saw blade. In many cases a carbide rip blade will give a good cut for gluing that will not need to be run through a thicknesser. Stock cut with a normal rip blade will need to be thickness-planed.

Wide laminations that can't be cut in one pass on the table saw can be cut on a band saw using a resaw jig. Another tablesaw method involves dressing stock normally, cutting from opposite sides of the board with the blade height set to cut halfway, and thicknessing the cut-away pieces. Because there is one smooth face they can be surfaced as is, ignoring warp if they are thin. The center portion of the board is left rough and should be resurfaced before repeating the operation.

Resawn stock may warp or cup. If this is not desirable the stock must be left thick enough to plane warp out. There is a tendency to overestimate the number of resawn layers available from a board. Therefore take careful account of kerf loss and warp. Be sure to laminate resawn stock in the same order it was cut. A vee marked on the ends of the laminate boards makes it easy to keep them in this order when they are glued to the curve. For wide laminations, the resawn pieces can be folded apart, or bookmatched, to keep the grain in a pattern.

2-INCH STOCK SAWN INTO 5 LAYERS.
VEE MARKED ON END BEFORE SAWING KEEPS LAMINATE IN ORDER.

Almost any glue works for flat laminations where the only stress is the seasonal movement of the wood. However, I prefer a slow-setting glue for a lot of layers or a large surface area. I do not recommend white glue for fine furniture because of the variation in quality from one brand to another. A yellow glue such as Franklin Titebond (an aliphatic naphtha-based glue) is good for shallow bends or curves without a lot of stress. Cold creep (slippage after drying) occurs to a lesser extent with yellow glue than with white glue. A chair leg laminated with yellow glue will slip minutely and show the layers after about nine months. The layers are trying to become straight again—you can see and feel the unevenness.

If a lamination is sharply bent and under stress, a urea formaldehyde glue such as Weldwood or Cascamite is called for. I have had good results with Urac 185, made by American Cyanamid Co., Wayne, N.J. 07470. (It is available in retail quantities from Nelson Paint Co., PO Box 907, Iron Mountain, Mich. 49801.) I recommend a two-part resorcinol formaldehyde where wetness is a problem, but the dark glue line may be objectionable. These glues don't suffer cold creep.

Springback is normal as the layers try to straighten out against the formed curve. It is slightly greater with yellow glue than with urea glue. But the amount of springback is usually small and can be estimated with practice. In many cabinet or chair parts it can be ignored. Joint angles should be checked after laminated parts are made. Where a precise curve is needed one could use thinner (and therefore more) layers, which will tend to reduce or eliminate springback, or test-glue the part and adjust the form before laminating the actual piece.

In lamination, as in all gluing, there are four potential trouble areas: moisture content of the wood, temperature, oily woods, and dull thickness-planer blades. Opinions may

Chair by Tom Hucker: Quick-action clamps hold thin layers of maple in two-part chipboard form, above. Outer part of form is segmented for easier assembly. Then eight identical staves are joined and shaped to make seat of chair. Legs are also laminated.

Hardwood board under screws of veneer press distributes pressure and keeps form from crumbling at center.

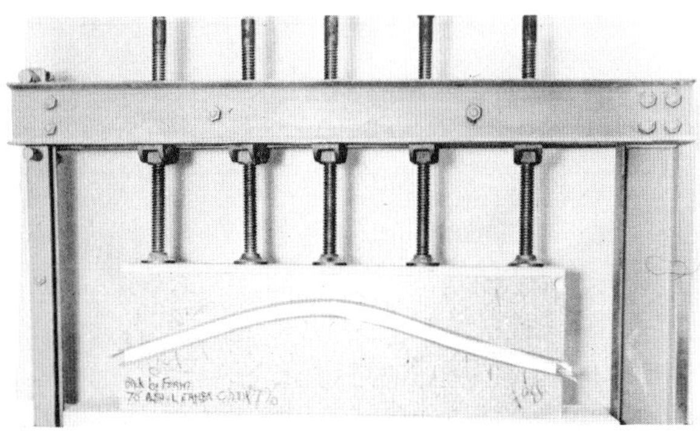

vary, but below 6% moisture content is risky.

Temperature is another important factor. While yellow glue can set at a lower temperature, 70° F is about the lowest for the urea type, and at that temperature about 12 hours of clamping time are required. For urea-resin glue a temperature of 90° F reduces the pressure period to about five hours. One easy way to increase temperature in a workshop is to throw a drop cloth over the clamped work and put a 150-watt bulb underneath. Be careful, because most glues don't reach maximum strength for 48 hours.

Oily woods such as teak or rosewood can be laminated in several ways. Titebond is more likely to succeed than a urea glue. Another way to achieve a bond is to roughen the glue surfaces with a toothing plane or 40-grit garnet paper. Narrow pieces cut with a carbide table-saw blade which are not cleaned up or jointed may glue better. Another method is to clean the surface with lacquer thinner or carbon tetrachloride before gluing. Oily stock should be tested first, before committing an expensive lot of wood.

Another area of potential trouble that is often overlooked is a dull thickness-planer blade. Dull knives beat and mash down the wood fibers; sharp knives slice them off cleanly. Microscropic differences in the surface greatly affect gluing.

A simple flat lamination can be done with two cover boards and a few quick-action clamps. An alternative to this is a veneer press. In addition to flat pressing, the veneer press can be used for curved parts with a two-part form.

For simple parts a one-piece form can be used. The layers are held in place under pressure with quick-action clamps.

Free clamping without a heavy back-up form can be done for parts requiring a spiral or otherwise impossible compound curve. A lamination of several layers can be held in place with 1/4-in. Masonite strips as cover pieces on either side of the layers of wood. Masonite of this thickness twists easily.

On a wide piece, a good rule is to begin clamping from the center out to the sides or from one side to another so that air or glue pockets aren't trapped between the layers.

The cheapest material for making forms is particle board, chipboard or floor underlayment, all basically the same material. Fir plywood is the next most economical choice and should be used where strength is required. Particle board has an advantage over fir plywood in that the band saw won't track off the pencil line into some strong grain configuration.

I usually face my press or forms with Masonite to help obtain even gluing pressure and to compensate for slight irregularities in bandsawing. I use 1/8-in. or 1/4-in., depending on the severity of the curve. Masonite is cheap and its surface resists glue.

In determining the curve to be drawn on the form, the actual piece plus the thickness of the facing must be considered.

Forms five or six inches thick could be made from solid, but it is often more economical to make the form as a series of ribs with spacers in between each rib. The form can be made as a one-part, open-face jig or constructed as a two-part form. Usually the decision depends on the gluing process. Clamping pressure must be maintained approximately perpendicular to the work. While I prefer a two-part form that fits in a press for most work, there are many cases where the curve is too great or the piece is too large. For example, the semicircular apron for a round dining table can be made most easily with a one-piece form.

A two-part form with a shallow curve, such as for a drawer

front with a one-inch deflection over a three-foot distance, requires bandsawing only along a single pencil line. The form will flex enough over that length to give even clamping pressure. For a drawer front of the same length but with a two-inch deflection, it would probably be necessary to calculate the various radii by the method described below.

The first step is to thickness-plane the laminates to the desired thickness and check the true combined thickness with calipers. For example, four 1/4-in. layers might actually measure 1-1/16 in. together, and a one-inch form would be off. The form needs to be that precise. The two band-saw lines are established by taking the curves of each side of the desired piece, adding the facing thickness to each side and transferring the total dimensioned curve to the form. For a compound shape, the bottom curve line is taken from a full-size shop drawing. Then a compass is set to the total laminate thickness plus the two layers of Masonite. The compass is lined up with the bottom line and small arcs are swung at the

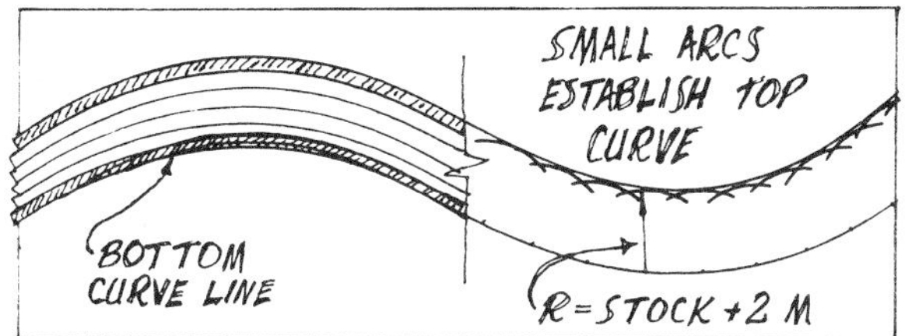

correct distance from points all along the bottom line. The crests of these small arcs are connected using a flexible curve, to establish the correct top line.

When laying out the curve onto the form, the normal inclination is to work from a vertical or horizontal reference on the drawing. This does not necessarily ensure perpendicular gluing pressure. Often the curve layout on the form must be tilted to center the curve.

Most of the directions so far have been for narrow furniture parts of up to five inches. Another method is suited to larger pieces such as door panels, cabinet ends and bench seats. The same method would be used to veneer the panels. After establishing the curve on the form, band-saw lines are drawn onto the end piece of a stack of ribs that have been carefully cut to the exact length and width and then dadoed. These ribs are not glued together, but held by four spacer strips press-fitted into the dadoes. The idea is to make a short, easy package to bandsaw. For example, a 20-in. form can be made of eleven 3/4-in. ribs which would make a stack 8-1/4 in. high to bandsaw. The stack can be kept uniform by inserting short, temporary spacer strips into the dadoes. After bandsawing, the short strips are replaced by strips of the total length. Masonite sheets are then used to line the form, and finally two sheets of particle board or plywood are cut for top and bottom plates. □

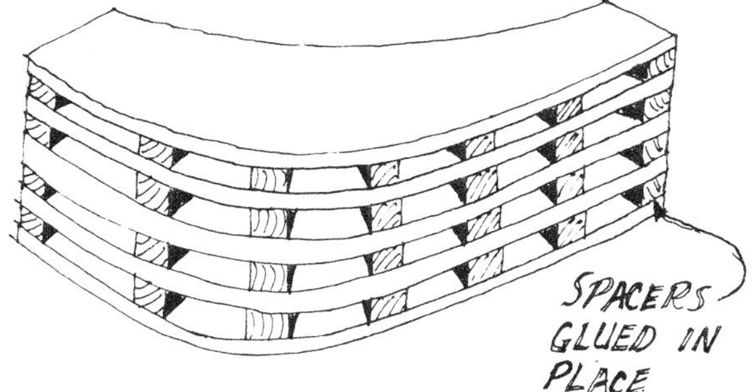

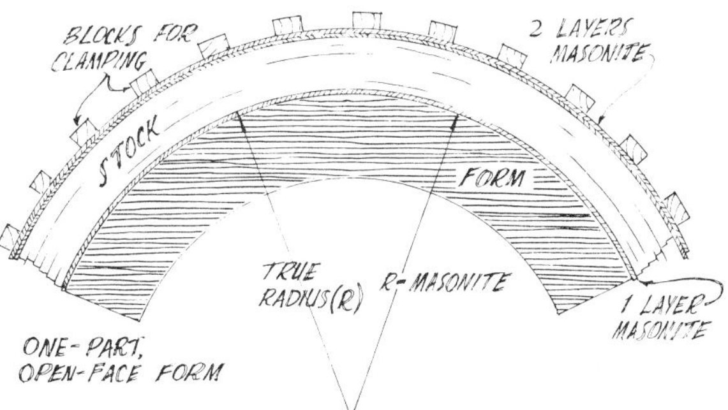

One-part, open-face form is used with quick-action clamps for parts that are too large for veneer press. Masonite regulates pressure, but must be accounted for in layout.

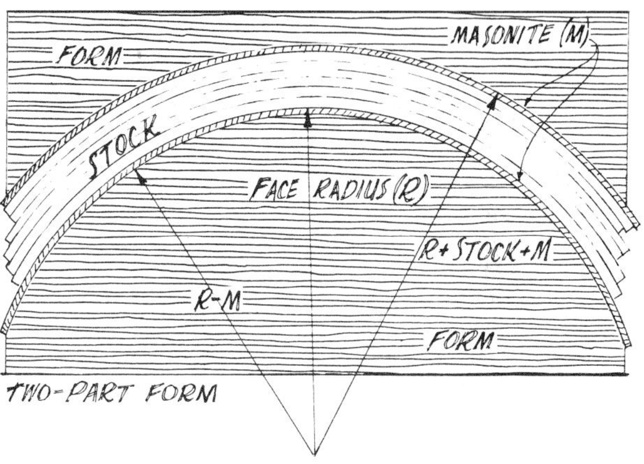

Two-part forms provide most even squeeze with either clamps or veneer press. Again, accurate layout is essential.

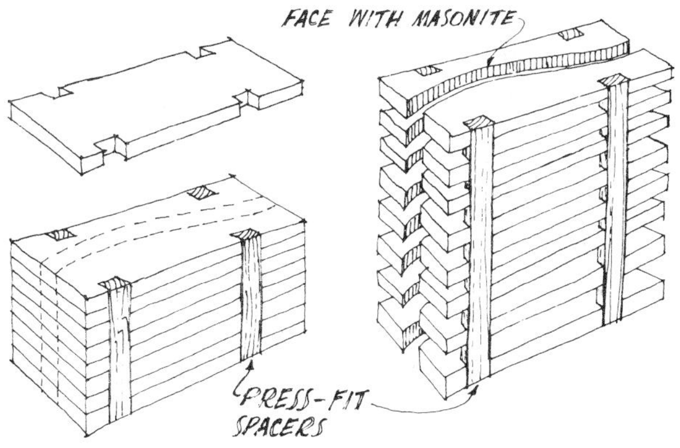

Rib-and-spacer forms bandsawn from a stack of boards are best for wide, curved panels. At left, an open-face ribbed form is made from chipboard with pine spacers.

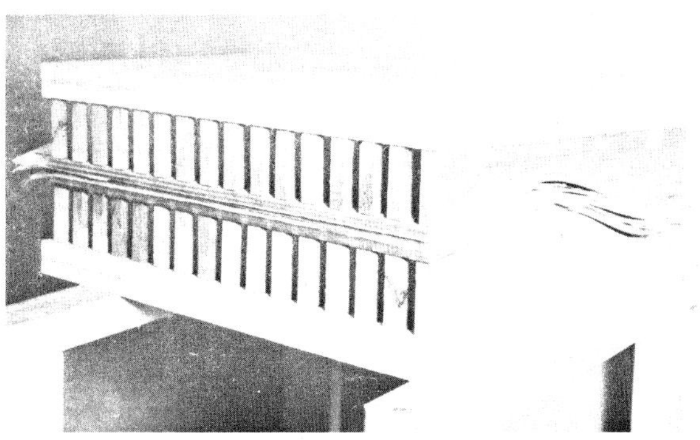

Tapered Lamination

Slender curves have necessary bulk for joinery

by Jere Osgood

Thin layers of wood are easy to bend. Several thin layers, all with the grain running in the same direction, can be bent on a form and glued together. The resulting curved laminate is much stronger than a piece sawn from solid stock would be, and much less wasteful of material. It is also stronger than a steam-bent piece, because the glue adds to the strength of the wood. Lamination has the additional advantage of stretching rare or highly figured boards, since the best stock can be resawn and used to face all the legs of a chair or table.

I discussed the basics of simple bent lamination, the necessary forms and the various gluing techniques in the preceding article (see pages 62 through 65). This article will cover layers of wood that are not of uniform thickness—tapered laminations and double tapered laminations. These techniques permit you to make a curved piece whose width and thickness vary, whereas a simple bent lamination can vary only in width. If the design requires cutting through the thickness of a layer of wood at any point along a curve, the whole part is weakened. The severed layers no longer contribute to the strength of the assembly. The problem is avoided by tapering the layers of wood, so the variation in thickness is built right into the lamination. It is important to make each layer of wood as thick as possible although still thin enough to follow the desired curve. It is much better to resaw stock to optimum thickness than to use many layers of thin veneer.

I know that my methods are liable to appear fussy or confusing to people who are accustomed to bandsawing curves from heavy, solid stock, but they will appeal to assemblers and people who enjoy complicated joinery. I prefer to spend time on the planning and drawing, instead of on carving huge amounts of waste from unformed heavy stock. Once a curve has been laminated, it is hard to alter the outward shape. It is simple to revise the shape of a bandsawn part. Because accurate previsualization comes with experience, I don't find being locked in a disadvantage. When I teach, I mention many times the absolute necessity of making full-size shop drawings. Many part-time woodworkers don't do this, but it is the key to seeing the shape of the finished, three-dimensional object. And it is the only way to be sure from the start that the joinery is possible.

This method of working has also been criticized as less than true to the material. Obviously I don't agree, and I don't think the things I make are any less woodlike than more traditional construction. If anything, a simple chest with curved sides and a bow front (obtainable by the compound staved lamination system, as seen on pages 70 through 73) is much more like a curving tree than is a chest with flat board sides, carved to represent folded linen. Although I make contemporary furniture, I should add that this method has nothing to do with style or design. Tapered laminates can make a traditionally curved leg, and compound staved laminates could be put to good use in producing a French bombe chest.

Tapered lamination Once you have made a shop drawing—for example of a table—and decided that a tapered lamination would make the strongest leg, you need to figure the measurements of the thickness-planer jig that will produce the necessary laminates. From the shop drawing, you need to know the thickness of the curved leg at both ends, and the length of the curve if it were straightened out.

To find the length, draw a center line on the curved part. Set a pair of dividers at an inch or less and walk the dividers down the center line. To decide the number and thickness of the layers of wood, look first at the small end of the leg. Suppose it is 1 in. thick—eight layers, each ⅛ in. thick, would be

---

Jere Osgood teaches woodworking and furniture design at Boston University's Program in Artisanry.

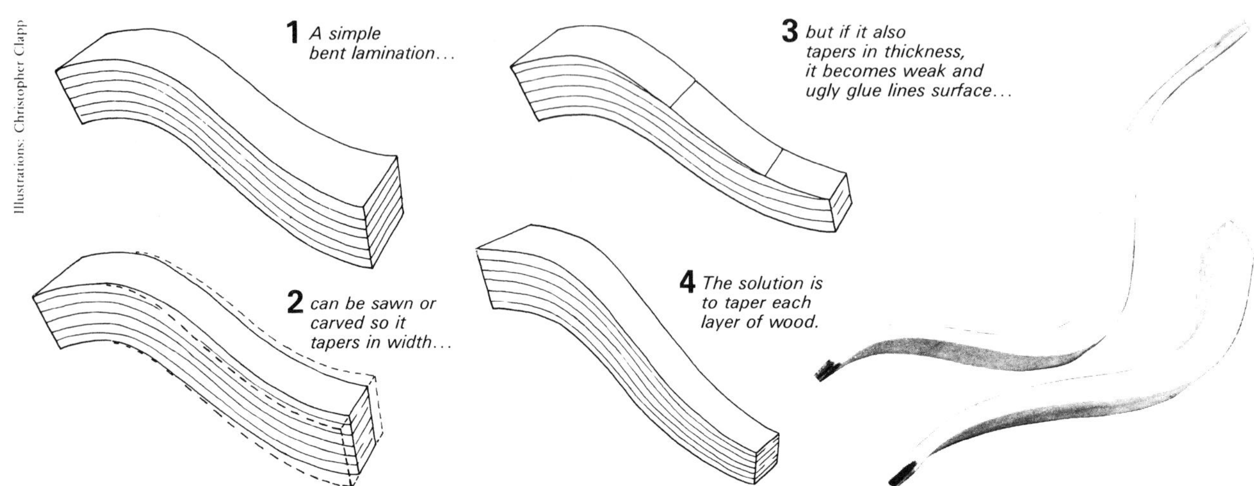
Illustrations: Christopher Clapp
1 A simple bent lamination...
2 can be sawn or carved so it tapers in width...
3 but if it also tapers in thickness, it becomes weak and ugly glue lines surface...
4 The solution is to taper each layer of wood.

Photos: Jere Osgood

Ash legs of table are single-tapered lamination. Table top is teak, and measures 57 in. diameter. Table is 29 in. high.

convenient. Now look at the thick end, perhaps 2½ in. thick, and divide by eight to get 5⁄16 in. Bear in mind here that the thin layers must turn the curve you have drawn, both at the thin end and at the thick end. There are no rules, but a little experience will give you a feel for the bending radii of different woods of various thicknesses.

The thickness-planer jig is a sloping platform that carries the stock through the machine. It should be a few inches longer than the finished length of the stock, and the laminates should be cut to the same oversize length. If each laminate is to taper from ⅛ in. at one end to 5⁄16 in. at the other, the slope of the jig has to express the difference, or 3⁄16 in.

The most accurate way to make a thicknesser jig is with top and bottom boards of some sort of plywood and several central ribs of plywood or particle board running the length of the jig. Since the support ribs are all exactly the same, I would nail or tape them together and carefully cut them as a package on the band saw or with a table-saw taper jig. Spread the ribs out on the base and glue them down, then glue on the top board. It might seem easier merely to sandwich a 3⁄16-in. wedge between two boards, but it isn't. The boards would deflect under the pressure of the planer's feed rolls and create a hump on the finished leg. Remember, each little error in the thicknesser jig multiplies by the number of layers in the lamination. Saw the stock for the laminates thicker than the thick end of the taper, and plane it smooth on one side before tapering in the thicknesser. This ensures uniform pieces. Feed the thinner end of the jig into the machine first, and you'll find that it doesn't require a stop block—the feed pressure against the taper will easily hold the laminates in place.

If you plan to use a one-part, open-face gluing form, the form line can probably be taken directly from your original shop drawing. Remember, though, to face the form with several layers of hardboard and to use more hardboard between the clamps and the laminates to even out the pressure. Account for the thickness of the hardboard in your layout. I'll return to forms later, after giving layout directions for a two-part form, which provides the most even pressure in gluing.

After the laminates are made, clamp them into a package that includes a piece of ¼-in. hardboard (or two ⅛-in. layers) on each side as a form liner. Trace the outline of the whole package onto a piece of drawing paper, or be more precise by measuring the thickness of the ends with calipers and transferring the size to the paper. Now draw in a center line and cross it with uniformly spaced perpendicular sections. I usually make them an inch apart and number them.

From the full-size shop drawing, transfer the center line of the curved part onto a heavy piece of drawing paper. If you

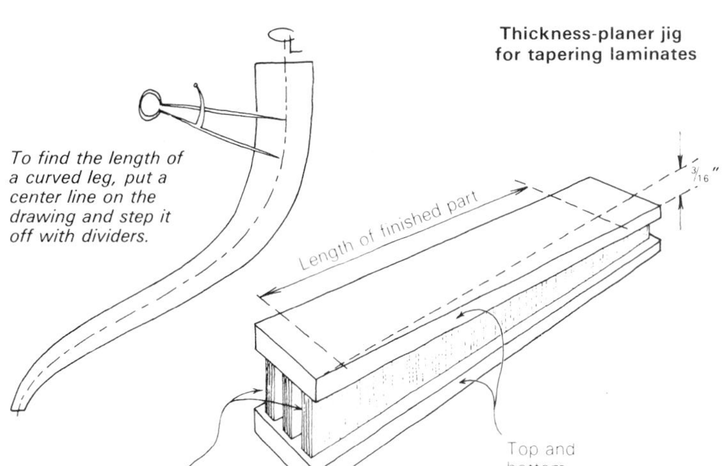
Thickness-planer jig for tapering laminates
To find the length of a curved leg, put a center line on the drawing and step it off with dividers.
Length of finished part
3⁄16"
Tapered ribs
Top and bottom boards

Thin end of jig is fed into planer first—pressure holds laminates in place, and no stop block is required.

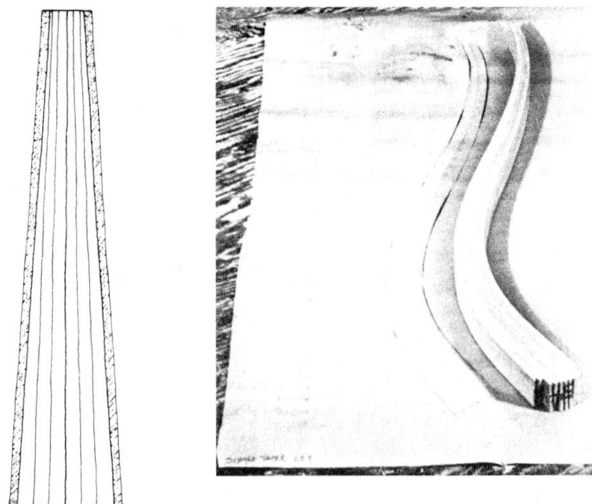

To lay out a two-part gluing form, clamp the hardboard facings and the tapered laminate into a package and trace its outline.

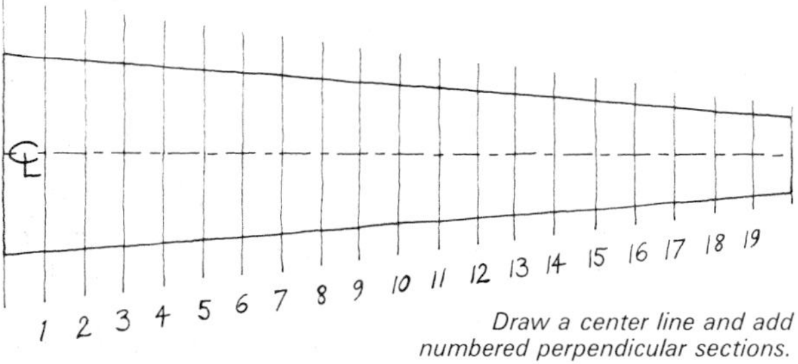

Draw a center line and add numbered perpendicular sections.

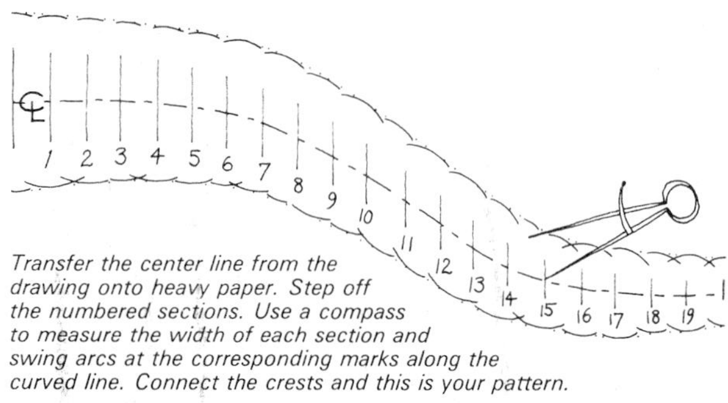

Transfer the center line from the drawing onto heavy paper. Step off the numbered sections. Use a compass to measure the width of each section and swing arcs at the corresponding marks along the curved line. Connect the crests and this is your pattern.

Laminates clamped in the gluing form are protected top and bottom by a hardboard liner.

anticipate a problem with springback, now is the time to consider it: Bend the center line a little farther at each end to compensate. Now on the center line walk off with dividers the same spacing you used for the perpendiculars on the flat package, and transfer the numbers too. With a compass, transfer the width at each numbered section, one section at a time, and swing arcs on both sides of the center line. The radius of each arc is the distance from the center line to the edge of the package of laminates, plus the layers of hardboard. When all the arcs are drawn, connect their crests with a flexible curve or a thin, springy piece of wood. This now is the pattern for the gluing form. For a narrow part such as a chair or table leg, I would bandsaw the form itself from a solid block glued up of several layers of chipboard or plywood. After gluing, check the finished leg against the shop drawing. If there is any difference, alter the drawing to conform, as this slight change might alter the measurements and the joinery of the piece of furniture you are making.

Double-tapered lamination A double-tapered lamination is often used for chair legs, where lightness is required along a delicate curve that might reflect the shapes of the human body. The curve still must be very strong, and the part must thicken at the joints. For example, the back leg of a chair might be of one thickness where it touches the floor, another at the seat rail, and a third thickness at the top. The laminates have to bend easily to the curve and must not have an odd thinness at one end. The initial calculations might yield laminates $\frac{1}{8}$ in. thick at one end, $\frac{1}{4}$ in. at the middle, but only $\frac{1}{32}$ in. at the other end. This would be too fragile to machine, and you would have to decrease the number of laminates. This would make them thicker, perhaps too thick to turn the radius—you must revise the design.

For the sake of the discussion, suppose you arrive at a laminate that is $\frac{1}{8}$ in. thick at the top end, $\frac{5}{16}$ in. at its thickest point and $\frac{3}{16}$ in. at the bottom. Use dividers to take the overall length of the curved piece from the shop drawing, as before. This will also locate the thickest point along its length. Now you can make a thickness-planer jig as before, except its top surface will be curved. The machine's feed rolls force the stock against the curve and the resulting laminate will taper uniformly from thin to thick and back to thin. To do it, start with a piece of plywood or particle board that is 3 in. overlong and perhaps 3 in. wide. Draw a center line. Subtract the thickness of the laminate at the small end from the thickness limits. The $\frac{1}{8}$ in. becomes zero, and the other two differences represent deflection from the center line along the length—in this example, $\frac{3}{16}$ in. and $\frac{1}{16}$ in. Mark these points along the center line. Put a brad into the particle board on the center line at one end, and another $\frac{1}{16}$ in. down from the line at the other end. Set a good steel or wood straightedge on the brads, and push it down to the $\frac{3}{16}$-in. mark at the thickest point. Draw a line carefully along the bent straightedge. Now bandsaw several rib supports along this line (in a package, as before) and glue them to a base board. Face the top of the form with a couple of layers of hardboard, glued together and glued to the ribs.

With the stock planed on one side and in place, feed the thin end into the planer, as before. Unlike a single taper, where planing downhill makes tearout unlikely, a double taper sometimes shreds. Therefore cut extra stock before you start to plane, and carefully check the grain direction of each

Double-tapered lamination (top) and one of its components.

To lay out ribs for double taper jig, measure the necessary deflection from a center line and connect the points with a bent straightedge.

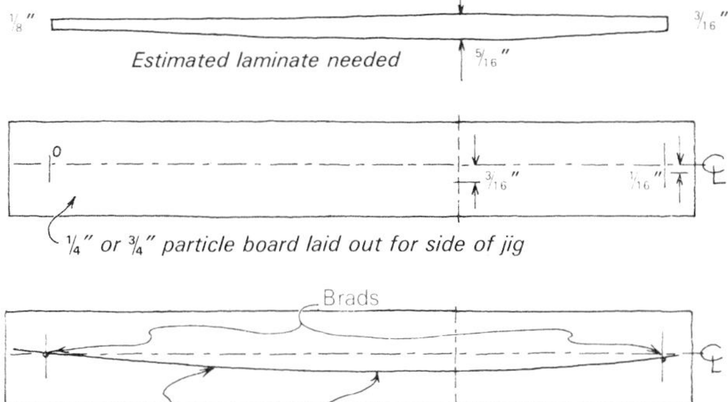

piece. If the grain tears out on the first pass, try reversing it on the jig. It may seem like a good idea to make the jig and the stock wide enough for several legs to be sawn out of a wide laminate. This usually doesn't work—tearout becomes a more serious problem, and inaccuracies in side-to-side thickness creep in.

It is usually better to glue up a double taper on a one-part form, facing both sides with hardboard and using as many quick-set clamps as will fit along the curve. A two-part form would give more uniform pressure, but the complications of making and testing may not be worth the effort.

Notes on laminating Press forms can be made of particle board, plywood or any sturdy material that can be sawn evenly. Form stock is better if it has no strong grain for the band-saw blade to track off into—construction fir is unsuitable. Forms are difficult to sand or rasp clean without introducing error. It is better to use them straight from the saw.

When making forms, you can save material by spacing the parts. For example, three ½-in. layers of particle board could be spaced out to 3 in. with two ¾-in. spacers. But be sure you don't weaken the form so much that it might break in the clamps or the press.

Forms must be lined with a hardboard-type material (Masonite is one brand name), and the thickness of the liners must be accounted for in layout. You can use ¼-in. hardboard, or several layers ⅛ in. thick, tempered or untempered, depending on the tightness of the curve. Thin plywoods are not suitable because they have a grain direction (due to the uneven number of plies and the wood itself) that interferes with bending to a particular curve.

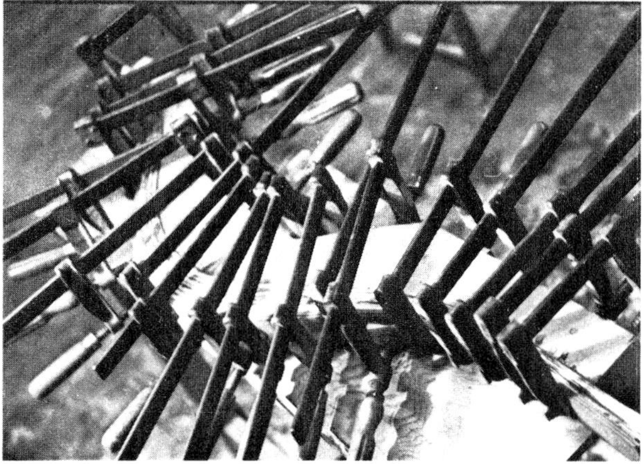

Double-tapered laminates are clamped to a one-piece form.

A two-part gluing form must be precisely cut or it is not worth the bother. If the curve is difficult or the taper becomes a complicating factor, use a one-part open-face form with several layers of hardboard to distribute the clamping pressure. Attempts to pad out forms with layers of rubber, felt or cork don't work, although small discrepancies can be repaired with two or three layers of brown paper or newspaper.

Forms and hardboard facings should be waxed. This gives easy slippage as the wood bends to the curve, and prevents dry glue from sticking. Use plastic-resin glue or Urac 185 (see page 63 for source), or a two-part resorcinol formaldehyde, because these glues don't suffer cold creep. Yellow glue and white glue aren't suitable because they will allow the wood to creep under strain. Spread the glue uniformly with a paint roller or a good brush. Be sure the shop is warm enough for the glue to cure.

It is easier to align the layers of wood, and to dry-clamp the setup to be sure it will work, if the forms and the laminates are the same width. If the width of a finished part is to be 2 in., make the stock and the form about 2¾ in. wide. When the glue has set it is easy to cut a ¼-in. layer off both sides of the blank and joint or hand-plane the sawn faces. This avoids the necessity of scraping off squeezed-out glue and the risk of nicking a good plane iron on hardened dribble.

After some experience with these methods, it is tempting to introduce all sorts of perturbations and various odd lumps of wood to go around joints here and there. But I have found that it is better not to introduce many complex forms, and to prefer simpler design. □

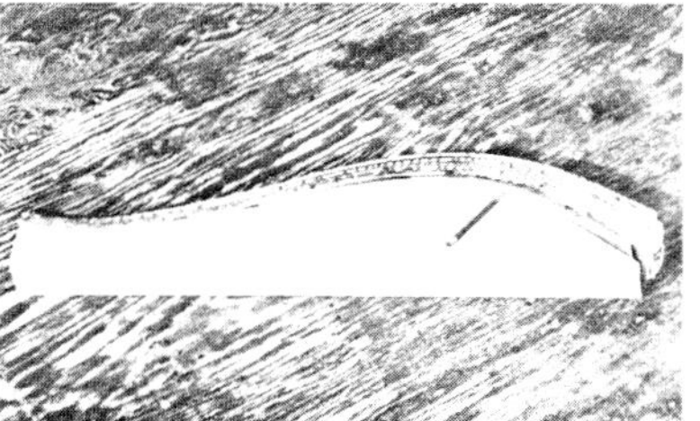

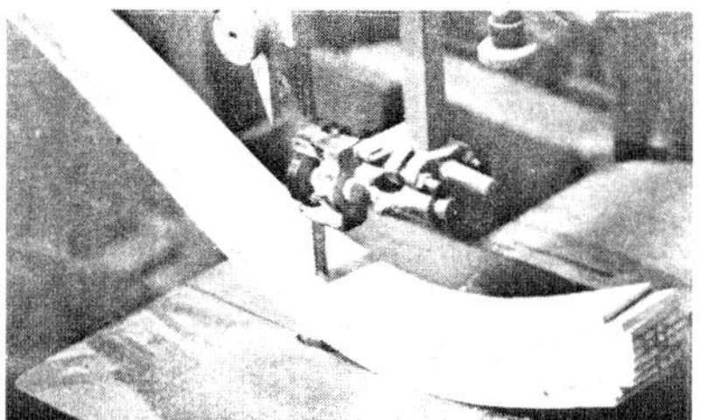

Use the form and shims to lay out the finished width on the lamination and bandsaw to size.

Bending Compound Curves

Laminated staves make bulging cabinets

by Jere Osgood

Sides of this chest curve from front to back and bow outward toward the middle.

Thin layers of wood are easy to bend into a variety of simple curves—that is, surfaces that bend in only one plane. The basic techniques of layout, stock preparation, making press forms and gluing up have already been described in the preceding articles (see pages 62 to 65 and 66 to 69). Now we will see how the same approach can be used to create thin-walled panels that curve in two planes; these panels can be used for cabinet fronts, doors or sides, for drawer fronts, or for any other application requiring a compound-curved form. It is done by gluing layers of wood face to face into relatively narrow staves, making each stave take the shape of a different but related curve, and then joining the staves edge to edge. The key to the compound-staved lamination system is realizing that flat layers of wood can be bent to one radius at one edge, and to a different radius at the opposite edge.

Keep in mind that the surface of each stave is a portion of the surface of a cone, straight across its width. A single stave cannot take the shape of a section of a sphere or of any other surface that curves in two directions. Wood is not normally elastic and it will bend in only one plane at a time. However, a number of staves, each bent to a different radius, can be edge-joined together to produce an approximately spherical form (like a barrel or even a pumpkin) or almost any other three-dimensional surface. This assembly will be made up of a number of flats, like the outside of a barrel, but as long as the radius of curvature is not too sharp and the outer laminate is thick enough, you can plane, spokeshave, scrape and sand the surface to a smooth, continuous curve.

When I want a slightly convex stave, there is a little trick that is helpful, although fallible. I resaw and plane the lamination stock and sticker it overnight. The thin layers usually cup slightly as the moisture gradient within the original board reaches atmospheric equilibrium. I then mark the convex face of each laminate, and when gluing up the stave I stack all the convex cups in one direction. When the press form is opened after the usual glue-curing period, the stave will be perfectly flat across its width. But within 24 hours it usually resumes the cup.

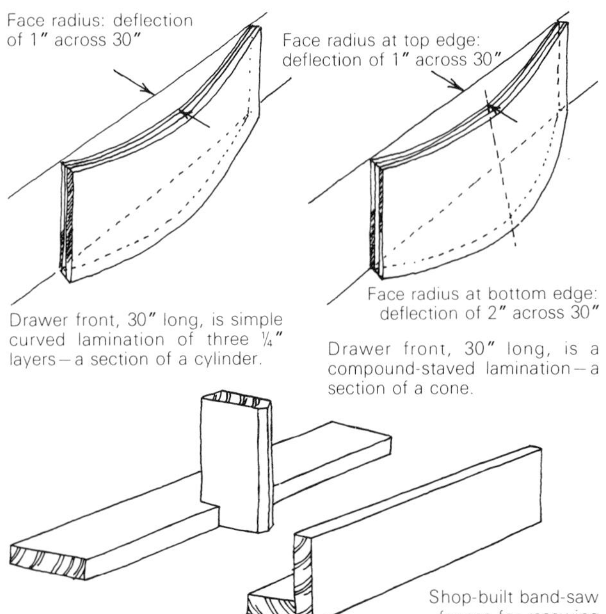

Drawer front, 30" long, is simple curved lamination of three ¼" layers—a section of a cylinder.

Drawer front, 30" long, is a compound-staved lamination—a section of a cone.

Shop-built band-saw fences for resawing

Compound-curved lamination is a forming process. Panels for cabinetry can be manufactured either as solid-wood laminates or by the veneer-plywood technique. In the former, the thickness of the layers is arbitrary and usually ranges from about 1/16 in. to ⅜ in. or more. A thin layer will bend around a smaller radius than will a thicker layer, but the thinner you resaw the stock, the more good wood you waste in the kerf. When using solid wood the grain of each layer is oriented in the same direction, and the laminated stave behaves and moves just like solid wood. In the veneer-plywood approach layers of thin veneer are cross-banded within each stave, or fancy face veneers are glued to multiple layers of ⅛-in. or ¼-in. plywood. The alternation of grain direction stabilizes the unit and there is little or no movement across the grain. But springback errors can be disastrous and the need for accuracy is acute.

I usually prefer a subtle curve and therefore find using solid wood laminates more congenial. For example, drawer fronts with a gentle curve might be made from two ⅜-in. thick layers glued together. Carcase sides to accommodate a slightly greater bulge might be made of three ¼-in. layers, the outer layer resawn and bookmatched from some sacred old stock, the two inner layers from a more common unmatched stock.

When resawing planks on the band saw, best results come from a new blade, preferably no finer than four or five teeth to the inch, and ¾ in. or 1 in. wide. Make sure the blade guides are firm and tight both above and below the table, and that the blade is tensioned to specifications. Most band-saw blades lead to one side or the other, especially when they get dull, so you can't use the rip fence that comes with the saw. Instead, you have to make a wooden equivalent that you can clamp to the table, as in the drawing at left, and angle it one way or the other to compensate for the blade's lead. Or, you can use a vertical *V*-block or rod set in line with the teeth, swinging the end of the stock to compensate for lead. In either case, set the fence for the thickness of the laminate you want, and saw all the stock at this one setting.

If the wood is plain and straight-grained, I usually just resaw it thick enough to run both sides through the thickness

Photos and illustrations: Jere Osgood

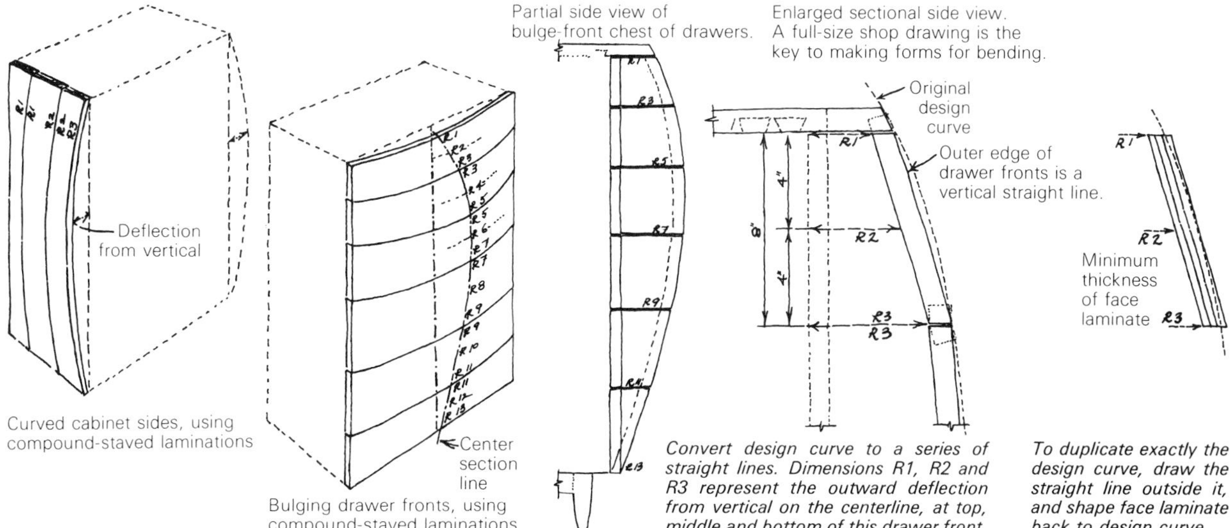
Deflection from vertical
Center section line
Partial side view of bulge-front chest of drawers.
Enlarged sectional side view. A full-size shop drawing is the key to making forms for bending.
Original design curve
Outer edge of drawer fronts is a vertical straight line.
Minimum thickness of face laminate

Curved cabinet sides, using compound-staved laminations

Bulging drawer fronts, using compound-staved laminations

Convert design curve to a series of straight lines. Dimensions R1, R2 and R3 represent the outward deflection from vertical on the centerline, at top, middle and bottom of this drawer front.

To duplicate exactly the design curve, draw the straight line outside it, and shape face laminate back to design curve.

planer. If it is highly figured, it is better to joint the face of the board before each cut. Use a stand or roller to support the wood as it leaves the band-saw table, and always have a push-stick handy for the last few inches of cut. The wood is liable to split suddenly near the end of the cut, and without a push-stick your thumb would plunge into the blade. Most small band saws are underpowered for resawing wide boards. I solve this problem by table-sawing a deep kerf on each edge of the plank. The remaining wood separating the two kerfs will be within the band saw's capacity. No fence is necessary because the band-saw blade tracks in the kerfs.

Most of the time I make bending forms from particle board because it is cheap and strong. I face the forms with layers of Masonite (hardboard) to distribute the pressure evenly, and clamp up with either quick-set clamps or a single five-screw unit from a veneer press. A vacuum press (see pages 92 through 97) is ideal for this application, especially when using the veneer-plywood process. When bending solid wood, avoid white glue because it suffers badly from cold-creep under the stress of the wood attempting to straighten out. Yellow glue is better, although it is still subject to some cold-creep, but a urea-formaldehyde such as Weldwood plastic resin or Urac 185 is best of all. In all lamination processes, good gluing habits are critical. There are four trouble areas: wood moisture content, oily woods, temperature and dull thickness-planer blades. The wood should be uniformly dried to about 8% moisture content—below 6% is risky, and so is above 12%. The curing time of most glues is sensitive to temperature, and many won't cure in a cold shop. But a drop-cloth tent over the work, with a light bulb suspended inside, usually solves the problem. Oily woods should be carefully tested before proceeding to the real thing, and here yellow glue will hold better than urea. Dull planer blades mash the wood fibers, while sharp ones cut them cleanly. A clean, newly machined surface always yields the best glueline. The surface of stock that is resawn and planed and then left sitting around the workshop for months oxidizes slightly, jeopardizing the glue bond.

The first drawing above shows a cabinet whose side is straight at the back edge and bows gently toward the front. The back stave is straight along its rear edge, with the curve (R1) beginning along its front edge. The next stave has the same curve R1 along its back edge, but continues the outward movement toward curve R2 at its front edge. The third stave matches the second along curve R2, and goes a final bit further outward to R3. A variation on this would be returning the front curve R3 to a straight line, although with straights that move to a curve you must take care to avoid too great a change too quickly. In this example, to have a straight vertical at the back and front edges might require one or two more staves. There is no limit to the number of staves, and return curves or *S*-curves can also be used, although the more surfaces you have curving in and out, the harder it becomes to keep all the parts in phase with one another.

The next sketch illustrates a set of drawer fronts designed to bulge outward toward the middle. The top edge of the top drawer is slightly curved, while the bottom drawer line is straight. The carcase sides are shown vertical and straight, but they need not be so. Here each drawer front would be a single stave, with the curve of its top edge matching the bottom edge of the drawer above, and the curve of its bottom edge matching the one below. The intermediate radii shown (R2, R4, etc.) designate the curvature of spacing ribs for the bending forms. In the sketches and photographs to follow, I will describe the procedure for making a cabinet whose drawer fronts bulge outward like the one shown here.

Any project involving compound-staved laminations absolutely requires a good, full-size shop drawing. Front, side, top and sectional views are usually needed. The shop drawing makes it possible to visualize accurately the curves, and measurements for bending forms can be taken directly from it.

In this example, start with the usual front and side elevations and plan view, and construct an accurate side sectional view at the part of the curve furthest forward (on the centerline, in this case). Because the wood will bend in only one plane at a time, you have to convert the vertical curve of each drawer front into a straight line. I draw the straight line just inside the design curve, and leave the drawer fronts flat on the finished piece. But if you want to duplicate the design curve exactly, draw the straight line tangent to, but outside, the design curve. The largest variation between the curve you want and the straight face of the bent stave is the minimum thickness of the face laminate, since you will want to shape the wood back to the true curve without encountering an ugly

Bending forms

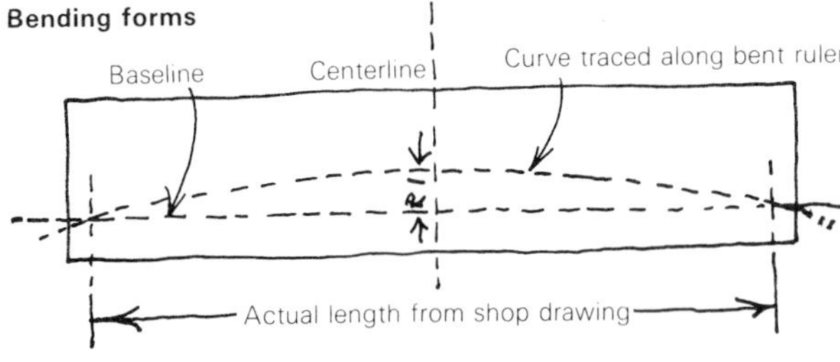

Example: press-form rib R1

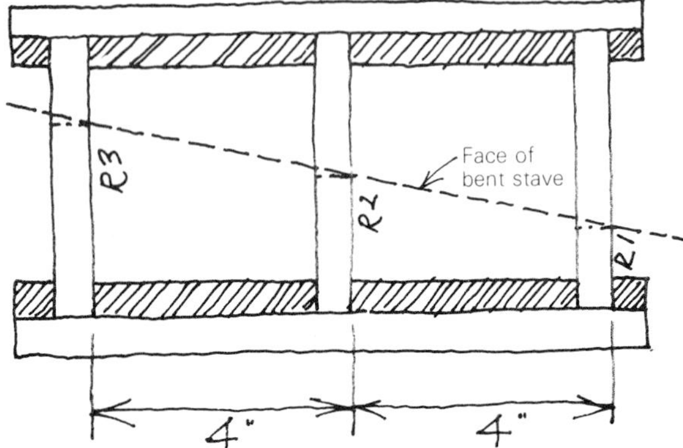

End view of typical form. Note construction for removable ribs.

Spacing is measured from the front face of the form ribs. Be sure to keep all the ribs oriented the same way.

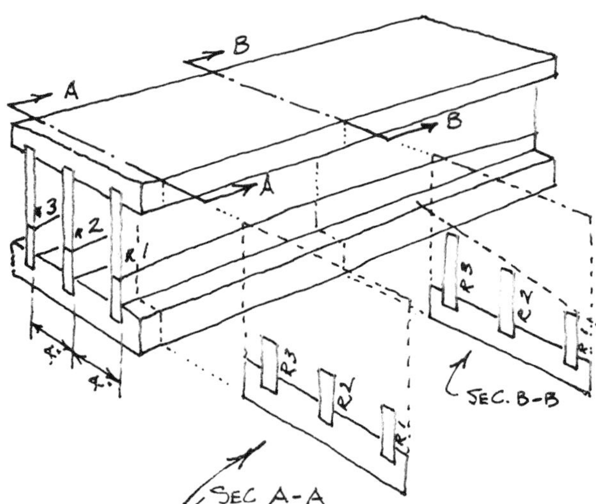

The sections A-A and B-B show deflection from the edges toward the center of the drawer front.

glue line. If this thickness is too great for the bend you have in mind, you will have to redesign the curve or divide the drawer front into two (or more) staves.

From this sectional drawing, you can measure the deflection at the center of each drawer front, with respect to a vertical line on the plane of its straight outer edges. On this drawing, these measurements are R1, R2 and R3. This is the information you need to lay out and construct the forms for bending each drawer front.

Drawers are often of different heights within a carcase. You can make a different bending form for each drawer front, or you can devise a modular form base to receive at the correct spacing the ribs for all the drawers. Drawer-front heights in multiples of 1½ in. or 2 in. will fit this concept nicely. The form ribs can be on any convenient spacing, as long as the base form is made to accept them all at the correct distance. The maximum distance is about 4 in., as shown at left. Beyond that, the gluing pressure might become spotty.

The sections R1, R2 and R3 need to be converted precisely to particle board or plywood ribs for the bending forms. There are only two measurements needed for this: the length of the drawer front (or of the cabinet side stave) and the amount of deflection in the curve. The bending forms should be made slightly overlong, and the resawn stock should be both overlong and overwide. The extra width in the form is gained by extending the Masonite form liners because the distance between sections R1, R2 and R3 cannot be changed. A typical two-part form would use a Masonite liner on each side: two or three layers of ⅛-in. tempered Masonite, or a single layer of ¼-in. tempered or untempered, depending on the sharpness of the curve.

In this example, prepare some pieces of particle board 2 in. longer than the finished length of the drawer front, and about 3 in. wider than the greatest deflection of the curve. That is, if R3 is 2 in., cut the particle board 5 in. wide.

For press-form rib R1, draw a base line and a vertical centerline on the particle board. At the actual length of the drawer front, drive two brads into the base line. Transfer the bulge height (R1) to the vertical centerline. Find a steel, plastic or straight-grained wood straightedge (aluminum does not bend evenly). Rest the straightedge against the nails and bend it up to the limit of R1. Then bend it a little more, say ¼ in. for a deflection of 2 in., for springback. The exact amount to allow depends on the wood species, the severity of the curve, and the number and thickness of the laminates—you need experience with this technique to judge. Trace the curve of the straightedge onto the particle board. I suggest

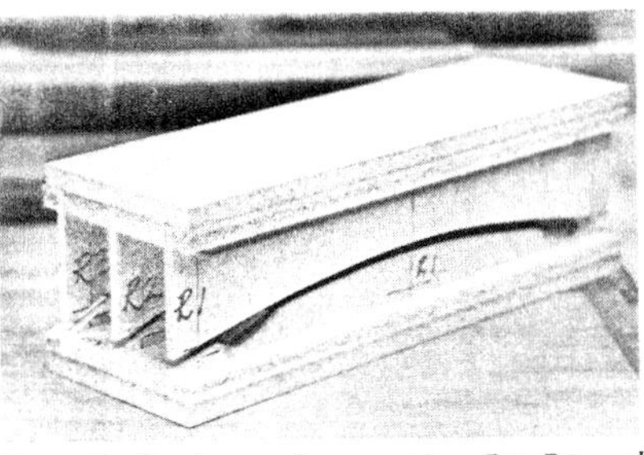

Full-size shop drawing (left) and resulting press-form ribs for drawer-front sections R1, R2 and R3. The press form (center) with ribs in place. These ribs are removable, so the same base pieces can be used with the ribs for the other drawers in the carcase. One section of a veneer press is used to bend the drawer-front laminates (right). The wood and the form are separated by a layer of Masonite to distribute the pressure.

drawing all of the curves for all of the form ribs in the same session. This ensures that you use the same straightedge, and that the same face is bent outward (or inward). It is particularly important to draw everything at once if the design calls for a return *(S)* curve.

When bandsawing the form ribs, it is not a good idea to tilt the band-saw table. The staves do twist from end to end, and accurate sectional contact might be lost. The square edge in conjunction with the Masonite form liner will distribute the pressure adequately. Note that top and bottom form ribs are cut on the same line. In work like this I would not attempt to make true two-part forms, bandsawing to a different radius for each half. It would be too confusing, and if the curves are so tight that it is necessary, you are probably leading to distortion problems anyway. Such a design is stretching the limits of this procedure.

Use the bending form base as a jig to trim drawer fronts to width. The curve can often be freehanded over the jointer.

Joint line bisects angle between staves. Set locating spline just back of center.

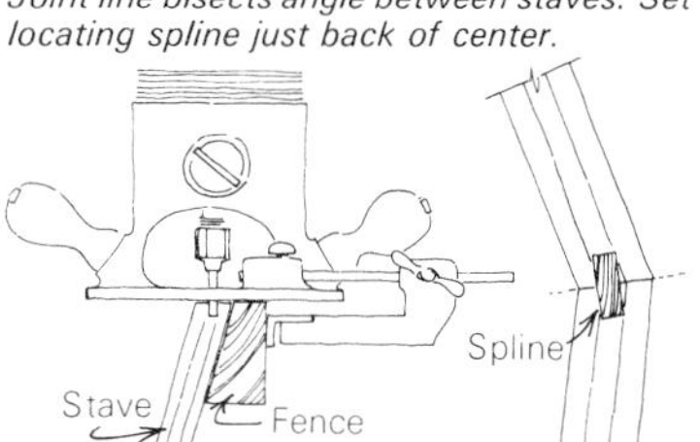

To rout slots for locating splines in staved cabinet sides, use a ¼-in. straight bit and fence blocks beveled to the appropriate angle. A straight fence will follow a convex curve, but a concave curve requires a shaped fence. Always work from the outside face of the staves, to keep them in the same plane.

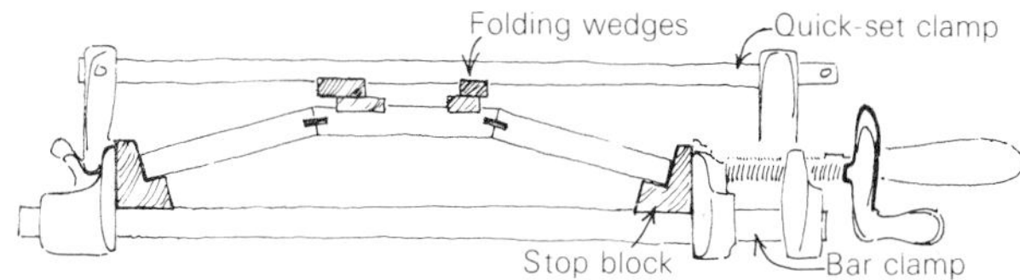

A combination of clamps, folding wedges and end blocks makes it possible to glue up a staved assembly. The wedges can be driven in and out, and the clamps tightened or released, to manipulate the curve. Always make a full-size cardboard template to check the curve during glue-up.

After the laminates are glued to shape, they need to be trimmed to width at the correct angle, on the section line. An easy way to do this is to use the base of the press form as a jig. Clamp the piece to the form so it overhangs (you'll have to cut a notch in the base so the clamp can clear the table) and feed it into the band saw or table saw. Because these pieces are curved, they can usually be freehanded over the jointer for a clean and true edge.

The angles that compound-curved laminations generate need to be understood. For drawer fronts, all the edges would be cut perpendicular to a real or imagined vertical, because the drawers need to slide straight in and out without interference. For cabinet doors or sides, I prefer a joint that bisects the average angle of the staves to each other. It is easier to glue and also easier to rout slots for splines.

A cross-grain spline is not needed for strength because the mating stave edges are all long grain and glue together well. The spline is only a locator, so it can be ripped from the edge of a board. The twist imparted by the compound curve makes the width of the stave edges vary, and the splines keep flush the face side of the staved assembly. The back side will need to be scraped down level, or the stave edges chamfered to disguise discrepancies.

Gluing up the staves that form curved panels often seems an impossible task, but it yields to experience. The method I have found best is to presand the insides of the panels and chamfer the mating edges slightly. To make clean-up easier I rub a little paraffin on the chamfer so the squeezed-out glue that collects there will pop right off after it dries. Then I use two stop blocks resting on pipe clamps to establish and control the overall width of the staved assembly, and a large quick-set clamp over the top to provide downward pressure, tightened with wedges. The drawing shows what I mean. It's very important to make a cardboard or Masonite template to check the angles between staves when gluing. This arrangement permits you to manipulate closely the pressure and the angle at which the staves meet when gluing up all sorts of curved or coopered panels.

These methods will seem to be fussy and confusing to people accustomed to roughing out curves from solid stock on the band saw. It will appeal to assemblers and to those who like complicated joinery. Here the time is spent on conceptualization, on accurate planning and drawing, instead of on carving off large amounts of waste from heavy unformed stock.

As I've said before in this series of articles, you must use discretion when designing for bent lamination. Consider the overall design appearance first and have the technique evolve from it. Once you master the basic techniques, it is all too easy to conceive of a piece that could be executed in theory, but that in practice would be simply too hard to handle. Such a piece would probably be disorienting as well, so busy that one couldn't bear to be in the same room with it. I have found it best to stay with one design experiment in one piece of furniture, and to keep the rest of the piece restrained. Being able to build a piece of furniture that bulges wildly in all directions at once is not a good enough reason for doing so. □

Jere Osgood is professor of woodworking and furniture design at Boston University.

Letting the Wood Bend Its Own Way

A flexible method for laminating compound curves

by Seth Stem

Wood sawn into thin strips and bent is almost animate in its flexibility. With the rudimentary formwork shown in the photo below, author Seth Stem laminates a stack of strips into a sweeping compound curve.

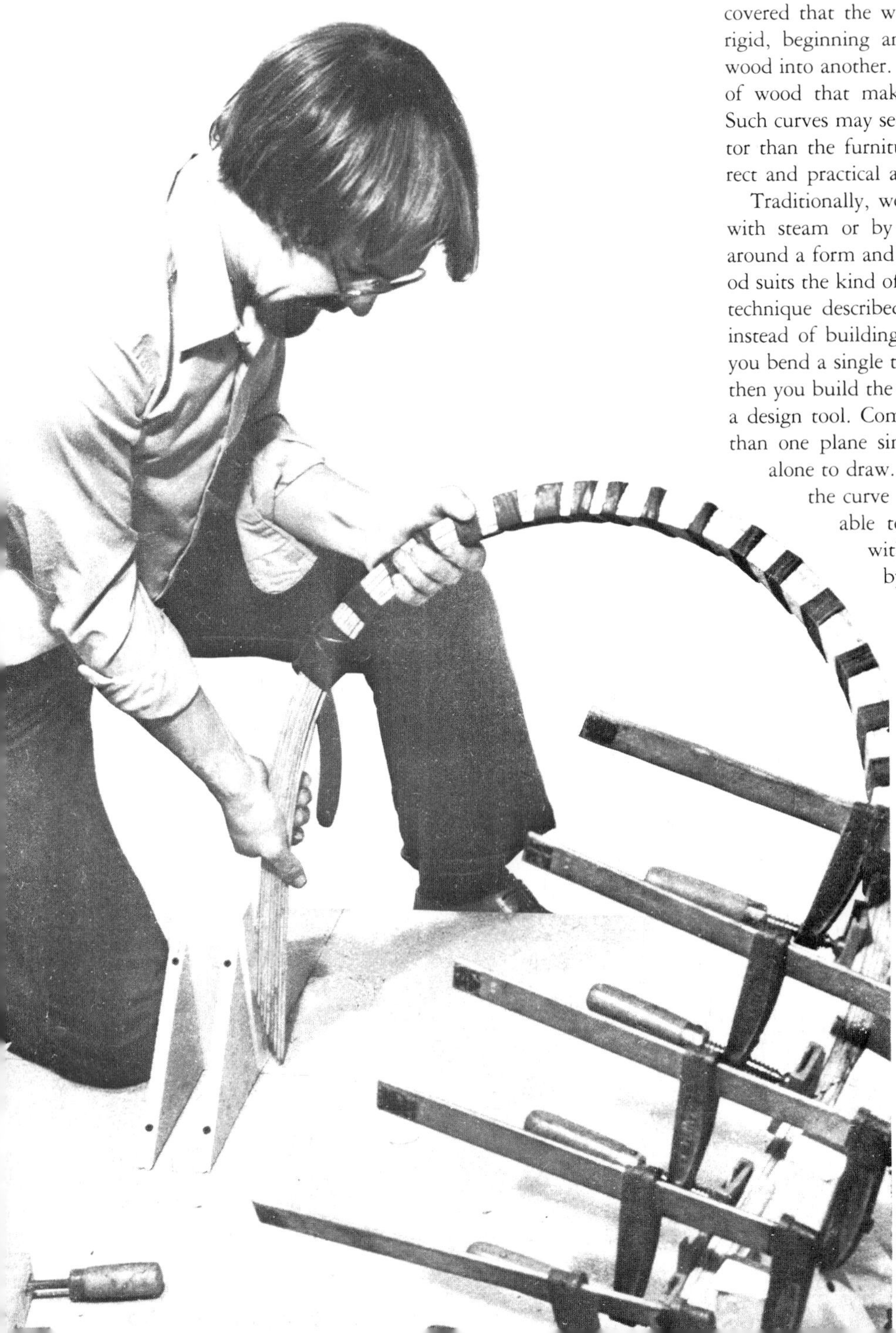

One of the most exciting ways to design with wood is to bend thin strips freely in space, letting form and line depend as much on the wood's natural flexibility as on any preconceived shape. When I first started bending wood, I discovered that the woodworking I had done before was really rigid, beginning and ending with fitting one flat plane of wood into another. I had learned little about the pliant nature of wood that makes dramatic sweeps and curves possible. Such curves may seem to be more in the domain of the sculptor than the furnituremaker, but I've found challenging, direct and practical application of these forms.

Traditionally, wood has been bent either by plasticizing it with steam or by cutting it into thin strips for wrapping around a form and layering up to thickness. This latter method suits the kind of furniture I design and build, although the technique described in this article is considerably different—instead of building the form and forcing the wood to fit it, you bend a single thin strip until you get a curve you like and then you build the form to suit. This method's real value is as a design tool. Compound curves—those which bend in more than one plane simultaneously—are difficult to envision, let alone to draw. I often find considerable disparity between the curve I imagine and the one the wood is actually able to assume. I start my lamination projects with a series of thumbnail sketches, followed by a scale model made of 12-ga. copper wire held together with hot-melt glue or tape. The model, though, takes me only part of the way through the design, because to bend thin strips of wood compoundly, you have to twist them. This process creates shapes difficult to predict with a model. I really don't know how a compound curve will come out until I actually begin bending the wood. My model, then, serves only as a guide for making a full-size, mock-up bend. Once I've bent a single strip to the curve I want, I build a simple but sturdy framework to both guide the shape of the curve and support the weight of clamps when I glue on more strips. When the bend has cured, I shape it to the desired cross-section with hand tools.

Cutting the strips—After I've made the sketches and models, I select the wood. Color and figure are a consideration, but the species' ability to bend is just as important, particularly if I'm planning tight curves. Oak, ash, hickory, beech and elm bend well. Maple, poplar, teak, mahogany, and softwoods such as pine and fir should be limited to gentler curves.

Ideally, lumber should be knot-free, straight-grained and, if possible, air-dried, since it will be less brittle than kiln-dried lumber and will bend better. If you plan severe bends, cut your laminate strips so the annual rings run across their width, and position the heartwood toward the inside of the curve, as in figure 1. If you have rift-sawn (quartersawn) lumber and you plan a severe bend, simply rip your laminae from the edges of the boards. This method is quick and you'll be able to maintain grain continuity. If you have only plain-sawn lumber, first rip the boards to the laminate width and then resaw to the proper thickness. This method is quite wasteful, and grain continuity is sacrificed if you have to build up a thick lamination.

Strips sawn from the center of a plain-sawn board will have short grain, which is more likely to break, particularly in a severe bend. Put the fragile short-grain pieces to the inside of the curve, with the more pliable long-grain pieces supporting the outside.

Expect about 50% waste in converting rough stock into strips. That means a board 6 in. wide in the rough will make a stack of ⅛-in. thick laminae 3 in. high. The strips should be cut a few inches longer than the length of the finished curve and about ¼ in. wider to compensate for slippage, splaying, glue removal and subsequent shaping of the bend. Before sawing, I witness-mark the face of the board with a large V, as a guide in maintaining grain continuity during assembly.

How thick should the strips be? That depends on the severity of the bends. You can get a good idea of the right thickness by cutting a test strip and bending it to the breaking point. Keep in mind, though, that the moisture in the glue will relax the wood's fibers, so a sharper curve is possible than with a dry strip. Curved laminations spring back slightly; if this will create problems in your design, you can minimize it by using thinner strips. If radical curves are wanted, dry-bend the laminae in your form after they've been soaked in hot water for an hour or steamed for 20 minutes. This will make the strips easier to bend and it will lessen springback by giving the wood fibers "memory." Let the strips dry for a day or two before gluing them.

I find that a bandsaw fitted with a 4-TPI, ½-in. or wider blade is the most efficient tool with which to cut laminate strips. It's fast and safe, and the saw's narrow kerf minimizes waste. I rig the saw with a fence or guide block set to cut a strip about $^{1}/_{32}$ in. to $^{1}/_{16}$ in. thicker than the final size I want. The extra material will be planed off later when the strips are smoothed for gluing. Rip a strip off each edge of the stock, joint both edges of the board to remove the sawmarks, and rip two more strips, continuing until the board is too narrow to be jointed safely.

The strips will be smooth on one side, but you'll have to remove the sawmarks on the other side. To do this, I use either a tablesaw set up with a 40-tooth carbide blade or a thickness planer. The carbide blade acts as a planer, producing a clean surface excellent for gluing. Install a wooden throat plate on your saw and run the blade up through it, so the slot is the exact thickness of the blade. This way, thin strips will be supported as they pass by the blade.

The advantage of the tablesaw method is that thin or ir-

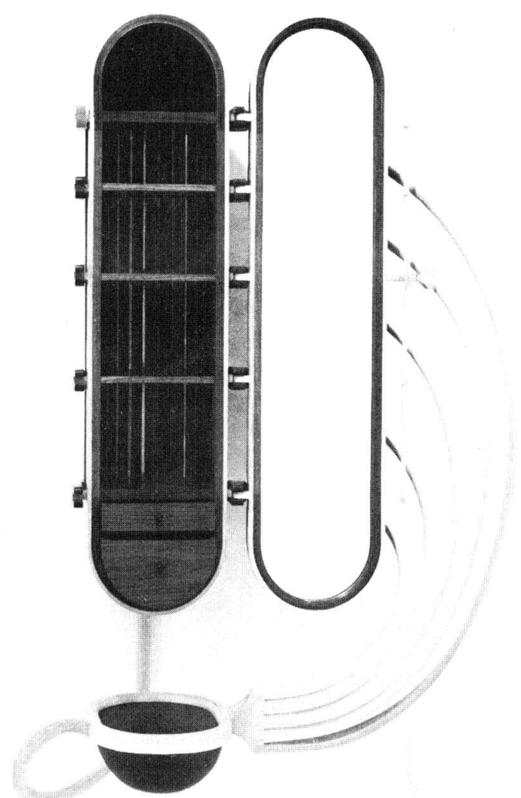

Laminated compound curves can be strong visual and structural elements of functional furniture. For this wall cabinet, Stem laminated maple strips into fluid arcs that connect the tray at the base of this cabinet to its sides.

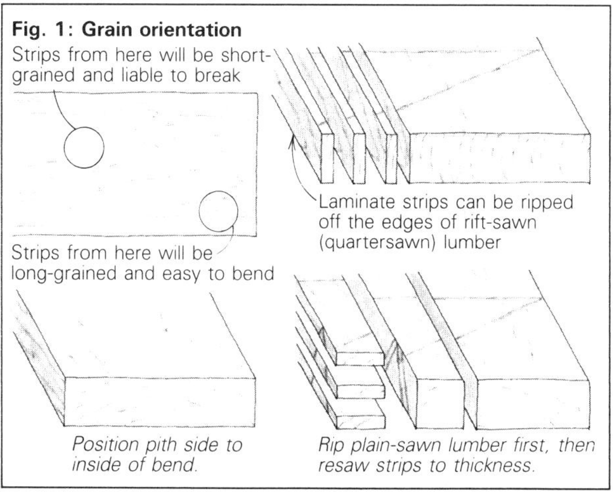
Fig. 1: Grain orientation
Strips from here will be short-grained and liable to break
Laminate strips can be ripped off the edges of rift-sawn (quartersawn) lumber
Strips from here will be long-grained and easy to bend
Position pith side to inside of bend.
Rip plain-sawn lumber first, then resaw strips to thickness.

For a good glue bond, laminate strips must be free of sawmarks. One way to remove them is to attach a wooden auxiliary fence to the tablesaw and, with the strips held against the fence by featherboards bolted into holes tapped in the saw's table, pass the strips by the blade. A 40-tooth carbide combination blade will leave an excellent gluing surface.

regularly grained strips can be smoothed without tearout or breakage. But make sure the blade is parallel to the fence (not just square to the table), because any thickness error will be multiplied in a stack of strips. Check for uniform thickness by trimming two strips and laying them side by side on a flat surface. Feel the adjacent edges for a ridge. Flip one strip over, and feel for a ridge again. Any thickness discrepancy will be apparent.

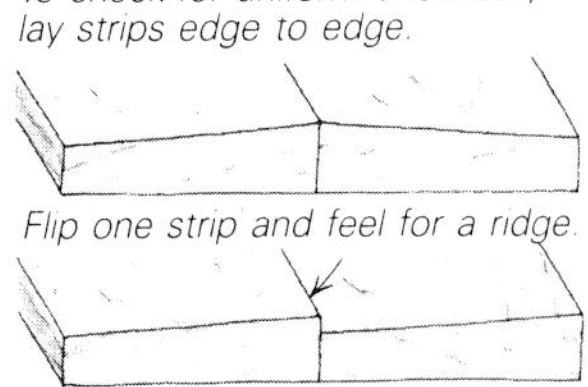

To check for uniform thickness, lay strips edge to edge.
Flip one strip and feel for a ridge.

The thickness planer does a good job of removing sawmarks from straight-grained material, but it's likely to chew up figured wood, in part because thin strips bear unevenly against the machine's bed rollers, which results in uneven, grabby planing. Bridging the planer's bed rollers with an auxiliary bed made of Formica-covered particleboard or a similarly smooth material should solve this problem. I've planed veneer as thin as $\frac{1}{28}$ in. with an auxiliary bed on a Makita 2040 planer. Sharp knives, of course, will limit tearout and will leave a better surface for gluing.

Though it's more hazardous and wasteful, strips can be ripped directly on the tablesaw, without planing off the sawmarks. But I don't recommend setting the fence to the strip thickness and then ripping with little space between the blade and the fence—a repetitious operation that invites an accident. A safer way is to support the stock with a wooden form, as in figure 2. Push the form and stock forward with your right hand while applying pressure against the form, in front of the blade, with your left.

You can save yourself the waste and the relatively hazardous work of milling strips by buying $\frac{1}{10}$-in. thick veneer, a material especially well-suited for making wide bends. These sliced veneers are available in many species from Chester B. Stem, Inc., Grant Line Rd., New Albany, Ind. 47150. You may have to purchase a complete flitch, which is expensive, at least \$150 (1983) plus shipping. But getting out your laminae from flitches saves time and makes grain-matching automatic. To cut the strips, I clamp part of the flitch to a bench, chalk lines to mark the strip width on the top piece of veneer and cut the whole stack with a portable circular saw.

Bending form—The key element of successful compound-curve lamination is the bending form. It must be versatile enough to conform to the curve, yet strong enough to hold the laminae rigidly in place during glue-up. A bend even 3 ft. long acts as a powerful lever, exerting tremendous force when a stack of laminae are bent. Nothing is worse than having parts of the form pop loose during glue-up. The fixture I describe here shows one way to support and clamp the laminae; see the boxes on pages 78 and 79 for other ideas. Any device—2x4s tacked to the ceiling and floor, steel pipes, even the shop's supporting posts—can be pressed into service, so long as it supports the laminae and remains firmly in place.

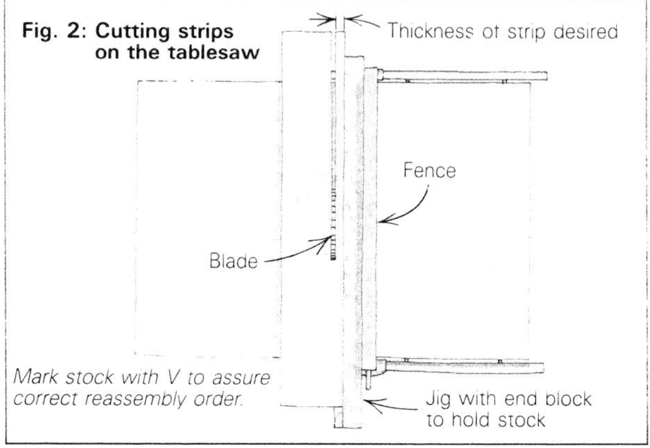

Mark stock with V to assure correct reassembly order.
Jig with end block to hold stock

Fig. 2: Cutting strips on the tablesaw

Begin the form by making a base plane, which can be particleboard or plywood if your design is small, or the shop floor if it's larger. I sometimes strike a grid pattern on the base as reference points to aid the layout of the curves, but I translate the model lines to the form mostly by eye—the spontaneous nature of this method makes it difficult to more exactly duplicate the model.

Once you've laid out the curve on the base, mark reference points where both ends of the curve will rest on it and temporarily screw down two 2x4 blocks to serve as anchors for clamping both ends of a laminate strip, as in the photo at the top of the facing page. You're now ready to try a mock-up bend—a single strip that will illustrate the actual form, and will tell you what kind of radius can be bent with a certain thickness strip and what sort of compound curve is possible.

With one end of the test strip clamped down, start bending it in the direction you want it to go. Remember, strips of wood will bend easily only in one direction; you'll have to twist them to get compound bends. Take your time. Experiment with strips of varied thickness and try different bends and twists. Once you've got a pleasing curve, stand back, look it over from various angles and compare it to your model. The mock-up strip should describe fair, consistent curves with no unintended kinks, flat spots or quick turns. Don't be afraid to play around with the strip and form until you get just the curve you want.

Using the mock-up strip as a guide, you can now make the bending fixture from construction lumber (2x2s, 2x4s, plywood, etc.), fastened together with hot-melt glue and drywall screws. But first rebuild the end blocks, anchoring them with stouter stock, or at least reinforce them with corner blocks and screws. Then make a series of 2x2 braces and locate them on about $2\frac{1}{2}$-in. centers, as in the middle photos on the facing page. These braces will hold the curve's position in space and will also support the weight of the clamps. You should support the curve anywhere along its length where the weight of the clamps is liable to distort the bend. But if you use lightweight clamps, such as the rubber inner tubes and bolt-clamps I'll describe later, you won't need to brace the curve as stoutly. I like to keep 2x2s, screws and hot-melt glue handy during the glue-up to shore the curve if it sags unexpectedly. To keep from gluing the bend to the form, cover with masking tape those parts of the supports that may come in contact with glue. Mark the point at which your mock-up strip intersects the braces, so you'll have a way to line up the laminate stack when you make the actual bend. Then remove the mock-up strip from the form.

Clamping and gluing—Each compound curve calls for its own clamping scheme, depending on the severity of the curve and thickness and width of the laminae. Quick-action or C-clamps will work, but if you're attempting a large bend you may not have enough, or there may be insufficient space

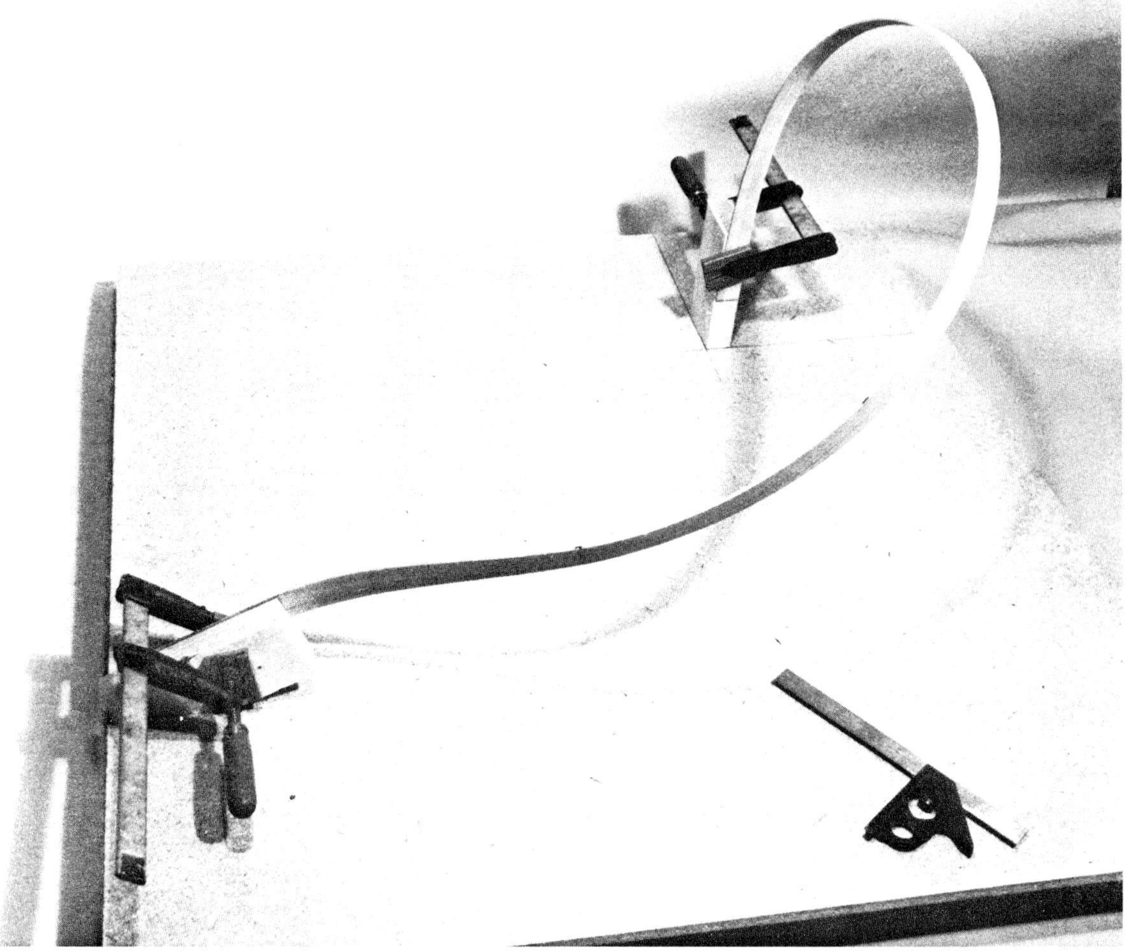

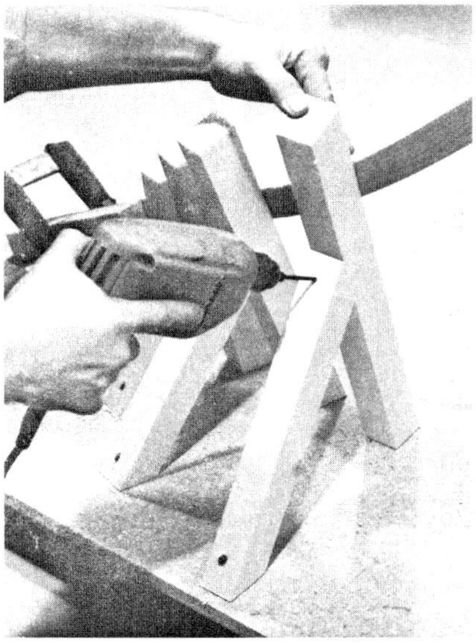

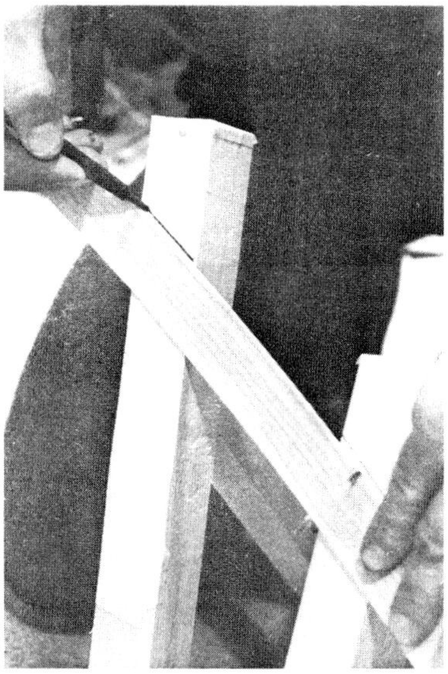

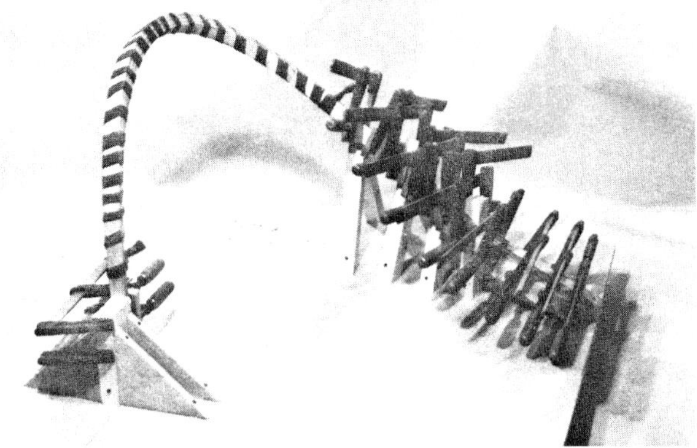

A mock-up strip determines the actual shape of the compound curve around which the bending form is built. Establish a base plane first, as in top photo—a piece of particleboard for small bends, the shop floor for larger ones—then tack down temporary anchor points. Clamp one end of the strip and start bending, twisting the strip to make it curve compoundly. When you've got the bend you want, build a form out of 2x2 lumber to support it. A scrap held against the bottom of the 2x2s, above left, provides reference for marking the base angles, which can then be cut on the bandsaw. Fasten the supports with hot-melt glue and screws, then add 2x2 braces for additional strength, above center. Before removing the mock-up strip, mark its position on the formwork, above right, so you'll be able to relocate the strips for the glue-up. Compound bending calls for clever use of clamps. For the bend shown at right, Stem used quick-action clamps, an old bicycle inner tube wrapped candy-cane fashion around the laminate stack, and shopmade bolt-clamps. Let glue cure overnight before you remove the bend from the form.

to fit them all in. Here are alternative clamping methods:

Cut the valve stems out of an old bicycle inner tube, tie off one end and wrap the tube around the laminae in a spiral, candy-cane fashion, stretching the tube as you pull it tight. Inner-tube clamps don't work well on laminations over 2¼ in. wide because the pressure bears mostly along the edges of the strips. Laminations wider than 2¼ in. can be clamped by this method if a ¼-in. thick strip is used as a batten between the inner tube and the laminae, as in the drawing at right. Rope or heavy string can be used similarly, though it doesn't have the elasticity. It is good for adding pressure to trouble spots.

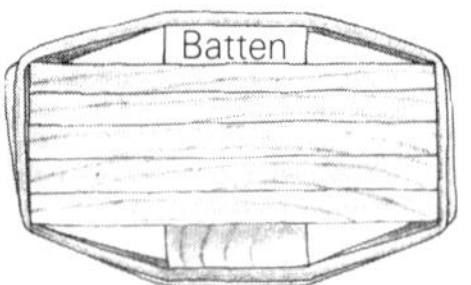

Lightweight, inexpensive clamps can be made of two 1-in. by 1-in. by 3½-in. wood bars connected by two ¼-in. or ⁵⁄₁₆-in. bolts or threaded rods, as in figure 3 on the facing page. A slot in the top bar allows the clamp to be put in place quickly, with both top nuts already started. Wax the wood parts to resist glue. The bolts can be spun on quickly using an electric drill fitted with the socket adapter shown in the drawing. As the laminae are bent, their edges will sometimes splay out of alignment, especially if clamps are tightened unequally. A handscrew, clamped across the edges of the

A platform fixture for a fancy table

by Baile Oakes

When I was commissioned to design and build the white ash dining table shown below, I worked out the forms and jigs as I went, starting with a sturdy, perfectly level platform fixture built of plywood and 2x4s, around which the bentwood table grew.

I first transferred to the fixture table a full-scale plan view of the bends that form the table's rails. Where the legs sweep up to join the rails, I fashioned a form and then anchored a single laminate strip which I bent and twisted until I got the leg shape I wanted. The legs were glued up by bending all the laminae at once, supported by a form of steel rods and angle iron. I put a strip of sheet metal between the clamps and the outermost laminae to spread clamping pressure and to protect the wood against marring.

So I would have less shaping to do, I tapered the leg laminae in a thickness sander, using a form similar to the one described in *FWW* #14 on p.*49. With complex compound bends like those on this table, I use epoxy glue from Chem-Tech, 4669 Cander Rd., Chagrin Falls, Ohio 44022—its 4-hr. working time is a necessary luxury because the bends take so long to complete. My shopmade clamps are similar to Seth Stem's, but instead of wood bars I use steel strap, angle or channel iron connected by ⁵⁄₁₆-in. machine bolts. To keep the laminae from splaying, I put the clamps in place finger-tight before I make the bend.

After the glue cures, I shape the laminae with a drawknife, Surform, spokeshave, file, cabinet scraper, and airbag sander, pretty much in that order. The table shown was dyed a rosewood color with powdered dyes and then finished with an oil/varnish mixture. □

Baile Oakes makes furniture in Westport, Calif. Photos by the author.

In compound-bend laminating, the bending form can sometimes be as involved as the object it's intended to produce. For this glass-topped white ash table, left, Oakes made a platform fixture from plywood and 2x4s. He made dozens of clamps out of steel strap, angle or channel iron connected by bolts or threaded rod.

*p.67 in this book

strips, will push the stack back into alignment.

The ideal glue for bent lamination should have a long working time and a high resistance to gradual slippage or cold creep, as the laminae try to straighten themselves out after the bend. The glue should also be sandable after curing, without it gumming up sandpaper or abrasive discs. An adhesive called Urac 185 (made by American Cyanamide) meets these requirements. It is sold in quarts and gallons by Nelson Paint Co., PO Box 907, Iron Mountain, Mich. 49801. Urea-formaldehyde glues (such as Weldwood's Plastic Resin) work nearly as well and are sold by most hardware stores. Urea-formaldehyde glues are powdered resins which, when mixed

Fig. 3: Shopmade clamp and socket wrench

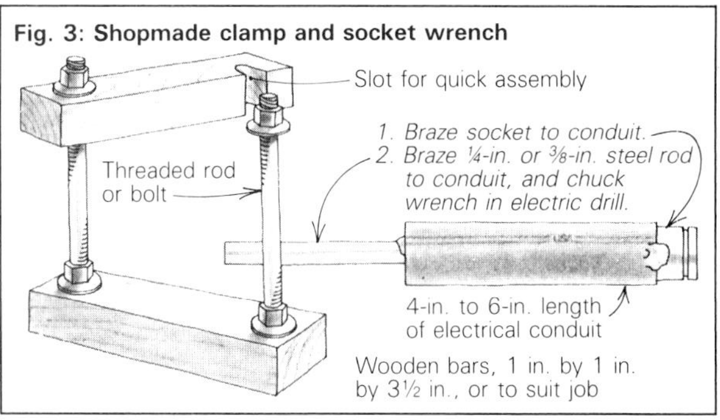
Slot for quick assembly
Threaded rod or bolt
1. Braze socket to conduit.
2. Braze ¼-in. or ⅜-in. steel rod to conduit, and chuck wrench in electric drill.
4-in. to 6-in. length of electrical conduit
Wooden bars, 1 in. by 1 in. by 3½ in., or to suit job

Bending with the help of steel hands

by Steve Foley

Playing around with a pliable strip of wood is an illuminating but sometimes frustrating way to arrive at compound curves. If you grab one end of a thin strip and start bending and twisting, any number of shapes will emerge—you'll sense, however, that even more would be possible if you could just grab the thing in the middle and give it a twist this way *and* that.

Having spent many hours yearning for more bodily appendages to do just that, I have developed this universally adjustable device which can lock onto various points of a wood strip twisted and curved in space. The idea is to bend a strip using the fixture as extra hands, and then build the necessary formwork around the strip to support clamps when you glue up more strips. This device is good for one-shot pieces, but I've also found it invaluable for building forms that can be reused.

All the materials were gotten from the local welding shop/junkyard—one of those places where they weld up leaky gas tanks with the gas still in them. You could substitute any kind of scrap parts you can get, so long as the device is adjustable yet rigid when all the parts are snugged down.

As the drawing shows, the fixture consists of a central column with adjustable telescoping arms that can be positioned anywhere to support a strip. Build as many collar-arm assemblies as you think you might need. Though my device is rather cumbersome, it works, especially with helical bends. And it was put together on a budget, always a preoccupation in the small shop. It can be modified for individual needs, and I'd like to hear about any improvements or refinements anyone can suggest. □

Steve Foley works wood in Lake Oswego, Ore.

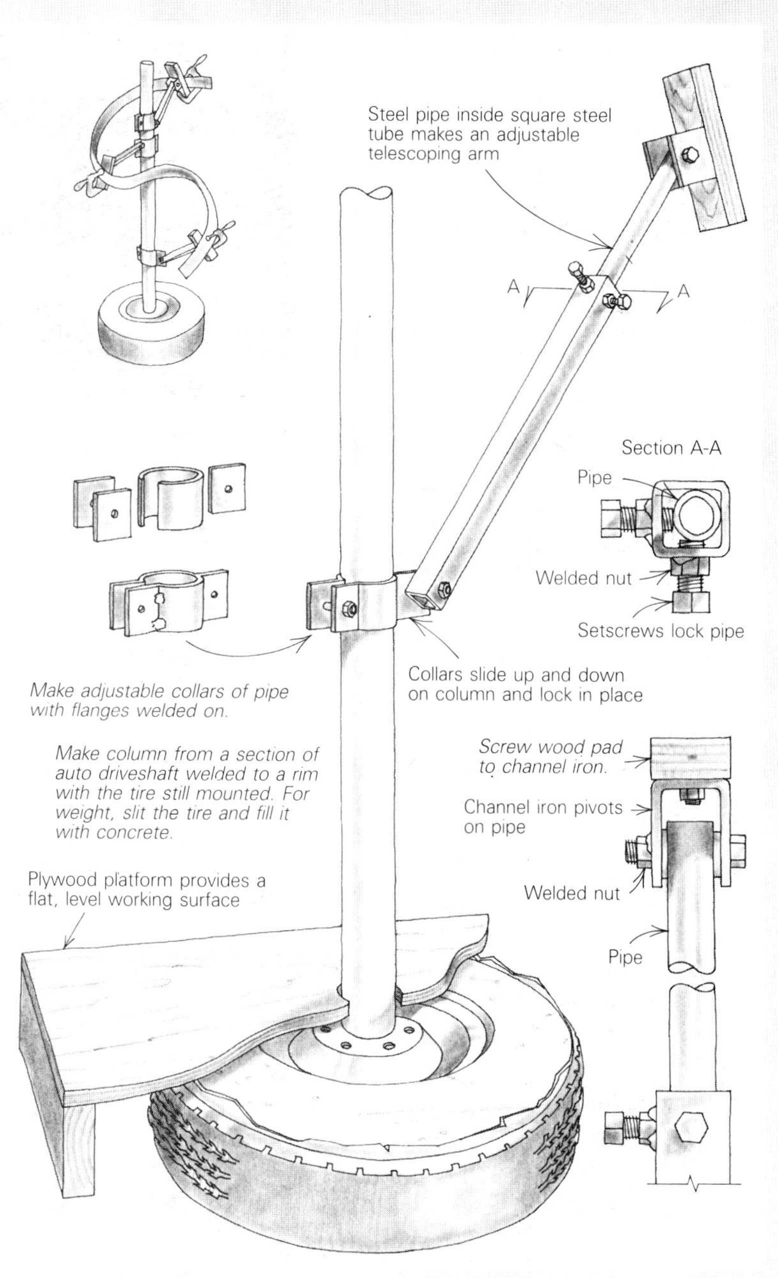
Steel pipe inside square steel tube makes an adjustable telescoping arm
A
A
Section A-A
Pipe
Welded nut
Setscrews lock pipe
Collars slide up and down on column and lock in place
Make adjustable collars of pipe with flanges welded on.
Make column from a section of auto driveshaft welded to a rim with the tire still mounted. For weight, slit the tire and fill it with concrete.
Screw wood pad to channel iron.
Channel iron pivots on pipe
Welded nut
Pipe
Plywood platform provides a flat, level working surface

with water, have a working time of about 20 minutes under normal conditions, less if you're working in a warm shop. Working time can be extended by chilling the glue in a refrigerator or by adding ice cubes to the mixture.

For a proper bond, the glue must be well mixed and lump-free. Also, make sure you store these glues in tightly sealed cans—premature contact with atmospheric moisture will crystallize the powder, ruining its bonding qualities. You could use yellow glue (aliphatic resin), but it is thermoplastic and thus quickly gums up and ruins sanding discs and belts. I never use white glue; it has little resistance to cold creep.

Glue-up is messy work. I suggest you do it on a bench covered with newspaper or plastic. With a brush or a 2-in. wide paint roller, apply glue to both sides of all but the outermost two laminate strips.

When all the strips are coated, align their edges and clamp one end of the stack in the form. As you make the bend, the glue-coated strips will resist, but you'll feel them sliding past each other as they seek mechanical equilibrium. Continue the bend, lining the strips up with the marks on the supports. Take your time—don't force the wood where it doesn't want to go, or you'll open up gaps between the strips.

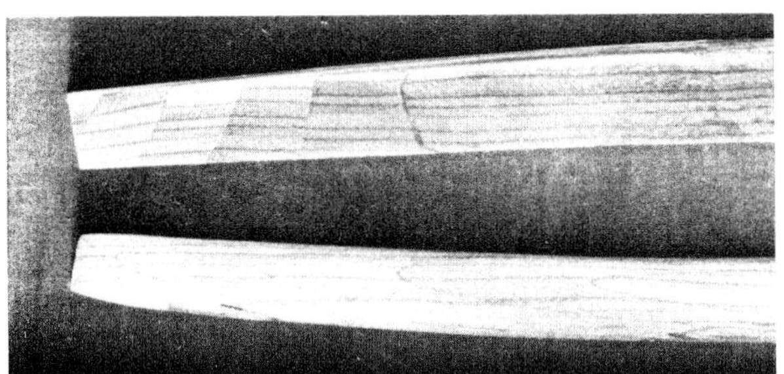

A graceful, dramatic compound bend can be ruined by insensitive shaping. Angular shaping of the top lamination in this photo has exposed gluelines and reveals a discordant grain pattern. The lower one was rounded and the resulting shape is more harmonious with the wood's figure.

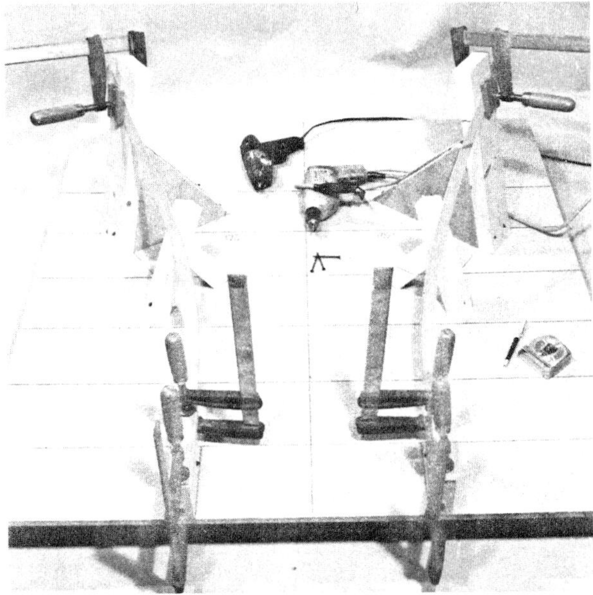

Furniture often wants symmetrical or mirror-opposite bends, for looks and strength. To make such bends, draw a grid on the formwork base as in the photo above, and locate the supports for both curves on the same lateral lines, equidistant from the grid's centerline.

Start clamping at one end of the bend and proceed to the other, thus forcing out gaps between strips. With inner-tube clamps, wrap the strips before you actually make the bend. This will reduce splaying and will also make tighter radii possible (the inner-tube wrapping supports the outer strips against breaking, and since the inner tubes stretch during the bend, they apply more clamping pressure). But bend *slowly*, so the individual strips can slide by each other to conform to the curve.

When the curve is all clamped up, check for open gluelines and use your finger to scrape off the oozing glue. Close any gaps with additional clamps.

Clamping time depends on temperature and humidity. Urac 185 and urea-formaldehyde adhesives will usually cure overnight. Check the cure with a chisel. If the hardened squeeze-out chips like glass, it's set; if it dents or gives, don't remove the clamps, or delamination is likely.

Shaping and sanding—After the glue has set, remove the clamps and unwrap the inner tubes. Sand off excess glue with a 16-grit to 36-grit abrasive disc on a body grinder or on an electric drill. Be careful not to remove too much material at this point. Once the glue has been cleaned off, you can further shape and refine your bend with a #49 cabinetmakers' rasp or a half-round Surform plane, followed by a cabinet scraper. Be sensitive about your shaping, however. Cutting into the face of the laminae is likely to reveal unattractive, randomly spaced gluelines. Better to use soft-edged, rounded shaping that will produce forms more sympathetic to the wood's grain patterns and to the shapes you are likely to build using this method of lamination.

Drawknives, spokeshaves, planes, knives and other edge tools can be used for shaping, though I prefer abrasive tools, especially for initial cleanup. Holding a bend for shaping sometimes calls for resourcefulness, but a quick-action clamp or a patternmakers' vise will usually do.

One or more completed bends can be joined together with conventional joints such as a mortise and tenon or a spline. As you would expect, these joints are difficult to lay out, so I prefer to simply design my bends so that they merge smoothly and can be glued long-grain to long-grain. For a better glue joint, flats can be planed on the bends along the length of the joint.

Used singly or joined together, laminated shapes can be strong elements—visual and structural—of chairs, cabinets, tables and other functional furniture. Before I learned this technique, I felt my woodworking constrained by method—my designs were too often dictated by the processes I was familiar with and, in retrospect, I had a lesser understanding of what wood as a material is truly capable of. Now I have a larger technical vocabulary with which to express my ideas, and one flat plane fitted into another is only a small part. □

Seth Stem teaches furniture design and construction at the Rhode Island School of Design in Providence, R.I. Photos by the author; drawings by David Dann. Two books on lamination are Tage Frid Teaches Woodworking: Shaping, Veneering, Finishing, *by Tage Frid, published by The Taunton Press; and* The Wendell Castle Book of Wood Lamination, *by Wendell Castle, published by Van Nostrand Reinhold Co.*

Form-laminating chair legs—*I want to make a chair with laminated legs shaped like a squared-off question mark. How do I make the forms? In what order should I make and glue the bends?*

—*Ettore Zuccarino, Deerfield, Ill.*

TAGE FRID REPLIES: First, make up a two-piece jig to fit the shape you want to laminate, as shown. Screw it to a plywood

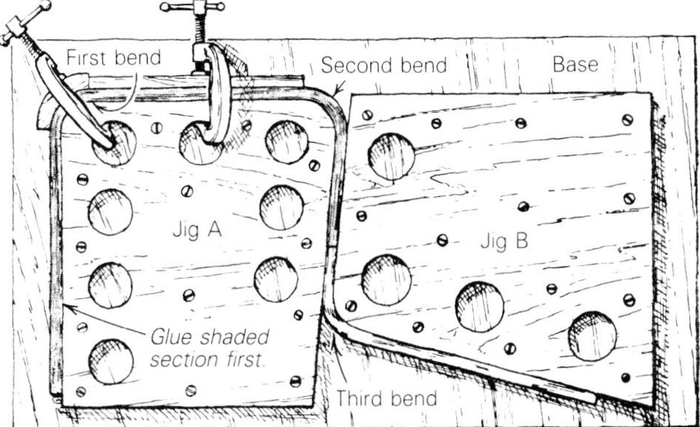
First bend
Second bend
Base
Jig A
Jig B
Glue shaded section first.
Third bend

or particleboard base. Make the space between the two jig parts exactly the thickness of the lamination and cut holes in the jigs for clamps. Wax the jigs and base to keep the laminae from sticking. Use wood as thin as possible, such as $\frac{1}{10}$-in.-thick veneer, so you won't have to steam it.

Begin by removing jig **B**. Apply glue to all the laminae that are shaded in the drawing, leaving the rest of the lamination straight for now. Clamp the leg on the top of jig **A** first, make the first two bends, and put clamps down each side of the jig. At the bends, make up a curved caul whose inside radius matches the outside radius of the bend; make it flat on the outside to give the clamp a solid bearing surface. Use as many clamps as you can and make sure you have good, tight gluelines. After the first glue-up has cured, remove the leg from jig **A**. Apply glue to the remaining laminae, using compressed air or a vacuum cleaner if needed to force it between the pieces. Put the leg back around jig **A**, screw down jig **B** and make the third bend. Remove jig **A** and clamp the leg, starting where you applied fresh glue. A clamp somewhere along the straight section of jig **B** will hold the leg in place while you remove jig **A** and set the rest of the clamps. I suggest a slow-curing glue such as urea-formaldehyde.

Making period legs—*The turned front legs on some late-Sheraton chairs and the square tapered legs on some Hepplewhite tables are bent at the bottom. What's the best way to make these legs?* —*Kenneth Glover, Mt. Pleasant, S.C.*

CARLYLE LYNCH REPLIES: Bend the round Sheraton chair legs after turning and reeding. This isn't hard when they are turned from green stock riven from the log, which is less liable to break while bending.

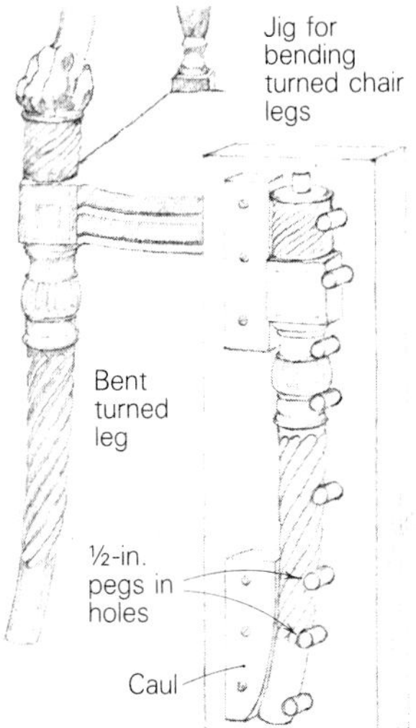
Jig for bending turned chair legs
Bent turned leg
½-in. pegs in holes
Caul

Make a bending form from a piece of 2x6; two cauls form the curve, and holes and pegs wedge the leg to the cauls. Make the cauls with a radius slightly smaller than the one desired, as the leg will spring back when removed from the form.

Steam the leg until it's pliable (see page 16), then place it on the bending jig, put in the first peg, and test the wood's pliancy. If the leg is not soft and yielding, steam it a bit longer. Bend the leg around the form, put in all the pegs, and let the piece dry for a few days.

Cut the curve in the square, tapered Hepplewhite table legs on the bandsaw. You'll need two patterns: one for the sides, and one for the front and back.

Follow-up: Form-laminating chair legs—I didn't quite agree with Tage Frid's answer to Ettore Zuccarino. During the seven years I spent doing nothing but designing and building plywood strip-laminated chairs, I developed some quick mold methods. The drawing at right shows my approach.

Make an open mold raised on a 2x4 rack. The underside of the glued-up parts will be open to the air, which speeds curing, and this gives you room to tighten the clamp handles. Also, the two parts of the mold can be "keyed" so they'll line up correctly for glue-up. A cheap way to build this mold is to draw the shape on any thickness of plywood you have around, and then build it up to the desired thickness with 2x4 scraps. Glue and nail the whole mess together, then bandsaw the mold sections to the final shape. Be careful not to put nails where you'll be sawing. To smooth out roughess left by the bandsaw, line the molds with birch doorskin material.

Curved cauls at the corners distribute pressure unevenly and this can break the laminae. The solution is to progressively clamp small sections of the curve to the mold with small, straight cauls, fitting in as many as you can to make the bend. Once the bend has been made and a clamp placed at each end of it, you can clamp the curved caul in place.

—*Michael Graham, Santa Barbara, Calif.*

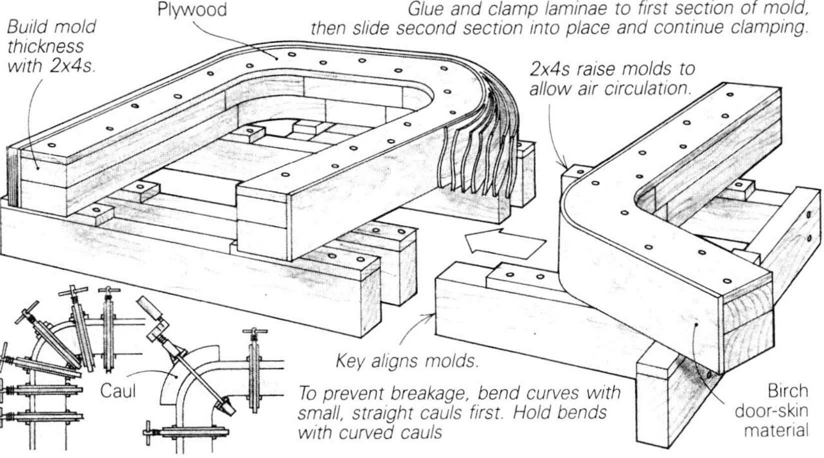
Plywood
Build mold thickness with 2x4s.
Glue and clamp laminae to first section of mold, then slide second section into place and continue clamping.
2x4s raise molds to allow air circulation.
Key aligns molds.
Caul
To prevent breakage, bend curves with small, straight cauls first. Hold bends with curved cauls
Birch door-skin material

Drawings: David Dann

Cross-Country Skis, the Easy Way

by George Mustoe

Though it took me a long time to make the discovery, cross-country skis are relatively simple to make. Ski building originally seemed intimidating because of the numerous laminations and the long curve from the tips through the arched or "cambered" bottom. However, in a recent and inexplicable attack of common sense, I stumbled upon a simple method for building skis that requires only a bare minimum of materials and effort. Based on 1980 prices, a pair of skis will cost about $20 for materials.

Preparing the laminations—Figure 1 shows a ski whose upper and lower surfaces, along with the thin wedge that fortifies the tail, are made from hardwood; hickory is most common, but birch, ash and oak work well too. Select straight-grained lumber with no knots, cracks or other defects. The two core laminations are of softwood to minimize weight; spruce, cedar, fir or pine will do. The final ski will be a compromise between a heavy, mountain touring ski and a light, racing model. However, you can modify the thickness of the inner layers to obtain just about any degree of durability and rigidity.

Saw the hardwood strips to a thickness of ⅛ in. and the softwood core strips to a thickness of 3/16 in., both from stock 2½ in. wide. Plane and sand the sawn surfaces smooth.

The lamination lengths given in figure 1 will vary depending upon the length of your ski. Feel free to experiment; significant variation exists among the various commercial brands, so if your skis come out looking unusual, just act smug. Starting about 6 in. from the ends, plane the core layers to a gradual taper so they will make a smooth joint.

The bending form—This form consists of three separate units: the base plate, the T-shaped form used for the main body of the ski, and the form used to bend the tip (figure 2a). When in use these three parts are bolted together into a single unit. To manufacture skis of other lengths you will have to make other main body forms. However, the same base plate and tip-bending form can be used regardless of the ski length.

The base plate is made from a length of warp-free 1x4 lumber, at least 4 ft. long. Glue or nail several pairs of wooden blocks to it for attaching the main body with machine bolts.

The main body form is also made from a warp-free 1x4. Draw an outline of the ski bottom along one edge of the board. The recommended method is simply to trace the contour of a commercially made ski. If a ski of the appropriate length is not available, don't be afraid to make your own pattern. The main consideration is that you include a reasonable amount of curvature, or camber. You can draw a smooth curve by tracing along a thin strip of wood bent around a series of tacks in the body-form blank (figure 2b). Cut along the line using a jigsaw or coping saw, and smooth with a plane and a sanding block. Make sure this surface is square with the sides of the board.

Once the correct outline has been shaped, cut a number of notches at 4-in. to 6-in. intervals for inserting C-clamps during lamination. The form is completed by nailing on a 2¼-in. wide piece of ¼-in. plywood (figure 2c). Align the center of the plywood with the 1x4. The result is a form that is T-shaped in cross section. The upper surface is only ¼ in. thick, thus only small C-clamps are needed to assemble a ski.

The form used to bend the curved tip consists of a sandwich made from three layers of ¾-in. thick solid lumber or plywood (figure 2d). The curvature can be copied from a commercially made ski, or it can be drawn freehand. Try to achieve a smooth curve that rises about 2½ in. vertically in a horizontal distance of about 8 in. Note that the tip form is designed so that it slips over the front end of the main body form as shown.

Assemble the base plate, tip form and main body form using machine bolts. Sand the upper surface and apply one or more coats of shellac or varnish. When the finish has dried, rub on a coat of paste wax, to prevent the ski from sticking to the form during lamination.

Lamination—Begin by sorting out the pieces of wood you will need to build one ski. Dampen the first 12 in. or so of the hardwood strips using a rag dipped in hot water. This will reduce the amount of force needed to bend the curved tip. Coat one surface of each strip with glue, and place the resulting sandwich on the bending form, aligning one edge of the wood strips with one edge of the form. The strips should extend slightly beyond either end of the form. Tighten the clamps of the tip form so that the two hardwood layers are pressed against the form surface. Coat with glue both surfaces of the softwood core layers and the wedge-shaped tail piece, and slide them into position between the two hardwood layers. Use C-clamps with wooden pads to press all of these strips against the form. If you don't have enough C-clamps, you can cut C-shaped forms from scrap plywood that will slip over the clamping platform of the main body form (figure 3). Wedges between these C-shaped forms and the laminations will provide adequate clamping pressure. Avoid excessive pressure that would squeeze out too much glue and produce a weak bond. Remove exuded glue with a damp rag to make clean-up easier. Leave the ski on the form for about 12 hours to allow the glue to harden completely, although this time will vary according to the room temperature. Do not remove the ski from the form until you are certain that the glue has thoroughly cured.

Shaping—Use a coping saw or jigsaw to cut the tip to a point and to trim the tail to the exact length. Sand the ski to remove glue stains, and if necessary plane the edges parallel.

Next cut the center groove in the ski bottom using a router with an edge guide. This groove serves as a rudder to keep the ski pointed straight ahead as it glides through the snow; on most models the groove begins about 12 in. back from the tip of the ski for maneuverability. A straight, ½-in. dia. bit can be used for this task, setting the depth to about 3/32 in. Alternately, a core-box bit having rounded corners will make a more professional-looking groove.

Finally, it is necessary to plane the edges of the ski to obtain the proper

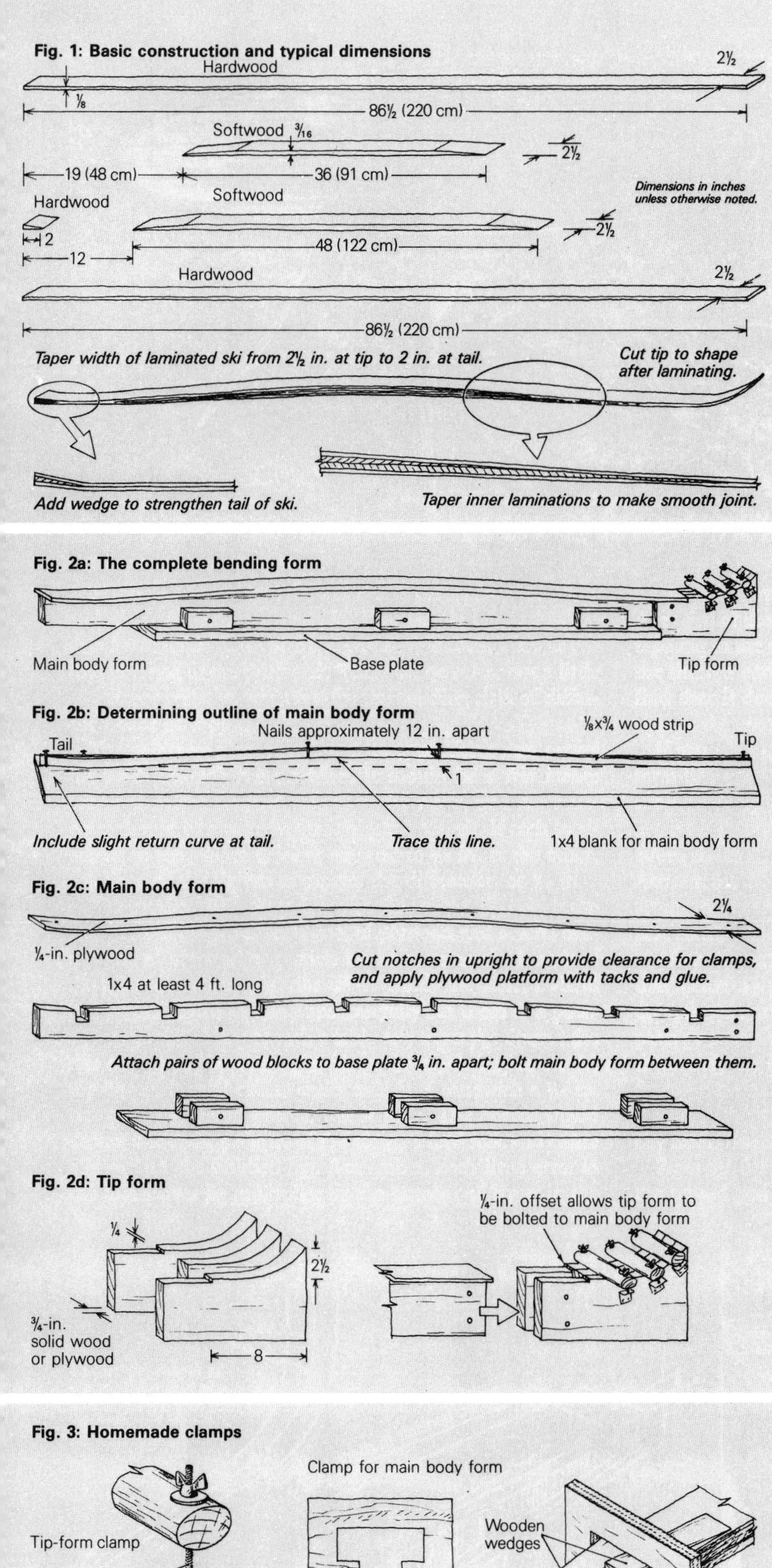

Drawings: Christopher Clapp

amount of side cut; the ski should be about ½-in. narrower at the tail than at the forward end, and the outline should be gently concave. Also relieve the bottom surface of the tail to produce a slight upswing that will enhance maneuverability. Perform whatever final sanding is necessary to remove tool marks or surface blemishes, then apply two or three coats of clear gloss varnish, sanding lightly between coats. Do not varnish the bottom surface of the ski, since this would prevent proper adhesion of ski wax. Instead, treat the bottom with a commercial base preparation such as pine tar.

Alternately, waxless skis can be made by routing the soles for mohair strips or multistep plastic bases. Both these materials are available from ski shops or the manufacturer—Rossignol, Industrial Ave., Williston, Vt. 05455.

To mount bindings, first locate the balance point of the ski by placing it across the edge of a thin wood strip. Pin bindings should be mounted so the leading edge of the binding is about 1 in. in front of the balance point. Heavy cable bindings should be placed on the ski in approximate position before determining the balance point. Then move the bindings slightly forward. When bindings are properly placed the ski tip should point downward at about a 20° angle when the user lifts the boot.

Now that your skis are completed, you can easily check the performance—just take them skiing. But before you leave the house it's possible to determine how well the degree of camber matches your weight. Place the skis side by side on a smooth floor, inserting a piece of paper between the skis and the floor directly beneath where your feet will be placed. Now stand on the skis as if you were actually out on a trail. If the paper can still be slid sideways with only slight friction, the camber is perfect. If it's not, there's not much you can do about it, except make adjustments in length and thickness of laminations in your next pair. But try your skis out first. Most cross-country skiers can tell little difference in performance from slight variations in ski lengths or degrees of camber. A less-than-perfect fit need not limit your fun. □

George Mustoe is a part-time geology technician and woodworker who lives in Bellingham, Wash.

Cross-Country Skis, Norwegian Style

by Richard Starr

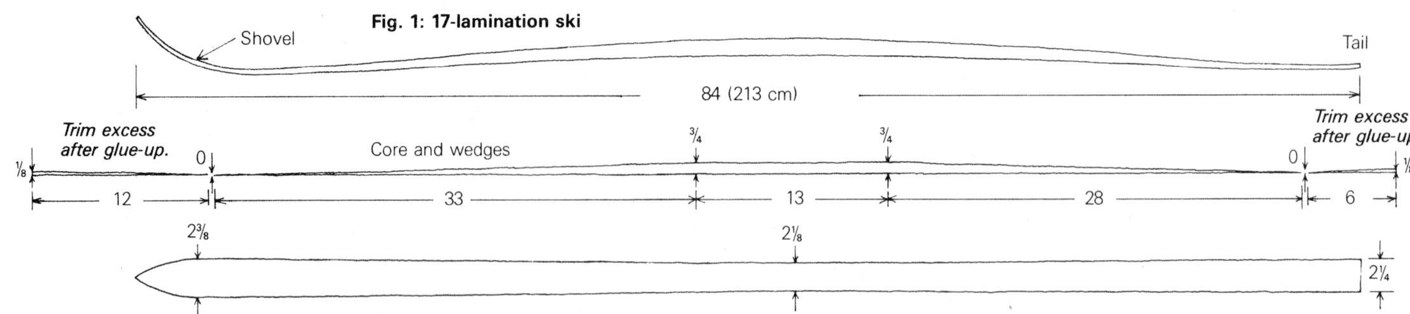

Walker Weed of Etna, N.H., has been making his family's cross-country skis since he learned the method in Norway some years ago. He taught the method at Dartmouth College where, until his recent retirement, he was director of the craft shops.

In the old days, when skis were of solid wood steambent to shape, you could stiffen your ski by rebending it to a deeper camber. Laminated skis hold their shape much longer than solid skis, but no adjustment is possible once the ski is glued together. The degree of stiffness must be accounted for during construction, and depends not only on camber but also on laminate thickness, type of wood and character of the particular pieces you use. There is an element of trial and error in learning to make well-tuned wooden skis. Modern skis, usually a combination of plastics or wood and plastics, perform better and require much less maintenance than those made of wood. You can buy a better ski than you can make, though high-quality skis are expensive. You'll save money and get extra satisfaction from running trails if you make the skis yourself.

Weed's method is a bit more complex than Mustoe's (page 82), but it produces stronger, lighter skis in pairs that will match more closely in balance and flexibility. This is achieved by laminating the ski across its width as well as across its thickness, and by systematic placement of matching laminations (figure 1). Also, the tips are reinforced with an extra lamination, and the sides of the softwood core are protected with strips of hardwood.

Weed uses hickory soles for toughness and birch tops to save weight. If you were to make both surfaces of the same wood, you could saw all four pieces for a pair of skis from a single piece of laminated stock. If you use different woods you must glue up separate pieces for tops and soles.

To make a 210-cm ski, the average size for adults, begin with a piece of straight-grained hardwood at least 86 in. long, 3½ in. wide, and an inch or so in thickness, depending on the thickness of your sawblade and on how many parts you will need from the lamination. Witness-mark the face of the board (figure 2), then rip it into six strips slightly more than ½ in. wide so that jointing or thickness-planing the sawn surfaces will yield ½-in. wide stock. Lay the strips in their original relationship according to the witness mark, then turn alternate strips end for end and upside down. By doing this you will distribute variations in grain and density through the lamination, resulting in a stronger ski. Glue the strips with a plastic resin glue (for example, Weldwood plastic resin).

When the glue has dried, you have a lamination 3 in. wide and an inch or so in thickness. Witness-mark a side and an end of the lamination, then joint one face and thickness-plane its opposite face. Saw a strip $^3/_{16}$ in. thick from one face, plane the newly exposed face of the lamination and saw off the next strip. If you are using a single laminated blank for soles and tops, number the strips as they come off and use adjacent pieces in matching positions in each ski. Plane each strip ⅛ in. thick, backing it with a piece of plywood while planing.

The stock for the core is 76 in. long, 3 in. wide and 2 in. thick, laminated across the 3-in. width. Out of this will come two blanks ¾ in. thick. The center is three ½-in. wide softwood strips (spruce is best), with outer layers of ¾-in. wide hardwood. You make this lamination from scraps, but for maximum strength and match, flip the central softwood strip end for end, as in the procedure described above, and use hardwood cut from the same board and arranged as shown in figure 3. After gluing, saw the lamination across the gluelines and plane the two pieces to ¾ in. by 3 in. by 74 in.

Cut the wedges and cores from these strips using the dimensions in figure 1. Supported on a wedge made from scrap, Weed puts these pieces through a thickness planer to get a perfect taper feathered down to zero thickness. (See Jere Osgood's article on tapered lamination, pages 66 to 69.)

Weed's bending form (figure 4) is simpler than Mustoe's, though it requires more material and larger clamps. Laminate a block of solid or fir plywood 3 in. by 7½ in. by 90 in. Square it up, then scribe the shape of a good ski on the wide face. After bandsawing, smooth the curved surfaces, checking across the curve for squareness to the sides. Cut a series of steps on the front end as clamp seats, screw five or six aligning blocks along each side and wax everything likely to come in contact with glue. To clear the clamp ends, rest the form on horses or support it off the workbench on blocks. Weed suggests using a clamp every 3 in. or closer. If you run short, make clamps from hardwood strips and carriage bolts as shown in figure 4. From ¼-in. plywood scraps, cut 3-in. wide strips and butt them up against one

Drawings: Christopher Clapp

another to cover the length of the ski and protect it from clamp damage.

When using Weldwood plastic resin, you should always be sure to dampen the wood with a rag to avoid dehydrating the glue. Apply adhesive to both surfaces with a brush and be sure to leave no dry spots. Clamp the ski from one end to the other or from the middle toward the ends, but never at random. Be sure the witness marks (top and edge) of corresponding pieces are in the same positions when gluing up the second ski.

Rather than scraping and chipping off dried glue, Weed saves time by belt-sanding it off, since plastic resins don't clog sandpaper. With the cleaned edge bearing on the table saw fence, he trims the other edge straight, using a carbide-tipped blade. Then, reversing the ski and setting the fence in a little, the sanded edge is sawn clean and straight. The ski now has parallel edges.

To cut the round-bottom groove in the bottom surface to help the ski track straight, Weed uses a molding head on a table saw (figure 5). The groove must be less than ⅛ in. deep to avoid cutting through the bottom lamination, and should be about ½ in. wide; a cutter whose radius is ½ in. will do the trick. Clamp a board about 8 in. wide to the saw as shown in figure 5, and raise the running cutter up through it; the board functions as a short table to accommodate the ski's camber. Set the fence so the groove is centered on the ski, and check the depth setting on a piece of scrap. The ski's groove starts just behind the shovel and ends just before the tail; mark these positions on the ski's top. By matching these marks with lines on the saw fence indicating the position of the cutter, you can start and end the groove quite accurately.

Relieving the sides to produce a concave contour in plan gives better edge bite in the snow and assures that the track cut by the shovel is wider than the rest of the ski. It is usually a gentle curve rather than a straight taper. You can take three width dimensions from an old ski, at the shovel, foot and tail, or use measurements given in figure 1. Be sure that the side camber is centered on the groove, and use a long, flexible batten through the three points to get a smooth curve. Bandsaw the sides, cut the tip shape, and smooth all edges with spokeshave and sandpaper. Chamfer the top corners but leave the bottom corners square. □

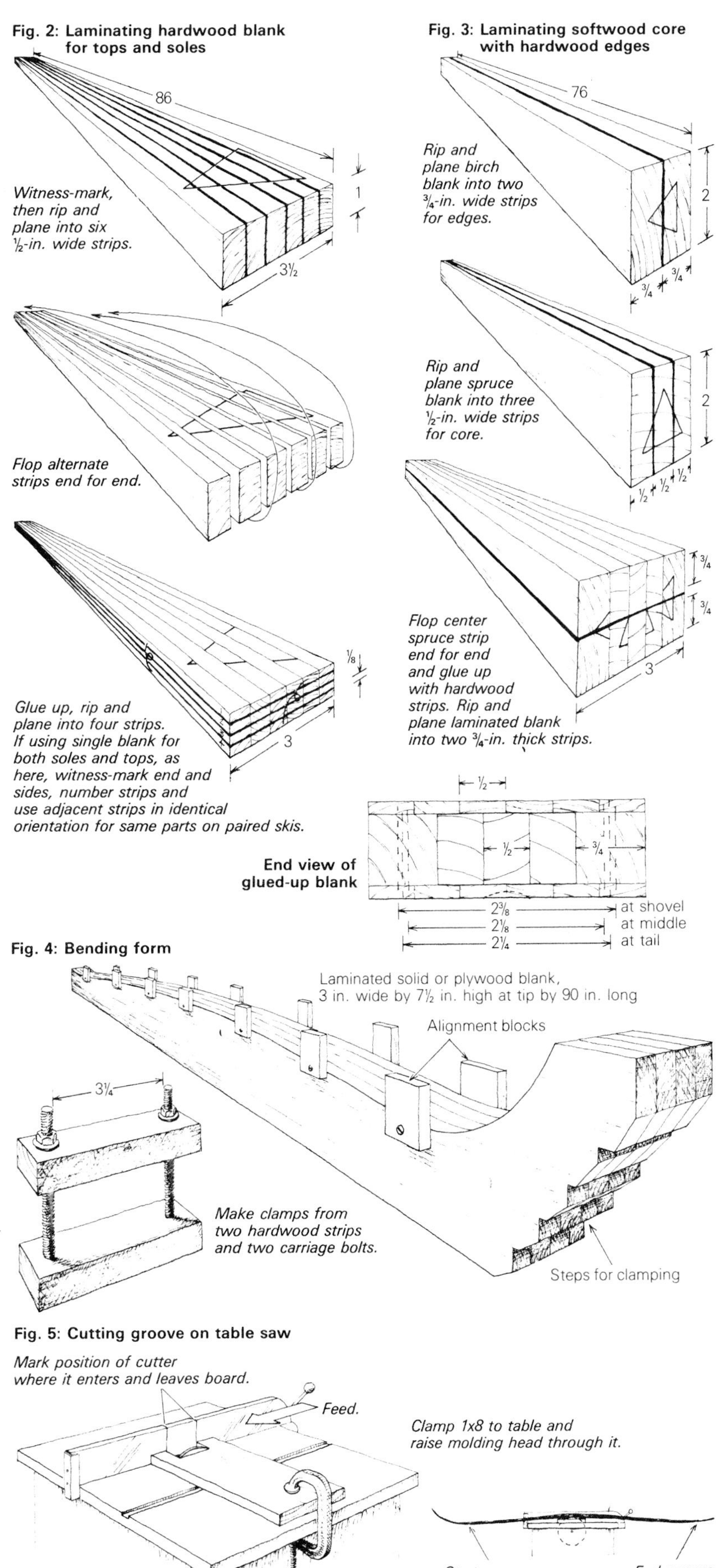

Fig. 2: Laminating hardwood blank for tops and soles
86
1
3½
Witness-mark, then rip and plane into six ½-in. wide strips.
Flop alternate strips end for end.
⅛
3
Glue up, rip and plane into four strips. If using single blank for both soles and tops, as here, witness-mark end and sides, number strips and use adjacent strips in identical orientation for same parts on paired skis.
Fig. 3: Laminating softwood core with hardwood edges
76
2
¾
Rip and plane birch blank into two ¾-in. wide strips for edges.
Rip and plane spruce blank into three ½-in. wide strips for core.
½
Flop center spruce strip end for end and glue up with hardwood strips. Rip and plane laminated blank into two ¾-in. thick strips.
End view of glued-up blank
2⅜ at shovel
2⅛ at middle
2¼ at tail
Fig. 4: Bending form
Laminated solid or plywood blank, 3 in. wide by 7½ in. high at tip by 90 in. long
Alignment blocks
3¼
Make clamps from two hardwood strips and two carriage bolts.
Steps for clamping
Fig. 5: Cutting groove on table saw
Mark position of cutter where it enters and leaves board.
Feed.
Clamp 1x8 to table and raise molding head through it.
Start groove.
End groove.

Bending a Tray

An experiment with lamination

by Jere Osgood

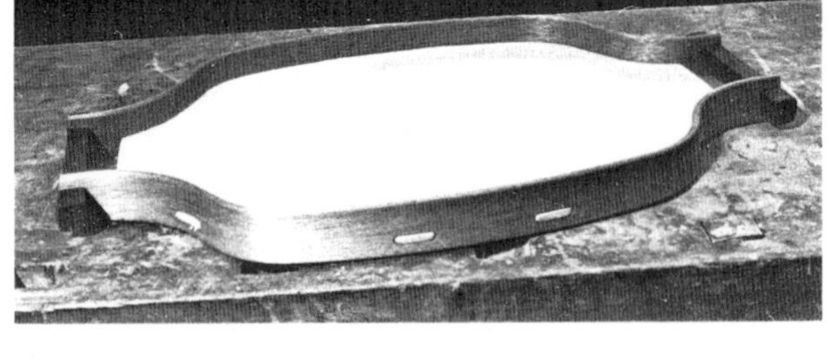

The serving tray described here is designed to introduce the woodworker to bending a simple lamination. The project is small and easily modified to suit your own taste, yet making it will give you the experience you need to apply the process to your own work. It can be made entirely with hand tools and clamps, although a table saw and a band saw or jigsaw are a great help.

The tray is symmetrical and combines a plan view of the work with the form layout. The curve is constructed by swinging a series of arcs with the centers and radii shown below. The important thing in making any two-part form is taking accurate account of the full thickness of the laminates and form liners (drawing and text, page 65). Because the curve of this project need not be absolutely precise, I have simplified the drawing process by using the outside line of the bent side as the face line of the concave half of the form. This means accounting for the total thickness of the liners on the convex half of the form. Where you need precision, you would construct the form drawing by dividing the total thickness of the liners, half on each side of the piece itself. In any case, you need a full-size shop drawing from which to make the form.

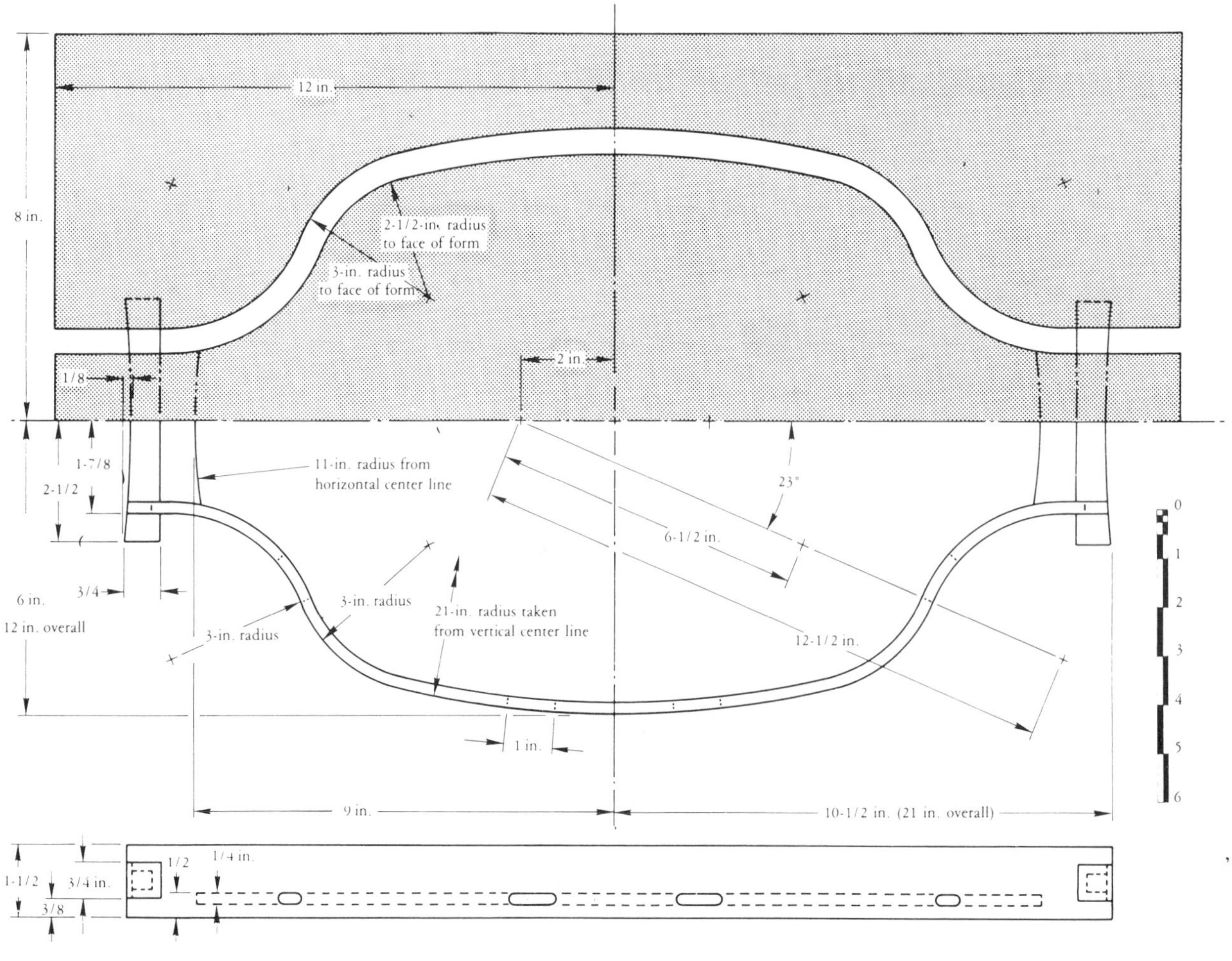

The bottom panel of the tray, shown in the photo at the top of the next page, does not lend itself to solid wood construction and is best made of good-quality plywood; I used 1/4-in. birch ply. The handles are of walnut and the sides are four laminations of 1/16-in. mahogany. This thickness turns the 3-in. radius well and the four layers are enough to minimize springback. Commercial veneers of 1/28 in., 1/30 in. or 1/40 in. could be used, but they are not the best because they often acquire lumps and bumps during glue-up. If you can't find thicker veneer, you can saw it from an 8/4 board on the table saw, using a hollow-ground planer blade or a carbide-tipped blade. Resawn stock might require five thinner layers to produce the 1/4-in. thickness, because it does not always bend as easily as sliced veneer.

To line the form I used four layers of 1/16-in. Formica, two on each side of the laminates, and the package totaled 1/2 in. You need to prepare your stock and form liners and measure the package before you can draw the line for the second half of the mold. Instead of plastic laminate liners, you can use an extra layer of veneers, springy metal, or, for shallow bends, Masonite. But if the material is bondable remember to insert paper or to wax the liners, or the whole business might just stick together.

The form shown at right, bandsawn but with the waste left in place for the photograph, is made of two layers of 3/4-in. veneer-core plywood. You could use particle board, a stack of Masonite, or even 2x10 lumber. But it is better to avoid solid wood with a strong grain pattern because the band-saw blade will track off the pencil line with variations in the density of the wood. Make the form as thick as the finished height of the bent sides, in this case 1-1/2 in., and make the stock to be bent a little oversize, perhaps 1-3/4 in., to allow for misalignment in gluing.

The glue I used was American Cyanamid's Urac 185, which is excellent for laminating (available from Nelson Paint Co.; see page 79 for address). You could also use Weldwood plastic resin glue, which is water-resistant, or even Franklin's Titebond (yellow glue) if you don't mind a little springback when the wood is removed from the form. But avoid white glue as it doesn't resist water and it creeps. Arrange the form on the clamps as shown, and double-spread each glue line with brush or roller. With the stock and liners in place, alternately tighten the center clamp and the two end clamps to bring the two halves together. A little glue should squeeze out all along each glue line. Tap the form with a hammer to keep everything aligned in the same plane. When doing any kind of laminating leave the clamps on overnight, longer if the workshop is chilly.

When both sides are glued and dry, clamp the wood to the convex half of the form, clean off the glue with an old rasp, and use a smooth plane to level one edge, as shown below. Turn it over so the finished edge rests flat on the bench and rasp and plane away whatever sticks up above the form to reach finished width.

Now carefully mark off and cut the sides to length. The tray bottom is held in the sides by four tabs in mortises, and the mortises are a little wider inside than outside. One mortise on each side will have to be pared at assembly in order to

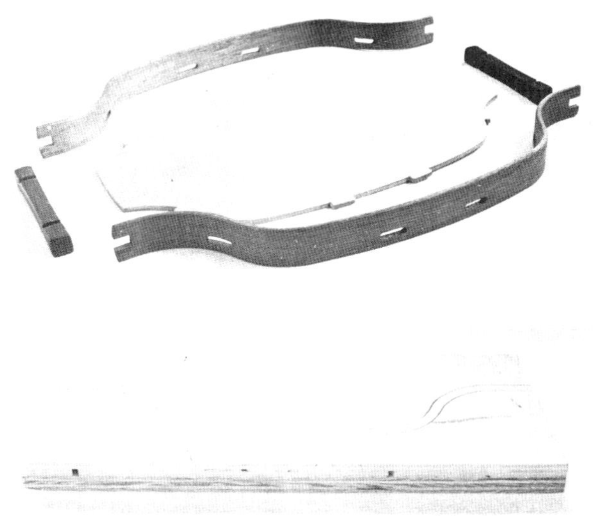

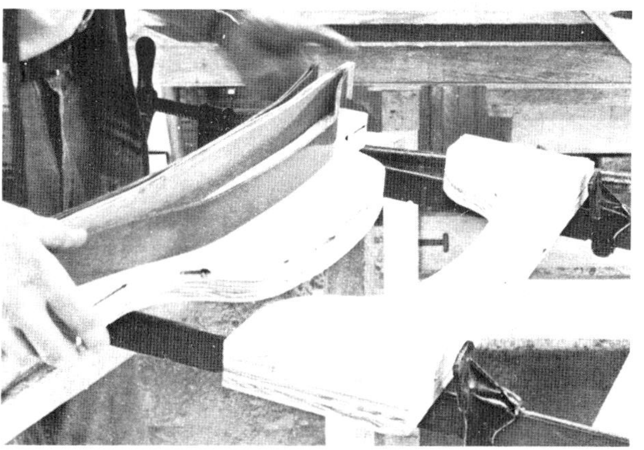

snap the bottom into place. The easiest way to lay them out is to place the side pieces on the shop drawing and transfer the marks, on both the inside and outside, and square them across the wood. The width of the mortise is laid out with a double-pin marking gauge, or a single one set twice; check the thickness of your plywood because commercial stock is noted for being only approximately 1/4 in. thick. The tabs must fit tightly. I used an eggbeater drill with a twist bit to take out the waste, starting with the two end holes and then the ones in between. Use a bit a little smaller than the tab thickness because the holes may wander and it is easy to clean up to size with rattail and straight files. Put masking tape on the back before drilling—it will minimize splitting.

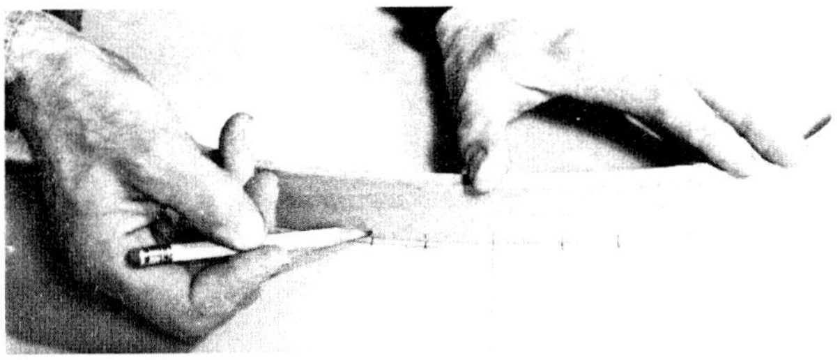

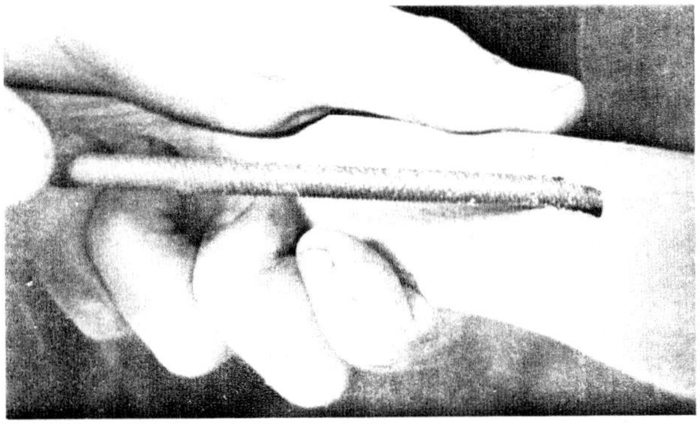

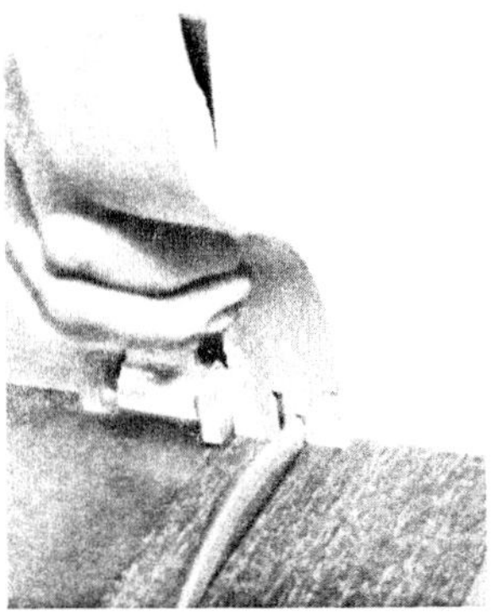

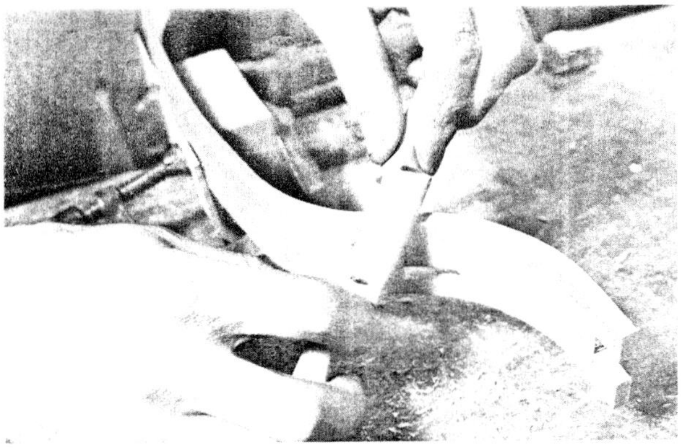

This joint is a through mortise and tenon, and I made the ends of the tenon flush with the outer surface and sanded all the edges slightly round. There are variations. The mortise could be squared off instead of being left round from the drilling, or the plywood tabs could be extra long and pinned with a tiny wedge to emphasize the joint. Or the tabs could be eliminated entirely by fitting the bottom into a shallow groove cut all around the sides with a scratch-stock.

The other joints to be cut in each side are the slots for the handles. I made them 3/8 in. wide and 3/4 in. deep, cutting the sides with the piece held vertically on the table saw and then chopping the ends with a chisel. Then I used a small spokeshave to round the top and bottom edges of the side pieces to a radius of about 1/8 in. It is best to put a radius on an edge like this, to accommodate wear.

I cut the matching dadoes in the handles (bottom photo) while the stock was still square, taking care to get a good fit as there is not much area for long-grain gluing. Then I rasped the handles slightly concave to give a better feel to the hand.

The next step is to lay out and cut the plywood panel. The way to deal with variations in the side curves is to fit the sides and handles together. Place the assembly on the plywood, and carefully trace around both the inside and outside. The plywood piece is 18 in. long and the arc on each end is swung from a center 11 in. away.

Since the tray is small enough to be easily picked up, both the top and bottom should be sanded and finished carefully. Start with 80-grit on the plywood and 50-grit on the solid parts, and sand through 120-grit and 220-grit on all surfaces.

The plywood bottom should be finished with lacquer or polyurethane to resist food and drink, and the sides and handles with oil to resist knocks and chips. I'd recommend putting masking tape on the tenons and finishing the plywood before assembly, and rubbing on the oil after assembly. If you put lacquer or polyurethane on the sides and handles as well as the bottom, do it before assembly. But mask all the spots that will have to accept glue. □

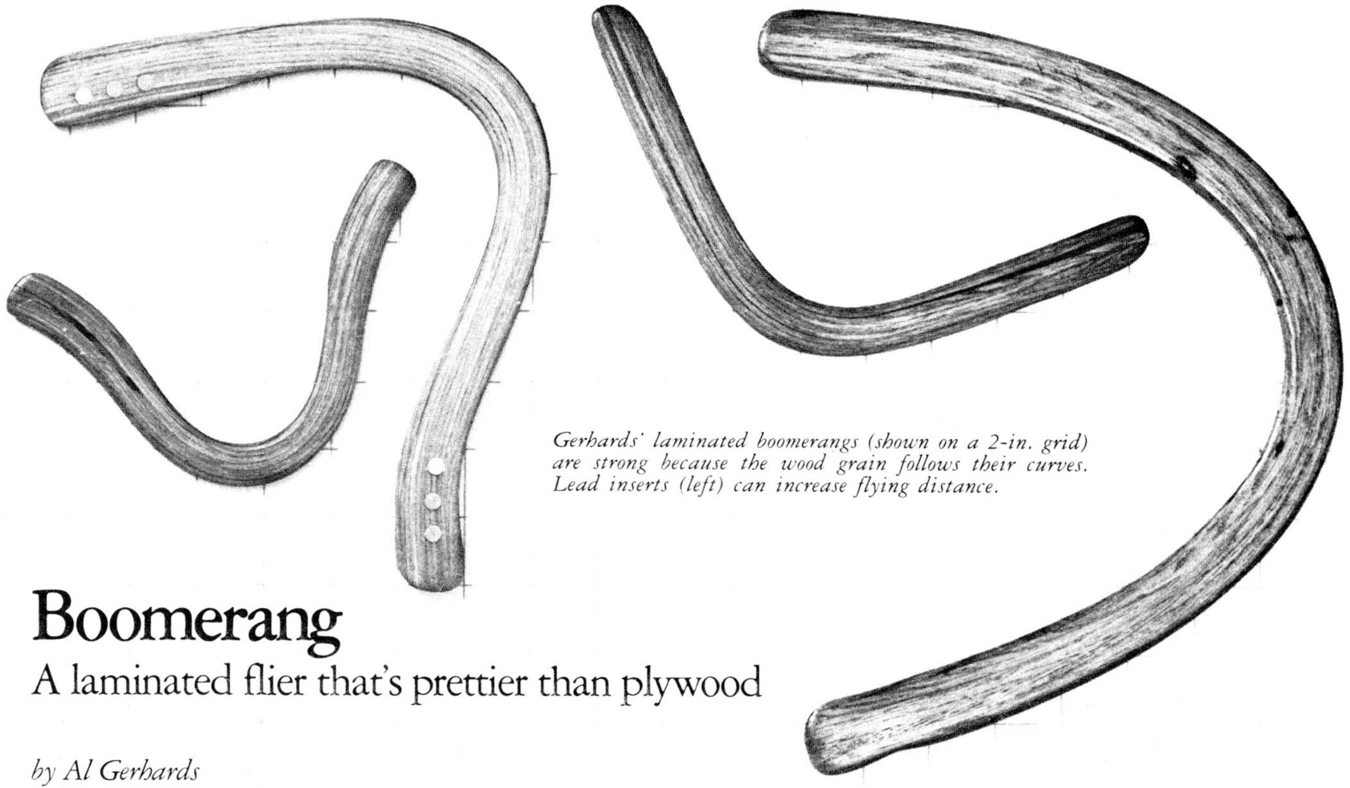

Gerhards' laminated boomerangs (shown on a 2-in. grid) are strong because the wood grain follows their curves. Lead inserts (left) can increase flying distance.

Boomerang

A laminated flier that's prettier than plywood

by Al Gerhards

A boomerang is an exercise in free-form woodworking. No straight lines, no corners to fit, no accurate measurements—just flowing lines and curves. Boomerangs can be made in many different shapes and sizes, besides the traditional shape. They're quick to make, fun to throw, and you can pack one along when you travel. To use it, all you need is a field and a little breeze.

The easiest way to make a boomerang is to cut the shape from 5-ply, ¼-in. birch plywood, then rasp and sand the edges to an airfoil section. I prefer to make a laminated boomerang by gluing up strips of wood on a form to build up not the thickness but the width. You can use any type of hardwood that will bend—so far, I've tried ash, hickory, oak, elm and locust. Where I live, these woods are inexpensive and available from local sawmills.

Since I make my boomerangs in batches, I start with a straight-grained, knot-free board, about 28 in. long, 2½ in. thick and 5 in. or more in width. I can get five of them from a board this size. Allow about ½ in. thickness for each boomerang. If you want to make two, you can start with a board 1 in. thick and 5 in. wide.

On the tablesaw, rip strips about 3/16 in. to ¼ in. thick from the edge of the board (see drawing, next page). Eight to ten strips, laminated together, should give you a thickness of 1¾ in. to 2 in. It's a good idea to cut a few extra strips, in case you break some while bending.

My boomerangs have sharp bends—less than 90°—so I steam and pre-bend my strips before gluing and clamping them on a form. If your boomerang doesn't have such a sharp bend, you can omit the steaming step. Place the strips in a preheated steam box for about 30 minutes (example, pages 45 to 46). When the strips are pliable, bend them freehand into a "U" shape and immobilize the ends to keep the strips from straightening out again as they dry. On my wall, I nailed lath strips about 16 in. apart, and when I compress the bent "U" and place the ends between two laths, the bent strip springs back a few inches and wedges in place. You could nail laths on a piece of plywood instead of on a wall. Whatever you do, let the strips dry for about a week.

To laminate the boomerang, you'll need to make a form by gluing and nailing together pieces of plywood or particleboard. You want a block about ½ in. thicker than the width of your strips, and about 4 in. longer than the length of the boomerang you want to make. The outside curve of the boomerang takes its shape from the concave surface of the form. Trace the outer edge of your boomerang pattern onto the plywood block, leaving about 2 in. of block at either end. Cut out the curve with a bandsaw or a bowsaw. Then glue and nail another piece of plywood to the form to make a base. Now you are ready to glue the strips together, but first coat the form with wax so that the glue won't stick to it.

You can get decorative effects by gluing up the strips in different ways. You can reassemble them in the order they were cut from the board, to match the original grain. For a different effect, you can alternate light and dark woods, or cut two long, thin wedges from wood of a contrasting color and slip them between the strips.

Coat both sides of the strips with epoxy (not quick-set epoxy) and allow the glue to cure for about an hour before assembling. This allows the glue to penetrate the pores of the wood and helps prevent a starved joint. I use T-88 epoxy (available from Chem Tech, 4669 Lander Rd., Chagrin Falls, Ohio 44022), but some other brands may set faster, so this technique may not work with all glues. The epoxy should still be tacky when the strips are assembled. Lay the glued-up strips in the form. To even the pressure from the clamps and to prevent them from marring the wood, I use a thin, flexible, steel strap about 2 in. wide and long enough to follow the curve. On a concave form, however, this isn't essential. Place the steel band (if you're using one) against the last

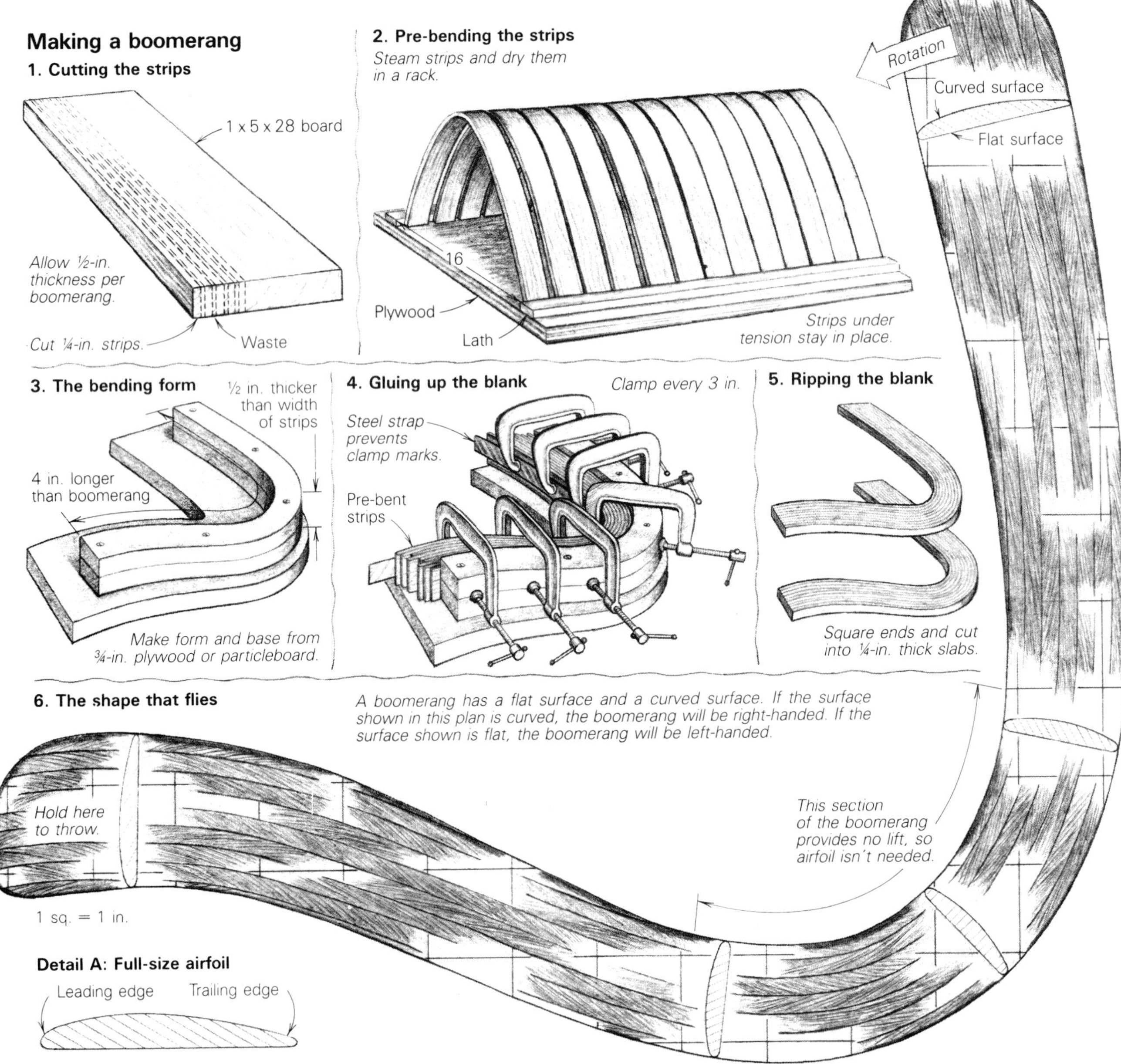
Making a boomerang
1. Cutting the strips
1 x 5 x 28 board
Allow ½-in. thickness per boomerang.
Cut ¼-in. strips.
Waste
2. Pre-bending the strips
Steam strips and dry them in a rack.
16
Plywood
Lath
Strips under tension stay in place.
Rotation
Curved surface
Flat surface
3. The bending form
½ in. thicker than width of strips
4 in. longer than boomerang
Make form and base from ¾-in. plywood or particleboard.
4. Gluing up the blank
Clamp every 3 in.
Steel strap prevents clamp marks.
Pre-bent strips
5. Ripping the blank
Square ends and cut into ¼-in. thick slabs.
6. The shape that flies
A boomerang has a flat surface and a curved surface. If the surface shown in this plan is curved, the boomerang will be right-handed. If the surface shown is flat, the boomerang will be left-handed.
Hold here to throw.
This section of the boomerang provides no lift, so airfoil isn't needed.
1 sq. = 1 in.
Detail A: Full-size airfoil
Leading edge
Trailing edge

strip. With a large C-clamp or bar clamp, start pulling in the midsection, snug it up and clamp each side at 3 in. intervals. Allow the epoxy to cure for a day at room temperature.

When the epoxy has cured, remove the laminated block from the form, and square up the sides where the edges of the strips may have slipped out of alignment. You now have a thick block shaped like a boomerang, from which you'll cut individual blanks. I cut mine on the tablesaw, but you can probably do this more safely and waste less wood with a wide resaw blade on the bandsaw. To increase the height of the tablesaw fence, I attach a piece of plywood wide enough to support the blank while ripping. Saw the blanks about ¼ in. thick. The blanks are now ready for shaping and sanding.

Here's how to determine which side gets rounded to form the airfoil. With your throwing hand, hold the boomerang upright by its arm, with the edge of its "elbow" toward your nose. Go through an overhand throwing motion. The side facing your ear is the top surface, which gets curved. The side away from you remains flat. As the boomerang leaves your hand, it spins, and the two edges that cut the wind as it spins are the edges you want to round. The rounded edge tapers to a thin trailing edge like the cross section of an airplane wing.

When shaping and sanding, I use a boomerang-shaped ¾-in. plywood backup to minimize flexing. Clamp the boomerang blank and the backup in a vise. Using a rasp, shape the top side of the blank into an airfoil shape. After you've roughed out the boomerang, finish it with sandpaper. I use an inflatable-bag drum sander for final contouring.

Every shape and size flies differently, so after flight-testing, you may need to tune your boomerang by slightly changing the shape of the airfoil. To make the boomerang travel farther before it returns, I sometimes epoxy ½-in. dia. lead inserts in holes near the ends of the arms. After the glue sets, I file the lead flush with the wood.

I finish my boomerangs with tung oil or boiled linseed oil, to bring out the wood's natural beauty. A boomerang gets a lot of hard use, and an oil finish is easy to repair. □

Al Gerhards is a dental technician in Downington, Pa. He's been making boomerangs for almost 25 years.

Drawing: Lee Hov

Throwing the boomerang

by John Huening

Hold the boomerang so it's nearly vertical and launch with an overhand throw. Snap your wrist on release to give it a good spin.

Rusty Harding took me to a field and considered the air and sky. "A boomerang is a gyroscope without a fixed point of gyration. It describes a circle, or whatever its flight path, depending on the design, velocity, spin, wind direction and thermal air currents."

Harding makes boomerangs for a living. Working in his backyard in Lebanon, Tenn., he produces fanciful, unorthodox shapes—a far cry from the familiar shallow "V" shape developed by the Australian aborigines.

There are right- and left-handed boomerangs, the difference being the location of the rounded edges and the direction the boomerang is thrown into the wind. A right-hander returns in a counterclockwise circle, while a left-hander circles clockwise. Hold the boomerang in your throwing hand, with the flat side against your palm, and imagine it spinning out of your hand, away from you. The rounded edge, like the front edge of an airplane wing, should be the edge that hits the wind first. If it's not, you've got a boomerang designed for the other hand.

"I usually pick up pieces of grass and drop them to see which direction the wind is blowing," Harding told me. "Throw about forty-five degrees into the wind. Stand so that the wind hits your left cheek." Since he's left-handed, Harding let the wind hit his right cheek.

"Spin is important," he continued, "so hold the boomerang as close as you can to the end of its arm. The boomerang should be nearly vertical when launched. Now, pick a target forty to fifty yards away, aim, and throw overhand, snapping your wrist to give the boomerang a good spin."

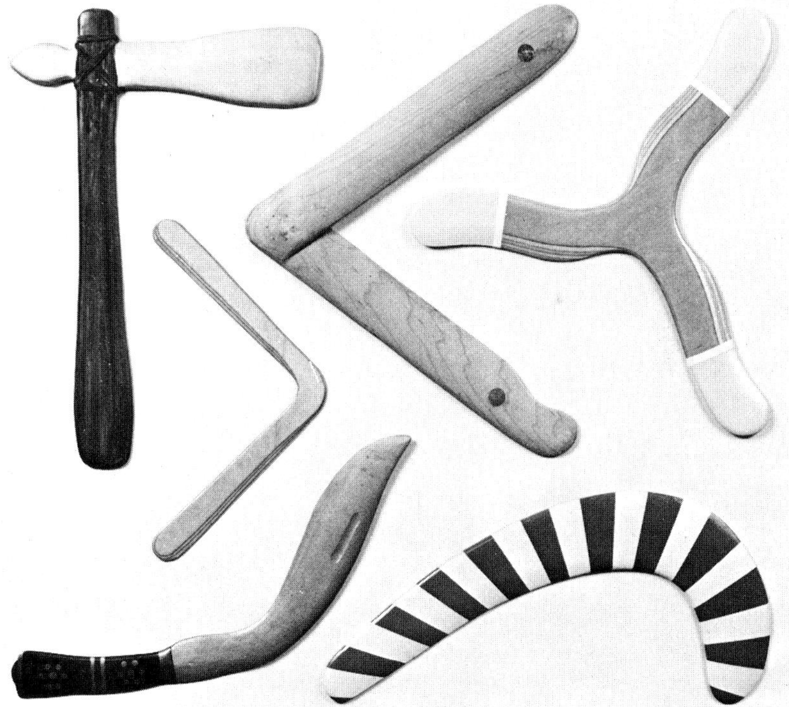

Harding makes his fanciful, unorthodox boomerangs from either hardwood or plywood.

That first throw was nearly miraculous—the boomerang actually returned and I almost caught it. There was a whirring sound as it cut the air. "Consistency is important," Harding said. "Until you can throw the same way each time, you won't know what you're doing wrong. If the boomerang lands consistently to your left, turn more away from the wind. If it lands to your right, turn more into the wind. Do the opposite if you're left-handed. If it lands consistently in front of you, throw a little higher or a little harder. If it lands in back of you, throw a little lower."

Boomerangs were originally used as weapons, and they do have the potential to be dangerous. When throwing one, you should allow between 50 and 75 yards of open space in all directions. □

John Huening is a pipe-organ builder and writer in Seffner, Fla.

Shop-Built Vacuum Press

Air pressure bends and glues veneers

by Donald C. Bjorkman

The author's vacuum-formed lounge chair, veneered in rosewood.

Photos: Donald Bjorkman

Vacuum presses are used in several disciplines, for example, the vacuum frame in printing and the thermo former for making sheet plastic into various three-dimensional shapes. The concept is also quite useful in woodworking, since air pressure can exert a force of up to 15 pounds per square inch. This is enough to bond veneers into plywood, and to bend veneers or sandwiches of veneer and other materials over curved forms. The idea is to evacuate all the air from a contained space, thus bringing the weight of the atmosphere to bear upon that space and whatever is in it. The problem is to create a container that will allow one to pull pressure over irregular forms, and if possible to let one see what is going on during the forming process.

Originally, vacuum presses used a cumbersome rubber blanket about ⅛ in. thick. One could not form items with much of a third dimension, because the blanket would have to be lapped over at the edges where it was clamped to the platform. It was hard to seal against leaks where the rubber was lapped, and one never knew what was happening—or going wrong—until the glue had cured and the blanket was removed. If there had been slippage or misalignment during assembly, it was too late. The work was ruined.

Some years ago, while doing graduate work at the School for American Craftsmen of Rochester (N.Y.) Institute of Technology, I came up with an idea that overcame both of these deficiencies. I have used this method successfully ever since. My idea was simply to substitute tough sheet vinyl for the rubber blanket, and to replace a complex plenum with a simple platform. The vinyl is easy to cement into various shapes, and it is transparent so one can see exactly what is happening as the vacuum is being drawn. My unit consists of a vinyl bag attached to a frame, which clamps to a platform. Any wood craftsman can construct this machine easily and relatively cheaply. Although many industrial pumps are sold for the purpose of drawing a vacuum, I converted my shop air compressor by a simple switching of the appropriate valves. The resulting machine permits projects that are limited only by imagination and ingenuity.

Building the press — Many woodworkers already have in their shops most of the materials necessary for this press. Everything should be available locally at lumberyards, industrial hardware stores and plastics outlets.

The press platform is a wide, flat sheet with a hole in the center for evacuating the air. I have found it unnecessary to use a perforated platform with a plenum (vacuum chamber) below, or a perforated pipe for uniform evacuation. Instead, I raise the form on skids inside the vinyl bag, which allows air to flow from all areas of the bag to the center exhaust port.

Don't make the platform from a plain sheet of plywood because it generally has internal voids that will leak air and could break out. Marine plywood is suitable, but I generally use a 3-ft. by 4-ft. piece of ¾-in. chipboard, skinned on both sides with ⅛-in. hardboard (Masonite). This sandwich not only airproofs the platform, but also strengthens it.

Gluing large, flat areas such as hardboard to composition board can be a problem if you don't already have a vacuum press or a screw-type veneer press. I suggest making up gently curved clamping members to span the platform, and compressing them with quick-set clamps. Cut scrap 2x3s to the shorter dimension of the space to be spanned, in this case 3 ft. A larger span needs more substantial stock. Allow about 6 in. between these members for the clamps. If you already have a strong, flat surface, such as a large bench, it can be

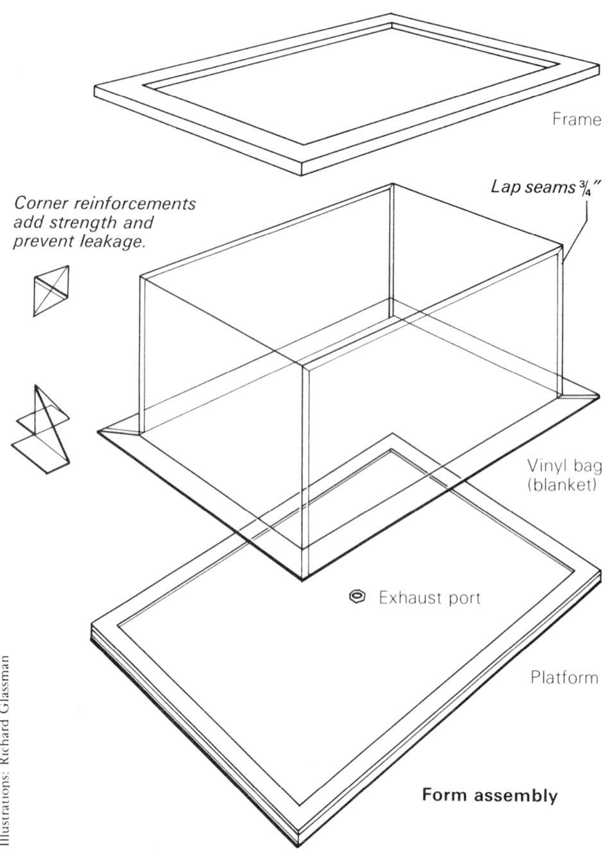

Form assembly

Illustrations: Richard Glassman

Simple veneer press for gluing up the hardboard/chipboard platform atop a wide bench. Slightly bowed clamping members squeeze glue outward from center, eliminating glue voids.

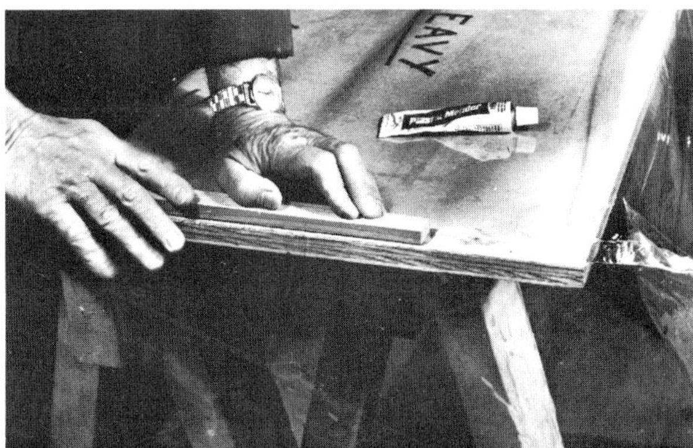

Makeshift sawhorse table supports vinyl sheeting while seams are glued. Wooden slat maintains pressure while vinyl adhesive begins to set. Seam takes time to gain strength.

used as one clamping surface. If not, you'll need twice as many clamping members because they will have to be used on both sides of the workpiece. Put a slight curve on the side of the clamping member that will contact the work. This can be easily done by taking a series of cuts, each about 1/32 in. deep, with the jointer. Start the first cut about a fifth of the distance toward the center from the end. Take the next cut two-fifths of the way to the center, and so on. Rock the piece with pressure at the back as you pass it through the jointer. With four cuts on each side of center, the clamping member will rock 1/8 in. both ways from center. This way, as the clamps are tightened, pressure will be transmitted first to the center of the work and gradually farther toward the ends of the members, forcing the excess glue to the edges and preventing voids. Use a 3/4-in. sheet of plywood next to the hardboard to distribute the clamping pressure. Glue-up will be a two-person job if you don't have a flat surface to clamp to.

After the glue has set, drill a 27/64-in. dia. hole in the platform center to receive the fitting that goes to the vacuum pump. Finish the platform edges to your liking and then place a gasket around the edge. A good material for the gasket is 1½-in. to 2-in. wide camper tape, a self-sticking, sponge-rubber tape to be used between pick-up beds and camper tops and sold by hardware stores and recreational vehicle centers. Buy the thinnest tape available. Make sure the joints at the corners are tight. Liberally dusting the top surface with talc prevents it from sticking to the bag, but be sure to remove all loose talc before applying vacuum to the unit.

Next, make the frame that holds the vinyl bag to the platform. The frames's outside dimension should be the same as the platform's, and made of stock about 2½ in. wide and 1 in. thick. It can be made of plywood or lumber, and a simple lap joint at the corners is strong enough to resist leaking between clamps and to withstand repeated clampings.

The bag is made of 16-mil or 20-mil clear or frosted vinyl sheet. This sheeting generally comes in 52 in. widths. Check the Yellow Pages under: "Plastics—Rod, Tubes, Sheets, etc., Supply Centers." Mail-order suppliers include Cadillac Plastics, 1221-T Bowers, PO Box P-2020, Birmingham, Mich. 48012, and AIN Plastics, Inc., 249 E. Sanford Blvd., Mount Vernon, N.Y. 10550. Vinyl adhesive is used to cement the bag together. This can be purchased from plastics supply centers or local hardware stores.

A bag about 18 in. high should be enough for most projects. If you plan to produce a quantity of one object, you may want to tailor the bag to its shape. This somewhat simplifies the pressing process, because there is no extra bag material to contend with. In either case, it is best to have some of the material touching the platform when it is under vacuum rather than stretching directly from the form to the frame. This relieves some of the stress on the bag. An oversize bag is better than one too small. When clamping a small bag down over the form the vinyl could pull away from the frame, creating problems in the middle of a glue-up.

Cut the vinyl to shape. If the bag is to be rectangular, as shown in the sketch, I recommend that it be cut out in three pieces: two sides and a piece that forms the top and two ends. Remember to allow material for lapping at the seams, under the frame and at the miters at the bottom corners. A marker pen works well for laying out the vinyl pieces.

A sheet of plywood slightly smaller than the top dimensions of the bag and set on sawhorses makes a good table for cementing the bag. It works the way a shoemaker's shoe jack holds a shoe—by holding the bag in place without wrinkles and overlaps. Allow a 3/4-in. overlap for the seams. Using a brush or the tube and your fingers, spread a good amount of vinyl adhesive over the area to be lapped. Quickly press together. Do one straight seam between corners at a time.

A wood slat about 3/4 in. by 1/2 in. is suitable for applying even pressure on the seam while the glue sets. Hold the seam together with the slat for a few minutes until the adhesive sets a little. Then if the slat can be removed without exerting any tension on the seam, remove it. Otherwise weigh it down for another five minutes. Then remove the slat and let the seam set another five minutes before handling the bag. The seam takes time to get strong.

Corners are hard to make airtight. A corner with a radius may look nice, but a right angle has fewer points at which to leak. Notch at the corner so that it may be tailored square. Reinforcing corner patches make a stronger, more airproof bag. When the bag is assembled, cement it to the frame. Allow seams to strengthen overnight before using. Acetone will clean up hands and brushes, but the fumes can be harmful—work in a well-ventilated area or use a good respirator.

The pump — A vacuum pump for this press should be a high-volume type, minimum 1/3 hp. It should be able to pull at least 3 cubic feet of air per minute. Mine pulls 5 cfm and works well with a press of this size. The lower the cfm, the longer it will take to evacuate the bag. Any pump that can

New valve/fitting arrangement controls vacuum to press.

maintain a vacuum of 15 in. of mercury will work, whether it be reciprocal, diaphragm or whatever—you might even try the pump from a milking machine. One can rent pumps, but generally only in large cities. The pump can be hooked up directly to the press, or a unit with a tank reservoir and a vacuum switch can be used. The latter creates a vacuum quickly and lets the pump rest once it reaches the point the switch is set for. Without a vacuum switch the pump runs continuously, equilibrium being maintained by leaks in the system.

The difference between an air compressor and a vacuum pump of the same horsepower is slight. The pump generally has larger pistons, because the pump runs at lower internal pressures, the extreme being a bit under 15 psi. Compressors operate at much higher pressures, so I can see no harm in converting a compressor into a pump. I never got a straight answer from compressor salesmen or repairmen on this subject, so I finally went ahead and converted mine.

I have a Bell and Gossett ¾-hp compressor. To convert it, I switched the exhaust valves with the intake valves, keeping the exhaust valve plug and the intake filters in the same ports as they were. The check valve was also reversed so that the compressor was now pumping. The check-valve spring had to be replaced with a lighter one from a comparable pump. The pressure switch was replaced (it could also be bypassed) with a vacuum switch, and the conversion was complete. I have used this unit as both a pump and a compressor over the past five years with no bad effects.

Finding proper fittings to connect the pump to the press can be a hassle. The drawing below shows fittings obtainable from good hardware and auto parts stores. The filter may be purchased from an auto parts store or from the pump supplier. If a ¼-in. to ⅛-in. pipe reducer can't be found, a 5⁄16-in. O.D. tubing to ⅛-in. male pipe fitting may be used by removing the flare end area of the fitting.

A thin ring of plumber's putty under the washers that clamp the nipple to the platform helps seal that connection. A loop bent into the tubing between the pump and the platform lessens the chances of work-hardening the tubing from vibration. The globe valves are to control the vacuum. The valve nearest the pump can be closed while the tank is brought to vacuum, or to stop air removal from the bag.

Materials to bend — One can vacuum-bend veneers, paper honeycomb, thin sheets of rigid foam, polyester resin and glass cloth, sheet aluminum, or virtually anything that bends relatively easily and can be cemented together with a time-lag adhesive. I find ⅛-in. poplar bending plywood imported from Italy easiest to use. It is three veneers thick, each veneer being about 1 mm thick, and comes in 4x8 sheets. This plywood will bend along the grain of the outer veneers to a minimum radius of about 2 in. When bent across the grain of the outer veneers, the radius has to be quite a bit larger. The plies are glued with waterproof glue, so tighter bends can be achieved by soaking the plywood.

The strength of a single sheet of this bending plywood won't set any records, but three or more sheets laminated together form a material strong enough for most applications. This is especially true if curves are incorporated into the design, and that's what this process is all about. Poplar is a white, bland wood with little character, but it veneers well and the multiple veneers of the edges are quite attractive.

A few years ago there were several suppliers of this material, but now I can find only one: North American Plywood Corp., with branches at 800 Third Ave., New York, N.Y. 10022; 3333 South Malt Ave., Los Angeles, Calif. 90040; and Box 24454, Oakland, Calif. 94623. No warehouse will sell less than a bundle of 60 sheets. To find the retailer nearest you, contact the closest branch.

The advantage of Italian plywood is the ease with which it bends. Several ⅛-in. pieces are easier to glue up and handle than three times as many 1⁄24-in. pieces of veneer. The disadvantages are the rather high cost and sometimes the difficulty in finding a retail source. Other types of ⅛-in. plywoods or door skins are available and will work. Door skins come in 3-ft. by 7-ft. pieces. The most common and usually the cheapest is Philippine mahogany. One-eighth-inch plywood in birch, beech, ash, oak, walnut or other hardwoods is often available at local lumberyards. Unfortunately these materials do not bend as easily as the poplar without fracturing. The tightest possible radius for mahogany ply, bending with the

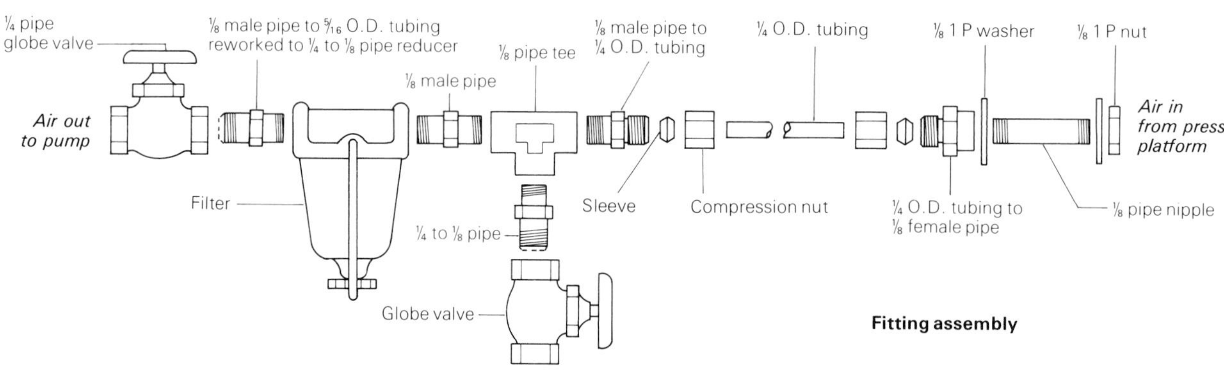

grain of the outside veneers, is 4 in. or more. With birch it is much larger, and of course they all bend to larger radii against the grain. For large simple bends I've used poplar for the core material and a hardwood plywood for the faces, thus eliminating the veneering process. The reason these materials do not bend as easily as poplar is their construction. Poplar has three plies of even thickness, but the others have a core twice as thick as the face veneers. And the woods themselves have different bending characteristics.

Hardwood plywoods create very strong units when formed. A vacuum-bent piece, say of birch, is almost indestructable.

You may also want to consider veneers. I avoid using thin face veneers for core material, but core veneers about a millimeter or 1/24 in. thick work well. Single veneers allow good control over forming curves because one can control the lay of the grains of the veneers as they are built up into plywood.

Design considerations — You must design to the limitations of the material you are using. If birch plywood is used, the curves must be large and simple; with 1/24-in. poplar veneer, the radii can be much smaller and might possibly include compound curves.

Straight, flat surfaces can be obtained from sheet plywood. Vacuum-bending permits curves that can add strength and beauty to the piece. Straight flat surfaces also have a tendency to show up irregularities and flaws, whereas curved surfaces are less likely to do so. Flat surfaces though, are sometimes necessary to a design, as in a sofa back. When confronted with such a situation I vacuum-bend the curved areas, then splice them to flat areas of standard plywood with a spline or tongue and groove joint. The joint is then made flush on both sides and the complete unit face veneered. This eliminates the need for a large form and press.

As you design, keep in mind what the form and press are forcing the material to do. Thin sheets of wood will bend to a point, then fracture. Slight compound curves can be formed without tailoring the pieces, but smaller curves require tailoring. Tailoring means notching the individual sheets that will make up the finished piece, as in tailoring clothing, so that they will bend over the form into a compound curve. The joints of the notches in one sheet must not fall in line with the joint in the sheet next to it or the piece will have no strength at these points.

Forms — One might think that a simple pine form would suffice, but this is inviting catastrophe. The atmosphere exerts tremendous pressure when air is evacuated from a contained space. This system should be able to maintain 15 in. of mercury, which works out to 1,060 pounds of pressure per square foot, enough to crush a simple pine form, especially when you consider that the pressure is exerted in all directions, not just downward. I generally make forms of odds and ends and scraps of plywood and chipboard. I usually make an egg-crate framework and face it with hardboard or with poplar plywood. Composition boards work nicely for shapes with somewhat flat areas and are easy to shape with Surform rasps. If you use bending medium for face material, it should be glued and nailed in place one sheet at a time, with the last sheet vacuum-pressed into place. This way, no nail heads protrude and no frame ribs show through. If all the pieces were vacuum-formed onto the framework in one process, the blanks would not yet be bonded together and would have only the strength of individual sheets. When pressure was applied they would give between supports and bond in that shape. This would most likely create a rippled or checkerboard effect that would be transferred to the finished piece.

A set of skids glued and nailed to the bottom of the form allows it to set over the fittings in the platform and prevents the form from blocking the air passage out of the press.

If the piece to be formed is irregular in shape I suggest covering the form with heavy paper, such as kraft wrapping paper, and taping it in place. The outline of the piece can then be laid out directly on this. This creates a template for

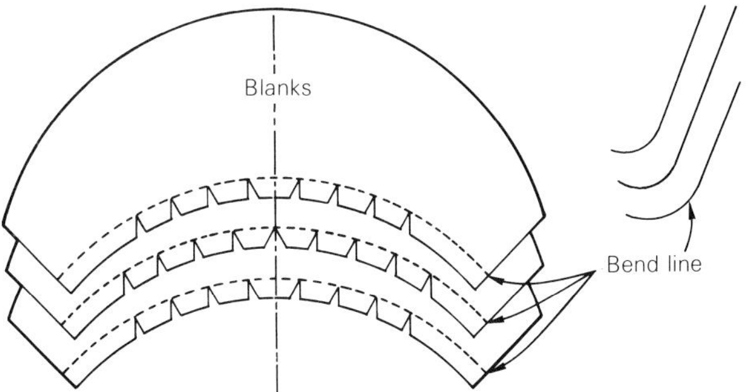

On tight compound curves, blanks must be tailored, or notched, so they can bend around the form. If the notches are not staggered from layer to layer, the finished laminate will be weak.

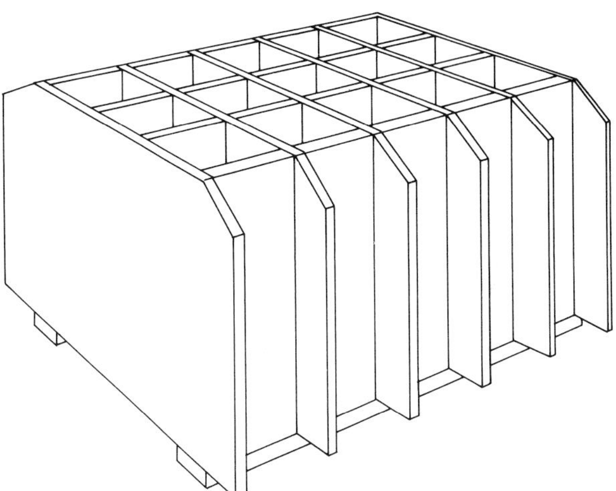

An egg-crate framework made of plywood scraps supports the exterior part of the form, and must be strong enough to withstand pressure from all directions for vacuum-forming.

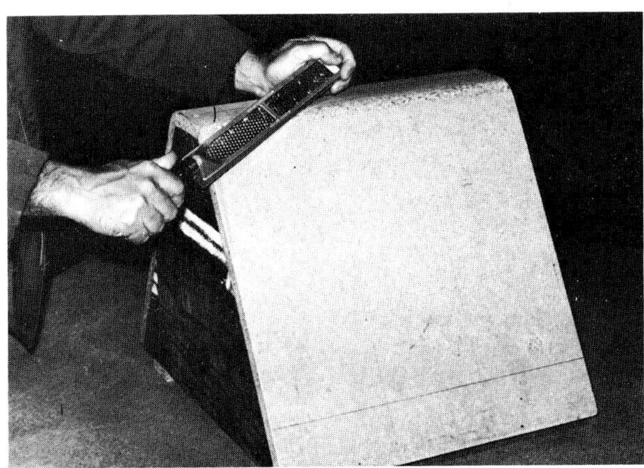

Surform easily shapes chipboard face of form.

cutting the stock, and also tells you whether the plywood will bend into the shape you want without crinkles, overlapping or spaces between the form and the piece. If the paper won't conform to the form, the form may have to be reworked to compensate. If the shape of the form is simple, the stock can be sized directly from your drawings.

Transfer the template outline or its dimensions to the bending plywood and cut. Allow extra material at the edge for trim, and don't forget the increase in dimension needed to pass over radii as the thickness of the piece increases. To position the blanks on the form, place index points on the blanks that relate to points on the form. These should be placed in positions where the blanks will be secured to the form, generally at center lines.

Using the press — The importance of having all your equipment ready has been stated many times, but is worth repeating. Clear off a table or bench other than the press platform for rolling the glue onto the blanks, which should already be cut to size, cleaned, indexed and (if desired) veneered. A hammer, wire nails and wood washers should be ready, along with masking tape, brown paper tape and a piece of light rope. A helper would be welcome.

Now a dry run should be made. The blanks are indexed in place on the form and secured. Wire nails, with washers made of ⅛-in. ply scrap, work best when driven in at strategic points. The washers permit easy removal. Put the nails in areas that will be trimmed off. If the piece is to be veneered, put the nails wherever you want because the veneer will cover their holes. Don't put nails where they would prevent the layers from being pulled down tight against the form. Be sure no nails protrude, or they may puncture the vinyl blanket. A couple of nails along the center line are usually enough to hold the blanks in place. Masking tape can be used instead of nails (or to supplement them), but the vacuum pressure drives the adhesive into the grain of the wood and it is very difficult to remove. Another way is to countersink flathead screws with a brace and screwdriver bit.

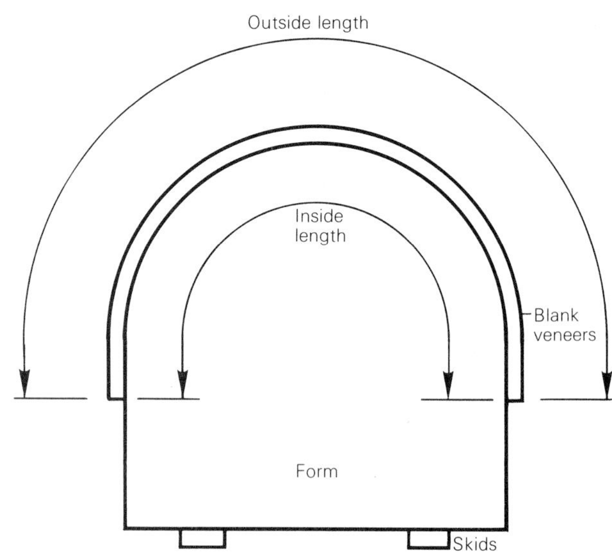

The thicker the piece, the longer the outside blanks will progressively have to be to wrap around the form.

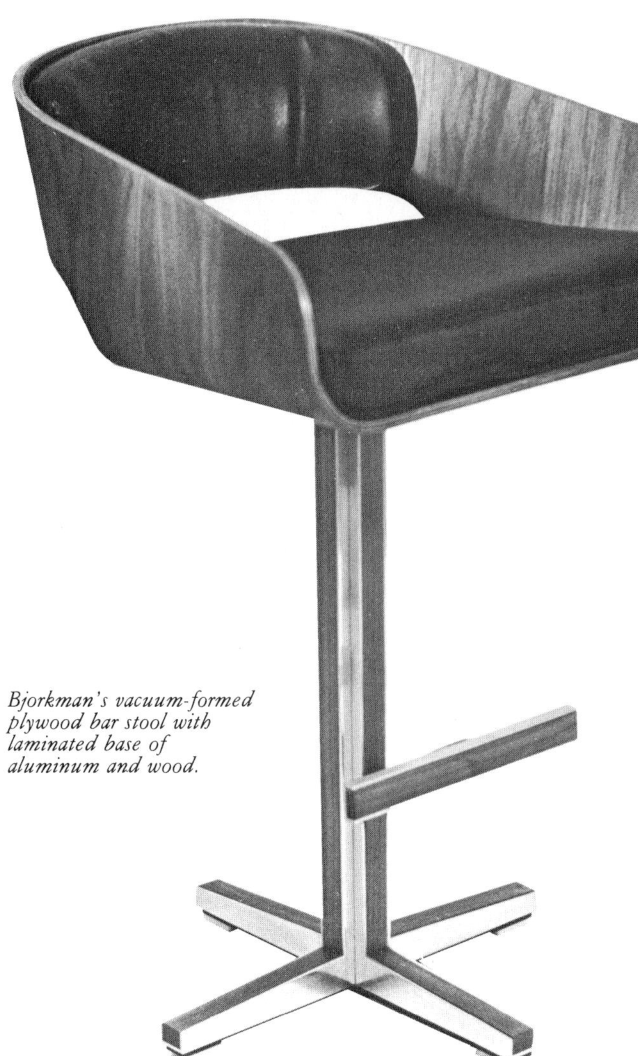
Bjorkman's vacuum-formed plywood bar stool with laminated base of aluminum and wood.

Now clamp the bag into place and work out all the air you can. Clamp about every foot along the frame. These clamps hold the bag in place until the vacuum is up and prevent the gasket from being sucked off the platform.

Constructing a completely airtight system is nearly impossible, although I have managed to get fairly close a couple of times. It is a good idea to have handy the vinyl cement and some vinyl sheet scrap from which to cut patches, in case a larger than tolerable leak occurs. The vacuum within the bag will pull the patch into the leak. Just don't overdo with cement—the vinyl can soften and the vacuum will pull it apart. For small leaks a dab of adhesive will generally do the job.

When the bag is clamped down, turn on the suction. As the bag collapses, smooth it over the workpiece and fold the excess blanket neatly around the form. Take tucks in such a way that the bag can be pulled taut as the air is evacuated. Don't let excess bag pull under the mold—it is hard on the bag and could block the air outlet at the platform center.

Sometimes the vacuum builds too fast and it must be shut off. The valve closest to the tank should then be closed. This will stop evacuation of the press, but not of the tank. Therefore, if vacuum is needed later, a reserve will be available quickly. If the vacuum is still too great inside the bag to make adjustments, open the second valve to bleed air in and relieve

1 *Wire nails and wood washers hold correctly aligned plywood blanks in position.*

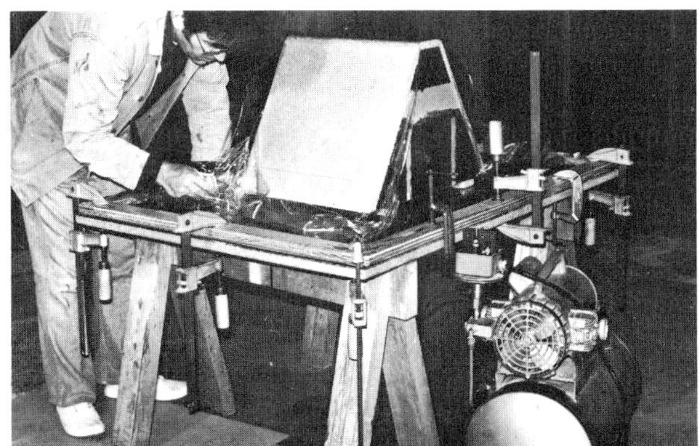

2 *Bag is smoothed over workpiece in dry run. Tucking excess blanket neatly around form prevents blockage of air outlet.*

3 *The workpiece under pressure: Extra sheeting is tucked neatly around form and away from clamps, air exhaust.*

4 *Taped veneer is bent and glued to curved plywood in one vacuum operation.*

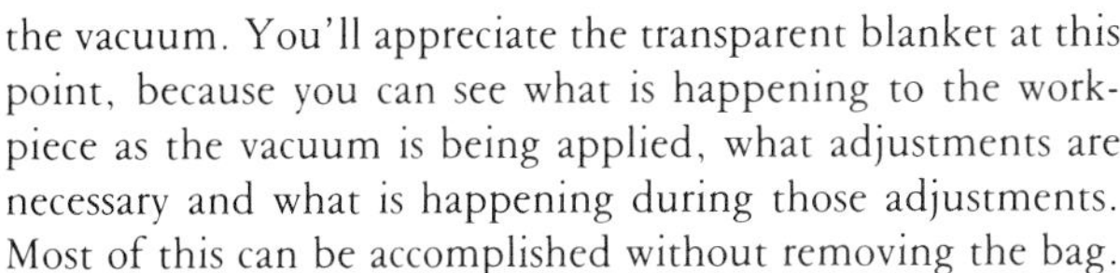

the vacuum. You'll appreciate the transparent blanket at this point, because you can see what is happening to the workpiece as the vacuum is being applied, what adjustments are necessary and what is happening during those adjustments. Most of this can be accomplished without removing the bag.

When the dry run is satisfactory, remove the workpiece and roll glue onto the contacting surfaces. Be careful not to apply glue to the surfaces that will touch the form or blanket. A medium coat of glue on each side is best, but a heavy, even coat on one side will suffice. Then proceed as with the dry run. I have found aliphatic (yellow) glues the best because of their relatively short setting time. Contact cement should never be used in vacuum-bending. The latex binder will sooner or later fatigue under stress and let go. An hour's press time usually does the trick, depending on room temperature and humidity, wood moisture content, and the amount and type of glue. Pieces with small radii or complicated curves may take longer. There will be some springback when the piece is removed from the form. The piece should be clamped to shape until thoroughly dry, because the bond can still creep from the forces exerted by the ply trying to return to its flat configuration.

If the piece is to receive a face veneer, it could be applied with hot glue and a hammer. But now that we have constructed a vacuum press, let's veneer with it. First, cut the face veneers to shape and index them, as with the plywood blanks. Apply glue to the contact surface of the workpiece only. Position the veneer on the piece and tape it in place with mucilage (brown paper) tape. Then vacuum-form as before. A ⅛-in. thick sheet of foam rubber or flexible foam urethane

5 *Left to right: blanks and veneer, the finished piece, the form.*

placed between the workpiece and the form will eliminate any variation between the match of the form and the workpiece and thus ensure a tight bond. One could even veneer while forming the plywood, especially if the item is rather simple, but it's better to gain experience with the press before attempting this.

If you don't like an exposed ply edge, apply a ¼-in. thick lumber edge before the veneering—it will take more abuse than a veneer edge. The existing ply edge, because of its many layers and solidity, is not visually unpleasing, however, and it will take stains that match the veneer. □

Donald Bjorkman is associate professor in wood design at California Polytechnic State University in San Luis Obispo.

A One-Piece Chair

They said it couldn't be done

by John Kelsey

One afternoon several years ago, furniture maker Peter Danko sat in a bar near his shop in Alexandria, Va., slicing up the menu card with a Swiss Army knife. A few slits and folds, and there it was—the one-piece plywood chair he had been musing about ever since touring the Thonet plant in Statesville, N.C. (see pages 60 and 61).

"I had thought it was so foolish, to cut up and bend all that wood only to glue it together again," Danko recalls. "After I had made my menu-card chair, I put it aside and forgot about it until a few months later when I cut my hand and couldn't work. I still thought it would be neat to make a one-piece chair so I fooled around some more. I tried the idea out in Plexiglas, and there was nothing to it. I added an arm and that worked too, so I tried it in wood at ¼ scale.

"Then I went back to Thonet with my idea, only to learn that most designers have tried to make a one-piece chair. Thonet had even put a couple of staff designers on the problem, but the three-legged chair they came up with wasn't stable and couldn't be molded efficiently. They had concluded it was impossible, and seemed to think I was crazy."

Thonet obviously doesn't think so anymore, for in 1980 the firm contracted with Danko to produce and market his chair in quantity. It debuted that year at the contract furniture show in Dallas. But before Thonet would take another look at his chair, Danko had to prove the design by tooling up to manufacture several hundred chairs himself. He also persuaded the Museum of Modern Art to add one to its study collection, which impressed the Thonet people, and he got the chair into the American Craft Council's New Handmade Furniture show for the 1980 national tour.

Danko recalls, "I went around to plywood jobbers, but they also refused to believe it could be done. So I showed my models to my dad, who used to be a pattern maker for the Navy. He thought it was nifty, and he agreed to build the press I'd need if I could come up with $1,800 for materials. I did, and three months later he'd done it." (See page 100.)

The chair consists of two face veneers sandwiching 10 layers of ¹⁄₁₂-in. poplar, glued with Franklin laminating glue 6W, for its long open time. It is formed in a two-part particle-board mold, lined with sheet aluminum, which weighs a half ton. Before pressing, the appropriate slots are template-routed into enough veneers for a batch of eight chairs. The piece that is later upholstered for the seat is cut out from between the chair's legs, and made only ½ in. thick by putting a piece of waxed paper in the middle of the stack before glue-up.

Another Danko invention is a spreader for coating the layers with glue. It's a contraption with rollers that looks something like an old-fashioned washing machine.

The chair cures for an hour in the press, then it's trimmed and finished with the aid of yet another of Danko's father's devices, a stationary pattern router. This machine consists of a horizontal pipe mounted about thigh-high, with a straight-flute router bit protruding through a hole in the top of the pipe. A template collar is welded to the pipe around the bit opening. Danko clamps a chair-shaped pattern to the rough stack that emerges from the press and runs the whole assembly over the pipe, the template collar guiding the pattern. About 15 minutes per chair and it's done.

In batches of eight, there are about 3½ hours' work and over $25 in materials in each side chair. A fire destroyed Thonet's Sheboygan factory, where the chairs were made, so Danko is again producing them himself. Since he has to gear up to make them, he accepts only large-quantity orders; the chairs sell for $375 each. Danko also works with veneers and laminates and makes sculptured furniture in his shop behind the Pond Gallery at 917 King Street, Alexandria, Va.

The sketch alongside is from an article about molded plywood in the January 1948 issue of the magazine *Woodworking Digest*. The author says the sketch was made from Scandinavian photographs "that turned up some ten years ago (late 1930s) and is evidence that molded plywood furniture, at least in the Baltic countries, dates back some years. . . . It is obviously one-piece construction and many arguments have taken place as to how it was cut and bent to the integral design illustrated."

Peter Danko's one-piece plywood chair, left, is made from a 10-laminate sheet of slotted veneer, center. The pattern for routing the veneers for the chair with arms is at right.

The two-part particle-board mold for the armchair: The wavy line between the halves is, from left to right, the chair's leg, front, arm and back.

Danko opens the mold by bolting its top half to the upper platen of the press, built by George Danko to his son's specifications, and checks alignment as it moves up.

The long wedge hanging down from the mold forms the chair's rear legs; the rounded curve pushes the seat downward.

Glue-spreader coats both sides of the veneer in one pass. White bucket holds glue; plywood guard normally covers pulleys.

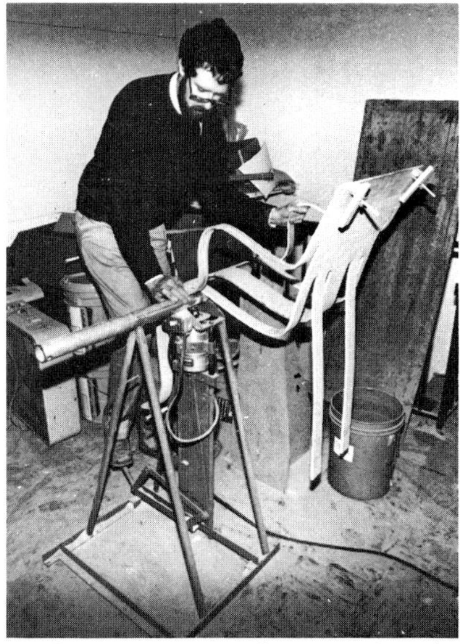

Danko runs jig over template router. Straight-flute bit protrudes through pipe; collar on pipe bears against jig.

Peter Danko

The Danko chair without arms.

Either version of the one-piece plywood chair can be stacked for storage.

Photos, except where noted: Staff

A Glue Press

by George Danko

My son's chair (page 98) was amazingly strong; to make it, a glue press was essential. His figures were out of this world: a 50-ton press with a 3-ft. by 4-ft. platen, with a lift of 80 in., for a shop with a 9-ft. ceiling. We discussed hydraulics, metering pumps and telescoping cylinders, but found their cost prohibitive. I am a devotee of simplicity. All that was needed was a huge, powerful clamp whose surfaces were always parallel, and long threaded rods would do.

A glue press is valuable in any woodshop as it can be used for an infinite number of operations. With this in mind we exceeded his minimum requirements: The final design consists of two platens 4 ft. by 6 ft., made of 7-in., 9.8 lb. channel iron, with a 2-in. dia. by 9-ft. long threaded rod at each corner. Roller-chain sprockets welded to nuts, driven by a single chain, provide the parallel clamping action. The power train is a 15-to-1 reduction gear and a 400 to 2,000 RPM variable-speed drive, powered by a 1½ HP, 1,750 RPM reversible motor. A bicycle sprocket and chain linked to the speed control can vary the speed of the upper platen from 4 in. to 22 in. per minute.

To simplify the construction, I ordered all the steel cut to size, then welded 16 steel plates, 7 in. square by ½ in. thick, to the corners. I drilled the plates on my Atlas lathe so the threaded rod could pass through: The eight plates on the bottom platen had 2-in. holes turned in them, and the plates on the upper platen were bored to a 2½-in. dia. on the bottom side and 2¾ in. on the top side, each to receive a brass tube measuring 2 in. I.D. by 2¾ in. O.D. (turned down to a 2½-in. shoulder on the bottom side, which secured the tubes in place). The brass tubes acted as bushings through which the threaded rods could slide. Four more steel plates, each bored through for the threaded rod to clear, were bolted through pipe spacers to the steel plates welded to the top of the top platen. These units trap roller-chain sprockets and washers welded to large nuts that fit the threaded rod. I added 4-in. squares of ⅛-in. bronze, machine-screwed into each plate, to bear the thrust. All the plates were aligned on the same ¾-in. by 4-ft. by 6-ft. plywood template before welding. Nuts with a setscrew welded to the underside of the bottom platen kept the threaded rod from turning.

About this point I learned that the channel-iron platens had warped during welding, so I built them up flat with ⅓₂-in. cardboard shims and added a ⅛-in. hump in the center to compensate for the 50-ton load. Then two pieces of ¾-in. plywood were glued together and bolted to the steel platens, with a sheet of 14-gauge steel plate secured to the bottom platen to make glue removal easier.

The press groaned and squeaked, but it worked. However, some parts of the chair showed spaces between the veneers because the press just did not exert quite enough pressure. The drive sprocket would actually turn inside the chain, and the chain would not move. Peter thought of laying flat lengths of fire hose on the bottom platen, attaching them to an iron pipe manifold, and blowing them up with 90 lb. of air pressure. Since the working area of the hose totaled almost 1,500 sq. in., this provided more than 130,000 pounds of force, plenty to close the joints. □

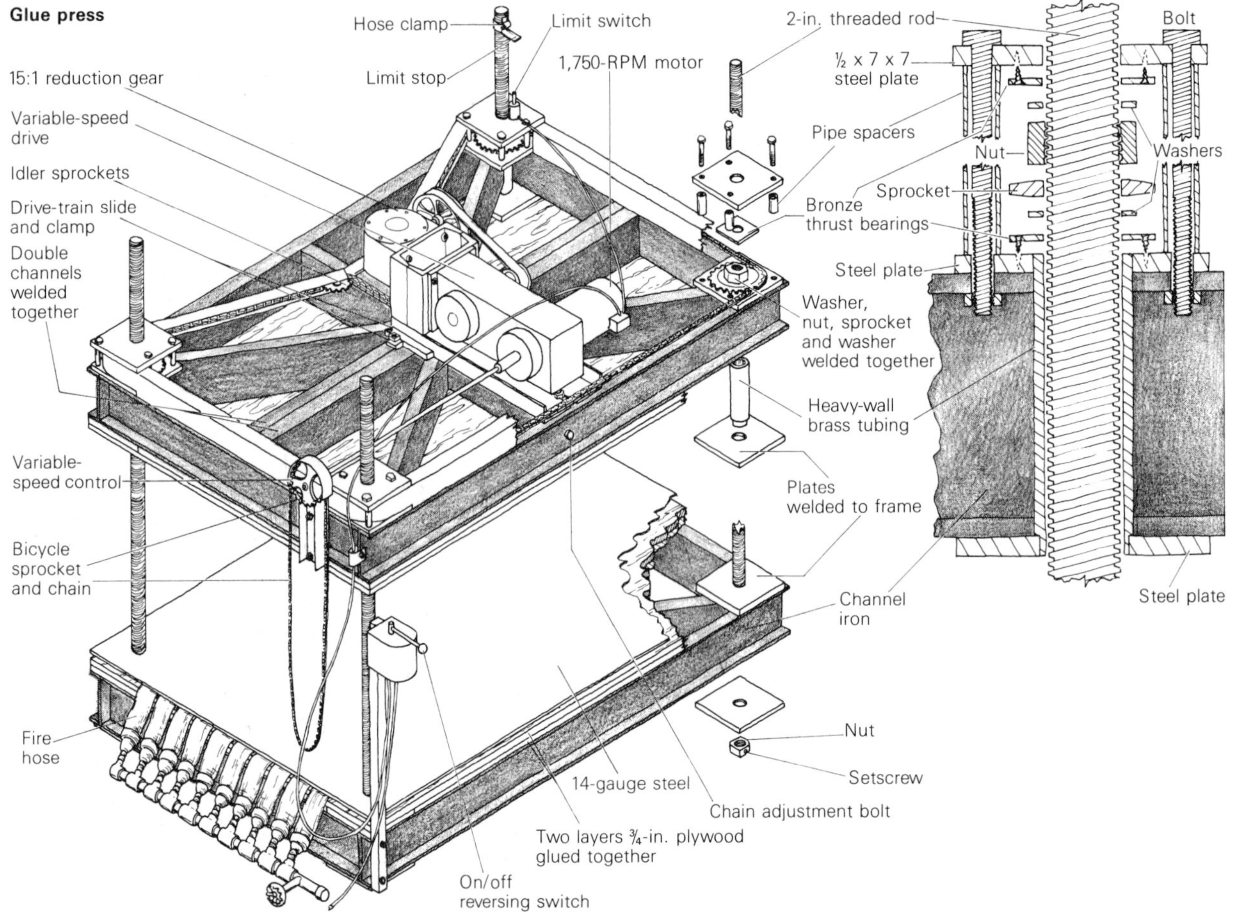

Illustration: Christopher Clapp

Circular Stairway

Laminate stringers around forming cylinders

by Laszlo Gigacz

I will tell you how I built a circular staircase, but before I begin I should tell you that I'm not a special stair builder by any means. I am Hungarian and have lived in the United States since 1957. I have made my living as a woodworker in Boston, New Haven, and for the past 16 years, in Jordan, N.Y., where I have had my own shop for 12 years now.

One afternoon a man and woman came into my shop and wanted me to turn two columns for a fireplace mantel and to carve an Ionic capital with a neck. I said, "Why not, that's what I'm here for." They seemed surprised, but when I delivered the job they were delighted and before too long they commissioned me for the staircase they wanted. The client was Porter Bachman, who lives in a fine house on Skaneateles Lake. Bachman himself did the design for the staircase.

Bachman furnished a dimensioned set of plans like the drawing alongside. Nothing about construction, so I worked on that. First I went to the library, a waste of time as there was nothing on circle stairs, or even straight stairs. My alternative was to think. I would like to remind you that this stairway was to be suspended in air, fastened to the upper and lower floors only, not a spiral staircase hung on a central column.

The first thing I did was to take down the loft in my shop to gain head room—16 ft.—and clear away a 15 ft. by 15 ft. area. The stairwell measured 10 ft. by 10 ft., and 108¾ in. from finished floor to finished floor. The stair was to be 9 ft. 10 in. at its widest, and the central space was to be 2 ft. 8 in. across. I put down ¾-in. plywood on the shop floor, and on it drew the floor plan of the stairway in actual size.

Next you work out the height of the risers, and it is basically the same as straight stairs. One rule of thumb is to divide the total height in inches by seven and forget about the remainder, to get the number of risers. Then divide the total height by this number of risers to get the exact height of each. There is always one less tread than there are risers. So in this case there are 14 treads and 15 risers, each 7¼ in. high, which equals the total height, 108¾ in. This of course includes the thickness of the tread. So when you decide the tread size, the riser height is minus that thickness. In the circle of stairs the width of the tread is governed by the radius of the stairwell, or by what part of the radius the stair is using. In this case, the stair winds less than three-quarters of the radius, as you can see on the floor plan. The bigger the radius the wider the tread, and the smaller the radius the narrower the tread. It is as simple as that, this is how I see the mathematics of it.

To make the stringer strong enough, it was merely speculation. I came up with 2½ in. thickness and 8 in. depth in white oak, which worked out swell. I made the stringers out of ¼-in. and ½-in. thick laminates of oak and here is how. First of all, you have to make up two cylinders, one as big as the outside diameter of the stairs less the thickness of the stringer, and one the size of the inside diameter. First you make the inside cylinder and after you have laminated the stringer onto it, you build the outside cylinder around it. Be sure you do it this way, otherwise you won't have room to swing your boards in between the two cylinders. To make the cylinders, I simply used 2x6 framing lumber, first putting the location of each upright piece on my floor plan, and also the size and shape of the horizontal bracing segments between the uprights. I nailed one segment on the floor, then nailed one 2x6 next to it, then nailed stiffening segments at about 24 in. height,

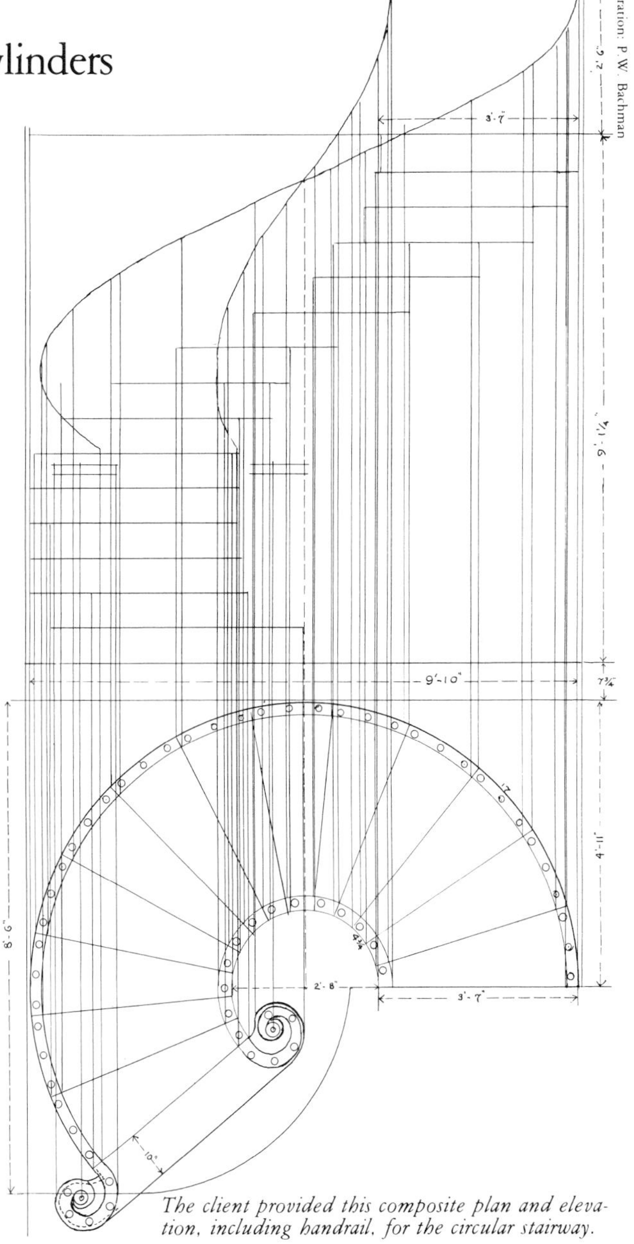

The client provided this composite plan and elevation, including handrail, for the circular stairway.

Illustration: P.W. Bachman

EDITOR'S NOTE: There aren't many books on stair-making, but these should get you started: *Stair Layout*, by Stanley Badzinski, Jr. (American Technical Society, 5608 Stony Ave., Chicago, Ill. 60637), for good technical advice; *Designing Staircases*, by Willibald Mannes (Van Nostrand Reinhold), for examples and ideas. Another basic reference is Time-Life Books' *Floors and Stairways*.

Laszlo Gigacz lives in Jordan, N.Y.

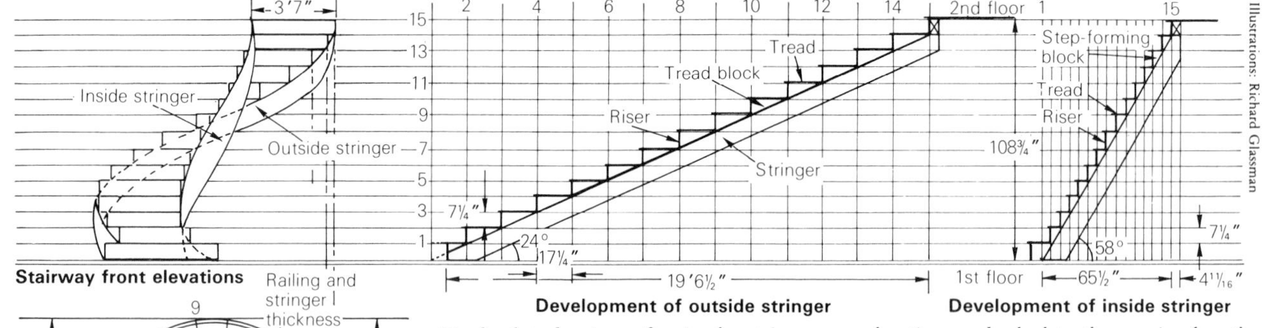

Stairway front elevations **Development of outside stringer** **Development of inside stringer**

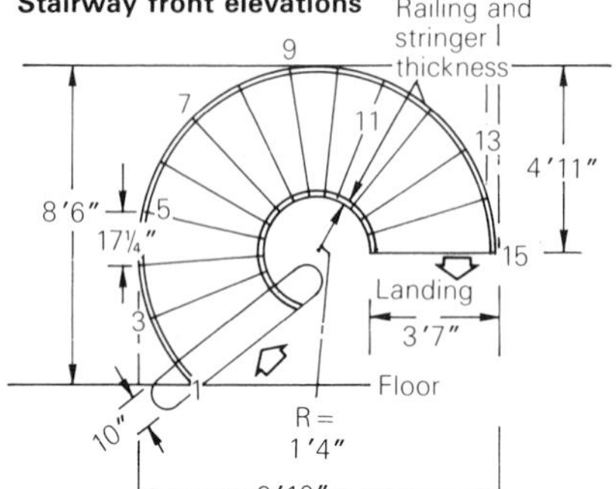

To develop drawings of a circular staircase, start with the plan (left) and the known distance between the floors. Calculate the rise of each tread, and directly above the plan view construct a horizontal grid of lines representing the top surface of each tread. Then project verticals from the plan to the horizontal grid, to locate each tread and riser as it would be seen in front elevation. The balusters and handrail are left off this drawing for clarity, but they can be projected in the same way. Then extend the horizontal grid to the right of the front elevation, and calculate the running length of the outside and inside stringers, from the known radius of the stairway. Since the number of treads is also known, the inside and outside width of each can be calculated, and the risers can be located by a grid of vertical lines. The stringers may now be drawn as if they were stretched out flat, along with the tread-supporting blocks, risers and treads. The slope of the stringers and the length of the stock needed to make them may be measured directly from these two developmental views.

Illustrations: Richard Glassman

again at 48 in., and so on. As you progress building up the cylinder you have to figure out where the segments should go, otherwise you might end up putting one where you would want to clamp. In other words, arrange the height of the horizontal stiffeners so that when you laminate they won't be in the way. The photos (next page) should help you understand.

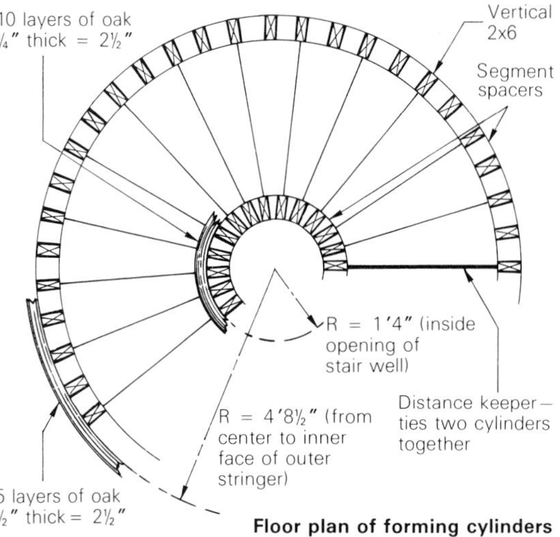

Floor plan of forming cylinders

Photos: Edward Krause

After you have the inside cylinder done, you nail a piece of ⅛-in. thick fiberboard that is 16 in. wide on the side of the cylinder, roughly where the stringer should be, and lay out the steps and risers to locate stringer position on the cylinder. I nailed small nails where the top edge of the stringer crossed each 2x6, taking the heads off the nails so I could remove the ⅛-in. board. The small nails remained in the 2x6s as the actual markers for the stringer. At this point I made 2 in. by 2 in. by 6 in. pieces of wood, cut at the angle the stringer was going, and nailed them to the 2x6 where I had the small nails. This block is preventing the stringer from climbing. It aids you in keeping the laminates in proper line.

I was able to bend ¼-in. thick boards of oak without any problem of breaking fibers. So I clamped the first board and on its backside I put little glue blocks to hold it to each 2x6 upright. After the glue set up I could take off the clamp and proceed with the next board. It took 10 laminations, each 12 ft. long, to make up the 2½ in. thickness. I clamped at each 2x6 upright and clamped in between, spreading glue as I went along. You have to have a good, even pressure distribution throughout your gluing. With the inside stringer done I built the outside cylinder and went ahead the same way. But it was nearly 20 ft. long, so I had to join the boards and stag-

Author finishes trim on circular staircase, which is supported only at the floor and landing. The sweeping railing was laminated on the same forms as the stringers, then carved to shape by hand.

Photos: Laszlo Gigacz

Gigacz built the outer forming cylinder after completing the inside stringer. Left, paper pattern for the outer stringer is pieced together on a layer of fiberboard. Center, the inner forming cylinder, seen from the top, is a forest of studs, spacers and clamps. Right, author twists clamps, dozens of clamps, as the outer stringer takes form. Curved blocks nailed to uprights keep the laminates from climbing upward.

ger the joints. I used a *V*-joint. The curve was easier so I could use ½-in. thick boards, five laminations.

While I still had the form up, I did a layout for the railing in the same fashion as for the stringer and laminated five strips of mahogany, each ½ in. by 2¼ in. After it was done I shaped the railing by hand, using gouges and rasps. I made a separate form to laminate the balcony railing. It was a simple bend. The volute and goose neck I carved out of solid. I bought the newel post and baluster.

Now that I'm done with laminating, I will talk about the so-called carriage. The carriage is a frame consisting of the two stringers, the step-forming members, and horizontal wooden members to tie the stringers together. I used 5/16-in. iron rod threaded for nuts and washers to span the width behind the horizontal members. As you see on the drawing, the horizontal member has nothing to do with the risers. I should say, as I was putting the horizontal members in place and tightening the rods, I was able to remove the 2x6 cylinder forming members. The stair was on its own. I cut the step-forming pieces out of 3-in. thick stock and placed them on top of the stringers by way of glue and wood screws, and shaped them to the same curve as the stringer. I used 1⅛-in. thick white oak for the treads, rounding the face and ends. The risers are ¾-in. thick pine. Keep in mind, the steps and risers are nothing more than an aid for walking on. The load bearing is in the carriage. The steps and risers I glued and screwed together in pairs, and later at the job site I glued and screwed the top of each riser to the bottom of the next step. I put the screws in from the face of the riser, which was covered later with a molding going all around under the steps. Fancy applique—you could call it fretwork—also went on the face of the inside stringer, for covering up the nuts and for looks.

Next is to take down the stairs, which are marked where each piece will go. Then a short ride on a flat-bed truck, the ride for home. I must say I was a little nervous but soon, as I started to put the pieces of the puzzle together, my nervousness went away. I worked about a month in the house. Bachman painted the risers and balusters, and varnished the treads and railing. A plasterer covered over the metal lath on the bottom side of the stair. Everything worked out fine. □

Illustrations: Richard Glassman

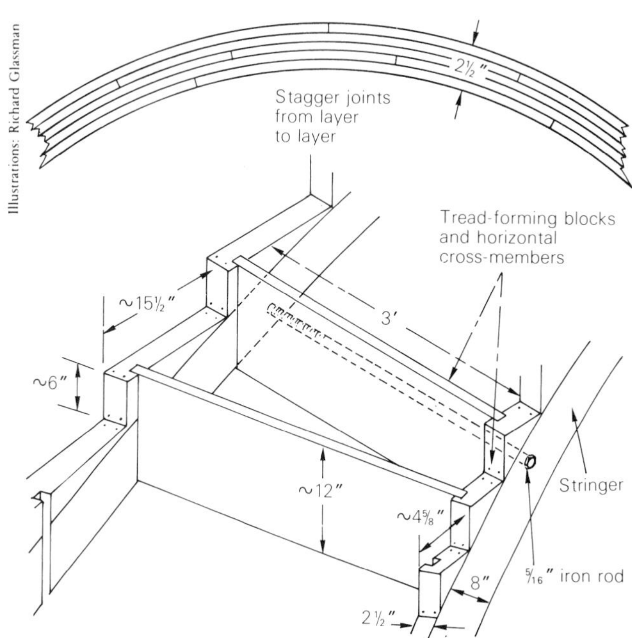

Laszlo Gigacz

Done with laminating, Gigacz adds horizontal tie-members reinforced by iron rod, and step-forming blocks, and removes the forming cylinders. The stairway is on its own.

Lapstrake Boatbuilding

The thousand-year-old way to keep afloat

by Simon Watts

Although she came off no drawing board, centuries of boatbuilding experience went into the design of Sea Urchin, above, a 10-ft. rowing boat made by Nova Scotian Jim Smith in 1963. As did generations of builders before him, Smith knew that lapstrake makes strong, light hulls that withstand the rigors of time and sea. Pictured below is Slippen, an English lapstrake pilot gig built in 1837 and still in daily use out of England's Scilly Isles. Lapstrake's relative ease of construction makes it ideal for a first boat. Simon Watts explains how to build the little Sea Urchin on pages 110 through 118.

©F.E. Gibson

The objective of much woodworking is to wrap wood around a hollow space. If the space is angular, the job is straightforward enough. We simply plane the edges of straight boards, glue them up until they are big enough and join them at the corners. But suppose the volume to be enclosed is curved? As boatbuilders and coopers know, the job then becomes a tricky exercise in cutting and planing constantly changing bevels and curves. And if the joints are to be watertight, as they must be on boats and barrels, the bevels must match perfectly.

Over the centuries, two basic approaches to boatbuilding have evolved. One is to construct a skeleton first and then cover it with a skin of planks, plywood or steel plates. The other is to make a shell of wood, fiberglass or concrete, and then stiffen it with an internal structure. The first method—called carvel—is roughly analogous to the cabinetmaker edge-joining boards. Carvel boats are smooth inside and out, their planks lie tightly edge to edge, and they are fastened to a rigid framework within, so the shape of the boat is determined before any planks are hung. With the second method, known as lapstrake or clinker, it's the other way around. First the planks are bent into place around molds, then ribs are added to stiffen the structure. Each of the planks overlaps the one below it, making the boat look like a clapboard house. The lapstrake shell is light but remarkably strong—a quality that would make this method of construction useful for other types of woodwork, including furniture or architecture.

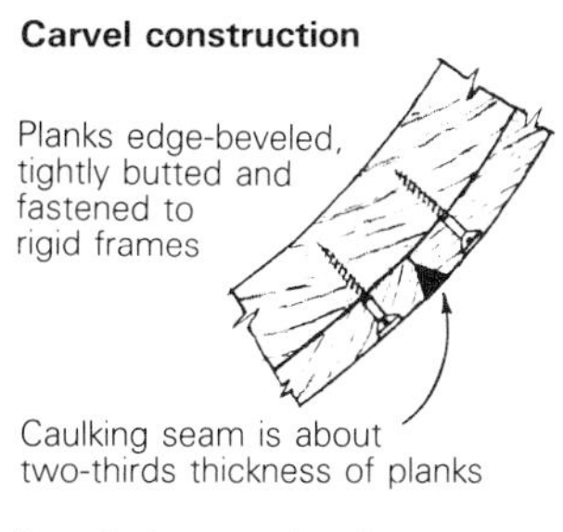
Carvel construction
Planks edge-beveled, tightly butted and fastened to rigid frames
Caulking seam is about two-thirds thickness of planks

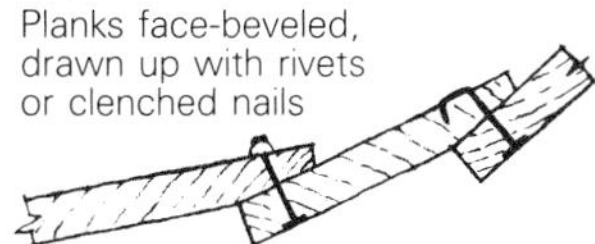
Lapstrake construction
Planks face-beveled, drawn up with rivets or clenched nails

Lapstrake's advantages were evident to early boatbuilders. Viking ships unearthed in Norway show us that the method has been used for more than ten centuries. Some of the most refined and practical workboats ever built, such as the English pilot gigs and American Adirondack guide-boats, use this method. In this article, I'll describe these craft and outline the principles of lapstrake construction. In the following article, I'll describe how to build a traditional 10-ft. lapstrake rowing boat—a type that developed in Nova Scotia over the past century. Such a basic lapstrake boat can be built by anyone with average woodworking skills, using locally available materials and simple tools. Small lapstrakes make elegant and practical little boats, safe, seaworthy and fun to row.

Basic lapstrake—Lapstrake construction meets a primary requirement of small boats—flexible strength combined with light weight. Where the planks overlap, the double thicknesses of planking act as stringers that strengthen and reinforce the hull. This makes for thinner planking than is possible with carvel, and thus a lighter boat. There is another reason why lapstrake planking can be thinner than carvel planking: planks butted edge to edge don't make a watertight joint. To keep out water on a carvel boat, a caulking of unspun cotton or oakum is driven into a small, vee-shaped groove (called a caulking seam) between adjacent planks. This means there is a limit to the thinness of carvel planking—anything less than ½ in. and the caulking is liable to be driven right through. There is no such limit with lapstrake because there is no caulking between the planks. The overlapping planks are beveled for a close fit and then tightly fastened together with rivets or clenched nails driven through the laps.

Forms or molds are often used in building a lapstrake boat, but only as temporary guides. The actual volume and shape of the boat are obtained by twisting and bowing the planks until they take on a form pleasing to the builder's eye. Traditionally, lapstrakes are built right side up on a strongback, a stout beam attached firmly to the shop floor. The keel, transom (back) and stem (front) of the boat are temporarily fastened to the strongback along with the molds. Then the whole assembly is securely braced before planking is begun. In carvel construction, the thicker planks can be wedged sideways and clamped to rigid frames for fastening. But trying to force the thinner planking of lapstrake into place will only cause it to buckle and spring away from the molds. The lapstrake builder must always work with the planking, not against it. Experienced builders often use only one mold giving the shape of the boat at its midsection. The rest of the boat's shape is made by twisting and bowing the plank until it looks right. Traditional Norwegian small craft are built by eye, entirely without molds, and so reflect the builders' idiosyncrasies more than a boat built around molds does.

While the planking lines on the smooth, painted hull of a carvel boat are barely noticeable, they are the most conspicuous feature of a lapstrake. Any errors in the way the planks are laid out are obvious—even to the untrained eye. This is a case where whatever looks right is right. Abrupt changes in width between adjacent planks appear awkward, as does excessive taper—it also may not leave enough room at the ends for fastenings. "Shapely" boats (a euphemism for tubby) are harder to plank than slender ones.

As each plank is bent into place, it must be fastened to its neighbor. There are several methods that can be used to pull the laps tightly together. Most often, copper nails are driven through the laps from the outside, a copper washer is forced

Lapstrake boats are built on a strongback attached to the floor. This is a Sea Urchin copy being planked up around molds. Keel, transom and stem are in place and firmly braced to one another and an overhead beam. Note rivets where planks overlap.

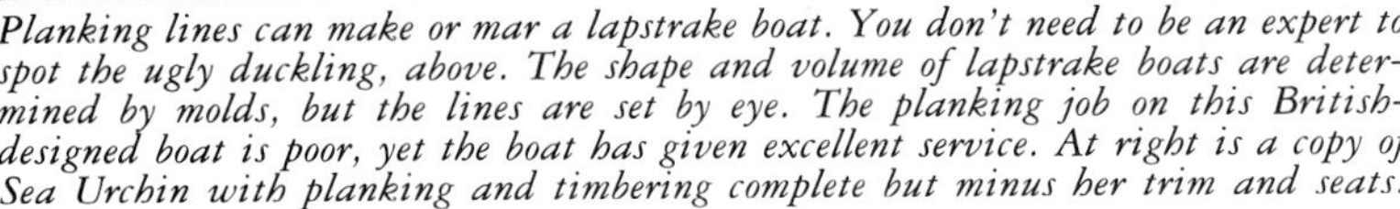

Planking lines can make or mar a lapstrake boat. You don't need to be an expert to spot the ugly duckling, above. The shape and volume of lapstrake boats are determined by molds, but the lines are set by eye. The planking job on this British-designed boat is poor, yet the boat has given excellent service. At right is a copy of Sea Urchin with planking and timbering complete but minus her trim and seats.

down over the point, then the nail is clipped off short. The cut end is then peened over, forming a rivet. Another way is to turn the point of the nail back so it reenters the wood. To make a watertight seal, the upper, outside surface of each plank is usually beveled so the plank above lies flat against it. This bevel varies along the length of the boat—the more curvature the boat has, the steeper the bevel must be. If the overlap were continued into the bow and stern it would look clumsy and let in water. A tapered rabbet, called a gain, is therefore planed into the ends of the plank so they lie more or less flush at stem and stern, as shown in the drawing below. This explains why the lines of planking seem to disappear into the stem at the bow of the boat. Bare, wood-to-wood joints, carefully fitted, should need no filler to be watertight. When first put in the water, or after winter storage, a lapstrake boat usually leaks a little, but as soon as the planks have had a chance to swell, they tighten. Many boatbuilders now use a bead of sealer such as polysulfide between the laps to act as a gasket.

After the boat has been planked, reinforcing ribs called timbers are installed. Usually, these are of white oak, steamed, bent, and clench-nailed or riveted to the planking.

Plank gains

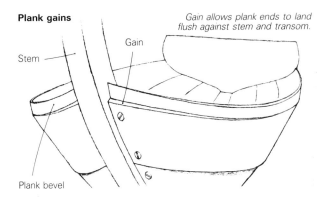

Gain allows plank ends to land flush against stem and transom.

Gain

Stem

Plank bevel

Lapstrake building is surprisingly fast. Carvel boatbuilders must "spile" to get the shape of their planks. This means bending a thin batten around the boat, marking on it the shape of the plank already in place and transferring that shape to the new plank. A carvel builder must work fast to accomplish more than one round of planking in a day. For a small lapstrake boat, the stock is limber enough to be wrapped around the boat and scribed directly, thus eliminating spiling. If the builder has continuous lengths of stock to work with and if he knows the boat, an 18-footer can be lapstrake-planked in three days. The method is also more forgiving—if the overlap varies slightly along the length of the plank, it's not critical.

In the water, lapstrake boats behave differently from smooth-skinned ones. They don't roll as readily because the laps "grab" the water and have more resistance to being pushed sideways. Norwegian fishermen, who have centuries of experience with lapstrake boats, talk of "packing" a layer of air bubbles in the laps as the boat moves through the water. This foamy water passing under the hull is thought to reduce drag and increase speed. Lapstrake hulls are supple and the larger ones flex noticeably in rough water. This quality makes lapstrake unsuitable for large cargo-carrying vessels; flexing can loosen rivets, opening the laps, causing the boat to leak. But lapstrake's combination of lightness and strength, not to mention good looks, makes it a sensible choice for small and intermediate-size boats.

Simon Watts is a cabinetmaker, boatbuilder and contributing editor to Fine Woodworking *magazine. Photos by the author except where noted.*

Viking ships

Norway has an unbroken boatbuilding tradition going back several thousand years, but the popular image of sleek, dragon-headed Viking ships is only part of the picture. Using lapstrake construction, the Vikings built a wide range of boats, from delicate *faerings* ("four oars") to large seagoing vessels for raiding and colonizing. The largest of these, the Long Serpent, which was built around 1000 AD, is thought to have been 160 ft. long. Viking leaders prized these ships so highly that they were often buried in them.

Much of what we know about these boats comes from the discovery and excavation of Viking ships in burial mounds in Norway. The largest and best preserved of these, the 76-ft. Gokstad ship, had remained buried for close to a thousand years. Although quite flattened by the weight of the mound, she was removed in fragments and reassembled in a specially designed museum near Oslo. Except for a pine deck and mast, the Gokstad ship is built entirely of oak. The 60-ft. keel was hewn from a single log and resembles a "T" in cross section. Instead of light, bent ribs or timbers, all Viking ships had sturdy "grown frames." These were selected from pieces of oak that naturally conformed to the required shape. Lacking sawmills, the Viking shipbuilders split their planks out of round logs. The resulting wedge-shaped boards were stronger than sawn wood, though, because the grain fibers inevitably followed the plane of the plank.

Each side of the Gokstad ship has sixteen of these overlapping planks fastened to each other with iron rivets. Below the waterline, the planks are not nailed to the frames but are lashed with thin spruce roots. A pair of cleats was hewn into each plank to serve as eyelets, so the lashings wouldn't pass through the hull. Above the waterline, planks are fastened to frames with an ancient device called a treenail—wooden pegs driven right through, then split and wedged at both ends.

Norse boatbuilding survives yet today. The Oselver boat, above, built by Alfred Sovik, is a descendent of early Viking lapstrake craft discovered in ancient burial mounds.

As early as the 10th century, the Vikings had developed lapstrake to a high art, and the boats pictured here are striking illustrations of their skill. The most complete example of the Norse boatbuilding technique is the Gokstad ship, below right. This large, seagoing vessel was owned by a Viking chieftan, and it became his tomb. So valued were these boats that they were frequently lavished with ornate carving, as shown in the stern view of the unearthed Oseberg ship, below left.

Pilot gigs

The Scilly Isles lie some 40 miles off the coast of Cornwall at the junction of two great shipping lanes—the English and Bristol channels. Incoming ships traditionally stopped here to pick up a pilot, fresh provisions and instructions from their owners. As soon as a vessel was sighted, pilots were rowed out in small boats to meet it and often this developed into a race, since the first boat out got the job, and the losers only a long pull home. The result of this constant competition was the creation and rapid evolution of a remarkable boat—the pilot gig.

A typical gig of the 1830s was 28 ft. to 32 ft. long and had a full bow with a high, narrow transom that effectively made it double-ended at the waterline. Gigs were built for seaworthiness and speed, but since the gig also had to be light enough to be picked up and launched by its crew, lapstrake was the best construction. The planking, which was always Cornish elm, was only ¼ in. thick, fastened with copper rivets and reinforced with slender oak timbers.

Gigs were the local equivalent of pickup trucks, ferrying cricket teams and wedding parties and delivering local produce to market. When a vessel went astray in fog or storm, the gigs went out for rescue and salvage. The speedy gigs were well suited for smuggling. Rowed by hardy, determined men, an eight-oared gig was more than a match for any revenue cutter of the day, and crews traded fresh produce for contraband, or rowed more than 100 miles across to France for spirits and tobacco.

Apart from the elegance of their construction, the most remarkable aspect of the gigs is their longevity. Workboats seldom last more than half a century, but several gigs—including the venerable Newquay, built in 1812 by Cornishman William Peters—are actually still in use. I asked the last boatbuilding member of the Peters family, Frank, about this. "The secret," he said, "was in the seasoning. Fresh water rots wood, but salt preserves it. The old boys selected their own trees—never took one more than half grown 'cause the nature was gone out of it." The boatbuilders would then chain the logs in creek mud where saltwater tides could soak them until worms had eaten away the sapwood—about four years. "Then they'd haul 'em out, adze 'em off and saw 'em," Frank told me. After four years of salt pickling and another year of drying, planks were ready for use.

Cornish elm is too small to make one-piece keels, so these were made of oak or American elm. The keels were not given the salt treatment and in the surviving gigs they have had to be replaced. As piloting declined toward the end of the century, so did the gigs. During the 1950s, though, interest in them reawakened; new rowing clubs were formed and funds were collected for repairing the survivors. Gig racing has become so popular that several new boats have been built.

©F.E. Gibson

This end-on view of the gig Active makes it easy to see why large lapstrake hulls flex noticeably in a rough sea. Active, copied from an existing gig, was built by Thomas Chudleigh in the Scillies. The Newquay, below, built by the Peters family in 1812, is the oldest pilot gig in existence. This six-oared boat has a full bow that rises to a sea rather than plowing through it. The almost vertical stem is characteristic of many British-designed lapstrake boats.

Ralph Bird

Adirondack guide-boats

About the time the English pilot gigs reached their final form, a very refined type of lapstrake boat appeared in America—the Adirondack guide-boat. Like the gigs, the guide-boats were working craft built for a special need. The Adirondack region in Upstate New York had few roads but many lakes and streams. The first settlers, hunters and trappers mostly, needed a lightweight, portable boat. Indian canoes were used at first, but as these wore out, plank boats gradually replaced them.

Guide-boats began as conventional lapstrakes but were too heavy to be carried by one man and were noisy in the water. Lighter, quieter boats were made by beveling the white pine planks at the joints instead of overlapping them. A smooth, uninterrupted skin was the result. Too fragile for nails or rivets, the joints were instead fastened with two staggered rows of copper tacks. Each row was driven from opposite directions and the points turned back into the wood. On the best boats, the laps are so perfectly fitted that they can barely be felt and are invisible when painted.

Construction procedures also differed from those for conventional lapstrake boats. Instead of timbers being bent into place after the shell had been completed, the boat was planked around a cage of L-shaped spruce crooks which extended and overlapped across the bottom plank. Finding and extracting suitable stumps to make these crooks was a considerable chore.

Two types of lap were used: a feather edge and a modified shiplap. The latter made a better joint but was harder to do well. Neither was as strong as conventional lapstrake because it didn't have the double thickness of riveted planks.

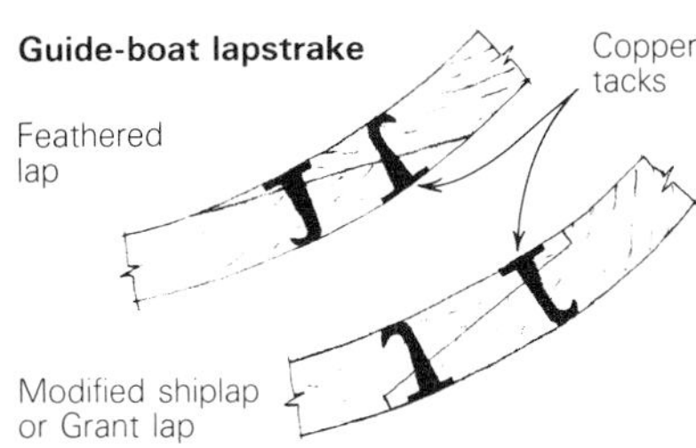

Lightness was so important in guide-boats that builders reduced the thickness of the pine planking to ¼ in. and replaced solid wood seats with caning. This constant refinement produced a boat akin to a fine musical instrument. "Resonance," write Kenneth and Helen Durant in *The Adirondack Guide-Boat* (International Marine Publishing Co., Camden, Maine), "was evidence of a boat in good condition. A guide-boat without resonance was a sodden hull passing into decay."

These boats were often built on a strongback that could be lowered and tilted as planking proceeded. They had no keel but started with an elliptical bottom board. The two stems were attached to this board and then the intermediate ribs. A 16-ft. boat typically had 36 ribs sawn from 13 different patterns. These largely determined the shape of the boat, instead of the molds used in conventional lapstrake.

For more than 60 years, the guide-boats served to carry the guide and his "sports" and their gear across choppy lake waters. As the Adirondacks became more accessible, such refined boats were no longer needed and they passed out of use. Fortunately, some of the finest examples have survived in private camps and at the Adirondack Museum at Blue Mountain Lake, N.Y. □

Helen Durant, courtesy of the Adirondack Museum

Adirondack Museum

Light weight was an essential quality of a guide-boat. Planking was reduced to ¼ in. and seats were caned for lightness, as in the photo above. The smooth hulls, which weighed as little as 65 lb., made for quiet movement through the water—vital to hunters and trappers. Guide-boats could be rowed or paddled. But unlike conventional lapstrake craft, the shape of a guide-boat was determined by pairs of ribs fastened to a bottom board, as in the photo at left, instead of molds on a strongback. Ribs were not steam-bent but cut from natural crooks in spruce stumps.

Building a Lapstrake Boat

A traditional design that's ideal for the beginner

by Simon Watts—drawings by Sam Manning

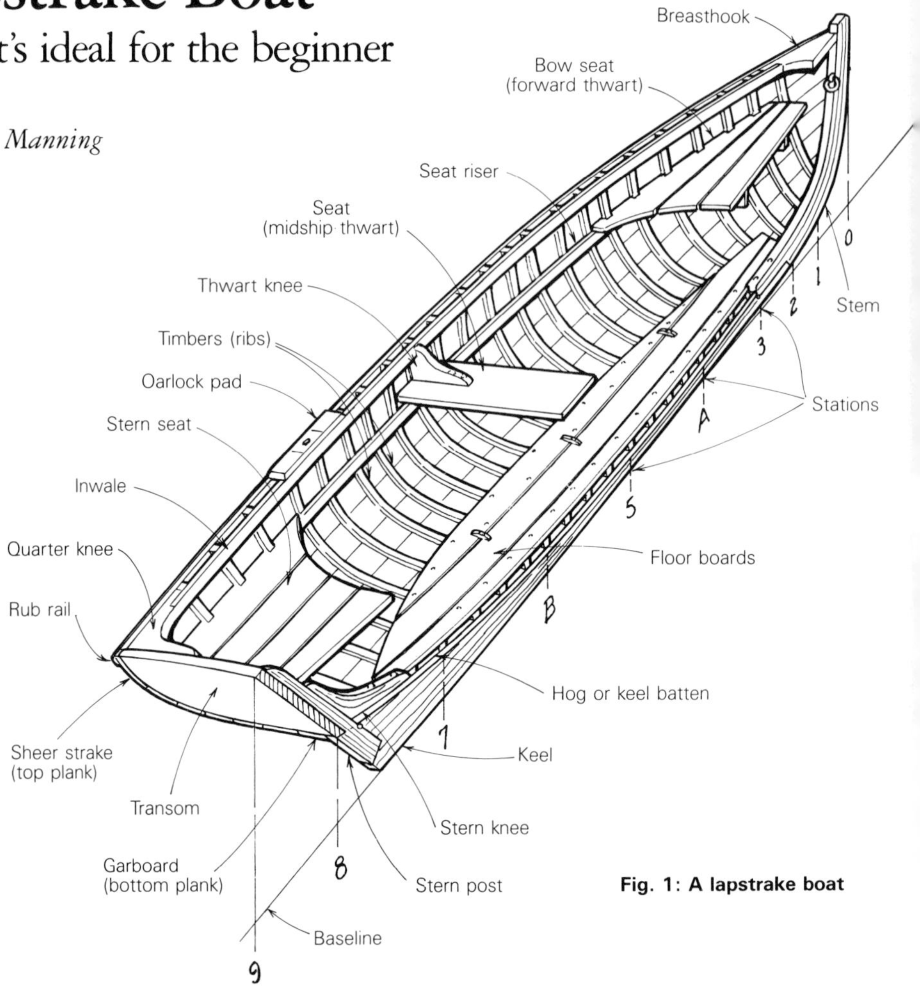

Fig. 1: A lapstrake boat

About 15 years ago, I bought a 10-ft. rowing boat secondhand from Jim Smith, a taciturn and rather crusty Nova Scotian. Smith was a traditional boatbuilder and not a conscious designer. He built boats out of his head and was impatient with paper plans. Yet he was proud of his work and swore he would never build a boat he wouldn't go to sea in himself.

Smith built this boat, christened Sea Urchin by my children, using a method called lapstrake. This construction, which I wrote about in the previous article, has a long history of producing strong, light hulls. Sea Urchin has been rowed in a variety of wind and weather—often inexpertly—and, like a well-mannered horse, has no vices. These experiences have given me the confidence to offer plans and instructions for building a copy of the boat.

Like all workboats, Sea Urchin can be built of locally available materials using a surprisingly small complement of tools: a saber saw or bandsaw, an electric drill and the usual assortment of hand tools. Building this boat is within the reach of even a novice woodworker. In fact, an amateur woodworker friend of mine built one as part of this article's preparation.

Using the traditional lapstrake technique, the boat is constructed right side up, on a hefty frame called a strongback. Two molds, which act as guides in setting the boat's shape, are mounted on the strongback, and the planks or strakes are laid up around them. After the planks have been riveted or nailed together at the overlaps, reinforcing timbers (ribs) are added to stiffen the hull.

Materials—The original Sea Urchin is planked with relatively heavy, ½-in. white pine, to withstand hard use and Nova Scotia's winters. But for recreational use the boat can safely be planked with ⅜-in. white pine, Northern white cedar, red cedar, or cypress. The other parts—transom, thwarts, keel, knees and timbers—are all red oak. In the cold, salt waters of Nova Scotia this combination gives a reasonable lifespan—20 years or more. For warm, freshwater service I suggest the more durable white oak instead of red.

Kiln-dried wood is seldom used for boatbuilding. It is much harder to work than green wood and isn't as amenable to steaming. Once in the water, planks swell to seal any leaks, but kiln-dried stock can swell too much, straining the fastenings. Planking lumber can be barely air-dry, verging on green. It will continue to dry out on the boat, which helps to "set" the boat's shape. All the oak parts should be air-dry except the timbers, which steam best when green. If you can't buy green oak, soak the pieces in salt water for a week before steaming and installing them—the salt inhibits the formation of fungus.

Butt logs with a natural curve or sweep to the grain make ideal planking—there's less waste and they're stronger since the grain follows the curve of the planks.

Sea Urchin has six knees—wooden brackets that brace the transom, seats and other structures that meet at angles—and they are best cut from natural crooks, wood with curved grain which occurs where tree limbs and roots join the trunk. Sea Urchin has red oak knees, but applewood, tamarack, spruce and locust are often used. You can rough the knees out with a chainsaw right on the tree, well in advance, and coat them with linseed oil so they'll season without checking. Knees and stems can be steam-bent or form-laminated using a waterproof glue such as Aerolite. If hardware, fittings and paint are not available locally from marine suppliers, they can be ordered by mail from Duck Trap Woodworking (PO Box 88, Lincolnville, Maine 04849) or Wooden Boat Shop (1007 N.E. Boat St., Seattle, Wash. 98105).

You should work in an environment that is cooler and more humid than is usual for a furniture workshop, as dry air will cause fresh-sawn oak to check.

Photos, except where noted: Brian Gulick

Lapstrake boats are usually built on a stout frame called a strongback. The photo above shows the strongback with the boat's backbone, molds and transom mounted. The diagonal bracing keeps the structure rigid during planking.

Strongback and molds—Lapstrake boats are best built right side up so each strake, or plank, can be fastened without the need of a helper underneath, and so you can see the evolving shape of the boat without standing on your head. Most boatmakers build these craft on a strongback frame like that shown in the photo at left and in figure 2. If you have a choice, place the strongback at right angles to and about 6 ft. from the workbench so you'll have access to the bench and both sides of the boat.

With the strongback built, construction of the boat begins with the molds, transom and backbone. These parts will form the basic shape of the boat, and the planks will be hung around them. See page 118 for an explanation of determining the mold and transom dimensions. I usually make full-size patterns on heavy paper folded in half, which assures symmetry when opened up. Make up the molds from ¾-in. dry pine, mark the centerlines and sheer lines, and leave "ears" projecting to attach bracing, as in figure 3.

Make the transom from two pieces of oak joined with cleats fastened with bronze screws. Don't

Fig. 2: The strongback

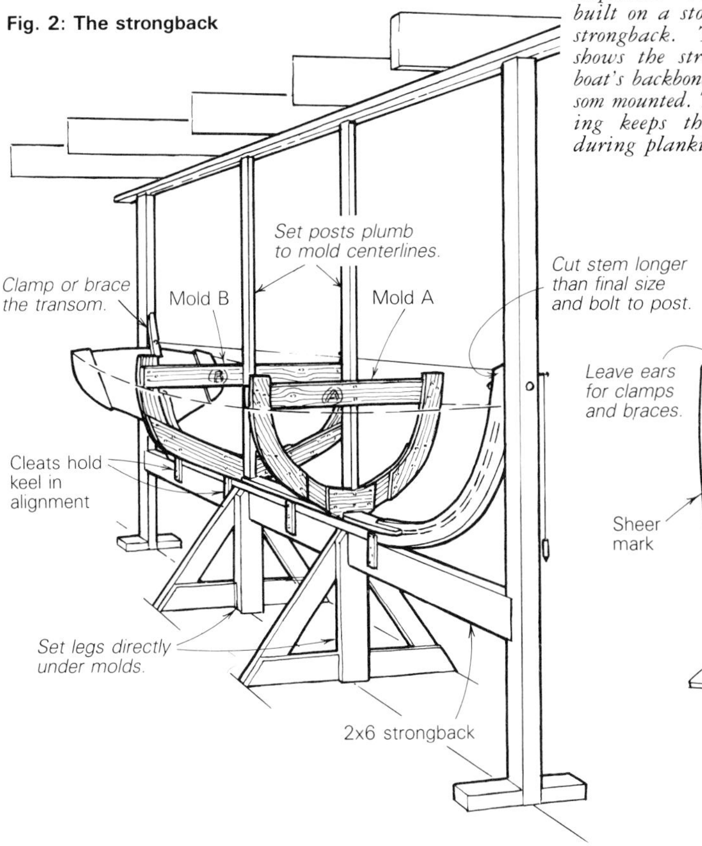

Set posts plumb to mold centerlines.
Clamp or brace the transom.
Mold B
Mold A
Cut stem longer than final size and bolt to post.
Cleats hold keel in alignment
Set legs directly under molds.
2x6 strongback

Strongback detail

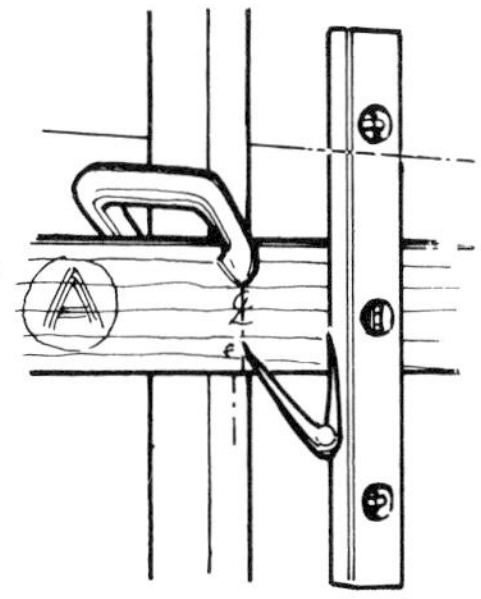

To plumb and align molds, check centerlines against an offset tight line before fastening molds to post.

Fig. 3: Hull mold

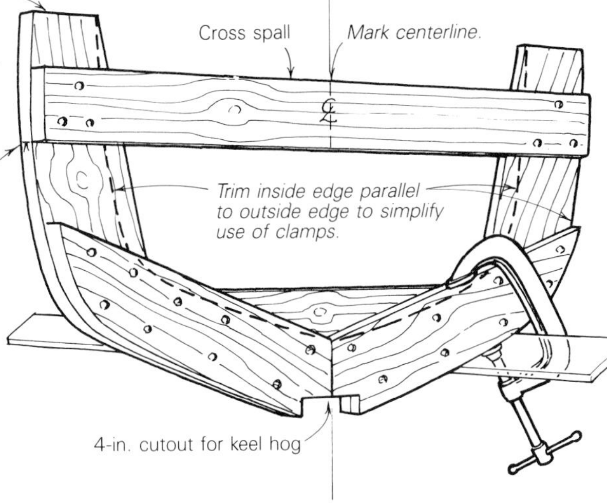

Leave ears for clamps and braces.
Cross spall
Mark centerline.
Sheer mark
Trim inside edge parallel to outside edge to simplify use of clamps.
4-in. cutout for keel hog

leave these cleats off in favor of simply gluing-up the transom, or you'll have only end grain to nail into when fastening the planks at the stern. After you have assembled the transom, set your bandsaw or saber saw to 32° and cut the bevel as shown in figure 4. You'll need to adjust this angle with a spokeshave later, to give the planks a solid landing.

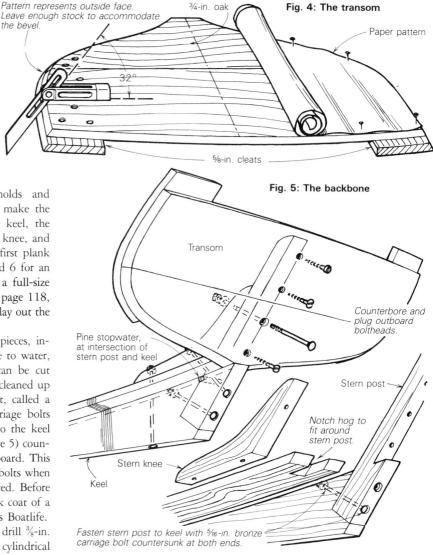

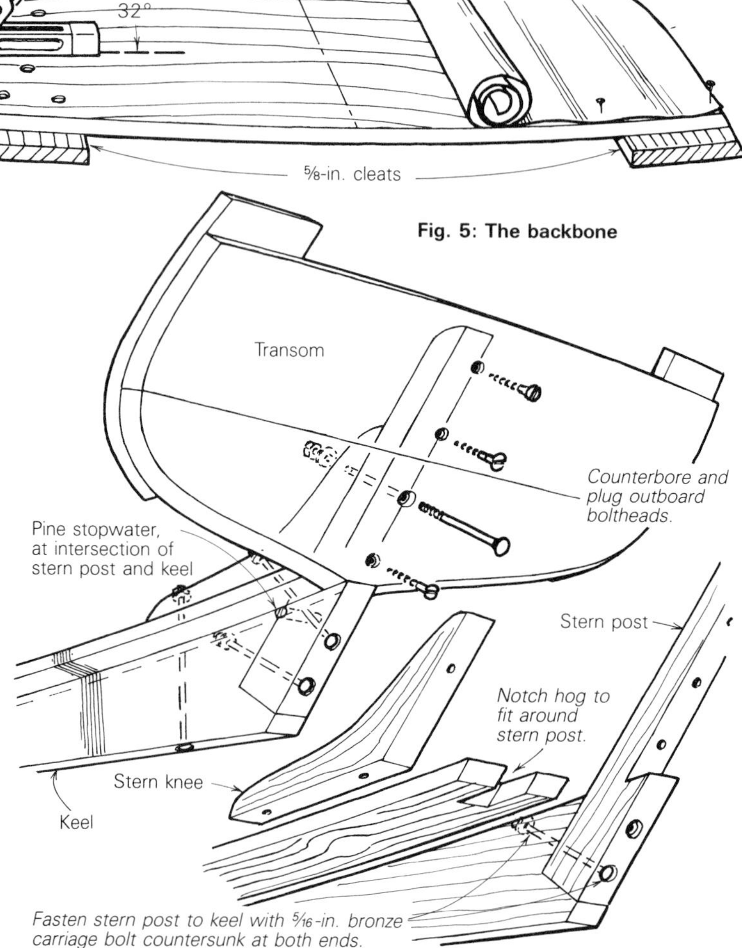
Fig. 4: The transom
Pattern represents outside face. Leave enough stock to accommodate the bevel.
¾-in. oak
Paper pattern
32°
⅝-in. cleats
Fig. 5: The backbone
Transom
Counterbore and plug outboard boltheads.
Pine stopwater, at intersection of stern post and keel
Stern post
Notch hog to fit around stern post.
Stern knee
Keel
Fasten stern post to keel with 5⁄16-in. bronze carriage bolt countersunk at both ends.

Backbone—Before attaching the molds and transom to the strongback, you must make the boat's backbone. This consists of the keel, the stem, the stern post and its connecting knee, and the keel batten, or hog, to which the first plank will be attached. Refer to figures 5 and 6 for an explanation of these parts, and make a full-size pattern from the drawing and table on page 118, which you can "loft" into templates to lay out the shapes directly on the stock.

The joints that connect these three pieces, intended to minimize end-grain exposure to water, are critical and must fit well. They can be cut with a bandsaw or handsaw, and then cleaned up with a plane or chisel. The stem joint, called a scarf, is fastened with two bronze carriage bolts and nuts. The stern post is fastened to the keel with a 5⁄16-in. bronze carriage bolt (figure 5) countersunk at both ends and bunged outboard. This joint will be further strengthened with bolts when the transom and stern knee are mounted. Before assembling the joints, give them a thick coat of a commercial bedding compound such as Boatlife.

After you've bolted up these joints, drill ⅜-in. holes through the joint lines. Drive a cylindrical plug of dry pine through the hole (see figures 5 and 6 for exact location), and cut it flush on both sides. This plug, called a stopwater, keeps water from seeping along the joint into the boat.

The next step is to make the hog and attach it to the keel with five through 5⁄16-in. bronze carriage bolts, located so they won't interfere with the placement of timbers later. The top surface of the keel must be planed and squared so the hog, when sprung down to it, lies flat.

Now cut and fit the hog, then remove it so that you can lay out the stem rabbet—a V-shaped step in which the plank ends land at the bow (figure 6). Experienced builders cut this out on the bench before planking, but to avoid errors I advise novices to cut a ¼-in. deep, 90° groove initially, and then to deepen and enlarge it to fit each plank as it's hung. The rabbet must be stopped at the top edge of the last plank (the sheer strake), so don't take it too far up—leave the last inch to be cut later.

To mark the stem rabbet, draw a pencil line along both sides of the keel, ⅜ in. (the planking thickness) down from the keel's top edge. This

The stern post is fastened to the keel with a bronze carriage bolt. Then the transom is attached with bronze bolts through the stern post and keel and into the stern knee. The small round plug between the stern post and keel is called a stopwater, but it is misplaced in this boat. It should be higher, just where the keel, hog and stern post intersect. Caulking cotton seals planks where they land on the transom, but bedding compound could be used instead.

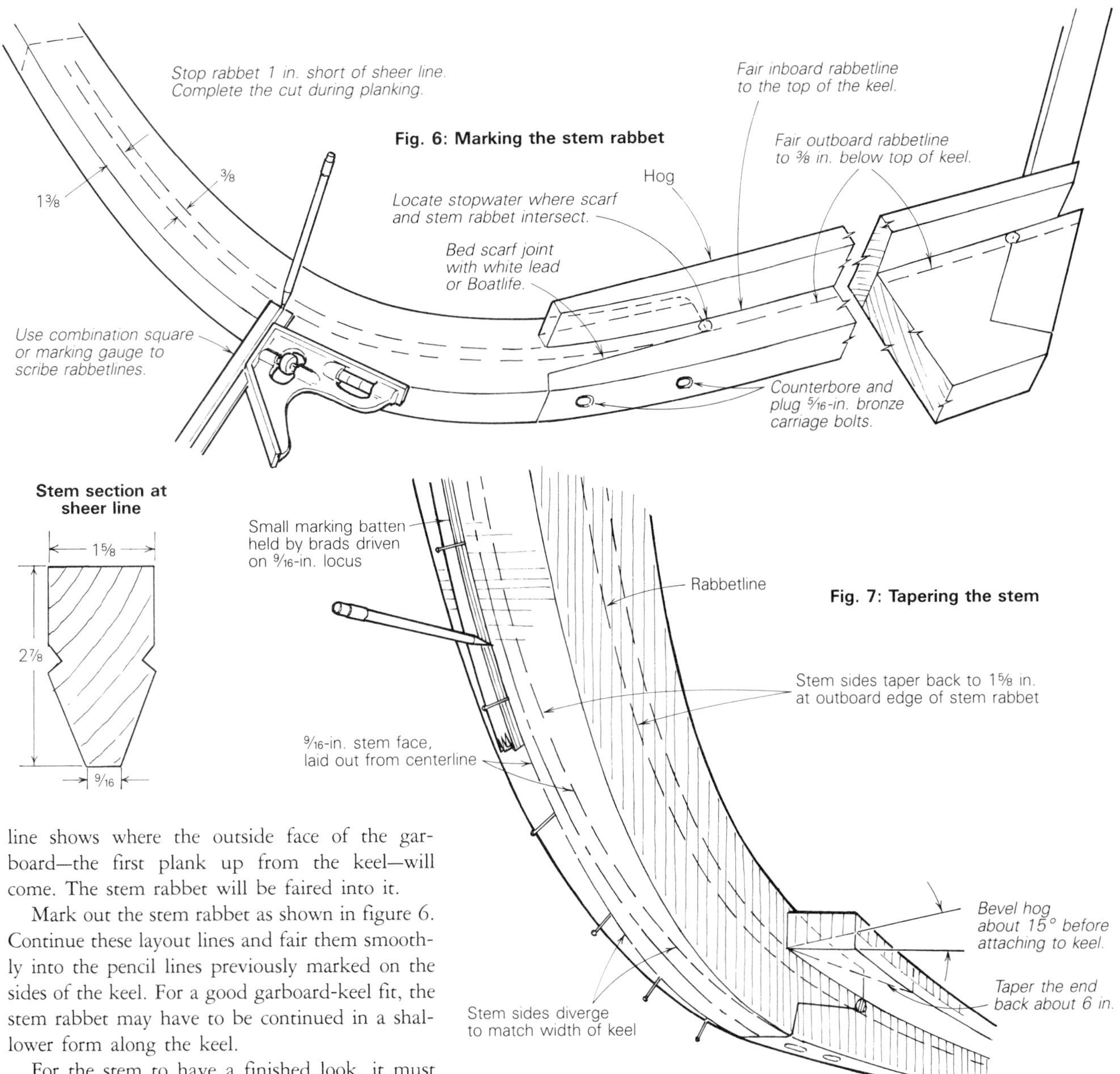
Stop rabbet 1 in. short of sheer line. Complete the cut during planking.
Fair inboard rabbetline to the top of the keel.
Fig. 6: Marking the stem rabbet
Fair outboard rabbetline to ⅜ in. below top of keel.
1⅜
⅜
Hog
Locate stopwater where scarf and stem rabbet intersect.
Bed scarf joint with white lead or Boatlife.
Use combination square or marking gauge to scribe rabbetlines.
Counterbore and plug 5/16-in. bronze carriage bolts.
Stem section at sheer line
1⅝
2⅞
9/16
Small marking batten held by brads driven on 9/16-in. locus
Rabbetline
Fig. 7: Tapering the stem
Stem sides taper back to 1⅝ in. at outboard edge of stem rabbet
9/16-in. stem face, laid out from centerline
Bevel hog about 15° before attaching to keel.
Taper the end back about 6 in.
Stem sides diverge to match width of keel

line shows where the outside face of the garboard—the first plank up from the keel—will come. The stem rabbet will be faired into it.

Mark out the stem rabbet as shown in figure 6. Continue these layout lines and fair them smoothly into the pencil lines previously marked on the sides of the keel. For a good garboard-keel fit, the stem rabbet may have to be continued in a shallower form along the keel.

For the stem to have a finished look, it must be tapered in cross section from 1⅝ in. in thickness at the outboard stem rabbetline to 9/16 in. at its leading edge. Mark out the taper, using a thin batten (figure 7) to draw a fair transition as the stem thickness increases toward the scarf and into the keel, then plane the taper.

Before bolting the hog to the keel, saw or plane about a 15° bevel on its lower edges. This angle will be correct only at the center mold, and must increase toward stem and transom to accommodate the changing angle that the garboard makes with the keel. It can be adjusted with a rabbet plane when the garboard is hung.

Now place the completed backbone on the strongback, and secure it temporarily with clamps. Then install the hog and transom. Place the two molds in their proper position and attach them to the hog with diagonal screws. Plumb the stem and the stern post, brace them firmly and then align the mold centerlines, using the method shown in the detail of the strongback on page 111. Everything must be securely braced so it cannot move during planking.

Planking—A lapstrake boat derives much of its strength from its planks, which are clench-nailed or riveted together lengthwise in overlapping joints. Jim Smith fastened the original Sea Urchin's pine planks with galvanized nails driven in from the outside and bent over (clenched) on the inside. This method is cheap and fast, but the nails can't easily be removed for repairs and they eventually rust. I used an alternative: copper nails with a copper washer called a rove, or burr, slipped over the point and forced down into the wood with a hollow punch. The pointed end of the nail is then clipped off close to the burr and riveted over with a ball-peen hammer. Bronze screws or bronze ring-barb nails fasten the planks at stem and transom.

Begin planking by making a full-size pattern of the garboard. Use a 10-in. to 12-in. wide piece of ¼-in. thick pine or ⅛-in. Masonite (the exact width will be determined later) to cut a rough pattern, and then twist it into place and clamp it lightly, using the method outlined in figure 8 to mark and trim the pattern. Once you've fitted the pattern well into the stem rabbet and along the keel, it's time to determine the widths of the garboard and the rest of the planks. Figure 9 shows a method of determining plank widths, which are then marked on the stem, transom and molds. (For another method,

Fig. 8: Fitting the garboard pattern

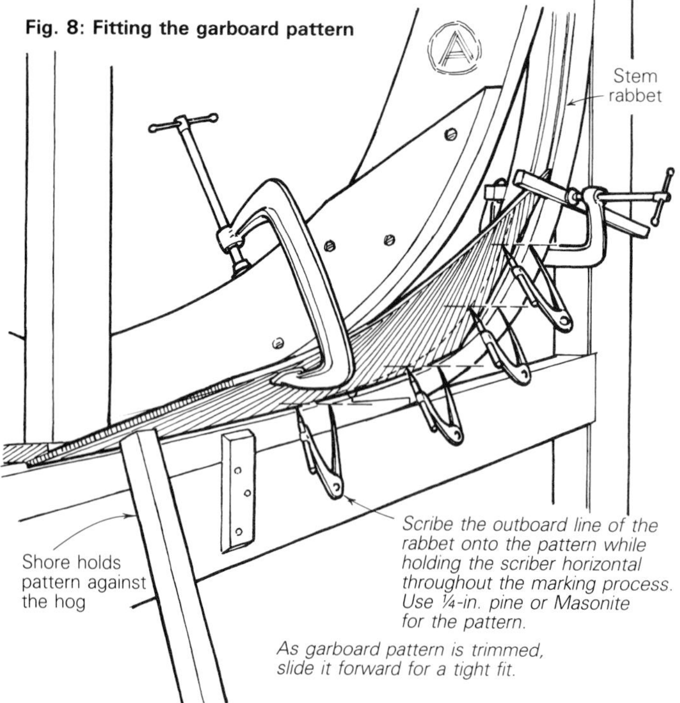

A
Stem rabbet
Scribe the outboard line of the rabbet onto the pattern while holding the scriber horizontal throughout the marking process. Use ¼-in. pine or Masonite for the pattern.
Shore holds pattern against the hog
As garboard pattern is trimmed, slide it forward for a tight fit.

Fig. 9: Laying off plank widths

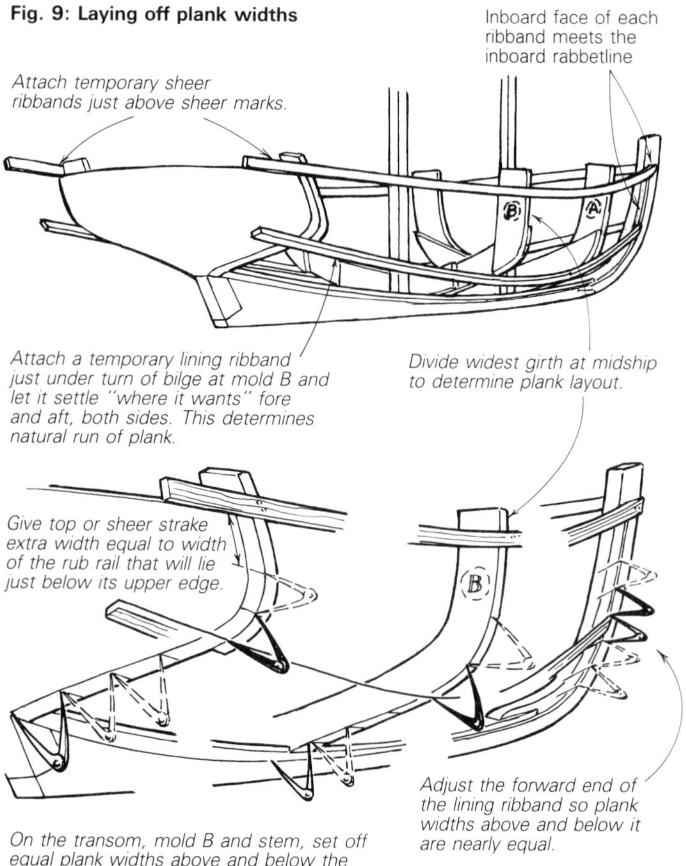

Inboard face of each ribband meets the inboard rabbetline
Attach temporary sheer ribbands just above sheer marks.
B
A
Attach a temporary lining ribband just under turn of bilge at mold B and let it settle "where it wants" fore and aft, both sides. This determines natural run of plank.
Divide widest girth at midship to determine plank layout.
Give top or sheer strake extra width equal to width of the rub rail that will lie just below its upper edge.
B
Adjust the forward end of the lining ribband so plank widths above and below it are nearly equal.
On the transom, mold B and stem, set off equal plank widths above and below the upper edge of the lining ribband, representing three planks below and four above. Check your marks for fairness with a batten before sawing plank stock.

refer to John Gardiner's *Building Small Classic Craft*—an invaluable book for amateur boatbuilders—which is published by International Marine, Camden, Maine 04843.) Use a straight-grained batten to mark a fair curve between the four width marks on your pattern, then saw and plane down to this line. With the pattern cut and fitted, transfer its shape to your plank (figure 10) so as to avoid dead knots, and try to take advantage of any natural sweep in the board. Any loose knots in the planking should be knocked out, and the hole reamed and plugged with a tapered pine plug dipped in Aerolite or resorcinol glue. The garboard has a considerable amount of twist toward the stem, and it is easier to do the final fitting after this twist has been steamed into it. The easiest way is to wrap it in a towel and pour on boiling water. Clamp it in place and leave it overnight to cool, then cut out the rest of the stem rabbet so the hood (bow) end fits nicely. Take time to fit the garboards properly—they are the most difficult planks to hang, and you can expect to break or otherwise spoil at least one in the process. Don't be discouraged if it doesn't go right the first time.

Before fastening the garboard, sand the inside surface, chamfer the inside corner and run a pencil line along the top outside edge of both garboards to mark the amount the next planks will overlap, ¾ in. Plane a 15° bevel away from this line. This can be done with a bench plane, but a rabbet plane with an adjustable fence is handier. To take the guesswork out of beveling laps, make a lap gauge (figure 12). Use the rabbet plane to cut the gains in the garboard and the other planks, which allow the strakes to lie flush at the stem and stern (figure 11).

Attach the garboard to the stem, hog and transom with 1-in. #10 bronze screws driven on 2-in. centers along the length of the keel and driven through the garboard into the hog. From now on, keep the boat balanced by planking evenly on both sides.

The planks on this boat are limber enough to be simply wrapped around the forms and marked directly from the edge of the plank already in place. Use slightly narrower planks where tight curves on the transom make splitting likely, or plane slight flats on the transom. Before committing planks to the saw, it's a good idea to line off one side of the boat with a batten for each intended plank-edge curve. This playing with battens until a curve "looks right" is a crucial part of lap-

Fig. 10: Marking the garboard template
(drawing is foreshortened for clarity)

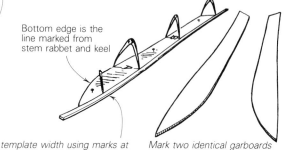

Bottom edge is the line marked from stem rabbet and keel

Mark out final template width using marks at stem, molds and transom. Top edge is the fair line run through these marks with a batten.

Mark two identical garboards from template; they will be mirror opposites.

strake construction. An unsightly line cannot be painted out later, whereas flat spots and "quick" turns are apparent at this stage and easily remedied by adjusting mold alignment or shimming flat spots.

Before continuing plank work, mark the centerlines of the timbers—the reinforcing ribs that fall every 6 in.—placing the first one on the centerline of the seat. Use a batten to carry these marks up from the hog to the sheer ribbands. Timbers in the middle two-thirds of the boat run straight up and down, but it is usual to lean them slightly forward as you approach the bow and slightly aft toward the stern.

Wrap the first plank around the boat so its lower edge overlaps the upper edge of the garboard by at least ¾ in. Run a pencil along the top edge of the garboard inside the boat, and also mark the position of the transom, each mold and the stem. If a wide plank must take a severe twist, you may have to cut it roughly to shape and then put it back on the boat for a more accurate line. Use the method in figure 13 to mark the plank's width. Then, using the first strake as a pattern, mark out its mate on the opposite side of the boat. Make an identical pair by planing both edges with the planks clamped or tacked together. Then plane the bevels and the gains, making sure that the beveled surface is flat or even slightly hollow, not rounded.

When the second plank is fitted and clamped to the garboard, fasten it to the stem. Drill pilot holes for the copper lap nails roughly 2 in. apart, laid out from the center of each timber marked on the hog and ribband. Now rove and rivet the nails, leaving the nails out where the timbers will occur.

The remaining planks are marked, cut and fitted in the same way, except that the angle of bevel needed will increase as the curvature of the boat's side increases. Leave the top (sheer) strake about ½ in. wider than the marks indicate. Clamp it temporarily in place and tack a ¾-in. batten up to represent the upper edge of the sheer strake. Stand back and take a look. Starting at the transom, the curve should dip gracefully at the waist and rise jauntily toward the bow. Adjust it until the curve is pleasing, even if it misses the original pencil marks. Few things spoil the look of a boat more than a dead or an exaggerated sheer. A narrow strip called the rub rail will be attached to the outboard top edge of the sheer strake to strengthen and protect it, so this plank must be wider by an amount equal to the width of the rail.

The boat's bottom plank, called the garboard, gets a considerable twist, which can be achieved only by soaking the end in boiling water, or steaming it, and clamping it in place to cool. This bow-on view shows how the stem is tapered back from its leading edge.

Fig. 11: The gains

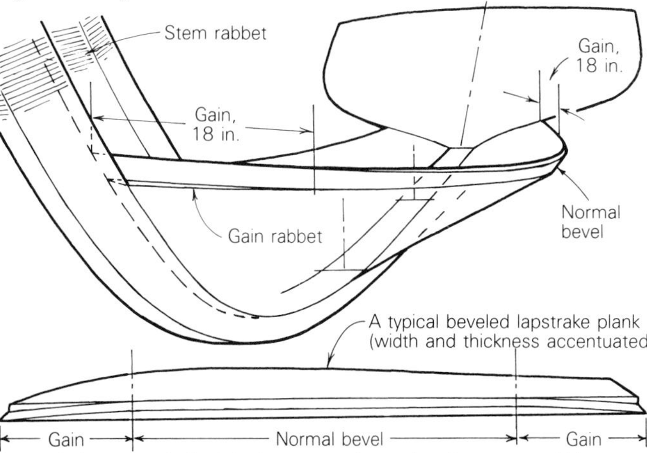

Lapped plank must lie flush in the stem rabbet and at the transom. This is done by cutting the plank bevel inward in the form of a rabbet until it runs out to a knife edge at the plank end. Transition between full lap and flush knife edge is called the gain.

Fig. 12: The lap gauge

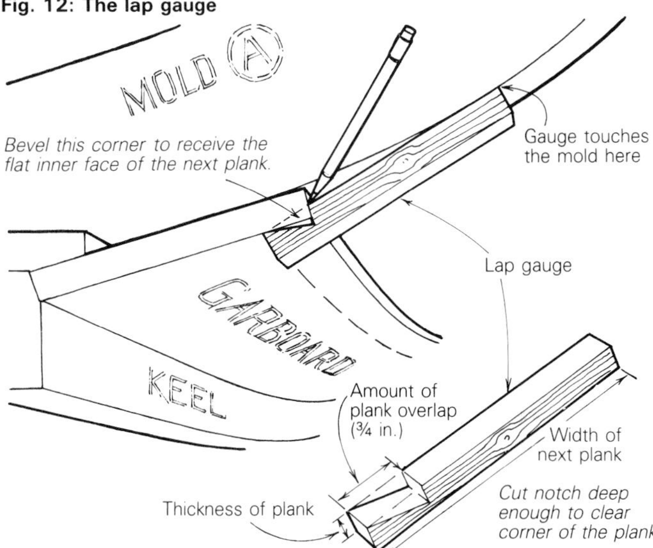

Use gauge to mark bevel angle at molds, transom and stem, and then fair to these marks by eye when planing the bevel.

Fig. 13: Marking and cutting planks

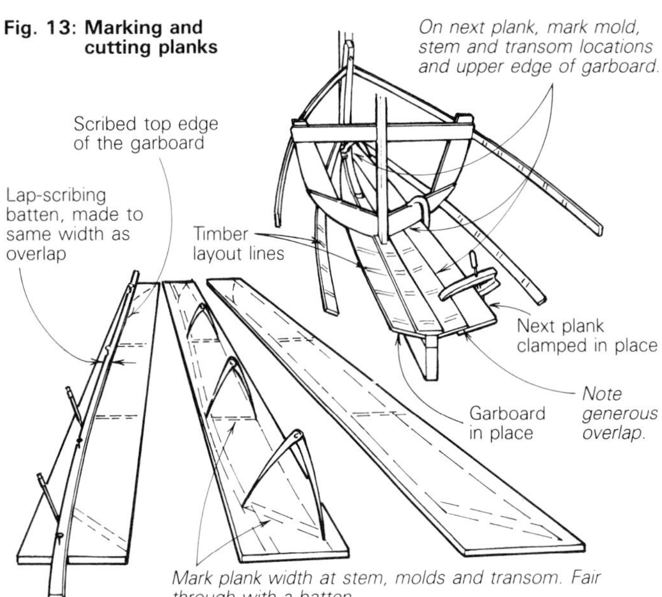

Mark plank width at stem, molds and transom. Fair through with a batten.

Fig. 14: Knees, breasthook and inwales

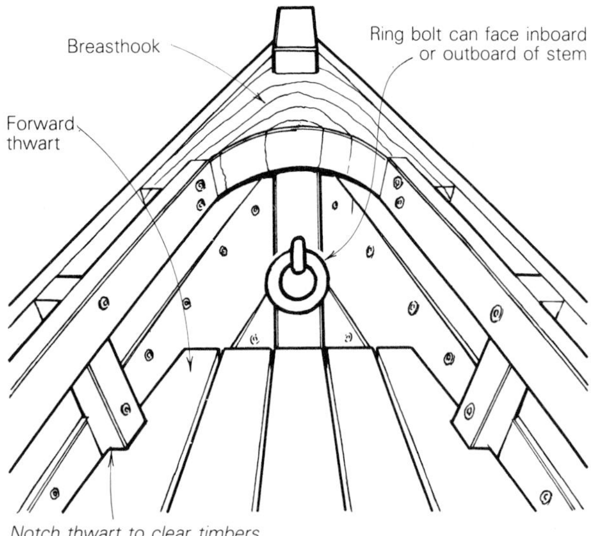

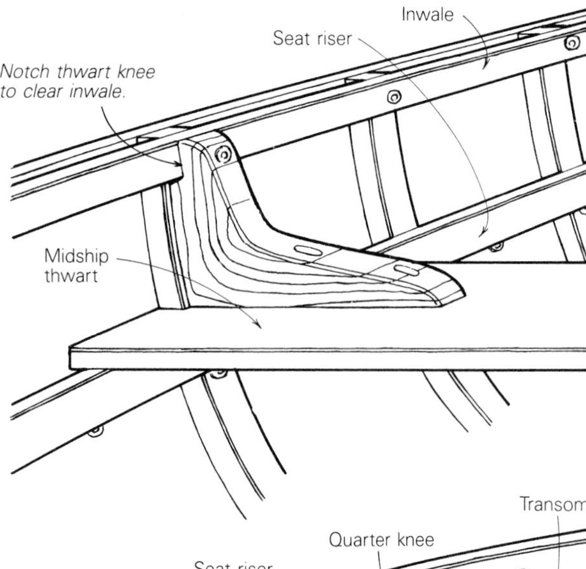

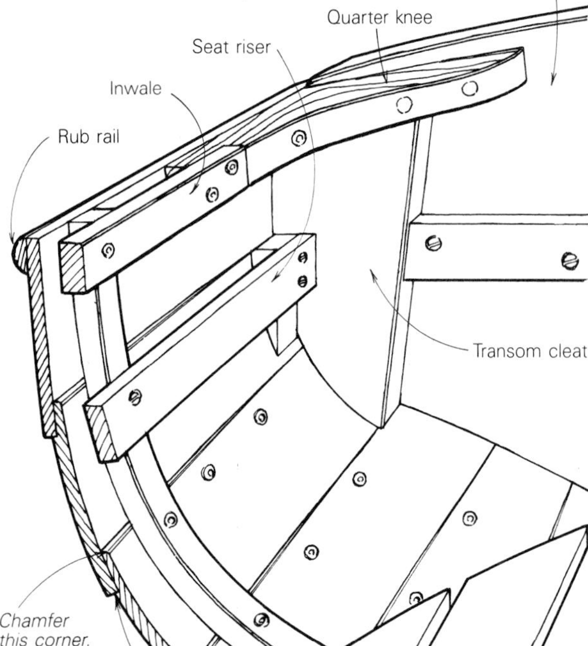

Timbering and knees—It's best to have three people for timbering, two to handle the hot timbers as they come from the steam box, one to drive in the nails from below. (For steam boxes and steambending basics, see pages 16 to 21.) Choose straight-grained oak for timbers; it will be less likely to break, and a coat of raw linseed oil before steaming will make it bend better. Cut the timbers extra long to give you leverage while bending. Leave the molds in place for timbering, but remove the crossbracing. Then start nails in from the outside so they are held firmly but do not stick into the boat through the planking. As each timber comes from the steamer, force it down into the boat and overbend it slightly so it will fit tightly. Then nail it to the hog with a single 1¼-in. bronze nail. Clamp it loosely to the sheer strake and hit the top end smartly with a hammer; this helps to get it lying flush against the planking. Then, working from the keel up, one person holds a backing iron against the timbers inside while another drives the copper nails through from the outside, as in the photo below. Speed is essential. If one timber cracks or begins to split, replace it. Don't be afraid to twist the timbers with an adjustable wrench so they conform to the changing angle of the planking. When all the timbers are nailed in place, let them cool overnight and then rivet them.

Now cut and fit the two quarter-knees and the breasthook, notching them out to receive the two inwales, as shown in figure 14. Inwales, which reinforce and stiffen the top edges of the boat, should be installed slightly proud of the sheer strake so they can be beveled to match the camber of the transom. The inwales are fastened through every other timber and are roved and riveted on the inside. The alternate timbers will be drilled for fastening the rub rail later.

Next install the two seat supports, called risers, which run roughly parallel to the sheer line (figure 14). Nail them to each timber with two small ring-nails or screw them. Install the thwart and the thwart knees, using roved nails through the inwale and thwarts, or screws if the nails are too short.

Rub rails, which mount outboard along the top edge of the sheer strake, should be straight-grained oak shaped to a half-round with a router or molding plane. Nail them through every other timber and set the nail heads far enough

With the planks in place, the reinforcing timbers (ribs) are added. It's a three-person job to bend the hot timbers into place and nail them. In this photo, Simon Watts and Alexis Nason install the aftermost rib. Note that the last two ribs are two pieces so they will clear the transom knee.

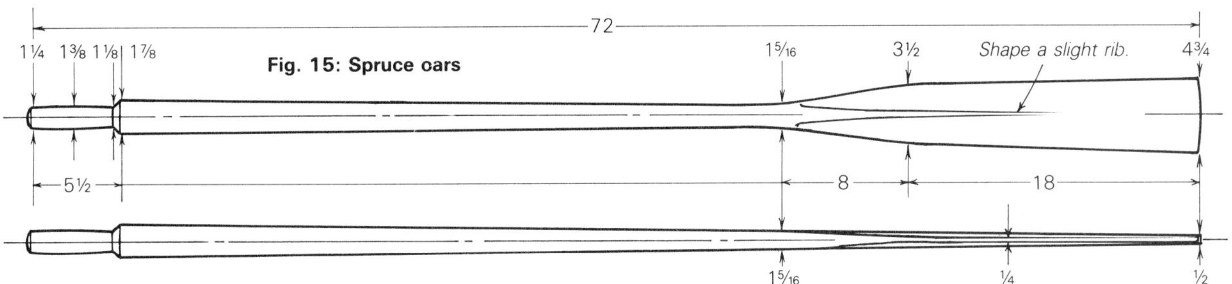

Fig. 15: Spruce oars

Simon Watts

The 10-ft. Nova Scotia lapstrake rowing boat described in this article was built by Jim Smith in 1963. A close copy of it was built by Alexis Nason of Brattleboro, Vt., as part of the preparation of this article. It took Nason about 160 hours to complete the job.

in so they can later be plugged with wooden bungs.

The floorboards are made of five pieces of ⅜-in. pine, as in figure 1. Cut the center floorboard 1 in. wider than the hog and nail it down. So you can bail the boat, make the floorboards to either side removable by fastening them with cross-grain cleats slipped under the center board and by hardwood turnbuttons screwed to the outer floorboards. Nail or screw the outer floorboards to the timbers.

Caulking and painting—This boat has only one seam to fill, the one that runs down the stem and along the keel. The other, running around the transom, has been sealed with bedding compound. Moisture-swollen planks will keep the laps tight. The traditional method of filling seams is to use caulking. This consists of one or more strands of unspun cotton driven into the seams with a wedge-shaped caulking iron. The seam is then filled up flush to the planking with putty or polysulfide. If the boat is going to be in and out of the water a lot, a bead of polysulfide run between the laps during planking will help keep it tight and will stay elastic through seasonal changes. Otherwise you can expect some leaking until the laps have swollen.

Some builders fill in the nail holes with putty. I prefer to sink them just enough to dimple the wood; they are a necessary part of lapstrake construction and nothing to be ashamed of. You can now bung all holes in keel, transom and rubbing strips. Sound knots can be shellacked to keep them from bleeding through the paint, or a shallow hole can be drilled with a centerless bit and bunged.

Before painting, it is a good idea to give the entire boat, inside and out, two applications of warm linseed oil, thinned half and half with turpentine. This helps keep the boat from getting waterlogged and heavy. The outside will need several coats of alkyd primer (give it plenty of time to dry and a thorough sanding between coats) before you put on the finish coat of marine gloss enamel. If you paint the inside, keep the number of coats to a minimum so you can get by each year with a light sanding instead of the considerable chore of removing the paint with torch or chemicals. If you want the inside finished clear, the oil finish Deks Olje, the marine equivalent of Watco oil, requires less maintenance than varnish, which tends to deteriorate rapidly in sunlight. It is usually available from the suppliers mentioned on page 110. Don't paint or varnish the floorboards—that would make for dangerous, slick footing. If left bare, the floorboards eventually turn an agreeable gray. I varnish the seats and pick out the edges in paint—a tradition in Nova Scotia. Spruce oars, 6 ft. to 6½ ft. long, are right for this boat—they're not difficult to make yourself. Dimensions are shown in figure 15.

I use Davis-type oarlocks because it's impossible to lose them overboard. Mount them on pads nailed to the inwale and sheer strake so the oars won't scrape the rubbing strip. Before launching, attach a ring bolt or pad eye to the stem for securing a mooring and towing line.

When your new boat goes into the water, expect some leaking until the planks swell and the laps close, a process which may take a day or so. Then she should stay tight and dry, and you'll have a craft with a pedigree that represents the accumulated experience of generations of boatbuilders.

Simon Watts frequently teaches week-long workshops on lapstrake technique in northern California and elsewhere. Sam Manning is a boat designer and builder who lives in Camden, Maine. For more on boatbuilding, see issues of WoodenBoat *magazine, published by WoodenBoat Publications, PO Box 78, Brooklin, Maine 04616. Plans for wooden boats are available from WoodenBoat, and also from The Rockport Apprenticeshop, PO Box 539, Rockport, Maine 04856; Mystic Seaport, Mystic, Conn. 06355; and Baker Boatworks, 29 Drift Road, Westport, Mass. 02790.*

Controlling shape: lofting Sea Urchin

by Sam Manning

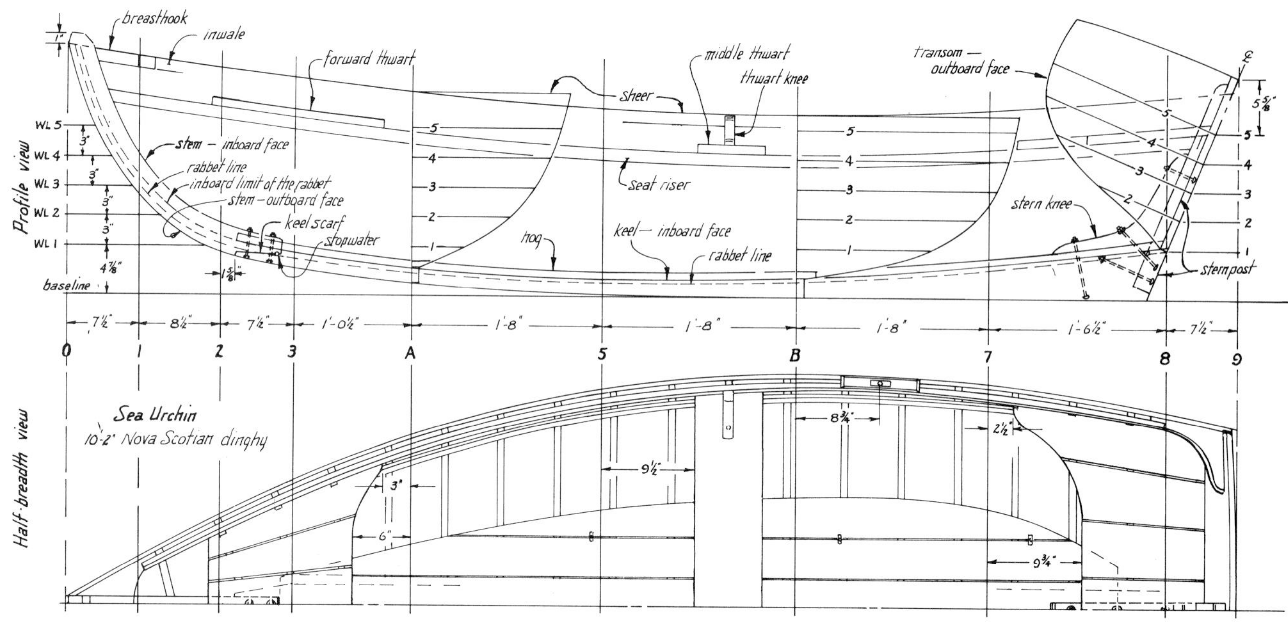

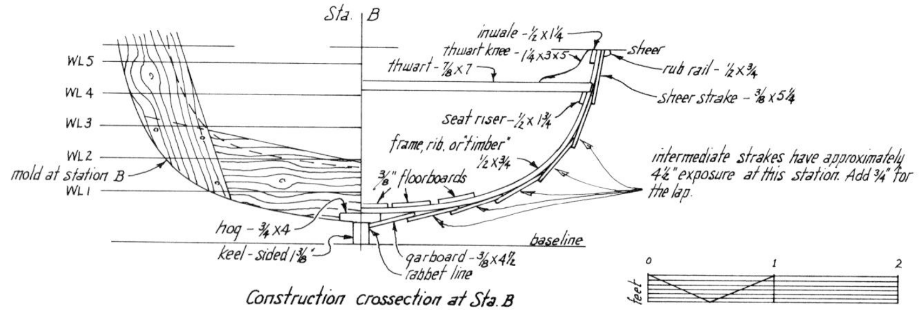

Construction crossection at Sta. B

Like all round-bottomed boats, Sea Urchin is made up from flat parts sprung and twisted into curves. Her overall shape is governed by two hull molds—A and B—spaced along the keel, and by the slant of the stem and transom. An experienced boatbuilder can set molds and end members by eye and come away with a functional, handsome boat.

I suggest, however, that the first-time builder of Sea Urchin follow the route used by professional boatbuilders who scale up, or loft, full-size the plans of a boat. If the plans of Sea Urchin shown here are lofted to full-size on heavy tracing paper, you will have a template from which to mark critical members directly on the building stock. Included here is a table of offsets (literally, distances set off from a measuring line) with dozens of perimeter dimensions that can be connected with a thin pine batten to form Sea Urchin's graceful curves.

Spread your paper on a large table or the long wall of a corridor. A boat's plan is laid out from station lines ruled perpendicular to a baseline shown in the profile (elevation) view and from the centerline shown in the plan view. Dimensions are shown for the two molds and the transom in half-breadth; the other half is identical. The offsets given are in traditional nautical nomenclature—feet, inches and eighths of inches—so 3 ft. 4¾ in. would appear as 3·4·6.

TABLE OF OFFSETS

STATION:	0	1	2	3	A	5	B	7	8	9
Heights above baseline (profile)										
Sheer line/top of rail	2·1·1	2·0·1	1·10·7	1·9·7	1·8·4	1·6·7	1·6·3	1·7·0	1·8·2	1·9·0
Inboard face of stem and hog		1·2·1	0·7·1	0·5·3&0	0·3·4	0·2·4	0·2·6	0·3·7	0·5·6	
Inboard face of keel				0·4·3	0·2·6	0·1·5	0·1·7	0·3·1	0·5·0	
Rabbet line		0·10·7	0·5·1	0·3·5	0·2·2	0·1·2	0·1·4	0·2·6	0·4·4	
Outboard face of stem and keel	2·1·0	0·10·0	0·4·2	0·2·6	0·1·2	0·0·2	0·0·0	0·0·0		
Distance out from centerline (half-breadth)										
Inside of plank at sheer	0·0·6	0·4·3	0·8·6	1·0·1	1·4·5	1·9·3	1·11·1	1·10·1	1·7·3	1·5·7

WATERLINE:	TOP OF KEEL	1	2	3	4	5	SHEER
Distance aft from station 0							
Stem - outboard face		1·2·3	0·9·5	0·6·6	0·4·4	0·2·7	0·0·0
- rabbet line		1·4·7	0·10·5	0·7·4	0·5·2	0·3·4	0·0·5
- inboard face			1·2·2	0·10·2	0·7·5	0·5·6	0·2·6
Distance aft from station A							
Mold (half-breadth) 'A'	0·0·6	0·5·4	0·10·3	1·0·7	1·2·5	1·3·5	1·4·5
Distance aft from station B							
Mold (half-breadth) 'B'	0·0·6	1·2·1	1·6·5	1·8·7	1·10·1	1·10·7	1·11·1
Distance out from C.L. of transom							
Aft face (half-breadth) of transom	0·0·6	0·0·6	0·9·3	1·3·1	1·5·5	1·6·3	1·5·7

Reading the table horizontally from the first to last station gives a series of points that are connected to form a particular line of the boat. The first line of the table, for example, describes the points which form the sweeping sheer line—the top edge of the top strake. Other parts of the table give point dimensions for the molds, transom, stem and keel. The drawings include other dimensions useful in building Sea Urchin. Take the time to be accurate; professionals strive for a tolerance of ⅛ in. over the length of a large hull. □

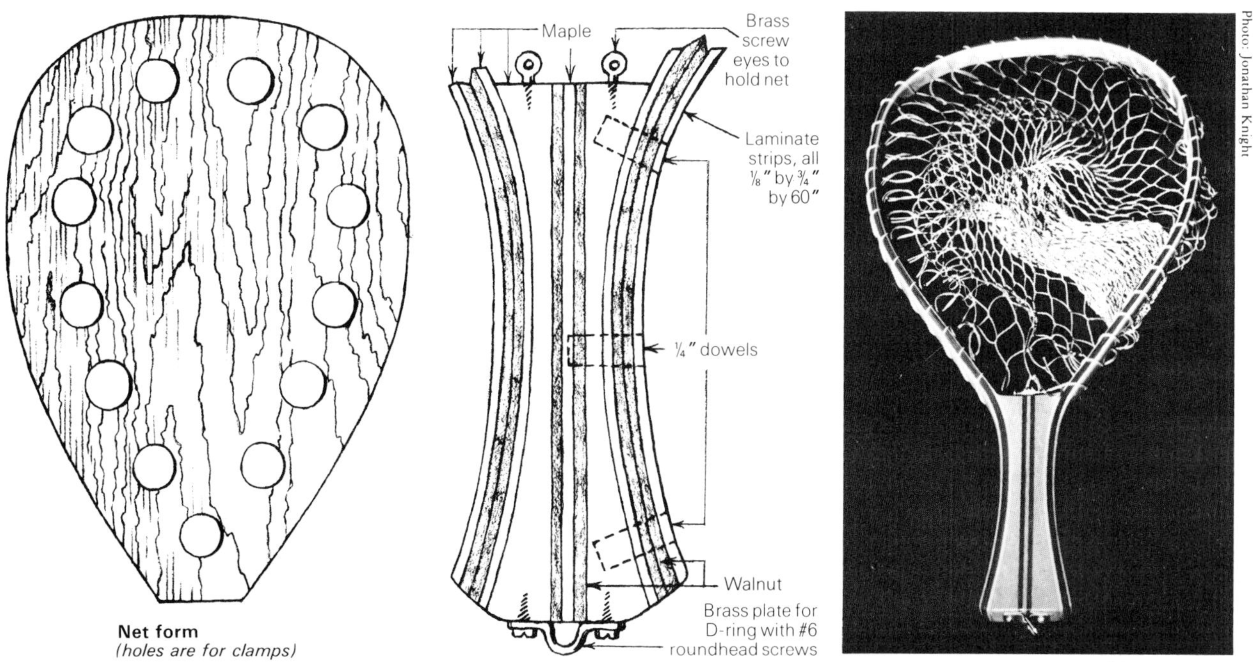

Net form
(holes are for clamps)

Laminated Fishing Net

A generous hoop pursues the noble trout

by Jonathan Knight

I am a recreational woodworker and don't have the expertise that many of the contributors to this magazine demonstrate. As a consolation, however, I do not have to produce in order to sustain myself, and this leisurely consideration of my projects lets me refine my ideas without time constraints. One simple project I have enjoyed is the fishing net shown here. It was a challenging design problem that bears dividends in all too infrequent use on the stream. I have made four or five of these nets now, for myself and a few good friends. The first was made five years ago and has seen seasonal use since with no ill effects or structural problems. It easily handled my largest trout, a four-pounder, and has bumped along many a stream clipped to my fishing vest.

The size of the hoop is generous, to match my optimism in pursuing the noble trout. The laminated hoop is constructed around a waxed plywood form, and composed of four ⅛-in. hardwood strips—two of walnut and two of curly maple. I cut them long enough to encompass the form plus the handle, usually 5 ft., and plane them. Then I bandsaw the two matching maple pieces for the handle and smooth them with spokeshave and files. The width of the walnut and maple spacing strips for the handle is important—the total width of the handle must just equal the throat of the hoop form, for a strong glue bond.

To assemble the net, I apply Weldwood plastic resin glue to all mating surfaces of the hoop strips, which are arranged with alternating grain in order to maximize stability. I use an extra maple strip as a caul to distribute the clamp pressure and to avoid marring the hoop. I begin clamping at the middle of the hoop and work around the sides until the hoop is fully secured. Then I apply glue to all the inner surfaces of the inner strips that join the handle, and with some fiddling and fussing I clamp the handle into position as well. Here precise cutting of the spacer strips pays off, because too little width will not permit adequate clamp pressure at the critical junction of the hoop and handle, and a poor gluing job will, of course, cause delamination.

After the glue has set for 24 hours, I remove the clamps and do preliminary shaping with a plane and spokeshave while the hoop is still around the plywood form. In this way I can remove excess wood and glue in a symmetrical fashion. A few blows with a mallet remove the form from the hoop, and I final-shape with spokeshave and scrapers. Then I reinforce the handle/hoop bond with ¼-in. maple dowels, three on each side of the handle.

I finish with five or six coats of Flecto Humicure catalyzed exterior finish, sanding between coats. It is a most durable finish. Then I attach the net with nylon cord around the hoop and anchor it at the throat with small brass screw-eyes inserted before finishing. A brass *D*-ring and mounting plate at the handle butt complete the net. □

Jonathan Knight practices orthopedic surgery in Seattle, Wash. An avid woodworker, he has recently completed a laminated oak couch and a lapstrake cradle along the lines of a Viking boat.

Illustrations: Mathilde Anderson

Index

FINE WOODWORKING
Editorial Staff, 1975-1984:

Paul Bertorelli
Mary Blaylock
Dick Burrows
Jim Cummins
Katie de Koster
Ruth Dobsevage
Tage Frid
Roger Holmes
John Kelsey
Linda Kirk
John Lively
Rick Mastelli
Ann E. Michael
Nina Perry
Jim Richey
Paul Roman
David Sloan
Nancy Stabile
Laura Tringali
Linda D. Whipkey

FINE WOODWORKING
Art Staff, 1975-1984

Roger Barnes
Deborah Fillion
Lee Hov
Betsy Levine
Lisa Long
E. Marino III
Karen Pease
Roland Wolf

FINE WOODWORKING
Production Staff, 1975-1984

Claudia Applegate
Barbara Bahr
Pat Byers
Deborah Cooper
Michelle Fryman
Mary Galpin
Barbara Hannah
Annette Hilty
Nancy Knapp
Johnette Luxeder
Gary Mancini
Laura Martin
Mary Eileen McCarthy
JoAnn Muir
Cynthia Nyitray
Kathryn Olsen